VEGETARIAN CUISINE

Published in Great Britain 1986 by Colour Library Books.

Display and text filmsetting by Acesetters Ltd.,
Richmond, Surrey, England.
Printed and bound in Barcelona, Spain.
ISBN 0 86283 399 X Softback
ISBN 0 86283 400 7 Hardback

Dep.Leg. B-30.467-85

Text by
Anne D. Ager
Lalita Ahmed
Denise Jarrett-Macauley
Maureen McCall
Beverley Piper

Designed by
Philip Clucas

Produced by
Ted Smart and Gerald Hughes

Editorial Direction
David Gibbon

COOKING
in Colour

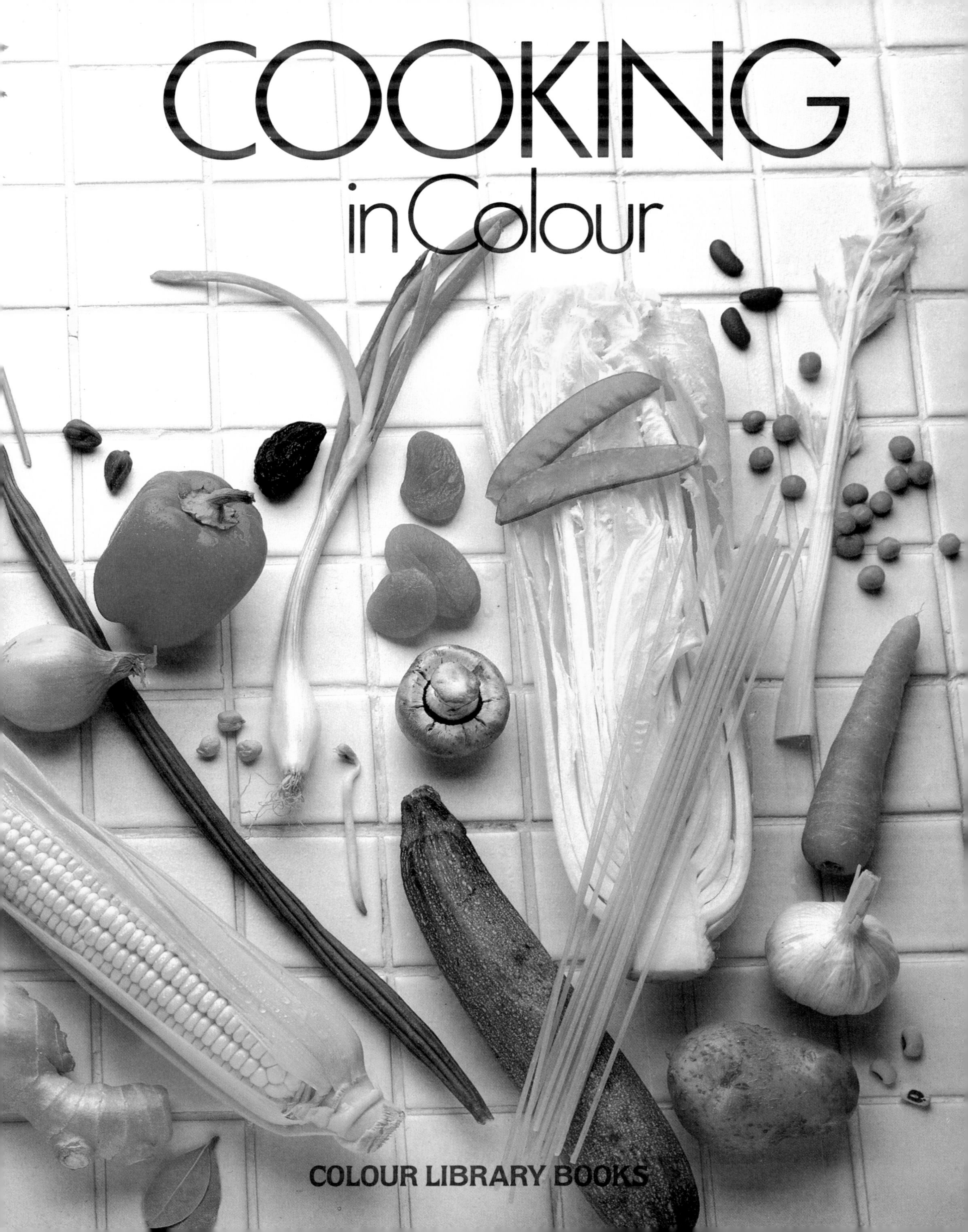

COLOUR LIBRARY BOOKS

Contents

Introduction to Vegetarian Meals

is amazing how rigid we are when it comes to the subject of food ıd what we eat. In all other aspects of life virtually anything goes: eople walk the streets with pink hair; sail the Atlantic single-handed r jog around the houses for two hours every morning and yet if we refer beans and lentils to beef and chicken we are considered as eing rather odd.

'egetarians are not cranks, and there is nothing weird and wonderful bout a pattern of vegetarian eating; they just prefer to eat dishes 'hich do not contain meat, poultry, game and, quite often, fish. Why don't they become ill?' you hear people say; 'Where do they et their energy from if they don't eat meat?'; 'How boring to live on ıst vegetables and those little dried peas!' As vegetarians will appily tell you, they feel perfectly healthy, have quite sufficient nergy to cope with day-to-day activities and, above all, *they really njoy their food.*

. vegetarian diet can be just as varied and interesting as one based n meat and fish. Meat is much the same the world over, which annot be said of the wide and wonderful range of fresh fruits and egetables. And it is variety which is very much the keynote of egetarian eating: different pastas, rices, cheeses, nuts and pulses are ıst a selection of the varied ingredients of a vegetarian diet. Most nportant of all, vegetarian dishes are every bit as nutritious as their meat-rich counterparts. The main difference lies with the types of food which provide us with the necessary nutrients. In a typical vegetarian dish, the protein usually comes from pulses, nuts or cheese, or a combination of these ingredients. Minerals, vitamins, fats and carbohydrates come from all the other basic foods, such as those already mentioned.

Eating 'the vegetarian way' has all sorts of advantages in its favour. A meatless diet is a very healthy one since it is nutritious, low in fat and high in bulk and fibre. Vegetarians rarely need to watch their weight as a diet that is high in natural fibre and low in fat is comparatively low in calories. The traditional pattern of Western eating is relatively expensive to follow, whereas vegetarian dishes are more economical to prepare and cook. In fact, meatless meals can simply make a nice change from the traditional pattern of eating. Vegetarian cooking is fun, and eating vegetarian meals is healthy and good for you.

Vegetarian food really can be exciting and delicious, and even if you are not a committed vegetarian many of the following ideas are well worth trying. The dishes combine unusual tastes with an imaginative use of spices and fresh herbs for extra flavour. If you served many of the recipes to your family and friends they probably wouldn't even realise that their meal was meatless.

Some recipes in this section suggest the use of beef or chicken stock cubes. Many vegetarians would not object, but those who do may just as effectively substitute vegetable stock cubes.

Soups

Cucumber Soup

PREPARATION TIME: 15 minutes
COOKING TIME: 8-10 minutes
SERVES: 4 people

1 large cucumber
250ml (8 fl oz) water
600ml (1 pint) chicken stock
15ml (1 tblsp) white wine vinegar
30ml (2 tblsp) cornflour mixed with
30ml (2 tblsp) water
30ml (2 tblsp) soured cream
30ml (2 tblsp) natural yogurt
Salt and ground white pepper to taste
15ml (1 tblsp) chopped chives or green spring onion tops
Chilli powder

Cut ¼ of the cucumber into wafer thin rounds and keep aside for garnishing. Puree the rest of the cucumber with the water in a liquidiser. Put the chicken stock and the pureed cucumber into a saucepan and bring to the boil over a medium heat. Add the vinegar and cook for 1 minute. Add the cornflour mixture gradually. Stir well until the soup starts to thicken. Simmer for 2-3 minutes. Remove from the heat and cool slightly. Blend in the liquidiser and add the soured cream and yogurt. Return to the saucepan and season with salt and pepper. Heat through gently to serve hot or chill to serve cold. Serve garnished with sliced cucumber and chopped chives or spring onion tops. Sprinkle with chilli powder.

Daal Soup

This is a thick and hearty soup, made from lentils. The lentils most often used for making soup are red lentils, or yellow lentils which are called Toor daal. The recipe below can be made with either variety.

PREPARATION TIME: 15-20 minutes
COOKING TIME: 15 minutes
SERVES: 4-6 people

350g (12oz) red lentils (see above)
900ml (1½ pints) water
4 canned tomatoes, drained and crushed
1 green chilli, sliced lengthways and seeded
30ml (2 tblsp) natural yogurt or soured cream
15g (½oz) butter
1 medium onion, peeled and chopped
salt and freshly ground black pepper to taste
1-2 sprigs fresh green coriander leaves, chopped

Wash the lentils in 4-5 changes of water. Drain the lentils and put them into a pan with the water. Cover the pan and bring to the boil; simmer for 10 minutes. Beat until smooth with an egg whisk. Add the crushed tomatoes and green chilli and simmer gently for 2 minutes. Stir in the yogurt or soured cream. Melt the butter in a small pan and fry the onion until golden. Season the hot soup with salt and pepper and pour into a serving bowl; sprinkle with the fried onion and chopped coriander. Serve immediately with buttered brown bread, crisp rolls or croutons.

Tomato Saar

This is a thin tomato soup from the South of India. It makes a refreshing and interesting starter.

PREPARATION TIME: 15 minutes
COOKING TIME: 17-18 minutes
SERVES: 4-6 people

10ml (2 tsp) butter
1 small onion, peeled and chopped
225g (½lb) tomatoes, skinned and chopped
1 litre (1¾ pints) water
15ml (1 tblsp) tomato puree
4-6 green curry leaves
Salt and freshly ground black pepper to taste
3 cloves of garlic, peeled and crushed

Garnish
1-2 sprigs fresh green coriander or parsley leaves, chopped
1 green chilli, chopped (optional)

Melt half of the butter and fry the onion for 3-4 minutes. Add the skinned and chopped tomatoes and cook for 5 minutes. Blend the water and tomato puree and add to the onion and tomatoes. Add curry leaves. Season with salt and pepper. Cover and simmer for 5-7 minutes. Heat the remaining butter and fry the crushed cloves of garlic until dark brown. Pour the mixture over the simmering tomato soup. Remove from the heat. Sprinkle over the chopped coriander and chilli. Discard green chilli before eating. Serve piping hot either with French bread or with a little plain boiled rice. Alternatively: blend the skinned tomatoes to give a smooth textured soup.

Mixed Vegetable Soup

This Indian recipe can include a wide variety of vegetables. One creates one's own dish by adding or subtracting one or more vegetables.

PREPARATION TIME: 15 minutes
COOKING TIME: about 20 minutes
SERVES: 6 people

10ml (2 tsp) butter
1 medium onion, peeled and chopped
6 cloves
2.5cm (1 inch) piece cinnamon stick
4 small green cardamoms
1 small bayleaf
1 medium potato, peeled and chopped
2 carrots, peeled and chopped
1 banana, peeled and chopped
6 florets of cauliflower
50g (2oz) shelled fresh or frozen peas
1 leek, washed and chopped
1 stick celery, chopped
50g (2oz) green beans (sliced or chopped)
1 litre (1¾ pints) water
Salt and freshly ground black pepper to taste

Garnish
1-2 sprigs fresh green coriander
1-2 green chillies chopped

Melt the butter in a large saucepan and fry the onion for 3 minutes. Add the cloves, cinnamon, cardamom, bayleaf and fry for 1 minute. Add the potato, carrots, banana and cauliflower. Fry for 3 minutes. Add the remaining vegetables and cook for 2-3 minutes. Add water and salt and pepper to taste. Cover and simm[er] gently for 8-13 minutes until vegetables are cooked. Adjust seasoning. Garnish with chopped coriander leaves and green chillie[s]. Discard green chillies before eatir[ng]. The vegetables should float in th[e] clear soup; do not blend.

Carrot Soup

PREPARATION TIME: 12 minut[es]
COOKING TIME: 20-25 minutes
SERVES: 4 people

4-6 carrots, peeled and cut into thic[k] slices
1 medium onion, peeled and quartered
1 medium turnip, peeled and cut in[to] wedges
2 cloves garlic, peeled
750ml (1¼ pints) water or vegetable stock
2.5ml (½ tsp) dried thyme
Salt and ground white pepper to ta[ste]
Hot pepper sauce to taste

Garnish
25g (1oz) toasted sunflower seeds, flaked almonds and pistachio nu[ts] (mixed together)

Put the carrots, onion, turnip, gar[lic] and water into a large saucepan. Cover and simmer for 15 minute[s]. Add thyme and salt and pepper t[o] taste and simmer for a further 5 minutes. Cool slightly and blend [in] a liquidiser. Return to the saucep[an] and heat the soup through. Ladle the soup into bowls. Add hot pepper sauce to taste. Serve garnished with toasted nuts.

Facing page: Tomato Saar (to[p] right), Daal Soup (centre left) and Mixed Vegetable Soup (bottom).

Minestrone Soup

This famous vegetable and pasta soup from Italy can be made in many different ways. The recipe below is a simple, but delicious one – served with bread, it is a complete meal in itself.

PREPARATION TIME: 20 minutes

COOKING TIME: 30 minutes

SERVES: 4-6 people

45ml (3 tblsp) olive oil
1 medium onion, peeled and chopped
2 cloves of garlic, peeled and crushed
2 medium potatoes, peeled and diced
3 carrots, peeled and diced
2 stems celery, chopped
175g (6oz) shredded cabbage
4-5 skinned or canned tomatoes, chopped
900ml (1½ pints) water or vegetable stock
1 bouquet garni

Quick Tomato Soup (above right), Minestrone Soup (right) and Onion Soup (far right).

75g (6oz) shelled fresh, or frozen peas
0g (2oz) boiled and cooked red kidney beans
00g (4oz) macaroni or any shaped pasta
alt and freshly ground black pepper to taste
0g (2oz) grated Parmesan cheese

Heat the olive oil in a saucepan and fry the onion and garlic until the onion is soft, 2-3 minutes. Stir in the potatoes, carrots and celery and fry for 3 minutes; add the cabbage and tomatoes. Cook for 5-6 minutes. Add water or stock and bouquet garni. Add peas, kidney beans, pasta and simmer gently, covered, for 10-15 minutes, or until the pasta is just tender. Season with salt and pepper and ladle into bowls. Sprinkle generously with grated Parmesan cheese before serving. Serve Minestrone soup with crusty bread.

Quick Tomato Soup

This is quite an exotic soup and is made within a few minutes. It is ideal for a hot summer's day.

PREPARATION TIME: 10 minutes plus chilling time

SERVES: 4-6 people

600ml (1 pint) chilled tomato juice
50g (2oz) fresh or canned tomato puree, chilled
2.5ml (½ tsp) hot red pepper sauce
2.5ml (½ tsp) grated lemon peel
2.5ml (½ tsp) grated orange peel
45-60ml (3-4 tblsp) dry white wine
Salt and ground white pepper to taste
Little iced water
45ml (3 tblsp) natural yogurt
60ml (4 tblsp) soured cream
6 balls of honeydew melon
6 balls of water melon
6 balls of ripe pear

Garnish
Mint leaves

Mix the tomato juice, tomato puree, pepper sauce, fruit peels and wine together. Season with salt and pepper, cover and refrigerate for 3-4 hours. Thin the soup with a little iced water if necessary. Whisk the yogurt and cream together until smooth and light. Divide the soup amongst 4-6 bowls. Spoon the yogurt and cream mixture into the centre of each portion and float the fruit balls on top. Garnish with mint leaves and serve.

Rice and Mushroom Soup

Ideal for a party or for summer afternoons.

PREPARATION TIME: 10 minutes
COOKING TIME: 40-50 minutes
SERVES: 6-8 people

125g (4oz) wild rice or brown rice
250ml (8 fl oz) water
25g (1oz) butter
1 medium onion, peeled and finely chopped
1 stem celery, chopped
100g (4oz) mushrooms, chopped
2.5ml (½ tsp) powdered garam masala
2.5ml (½ tsp) ground mustard seed
Salt and freshly ground black pepper to taste
1 litre (1¾ pints) water or stock
22ml (1½ tblsp) cornflour blended with
30ml (2 tblsp) water
75ml (5 tblsp) single cream

Garnish
1-2 sprigs fresh green coriander or parsley, chopped

Wash the rice in 3-4 changes of water; cook covered in 250ml (8 fl oz) water for 25-30 minutes, or until rice is tender. Keep on one side. Melt the butter in a large saucepan; saute the onion until tender for 3-5 minutes. Add the celery and mushrooms. Cook for 1-2 minutes. Stir in the powdered garam masala, mustard and salt and pepper to taste. Add the water or stock. Simmer for 5 minutes. Add the cornflour mixture and simmer for a further 3 minutes. Add the cooked rice and cream. Gently stir over a low heat for 2 minutes to heat through. Ladle the soup into bowls and garnish with coriander or parsley.

Carrot Soup (top), Rice and Mushroom Soup (centre right) and Cucumber Soup (bottom left).

Onion Soup

Onion soup has been made famous by the French. Here is a delicious recipe based on the French style.

PREPARATION TIME: 20 minutes
COOKING TIME: 1 hour
SERVES: 4-6 people

75g (3oz) butter
3-4 large onions, peeled and sliced into rings
30ml (2 tblsp) flour
900ml (1½ pints) beef stock
Salt and ground white pepper to taste
6 slices of French bread 1½cm (¾ inch) thick
2 cloves of garlic, peeled and bruised
75g (3oz) grated Parmesan cheese

Melt the butter in a saucepan and fry the onions briskly on a very low heat. Cover and simmer the onions in their own juices for 25-30 minutes, stirring occasionally until golden brown. Remove from the heat. Stir in the flour and add the stock gradually. Season with salt and pepper and return to heat. Bring to the boil quickly; reduce the heat and simmer covered for 15-20 minutes. Rub the bread pieces each side with the bruised garlic. Float the bread rounds in the soup and sprinkle grated Parmesan cheese generously over the top. Put under the grill and cook for 2-3 minutes or until the top is golden. Serve at once. Alternatively – fry the bread rounds or bread slices in butter prior to rubbing with garlic.

Snacks and Starters

lour Pancake

ıis is a favourite pancake from
e southern part of India and it is
ılly worth making; good,
ıolesome and nutritious.

EPARATION TIME: 10 minutes
OOKING TIME: 20 minutes
RVES: 6 people

5g (10oz) wholemeal flour
5ml (½ tsp) salt
0ml (¼ pint) natural yogurt
gg, beaten
mall onion, peeled and chopped
2 green chillies, chopped
prigs fresh green coriander leaves, chopped
ml (1 tblsp) grated fresh coconut, or desiccated coconut
ml (2 tsp) sugar
ive oil

eve the flour and salt and add the gurt and egg. Mix in sufficient ıter to make a thickish batter of ıuring consistency. Beat the xture well and add the onion, illi, coriander, coconut and sugar. ix well. Allow to stand for 2-3 nutes. Heat 15ml (1 tblsp) oil in mall frying pan or omelette pan. oon in a little of the batter to e a depth of 5mm (1¼ inch). over with a lid and cook over a v heat for 3-5 minutes. Turn the ncake over and pour a little oil ound the edge; cover and cook til the pancake is set and brown both sides. Repeat with the maining batter until you have veral pancakes. Serve piping hot.

osas

osas can be eaten plain or with a ing. Eat them as a snack, for eakfast, or as a main meal with a ing and accompanied by chutney d daal (lentil dish).

EPARATION TIME: overnight, ıs 20 minutes
OOKING TIME: 30-45 minutes
RVES: 6 people

0g (1lb) rice
5g (½lb) white lentils (urid daal)
25ml (¼ tsp) fenugreek seeds
5ml (1 tsp) dried yeast
5ml (1 tsp) sugar
2.5ml (½ tsp) salt
15ml (1 tblsp) natural yogurt
Olive oil

Wash the rice and white lentils separately in 3-4 changes of water. Soak in fresh water for 1 hour. Grind the rice with a little water to a thick, coarse paste. Grind the white lentils with fenugreek seeds and a little water into a fine paste. (Use a food processor, food liquidiser or food grinder). Mix the dried yeast with 15ml (1 tblsp) tepid water and the sugar. Mix well and leave to stand for 10 minutes until frothy. Mix the ground rice and lentils with the salt, yeast and yogurt and mix well. Cover with a cloth and leave in a dark, warm place overnight. Next day mix well with sufficient water to give a smooth, thickish batter. Heat a medium non-stick frying pan and grease well with 5ml (1 tsp) oil. Pour in 30-45ml (2-3 tblsp) of the rice batter, spread it around to make a thin pancake. Cover with a lid. Cook for 3-4 minutes; spoon a little oil around the edge of the frying pan and turn the dosa over.

Baisen Omelette (top right), Flour Pancake (centre left) and Dosas (bottom).

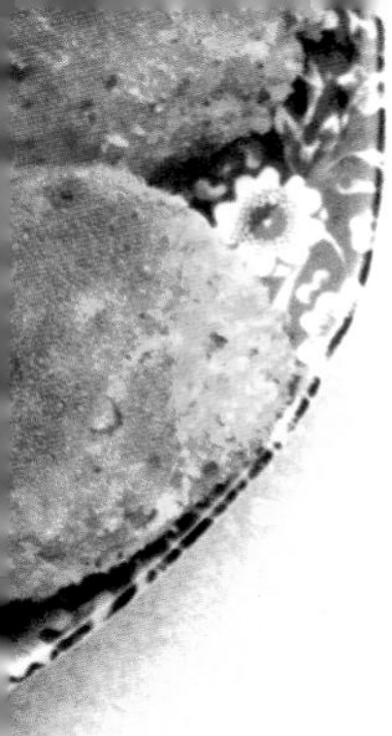

Cook for a further 2-3 minutes and serve hot. make the remaining dosa in the same way. Dosas can be made as large as 30-35cm (12-14 inches) in diameter.

Vegetable Filling

45ml (3 tblsp) olive oil
2 large onions, peeled and thinly sliced
5ml (1 tsp) white lentils (urid daal), washed and soaked in water for 5-10 minutes
2.5ml (½ tsp) mustard seed
8-10 fresh curry leaves
2 green chillies, cut into quarters
750g (1½lb) potatoes, boiled in their skins, peeled and cubed
Salt to taste

Heat oil and fry the onions for 4-5 minutes or until light brown. Add the drained lentils and mustard seed. Fry for ½ minute; add the curry leaves and green chillies. Add the potatoes and salt to taste. Cover and cook for 8-10 minutes, stirring occasionally. To serve: make the dosa as above and place 30ml (2 tblsp) of the potato filling in the centre; fold the dosa over like an omelette.

Samosa

These crispy triangles with a vegetable filling can be eaten hot or cold.

PREPARATION TIME: 40 minutes
COOKING TIME: 25 minutes
SERVES: 4-6 people

Pastry

275g (10oz) plain flour, sieved
1.25ml (¼ tsp) salt
1.25ml (¼ tsp) baking powder
Water

Make the dough by adding water, a little at a time, to the sieved flour, salt and baking powder. Mix to a soft pliable dough. Cover and allow to stand.

Filling

45ml (3 tblsp) oil
1 medium onion, peeled and chopped
450g (1lb) potatoes, peeled and cubed
2 carrots, peeled and grated
50g (2oz) shelled green peas
50g (2oz) green beans, chopped
5ml (1 tsp) chilli powder
5ml (1 tsp) salt
5ml (1 tsp) garam masala powder
2.5ml (½ tsp) ground turmeric
15ml (1 tblsp) dry mango powder, or lemon juice
Oil for deep frying

Heat the oil and fry the onions for 2-3 minutes. Add the potatoes and carrots and cook for 3 minutes. Add peas and beans and cook for 2-3 minutes. Sprinkle chilli, salt, garam masala, turmeric and mango powder. Mix well, cover and cook till potatoes are tender. Remove from heat and allow to cool. Divide the dough into 12-14 equal sized balls; roll each one out on a floured surface to a thin circle, 6-7cm (2½-3 inch) in diameter. Cut each circle in half. Apply the flour paste on the straight edge of each half. bring the edges together, overlapping them so as to make a cone. Fill the cone with the filling. Apply a little flour paste on the open edge and seal by pressing both the edges together. This will make a triangular shape. Make all the samosas in the same way. Heat the oil for deep frying. When the oil is hot, reduce the heat and fry the samosas, a few at a time, until golden brown on either side (about 4-5 minutes). Drain on kitchen paper and serve with chutney or tomato sauce.

Curry Puffs

Like sausage rolls, curried vegetable puffs make an ideal dish for snacks and cocktails. The size can be varied to suit the occasion.

PREPARATION TIME: 1 hour
COOKING TIME: 20 minutes
SERVES: 4-6

450g (1lb) ready-made puff pastry

Filling

45ml (3 tblsp) oil
1 large onion, peeled and chopped
5ml (1 tsp) cumin seeds
450g (1lb) potatoes, peeled and diced
2 carrots, peeled and shredded
100g (4oz) shelled peas
5ml (1 tsp) salt
5ml (1 tsp) freshly ground black pepper
2-3 sprigs fresh green coriander leaves, chopped
5ml (1 tsp) garam masala powder

Flour paste: mix together 10ml (2 tsp) flour with water to make a sticky paste.

Heat the oil and fry the onion for 2 minutes. Add cumin seeds and allow to crackle, then add the diced potatoes. Stir fry over a medium heat for 5-6 minutes. Add the carrots and stir fry for 2 minutes. Add the peas and season with salt, pepper and chopped coriander leaves. Stir well. Cover and cook for 5-6 minutes or until the potatoes are tender. Sprinkle with the garam masala and lemon juice. Mix well. Remove from the heat and allow to cool. Roll out the puff pastry thinly. Cut into 7.5cm (3 inch) by 15cm (6 inch) rectangles. Place 15ml (1 tblsp) filling at one end and roll up the pastry like a swiss roll. Secure the ends with the

Potato Cutlets (top), Samosa (above left) and Curry Puffs (left).

flour and water paste. Preheat the oven to 190°C, 375°F Gas Mark 5. Arrange the curry puffs on greased baking sheets and bake for 10-15 minutes or until golden. Serve hot with tomato sauce.

Potato Cutlets

PREPARATION TIME: 30 minutes
COOKING TIME: 30 minutes
SERVES: 6 people

15ml (1 tblsp) oil
1 medium onion, peeled and chopped
175g (6oz) shelled peas
750g (1½lb) potatoes, boiled in their skins, peeled and mashed
5ml (1 tsp) salt
5ml (1 tsp) freshly ground black pepper
30ml (2 tblsp) lemon juice
2 eggs, beaten
Breadcrumbs
Oil for shallow frying

Heat 15ml (1 tblsp) oil in a frying pan and fry the onion for 3 minutes; add the peas and fry for 2 minutes. Mix the onion and peas with the mashed potatoes. Add salt and pepper to taste and the lemon juice. Mix well. Divide mixture into 24-30 small even-sized cakes. Dip firstly into beaten egg and then coat evenly with breadcrumbs. Heat sufficient oil in a frying pan for shallow frying. Shallow fry the potato cutlets for 3-4 minutes or until golden. Serve hot or cold with chutney or tomato sauce.

Baisen Omelettes

These vegetarian omelettes are made with chickpea (baisen) flour and can be eaten as a quick snack. Easy to make and quick to prepare, they are ideal for unexpected friends or late night guests.

PREPARATION TIME: 10 minutes
COOKING TIME: 20 minutes
MAKES: 12

275g (10oz) sieved baisen flour
1 small onion, peeled and finely chopped
1-2 green chillies, chopped (optional)
2 sprigs fresh green coriander, chopped
2 tomatoes, seeded and diced
50g (2oz) shelled peas
2.5ml (½ tsp) salt
Pinch chilli powder
Olive oil

Mix the baisen flour with the onion, chillies, coriander, tomatoes and peas. Add sufficient water to made a thick batter, about 450ml (¾ pint). Season with salt and chilli powder, Mix well and allow to stand for 5 minutes. Heat a solid based frying pan or griddle pan and brush with oil. Ladle in sufficient batter to cover the base of the pan. Cover and cook over a low heat for 4-5 minutes. Turn the omelette over and cook for 3-4 minutes. Both sides should be browned evenly. Make the rest of the omelettes in the same way. Serve hot with tomato sauce.

Stuffed Marrow

Marrows can be stuffed with a vegetable or meat filling. Here is a delectable recipe for a vegetable stuffed marrow.

PREPARATION TIME: 15 minutes
COOKING TIME: 45 minutes
SERVES: 4-6 people

1 marrow 25-30cm (10-12 inches) in length

Filling
45ml (3 tblsp) oil
1 large onion, peeled and chopped
450g (1lb) potatoes, peeled and diced
5ml (1 tsp) crushed fresh root ginger
5ml (1 tsp) crushed garlic
5ml (1 tsp) chilli powder
2.5ml (½ tsp) turmeric powder
5ml (1 tsp) garam masala powder
100g (4oz) shelled peas
4 tomatoes, chopped
2.5ml (½ tsp) salt
2.5ml (½ tsp) freshly ground black pepper
1 green chilli, chopped
10ml (2 tsp) melted butter

Heat the oil in a wok or large frying pan and fry the onion for 2 minutes. Add the potatoes and stir-fry for 3-4 minutes. Add the ginger, garlic, chilli powder, turmeric and garam masala powder. Mix well and add the peas, tomatoes, salt and pepper and the green chilli; cover and cook until the potatoes are tender, about 6-8 minutes. Add the lemon juice. Remove a thin slice from each end of the marrow. Scoop out the centre pith leaving a 2cm (¾ inch) shell. Remove the skin in alternate strips to give it firmness. Fill the hollowed marrow with the prepared potato filling. Place the stuffed marrow on a rectangle of foil and brush with melted butter; season with salt and pepper. Wrap the foil around the marrow; bake at 180°C, 350°F Gas Mark 4 for 40-45 minutes. Remove the foil from to time and brush with the juices. Serve hot.

Vegetable Kebabs

This Turkish/Greek recipe makes an ideal side dish for barbecue parties.

PREPARATION TIME: 30 minutes
COOKING TIME: 30 minutes
SERVES: 4-6 people

1 aubergine cut into 2.5cm (1 inch) pieces
1 large green pepper, seeded and cut into 2.5cm (1 inch) pieces
12-14 small cherry tomatoes (or 6-8 tomatoes, halved)
12-14 small pickling onions, peeled and blanched for 5 minutes
12-14 large button mushrooms
2 medium potatoes, boiled in their skins, peeled and cut into 2.5cm (1 inch) cubes
Olive oil
30ml (2 tblsp) lemon juice
1.25ml (¼ tsp) salt
2.5ml (½ tsp) freshly ground black pepper

Put all the vegetables into a large bowl and add 60ml (4 tblsp) olive oil, lemon juice and salt and pepper. Mix together and leave to stand for 10-15 minutes, turning the vegetables once or twice. Thread the vegetables alternately onto skewers. Brush with the marinade. Grill for 3-4 minutes, until evenly browned. Brush the vegetables with oil or marinade during grilling. Serve piping hot.

Stuffed Peppers

PREPARATION TIME: 30 minutes
COOKING TIME: 30-40 minutes
SERVES: 6 people

6 even sized peppers (green or red)
45ml (3 tblsp) oil
1 medium onion, peeled and chopped
2 cloves garlic, peeled and chopped
2 tomatoes, chopped
1 green chilli, chopped
100g (4oz) plain boiled rice
1 medium potato, peeled and diced
1.25ml (¼ tsp) salt
2.5ml (½ tsp) freshly ground black pepper
50g (2oz) shelled peas
15ml (1 tblsp) lemon juice
15ml (1 tblsp) chopped parsley or coriander leaves
30ml (2 tblsp) water or vegetable st

Cut a slice from the top of each pepper; scoop out the centre see Heat the oil and fry the onion fo 1-2 minutes. Add the garlic, tomatoes and green chilli and sti fry for 2-3 minutes. Add the rice, potato, salt and pepper, peas and lemon juice and parsley. Cover a cook for 2-4 minutes. Arrange th peppers in an ovenproof dish an stuff the peppers with the rice mixture. Pour the stock around t peppers. Bake at 195°C, 375°F, Gas Mark 5, for 20-30 minutes, basting occasionally with the juic Serve hot.

Stuffed Tomatoes

Tomatoes stuffed with a vegetab filling and served with a tangy sauce make a good starter.

PREPARATION TIME: 20 minut
COOKING TIME: 15-18 minutes
SERVES: 6 people

12 medium size firm tomatoes
30ml (2 tblsp) oil
10-12 spring onions (only the whit part), chopped
10ml (2 tsp) chopped parsley or coriander leaves
100g (4oz) cooked rice
10ml (2 tsp) pine kernels, or skinne hazelnuts, chopped
10ml (2tsp) roasted sesame seeds
2.5ml (½ tsp) salt
1.25ml (¼ tsp) freshly ground blac pepper
1.25ml (¼ tsp) ground mixed spice
250ml (8 fl oz) vegetable stock
10ml (2 tsp) cornflour
30ml (2 tblsp) lemon juice
1 egg, well beaten

Stuffed Marrow (top), Vegetable Kebabs (centre right) and Stuffed Peppers (bottom).

Slice the tops off the tomatoes and scoop out the centre pulp, leaving a 2cm (3/4 inch) "shell". Reserve the tomato pulp. Heat the oil in the frying pan and fry the onions for 2-3 minutes. Add the parsley, cooked rice, nuts, sesame seeds, salt and pepper and allspice. Add the tomato pulp and any juice which may have formed. Cook, uncovered, for 3-4 minutes, until most of the moisture has evaporated. Stuff the hollowed tomatoes with the rice mixture and arrange in a large frying pan. Add the stock and cook for 4 minutes. Remove the tomatoes. Bring the liquid back to the boil and add the blended cornflour and lemon juice. Remove from the heat. Add the beaten egg a little at a time. Return the mixture to the heat and cook until thickened. Add the stuffed tomatoes and cook over a low heat for 5 minutes, spooning the sauce over the tomatoes from time to time.

Fritters
(TEMPURA)

PREPARATION TIME: 10 minutes
COOKING TIME: 10-15 minutes
SERVES: 4 people

Batter
225g (8oz) plain flour
15ml (1 tblsp) cornflour
1.25ml (1/4 tsp) salt
250ml (8 fl oz) chilled water
1 egg yolk
2 egg whites, stiffly beaten

Oil for deep frying
225g (8oz) fresh green beans, cut into 5cm (2 inch) pieces
10-12 fresh asparagus spears, cut in 5cm (2 inch) lengths
1 aubergine, cut into 2.5cm (1 inch) cubes
1 large potato, peeled and sliced 5mm (1/4 inch) thick
10-12 fresh mushrooms, halved
6-8 cauliflower florets, halved

Tempura sauce: A
250ml (8 fl oz) water
60ml (2 fl oz) sherry
60ml (2 fl oz) soya sauce
5ml (1 tsp) sugar
1/2 a vegetable stock cube

Mix the ingredients together and bring to the boil. Stir until dissolved.

Tempura sauce: B
2.5cm (1 inch) fresh root ginger, peeled and grated
30ml (2 tblsp) grated turnip
30ml (2 tblsp) grated radish
45ml (3 tblsp) prepared mustard
45ml (3 tblsp) soya sauce

Mix the ingredients together and keep covered.

To make the batter: mix together the flour, cornflour and salt. Make a well in the centre. Mix the chilled water and egg yolk together and pour into the centre of the flour. Stir in the flour and biend lightly. Fold in the whisked egg whites.

Heat oil for deep frying. Dip the vegetables into the batter and fry in hot oil for 2-3 minutes until golden. Drain on kitchen paper and serve hot with the Tempura sauces. Use the batter within a few minutes of making. Do not allow it to stand for long.

Cheese and Lentil Rissoles

PREPARATION TIME: 30 minutes
COOKING TIME: 1 hour
SERVES: 4 people

175g (6oz) red lentils
400ml (2/3 pint) water
100g (4oz) grated cheese
1 medium onion, peeled and chopped
2 large eggs
50g (2oz) fresh breadcrumbs
5ml (1 tsp) mixed dried herbs
15ml (1 tblsp) lemon juice
Salt to taste
2.5ml (1/2 tsp) freshly ground black pepper
Oil for shallow frying

Wash the lentils in 3-4 changes of water. Drain the lentils and put them into a pan with the water. Cook until the lentils are tender and the water has been absorbed. Remove from heat and allow to cool. Mix the cooked lentils with the cheese, onion, egg, breadcrumbs, herbs, salt and pepper and the lemon juice. Mix well and shape into rissoles. Shallow fry the rissoles for 4-5 minutes on each side until golden brown. Drain on absorbent paper and serve immediately.

Mixed Nut Rissoles

PREPARATION TIME: 15 minutes
COOKING TIME: 20-25 minutes
SERVES: 4 people

25g (1oz) hazelnuts, chopped
50g (2oz) shelled peanuts, chopped
50g (2oz) cashew nuts, chopped
25g (1oz) pistachio nuts, chopped
1 onion, peeled and chopped
75g (3oz) fresh breadcrumbs
3 eggs, beaten
Salt and freshly ground black pepper to taste
2.5ml (1/2 tsp) dried, chopped marjoram
1 carrot, peeled and grated
15ml (1 tblsp) lemon juice
Little milk
Oil for shallow frying

Mix the chopped nuts with the onion, breadcrumbs, eggs, salt and pepper, marjoram, carrot and lemon juice. Add a little milk to bind the mixture, if necessary. Shape into rissoles. Shallow fry the rissoles in oil, for 4-5 minutes on each side, until golden brown. Drain well on absorbent paper and serve immediately. Alternatively, brush the rissoles generously with oil, put them onto a baking tray and bake in the oven at 220°C, 425°F, Gas Mark 7 for 15 minutes. Turn the rissoles halfway through cooking and brush with extra oil.

Cashew Nut Pie

PREPARATION TIME: 20-25 minutes
COOKING TIME: 30-40 minutes
SERVES: 4 people

Filling
2 medium onions, peeled and chopped
30ml (2 tblsp) oil
225g (8oz) shredded cabbage
50g (2oz) carrots, peeled and grated

Pie Crust
100g (4oz) crushed cornflakes
50g (2oz) cashew nuts, coarsely ground
175g (6oz) grated cheese
5ml (1 tsp) mixed dried herbs
Salt and freshly ground black pepper to taste
2 large eggs
100g (4oz) fresh breadcrumbs
15ml (1 tblsp) oil
50g (2oz) butter

To make the filling: fry the onions in the oil for 2 minutes; add the cabbage and carrots and fry for a further 4-5 minutes. Remove from the heat and allow to cool.

To make the pie crust: mix all the ingredients together in a bowl, apart from the oil, butter and 50g (2oz) of the grated cheese. Grease a baking tray with the oil. Press half the pie crust ingredients out to form an even base. Spread the filling mixture on top, and then press over the remaining pie crust ingredients. Sprinkle with the remaining grated cheese and dot with butter. Bake in oven at 200°C, 400°F, Gas Mark 6, for 25-30 minutes.

Tomato, Onion and Mushroom Flan

PREPARATION TIME: 20 minutes
COOKING TIME: 40-45 minutes
SERVES: 6 people

225g (8oz) shortcrust pastry
225g (8oz) grated Cheddar cheese
4 tomatoes, skinnned and chopped
15ml (1 tblsp) chopped chives or parsley
100g (4oz) mushrooms, sliced
10ml (2 tsp) corn oil
1 large onion, peeled and chopped
3 eggs, beaten
150ml (1/4 pint) milk
2.5ml (1/2 tsp) salt
1.25ml (1/4 tsp) freshly ground black pepper

Roll out the pastry and use to line a 20-23cm (8-9 inch) flan dish. Put 50g (2oz) of the grated cheese into the pastry case followed by the tomatoes, chives or parsley and the mushrooms. Heat the corn oil and fry the onion for 2-3 minutes. Mix the beaten eggs with the milk, salt and pepper and fried onion. Pour into the flan case and top with the remaining grated cheese. Bake at 200°C, 400°F Gas Mark 6 for 35-40 minutes, or until set. Serve hot or cold.

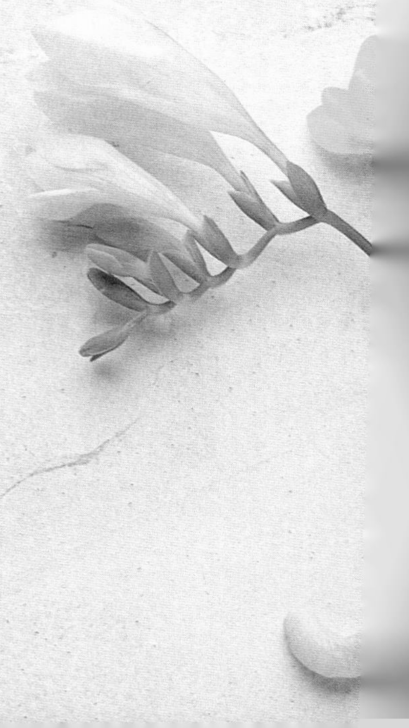

Mixed Nut Rissoles (left), Cheese and Lentil Rissoles (below) and Cashew Nut Pie (bottom).

Pakora

This is the Indian version of vegetable fritters. Fried with or without batter, they make an interesting starter or snack.

PREPARATION TIME: 15 minutes
COOKING TIME: 15-20 minutes
SERVES: 4-6 people

1 large potato, or
2 medium potatoes, peeled and cut into 5mm (¼ inch) thick slices
8-10 cauliflower florets, halved lengthways
6 carrots, cut into 5cm (2 inch) lengths and halved
1 aubergine, cut into 5cm (2 inch) cubes
6 courgettes, trimmed and cut into 5cm (2 inch) pieces and then quartered
1-2 green peppers, seeded and cut into 5mm (¼ inch) thick rounds or 2.5cm (1 inch) pieces
5ml (1 tsp) salt
5ml (1 tsp) red chilli powder
2.5ml (½ tsp) turmeric powder
Oil for deep frying
6 lemon wedges

Sprinkle the vegetables with the spices and rub well in. Keep on one side. Heat the oil for deep frying. When it is beginning to smoke, reduce the heat. Fry the vegetables a few at a time, in batches. Fry for 2-3 minutes and drain on kitchen paper. Serve piping hot with wedges of lemon and a sweet and sour chutney or tomato ketchup. (These uncoated fritters are called Bhaja).

Batter
275g (10oz) baisen flour, sieved
5ml (1 tsp) salt
5ml (1 tsp) chilli powder
5ml (1 tsp) ground cumin
15ml (1 tblsp) lemon juice
300ml (½ pint) water

Mix the sieved flour with the salt, chilli powder, cumin and lemon juice. Make a well in the centre and add the water; stir in the baisen flour until all the flour has been incorporated. Beat well to give a smooth batter. Adjust seasoning. Allow the batter to stand for a few minutes. Heat the oil as above. Dip the vegetables into the batter and then fry for 2-3 minutes. Drain on kitchen paper and serve piping hot with tomato sauce. Other vegetables which may be used: onions rings, raw banana slices, green tomato slices, spinach leaves.

Stuffed Mushrooms

PREPARATION TIME: 20 minutes
COOKING TIME: 10-15 minutes
SERVES: 4-6 people

Filling
1 small onion, peeled and finely chopped
10ml (2 tsp) oil
1cm (½ inch) fresh root ginger, peeled and crushed
2 cloves garlic, peeled and crushed
225g (8oz) boiled, peeled and mashed potatoes
Salt and freshly ground black pepper to taste
15ml (1 tblsp) lemon juice
10ml (2 tsp) chopped chives or parsley
20-24 large button mushrooms
175g (6oz) grated Cheddar cheese
Oil for brushing

Fry the onion in the 10ml (2 tsp) oil for 2 minutes; add the ginger and garlic. Fry for 1 minute and mix with the mashed potatoes. Season to taste with salt, pepper, lemon juice and chopped parsley. Mix well. Remove the stalks from the mushrooms; stuff the hollows with the potato filling and top with a little Cheddar cheese. Brush the mushrooms with a little oil and arrange them on a baking tray. Bake the mushrooms in a moderately hot oven, 190°C, 375°F, Gas Mark 5, for 10 minutes until the cheese is brown.

Aloo Bonda

This is an Indian potato fritter recipe made in the shape of spicy balls. Eaten hot or cold, they are ideal for parties, snacks and picnics.

PREPARATION TIME: 25 minutes
COOKING TIME: 30 minutes
SERVES: 4-6 people

Batter
225g (8oz) baisen flour, sieved
1.25ml (¼ tsp) salt
1.25ml (¼ tsp) baking powder
300ml (½ pint) water

450g (1lb) potatoes, boiled in their skins and peeled
1 large or 2 medium onions, peeled and chopped
2.5cm (1 inch) fresh root ginger, peeled and finely chopped
2-3 green chillies, chopped
4-5 sprigs fresh green coriander leaves, chopped
2.5ml (½ tsp) salt
1.25ml (¼ tsp) freshly ground black pepper
15ml (1 tblsp) lemon juice
Oil for deep frying

Mix the sieved flour with the salt and baking powder. Make a well in the centre and add the water. Beat well to give a smooth batter. Chop the boiled potatoes into tiny cubes; add the chopped onions, ginger, chillies, coriander leaves, salt and pepper to taste and lemon juice. Mix well and adjust seasoning to taste. Mould into even-sized balls with dampened hands. Heat the oi for deep frying. When hot, dip the vegetable balls into the batter and then fry for 3-4 minutes over a gentle heat until golden brown. Drain on kitchen paper and serve with tomato sauce.

This page: Aloo Bonda (top), Fritters (Tempura) (centre right) and Pakora (bottom left).

Facing page: Stuffed Tomatoes (top right), Stuffed Mushrooms (centre left) and Tomato, Onion and Mushroom Flan (bottom).

Salads

Onion Salad

This salad is usually served as an accompaniment to kebabs. Onion salad goes very well with a variety of main courses, as a side salad.

PREPARATION TIME: 5-7 minutes
SERVES: 4 people

2 large Spanish onions, peeled and thinly sliced
2-3 sprigs fresh green coriander, chopped
1 green chilli, sliced
Juice of 1 lemon
2.5ml (½ tsp) salt
Pinch paprika

Combine the onion rings, coriander leaves and chilli in a bowl. Add the lemon juice and salt and mix well. Put the onion salad onto a serving plate and sprinkle with paprika.

Tabbouleh

This is a Lebanese salad and it is very good for parties and picnics.

PREPARATION TIME: 2 hours 30 minutes
SERVES: 6 people

225g (8oz) bulgar or pourgouri (precooked, cracked wheat)
250ml (8 fl oz) boiling water
8-10 spring onions, chopped
1 green pepper, seeded and chopped
120ml (8 tblsp) chopped parsley
30ml (2 tblsp) chopped mint leaves

Dressing
45ml (3 tblsp) lemon juice
175ml (6 fl oz) olive oil
5ml (1 tsp) grated lemon peel
5ml (1 tsp) ground mixed spice
2.5ml (½ tsp) ground cumin
5ml (1 tsp) salt
1.25ml (¼ tsp) freshly ground black pepper
1 small iceberg lettuce, shredded
2 large firm tomatoes, cut into wedges
10-15 pitted black olives, halved
2-3 sprigs mint
1-2 sprigs fresh green coriander

Place the pourgouri or bulgar into a bowl and add boiling water. Cover and stand for 1½-2 hours. Drain the bulgar by squeezing out the excess water. Mix the spring onions, green pepper, parsley and mint with the bulgar. Combine all the dressing ingredients in a screw top jar and shake well. Pour the dressing over the bulgar mixture and mix lightly. Line a platter with shredded lettuce. Place the prepared bulgar in the centre. Garnish with tomato, olives, mint and coriander leaves.

Sweet and Sour Coleslaw

A variation on the usual theme, but a definite winner.

PREPARATION TIME: 20 minutes
SERVES: 6 people

½ small red cabbage, shredded
1 small green cabbage, shredded
1 large sweet carrot, peeled and shredded
3 spring onions, finely chopped
75ml (5 tblsp) cider vinegar
45ml (3 tblsp) brown sugar
2.5ml (½ tsp) salt
1.25ml (¼ tsp) freshly ground black pepper
75ml (5 tblsp) soured cream
5ml (1 tsp) French mustard

Combine the red and green cabbage, carrots and spring onions in a mixing bowl. Mix the vinegar, sugar and salt and pepper in a small saucepan and stir over the heat to dissolve the sugar. Pour the hot vinegar sauce over the cabbage mixture and mix well. Stir the soured cream and mustard together in a separate bowl; stir this mixture into the vegetables. Mix well and serve.

Mixed Bean Salad

This nutritious salad is made from a medley of beans and is very good for health conscious and athletic people. Either cook the dried beans at home or buy ready-cooked ones. Soak the beans separately overnight, and then boil them separately until tender. Drain well.

PREPARATION TIME: 15 minutes
SERVES: 4-6 people

175g (6oz) cooked red kidney beans
175g (6oz) cooked black eyed beans (Lobia)
175g (6oz) cooked chick peas
175g (6oz) cooked butter beans
100g (4oz) shelled broad beans
225g (8oz) sliced green beans, blanched

Dressing
30ml (2 tblsp) brown sugar
120ml (4 fl oz) white wine vinegar
2.5ml (½ tsp) salt
1.25ml (¼ tsp) freshly ground black pepper
120ml (4 fl oz) olive oil
2.5ml (½ tsp) dry mustard powder
2.5ml (½ tsp) dried basil leaves
1 large Spanish or red onion, peeled and thinly sliced into rings
30ml (2 tblsp) chopped parsley

Mix all the beans together in a large bowl. Mix the sugar and vinegar together with salt and pepper to taste. Stir in the oil, mustard and basil. Pour this vinegar mixture over the beans. Mix thoroughly. Refrigerate until ready to serve. Before serving, mix in the onion rings and parsley.

Nutty Salad

PREPARATION TIME: 20 minutes
SERVES: 4 people

450g (1lb) boiled potatoes, diced
175g (6oz) shelled green peas
100g (4oz) cooked carrots, diced
1 medium onion, peeled and chopped
1 small green pepper, seeded and chopped
8-10 radishes, chopped
2 stems celery, chopped
¼ cucumber, chopped
50g (2oz) roasted peanuts, coarsely chopped
50g (2oz) grated fresh coconut
15ml (1 tblsp) sunflower seeds
2-3 sprigs fresh green coriander leaves or parsley, chopped

Dressing
30ml (2 tblsp) lemon juice
60ml (4 tblsp) olive oil
5ml (1 tsp) salt
2.5ml (½ tsp) freshly ground black pepper
2.5ml (½ tsp) brown sugar

Mix all the vegetables together, except the nuts and sunflower seeds, in a large bowl. Mix the dressing ingredients together in a screw top jar and shake well. Add the dressing to the salad and mix throughly. Sprinkle with the nuts and sunflower seeds before serving.

Rice and Nut Salad

This salad has a very refreshing taste. The main ingredients are nuts, raisins, carrots and rice.

PREPARATION TIME: 15 minutes
SERVES: 4 people

30ml (2 tblsp) olive oil
30ml (2 tblsp) lemon juice
Salt and freshly ground black pepper to taste
100g (4oz) sultanas
50g (2oz) currants
275g (10oz) cooked long grain rice, well drained
75g (3oz) chopped blanched almonc
50g (2oz) cashew nuts, chopped
50g (2oz) shelled walnuts, chopped
425g (15oz) can peach slices, drained and chopped
¼ cucumber, cubed
100g (4oz) cooked red kidney beans
15ml (1 tblsp) chopped pitted olives

Mix the olive oil, lemon juice and salt and freshly ground black pepper in a screw top jar; shake vigorously. Soak the sultanas and

Facing page: Onion Salad (top), Nutty Salad (centre) a Tabbouleh (bottom).

currants in sufficient boiling water to cover, for 10 minutes. Drain the fruits. Mix the rice, nuts and soaked sultanas and currants. Add the chopped peaches, cucumber, red kidney beans and olives. Pour the dressing over the salad and toss lightly together. Serve on a bed of chopped lettuce.

Cheese Salad

This cheese salad originates from Greece and has many variations; it is popularly known as Horiatiki.

PREPARATION TIME: 10-12 minutes

SERVES: 4 people

½ a head of endive
½ iceberg lettuce
1 cucumber, peeled and sliced
3-4 large tomatoes, cut into wedges, or
15-20 cherry tomatoes, halved
8-10 pitted green or black olives, halved
1 medium Spanish or red onion, peeled and chopped
125g (4oz) Feta cheese, cut into 1cm (½ inch) pieces

Dressing
75ml (5 tblsp) olive oil
30ml (2 tblsp) red wine vinegar
5ml (1 tsp) chopped fresh oregano or
1.25ml (¼ tsp) dried oregano
2.5ml (½ tsp) salt
1.25ml (¼ tsp) freshly ground black pepper
2.5ml (½ tsp) brown sugar

Wash and dry the endive and lettuce leaves; tear into bite size pieces. Place the endive and lettuce in a large bowl and add the cucumber, tomatoes, olives, onion and cheese. Shake the dressing

Cheese Salad (bottom left), Mixed Bean Salad (below) and Rice and Nut Salad (bottom right).

ingredients together in a screw top jar. Pour the dressing over the salad. Toss lightly and serve.

Mixed Fresh Vegetable Salad

This salad can be prepared with any combination of vegetables, in any proportion. Add or subtract according to personal taste.

PREPARATION TIME: 20 minutes

SERVES: 6 people

1 large spring onion, peeled and chopped
½ cucumber, diced
3 carrots, peeled and diced
6 large tomatoes, diced, or
8 cherry tomatoes, halved
10 button mushrooms, diced
3 stems celery, diced
1 green pepper, seeded and diced
15-20 tiny cauliflower florets
15-20 radishes, quartered
15ml (1 tblsp) chopped watercress or mustard and cress
2 sprigs fresh green coriander leaves or parsley, chopped

Dressing

2.5ml (½ tsp) salt
2.5ml (½ tsp) freshly ground black pepper
5ml (1 tsp) brown sugar
30ml (2 tblsp) cider vinegar
15ml (1 tblsp) lemon juice
15ml (1 tblsp) honey
60ml (4 tblsp) olive oil
Pinch mustard powder
8 lettuce leaves

Combine all the vegetables in a large bowl. Mix together all the dressing ingredients. Pour the dressing over the vegetables and serve on a bed of lettuce leaves.

Pasta Salad

This is a popular salad from America. It can be eaten as a main dish or as a side salad – it is a wonderful combination of vegetables, pasta and kidney beans.

PREPARATION TIME: 15-20 minutes

SERVES: 6 people

450g (1lb) cooked red kidney beans, drained
350g (12oz) pasta shells or spirals, cooked
1 large green pepper, seeded and sliced into 2.5cm (1 inch) long pieces
1 large red pepper, seeded and sliced into 2.5cm (1 inch) long pieces
20-30 pitted black olives, sliced in half
15ml (1 tblsp) capers
4-5 sprigs fresh parsley, chopped

Dressing
200ml (⅓ pint) olive oil
45ml (3 tblsp) lemon juice
10ml (2 tsp) finely chopped fresh basil leaves
5ml (1 tsp) salt
1.25ml (¼ tsp) freshly ground black pepper
2 cloves garlic, peeled and minced
1 small head curly endive

Combine the beans, pasta, peppers, olives, capers and parsley in a large bowl. Mix all the dressing ingredients together; add to the salad ingredients and toss together. Line the serving platter or bowl with endive leaves; place the pasta salad in the centre. Alternatively: add 225g (½lb) of thinly sliced salami or Italian sausages or can sausages in brine cut into bite size pieces.

This page: Sweet and Sour Coleslaw (top left), Mixed Fresh Vegetable Salad (top right) and Pasta Salad (bottom).

Facing page: Kedgeree (top left), Sweet Savoury Rice (centre right) and Vegetable Pulao Rice (bottom).

Rice and Pulses

edgeree

EPARATION TIME: 15 minutes,
s soaking time

OKING TIME: 30 minutes

RVES: 4-6 people

5g (8oz) long grain rice
5g (8oz) red lentils
0ml (1¼ pints) tepid water
0g (4oz) butter (or an equivalent
amount of olive oil)
nedium onion, peeled and chopped
ml (½ tsp) crushed fresh root
ginger
ml (½ tsp) crushed garlic
cm (1 inch) piece cinnamon stick
loves
ayleaf
l (1 tsp) ground coriander
5ml (¼ tsp) ground turmeric
ml (½ tsp) salt
reen chillies, sliced in half
engthways

ash the rice and the lentils in 4 to hanges of water; soak them in 750ml (1¼ pints) tepid water 30 minutes. Heat the butter or in a large pan; add the onion d fry for 2-3 minutes. Add the ger, garlic, cinnamon stick, ves and bayleaf, and fry for 1 nute. Drain the water from the e and lentils; reserve the water. ld the rice and lentils to the fried ion, together with the coriander, meric, slt and green chillies. Stir er the heat for 2-3 minutes, until e rice and lentils are evenly ated with fat. Add the reserved ter and bring to the boil; reduce e heat and simmer covered for 8- minutes, without stirring, until e water has been absorbed and e rice and lentils are tender. rve with a vegetable curry.

'egetable Pulao Rice

REPARATION TIME: 30 minutes

OOKING TIME: 30 minutes

RVES: 4-6 people

50g (1lb) long grain rice (Basmati)
50-900ml (1¼-1½ pints) water
medium onion, peeled and diced
5cm (1 inch) piece cinnamon stick
bayleaf

6 cloves
5ml (1 tsp) black cumin (shah-zeera)
6 small cardamoms
2.5ml (½ tsp) crushed fresh root ginger
2.5ml (½ tsp) crushed garlic
1 medium potato, peeled and diced
1 carrot, peeled and diced
100g (4oz) shelled peas
75g (3oz) sliced green beans
5ml (1 tsp) garam masala powder
2.5ml (½ tsp) chilli powder
5ml (1 tsp) ground coriander
5ml (1 tsp) ground cumin
5ml (1 tsp) salt
30ml (2 tblsp) lemon juice
100g (4oz) butter (or an equivalent amount of olive oil)

Wash the rice in 4-5 changes of water and soak in the 750-900ml (1¼-1½ pints) water for 30 minutes. Melt the butter in a pan and fry the onion for 2-3 minutes. Add the cinnamon, bayleaf, cloves, black cumin, cardamoms, ginger and garlic. Fry for 1 minute, stirring, and add the potato, carrot, peas, green beans, garam masala, chilli, coriander, cumin and salt. Mix well. Drain the soaked rice, retaining the water and add the rice to the onion and spices. Stir the mixture gently and add the reserved water. Bring to the boil and then reduce the heat; cover and simmer gently for 10-15 minutes, until the rice is tender and the water has been absorbed. Do not stir during cooking. Sprinkle with the lemon juice and serve. To colour pulao: dissolve a pinch of saffron in 15ml (1 tblsp) warm milk; pour over the rice and allow to stand over a very low heat for 5 minutes.

Mixed Daal

This is a mixed lentil stew, using 3 or 4 varieties of daal. Add a few vegetables of your choice to turn it into a substantial meal.

PREPARATION TIME: 15 minutes
COOKING TIME: 30 minutes
SERVES: 4 people

75g (3oz) split Bengal grain (Channa)
50g (2oz) yellow lentils (Toor Daal)
100g (4oz) red lentils (Masoor)
50g (2oz) dehusked split mung (Moong), or any other daal
2.5ml (½ tsp) ground turmeric
7.5ml (1½ tsp) ground coriander
4 canned tomatoes, chopped
2 green chillies
3 sprigs fresh green coriander leaves
Salt to taste
100g (4oz) butter
1cm (½ inch) fresh root ginger, peeled and chopped
1 onion, chopped
1 clove garlic, chopped

As some of these pulses have different cooking times, wash each pulse separately in 3-4 changes of water. Drain. Soak separately in water for 5 minutes. Bring 600ml (1 pint) water to the boil; add the drained channa daal. Boil for 15-20 minutes or until the pulses are tender. Add the remaining pulses well drained, and simmer gently with the turmeric and ground coriander for 15-20 minutes, or until all the pulses are soft. Beat with an egg whisk. Add the tomatoes, green chillies and coriander leaves. Simmer for a further 5-6 minutes. Pour into a serving bowl and keep warm. Melt the butter in a frying pan and fry the ginger for 2 minutes. Add the onion and garlic and fry until golden brown. Pour this mixture over the mixed daal and serve immediately.

Sweet Savoury Rice

PREPARATION TIME: 20 minutes
COOKING TIME: 30 minutes
SERVES: 4-6 people

450g (1lb) rice (Basmati or long grain)
750-900ml (1¼-1½ pints) water
50g (2oz) raisins
75g (3oz) cashew nuts, chopped
50g (2oz) blanched almonds, split
50g (2oz) pistachio nuts, split
100g (4oz) butter (or an equivalent amount of olive oil)
2.5cm (1 inch) piece cinnamon stick
6 cloves
6 small cardamoms
1 bayleaf
2.5cm (½ tsp) black cumin seed (shah-zeera)
100g (4oz) sultanas
5ml (1 tsp) salt
5ml (1 tsp) sugar
Pinch of saffron

Wash the rice in 4-5 changes of water and soak in the 750-900ml (1¼-1½ pints) water for 30 minutes. Soak the raisins and nuts in a little water for 10 minutes. Drain the raisins and nuts. Melt the butter in a large pan and fry the cinnamon, cloves, small cardamoms, bayleaf and black cumin for 1-2 minutes. Add the nuts, raisins and sultanas. Drain the soaked rice retaining the water; add the rice to the saucepan. Fry for 1 minute. Add salt, sugar and the reserved water. Bring to the boil. Reduce the heat and add a pinch of saffron. Stir once gently. Cover and simmer gently for 10-15 minutes, without stirring, until the rice is tender and the water has been absorbed. Serve with curries.

Red Kidney Bean Curry

A popular dish from the Punjab province of India. It is similar to Chilli Con-Carne and makes a hearty meal with bread or rice.

PREPARATION TIME: overnight, plus 15 minutes
COOKING TIME: 20-45 minutes
SERVES: 4 people

225g (8oz) dried red kidney beans, washed and soaked overnight in sufficient water to cover
2 medium onions, chopped
45ml (3 tblsp) oil
1 bayleaf
2.5cm (1 inch) piece cinnamon stick
6 cloves
6 small green cardamoms
2 green chillies, quartered
3 cloves garlic, peeled and finely chopped
2.5cm (1 inch) fresh root ginger, peeled and finely chopped
2.5ml (½ tsp) chilli powder
1.25ml (¼ tsp) ground turmeric
7.5ml (1½ tsp) ground coriander
5ml (1 tsp) ground cumin
5ml (1 tsp) garam masala powder
425g (15oz) can peeled tomatoes, chopped
2.5ml (½ tsp) salt
2-3 sprigs fresh green coriander, chopped

Either pressure cook the red kidney beans for 5-6 minutes, or cook them in their soaking water for 15-20 minutes until soft. Remove from the heat; allow to stand, covered. Fry the onions in the oil in a large saucepan over a moderate heat until tender. Add the bayleaf, cinnamon, cloves and cardamoms and fry for 1 minute. Add the chillies, garlic and ginger and fry until golden. Sprinkle with the chilli powder, turmeric, ground coriander, ground cumin and garam masala. Avoid burning the mixture. Stir the mixture to blend the spices. Add the tomatoes and season with salt. Cover and simmer for 2-3 minutes. Drain th cooked beans and collect the thi red liquid. Add the beans to the spiced tomato mixture. Stir gentl and cook for 1 minute. Add the red liquid and chopped coriande cover and simmer for 3-5 minute Serve with bread or boiled rice.

Red Lentil Daal

There is an abundance of natural protein in pulses and there is a great variety of pulses now available.

PREPARATION TIME: 10 minut
COOKING TIME: 30 minutes
SERVES: 4 people

225g (8oz) red lentils
350ml (12 fl oz) water
1.25ml (¼ tsp) ground turmeric
5ml (1 tsp) ground coriander
1 green chilli, cut in half
Salt to taste
4-6 canned tomatoes, chopped
2 sprigs fresh green coriander leaves chopped
50g (2oz) butter
1 small onion, peeled and finely chopped

Wash the lentils in 3-5 changes o water. Put the lentils into a pan with the 350ml (12 fl oz) water; cover and cook over a low heat f 10-15 minutes. Remove any frot with a spoon. Once the lentils ar tender and yellow, blend until smooth with an egg whisk. Add t turmeric, ground coriander, chilli, salt to taste and chopped tomato Cover and simmer for 10 minute Add the coriander leaves and po into a dish. Keep warm. Melt the butter in a frying pan and saute t onion until golden brown. Pour t onions and butter juices over the daal. Serve with rice or bread.

Facing page: Mixed Daal (to left), Red Kidney Bean Curry (centre) and Red Lentil Daal (bottom).

Bread and Pizza

Puri

These deep-fried breads are simple to make once the art has been mastered.

PREPARATION TIME: 10-15 minutes

COOKING TIME: 20 minutes

MAKES: 30-32

450g (1lb) wholemeal flour
2.5ml (½ tsp) salt
250-300ml (8-12 fl oz) water
Oil for deep frying

Sieve the flour and salt into a mixing bowl. Mix to a soft dough with water. Knead well and leave to relax for 5 minutes, covered with a damp cloth. Divide the dough int 30-32 small even sized balls; roll out each ball into a small round about 6-7cm (2½-3 inch) in diameter. Heat the oil for deep frying and drop in a small piece of dough. If it rises to the top instantly then the correct temperature for frying has been reached. Place one puri at a time into the hot oil, taking care not to splash the oil. Gently stir the puri and it will begin to swell. Turn ove and cook on the underside until golden brown – about ½-1 minut The flip side is always the thick sid and it needs extra cooking time. Drain the puris on the side of the frying pan, and place them on

Puri (above), Roti (right) and Paratha (far right).

kitchen paper to drain, before serving. Puris are best when served piping hot. Puris can be served cold and they can also be reheated under the grill.

Paratha

These shallow-fried breads can either be made plain, or stuffed with a favourite filling, such as cheese, potato etc.

PREPARATION TIME: 15-20 minutes

COOKING TIME: 20-30 minutes

MAKES: 16-18

450g (1lb) wholemeal flour
2.5ml (½ tsp) salt
250-300ml (8-12 fl oz) water
Melted butter or oil

Sieve the flour and salt into a mixing bowl. Mix to a soft dough with water. Knead the dough well; leave to relax, covered, for 5 minutes. Divide the dough into 16-18 even-sized balls. Roll each ball into a small round about 5cm (2 inches) in diameter. Brush each round of dough with oil or melted butter and fold in half. Brush the upper folded surface with oil or butter and fold in half to form a small triangle. On a well floured surface roll out these triangles thinly. Heat a solid based frying pan or a griddle. Put the paratha onto the heated frying pan and cook for ½-1 minute or until small brown specks appear. Cook the other side in the same way. Brush a little oil or butter over the paratha and turn over. Fry for 1 minute and then brush the second side with oil or butter. Fry on both sides until the

paratha is golden and crisp. Make the rest of the paratha in the same way. Keep them soft and warm, well wrapped in a clean tea towel or foil.

Roti

Roti is best made with wholemeal flour; any variety may be used.

PREPARATION TIME: 20 minutes
COOKING TIME: 20-30 minutes
MAKES: about 24

450g (1lb) wholemeal flour
2.5ml (½ tsp) salt
250-300ml (8-12 fl oz) water

Sieve the flour and salt into a mixing bowl. Mix to a soft dough with water. Knead the dough for 2-3 minutes. Cover and allow to relax for 5-6 minutes before shaping the bread. Divide the dough into 25g (1oz) balls. Roll each ball into a thin round about 13-15cm (5-6 inches) in diameter. Place a solid based frying pan or a griddle over a medium heat; when the pan is hot, place the shaped roti onto it. Cook for ½ minute on each side and then place under a preheated grill to bloat (little brown specks will appear on the surface). The first 2 rotis do not usually bloat, so do not be alarmed. Make all the rotis and stack them one on top of each other. Keep them covered with a clean tea towel or foil. Serve hot with any curry or spicy savoury dish.

Banana and Nut Bread

PREPARATION TIME: 30 minutes
COOKING TIME: 1 hour
MAKES: 1 loaf

100g (4oz) butter
225g (8oz) brown sugar
1 egg, well beaten
225g (8oz) wholemeal flour
2.5ml (½ tsp) salt
7.5ml (1½ tsp) baking powder
60ml (4 tblsp) natural yogurt
2 ripe bananas, peeled and mashed
50g (2oz) raisins
100g (4oz) mixed nuts, chopped

Preheat the oven to 180°C, 350°F, Gas Mark 4. Cream the butter and sugar until light and fluffy and gradually beat in the egg. Sieve the flour, salt and baking powder together. Add half the yogurt to the butter and sugar mixture and then mix in half the sieved dry ingredients. Beat in the remaining yogurt, flour, mashed banana, raisins and chopped nuts. Mix well. Put the mixture into a greased loaf tin. Bake at 180°C, 350°F, Gas Mark 4, for 1 hour.

Crusty Loaf

PREPARATION TIME: 3 hours 40 minutes
COOKING TIME: 45 minutes-1 hour
MAKES: 2 loaves

300ml (½ pint) tepid water
15g (½oz) fresh yeast or 10ml (2 tsp) dried yeast
2.5ml (½ tsp) salt
15g (½oz) butter
15ml (1 tblsp) sugar
400g (14oz) sieved plain flour
15ml (1 tblsp) melted butter
25g (1oz) caraway, sesame or poppy seeds for topping (optional)

Sprinkle or crumble the yeast into the tepid water; stir to dissolve. Leave for a few minutes until frothy. Mix the salt, butter, sugar and flour together; stir in the yeast liquid and mix to a dough. Knead the dough for 10 minutes on a lightly floured surface. Place the dough in a greased bowl and brush the top lightly with melted butter; cover with a damp cloth and leave it to rise in a warm place (free from draught), until doubled in bulk (about 40-45 minutes). Punch the dough down and let it rise again until almost double its original size about (30 minutes). Punch down once again and turn out onto a floured surface, cut into two equal portions. Roll each one into an oblong about 20-25cm (8-10 inches) in length. Beginning with the wide side, roll up each oblong tightly. Seal the edges by pinching together. Holding each end of the roll, roll it gently backwards and forwards to lengthen the loaf and shape the ends. Place the loaves on a greased baking sheet lightly sprinkled with plain flour. Brush the loaves either with milk, or with cornflour glaze, and leave to rise for 1½ hours, uncovered. With a sharp knife, make 5mm (¼ inch) slashes at regular intervals. Bake in a hot oven, 200°C, 400°F, Gas Mark 6, for 10 minutes. Brush once again with milk or cornflour glaze and sprinkle with poppy seeds (or other seeds). Return to the oven and bake for 25-30 minutes or until golden brown.

To make cornflour glaze: mix 5ml (1 tsp) cornflour with 5ml (1 tsp) cold water. Add 120ml (4oz) boiling water and cook for 1-2 minutes until smooth. Cool slightly before use.

Wholemeal Bread

PREPARATION TIME: 2 hours 30 minutes
COOKING TIME: 50 minutes
MAKES: 1 large loaf

750g (1½lbs) wholemeal flour
2.5ml (½ tsp) salt
50g (2oz) margarine
25g (1oz) fresh yeast, or
15ml (1 tblsp) dried yeast (see below)
15ml (1 tblsp) granulated or brown sugar
300ml (½ pint) tepid water
150ml (¼ pint) tepid milk
15ml (1 tblsp) melted butter

Sieve the flour and salt into a warm bowl and rub in the margarine. Cream the fresh yeast with the sugar and stir in the warm water and milk. (If using dried yeast, sprinkle it onto the warm water and milk, with the sugar, and leave to stand for 10 minutes until thick and frothy). Make a well in the centre of the flour and pour in the yeast liquid; gradually mix in the flour to form a dough. Knead the dough well. Cover it with a damp cloth and leave to rise until double in bulk (about 1¼ hours). Grease a loaf tin, 23cm by 13cm by 7.5cm (9 inches by 5 inches by 3 inches). Turn the risen dough onto a floured surface and knead well; place in the loaf tin. Leave in a warm place to rise for 40 minutes. Brush the loaf with melted butter and bake at 200°C, 400°F, Gas Mark 6, for about 50 minutes

Wholemeal Pizza Dough

PREPARATION TIME: 50-60 minutes

200ml (⅓ pint) tepid water
7.5ml (1½ tsp) dried yeast
2.5ml (½ tsp) salt
5ml (1 tsp) sugar
5ml (1 tsp) olive oil
100g (4oz) wholemeal flour
150g (5oz) plain flour

Mix the dried yeast with the tepi[d] water. Add the salt, sugar and oil Mix in the flours a little at a time to make a dough. Use extra wate[r if] needed. Turn the dough onto a lightly floured surface and knead until smooth (about 5-8 minutes Cover the dough with a clean damp tea towel and leave to stan[d] for 15-20 minutes. Knead once more for 1-2 minutes. You can make either one large pizza base [or] several smaller ones. Grease one 35cm (14 inch) pizza pan and rol[l] out the dough to make a round large enough to fit the pizza pan. Shape the pizza dough with the hands to fit the pan. Top with th[e] chosen topping and bake.

Basic Pizza Dough

This is the basic recipe for pizza dough and although there are many variations, the making of t[he] dough is very important. Pizza originated in Italy, around the Naples area, but it is now eaten a[nd] enjoyed worldwide. Once the ba[sic] dough is perfected, toppings can [be] adjusted to one's taste. In fact, o[n] one single pizza, each slice can ha[ve] a different taste (i.e. with a differe[nt] topping). See Taco Pizza Topping and Mixed Vegetable Pizza Topp[ing] recipes.

PREPARATION TIME: about 1 hour 30 minutes

1.25ml (¼ tsp) sugar
15ml (1 tblsp) dried yeast
120ml (4 fl oz) tepid water
5ml (1 tsp) salt
225g (8oz) plain flour, sieved

Mix the dried yeast with 30ml (2 tblsp) of the tepid water and the sugar. Stir until dissolved. Leave stand for 10-15 minutes until frothy. Put the flour and salt into

Facing page: Crusty Loaf (top), Banana and Nut Bread (centre) and Wholemeal Bread (bottom).

bowl and make a well in the centre. Add the yeast liquid and the remaining tepid water; mix to form a dough. Kneed the dough on a floured surface for 8-10 minutes. Cover with a damp cloth and leave to rise in a warm place for 40-45 minutes, until double its original size. Knead once again on a lightly floured surface for 3-5 minutes until soft and elastic. You can make either one large pizza base, or several smaller ones. Grease one 35cm (14 inch) pizza pan and roll out the dough. Shape the pizza dough with the hands to fit the pan. Top with the chosen topping and bake.

Taco Pizza

This idea is taken from the taco (a Mexican pancake). The pizza base is made with a mixture of cornmeal and flour and some of the topping ingredients are the same as those used in a taco filling.

PREPARATION TIME: 30-40 minutes

COOKING TIME: 30-35 minutes

SERVES: 6 people

Dough

175g (6oz) plain flour
75g (3oz) fine yellow cornmeal
10ml (2 tsp) baking powder
5ml (1 tsp) salt
100g (4oz) margarine
120ml (4 fl oz) milk

Sieve the flour, cornmeal, salt and baking powder into a mixing bowl. Rub in the margarine. Add the milk, gradually, to form a medium soft dough. Knead the dough on a well floured surface for 4-5 minutes, until smooth. Roll into a circle to cover a 33-35cm (13-14 inch) pizza pan, with a 2.5cm (1 inch) high rim. Grease the pizza pan and cover with the dough. Shape the pizza dough to fit the pan. Pinch the edges to form a deep rim. Keep on one side until the topping is ready.

Topping

30ml (2 tblsp) olive oil
1 clove garlic, peeled and crushed
1 small onion, peeled and chopped
½ green pepper, seeded and coarsely chopped
4-6 mushrooms, sliced
225g (8oz) cooked red kidney beans (or drained canned ones)
2 spring onions, chopped
3 large tomatoes, chopped
6-8 pitted black olives, halved
3-4 pickled Mexican chillies, chopped
225g (8oz) Mozzarella, Cheddar or Monterey Jack cheese, cut into slivers
1 carrot, peeled and grated
150ml (¼ pint) soured cream
Bottled taco sauce

Heat the oil and fry the garlic, chopped onion, pepper and mushrooms for 2 minutes; add the kidney beans and stir fry for 1-2 minutes. Remove from the heat and stir in the spring onions. Spread the above topping mixture over the pizza base. Arrange the tomatoes evenly on top. Add the olives, Mexican chillies and slivers of cheese. Bake at 200°C, 400°F, Gas mark 6, for 15-20 minutes until the edges turn golden brown and crusty. Serve with grated carrots, whipped soured cream and taco sauce.

Mixed Vegetable Pizza Topping

PREPARATION TIME: 30 minutes

COOKING TIME: 20 minutes

SERVES: 4-6 people

30ml (2 tblsp) olive oil
1 small onion, peeled and chopped
2 spring onions, chopped
1 medium courgette, trimmed and thinly sliced
4 mushrooms, sliced
Salt and freshly ground black pepper to taste
6-8 canned tomatoes, chopped
10ml (2 tsp) tomato puree
8 pitted black olives
2 tomatoes, thinly sliced
1 green pepper, seeded and chopped
1 green chilli, chopped
5ml (1 tsp) dried oregano
175g (6oz) Mozzarella cheese, Cheddar cheese or a mixture of the two, cut into thin slivers
30ml (2 tblsp) grated Parmesan cheese

Heat the olive oil in a large frying pan; add the onions and sauté for 1-2 minutes. Add the courgette and sauté for 2 minutes. Add the mushrooms and salt and pepper to taste and stir fry for 1 minute to glaze the vegetables. Remove from the heat and cool. Mix the chopped tomato with the tomato puree and spread evenly over the pizza base. Spoon the vegetable mixture over the pizza and arrange the olives, sliced tomatoes, green pepper and green chilli on top. Sprinkle with the oregano, the slivers of cheese and the grated Parmesan cheese. Bake at 230°C, 450°F, Gas mark 8 for 12-15 minutes, or until the edge of the pizza is golden brown and crusty.

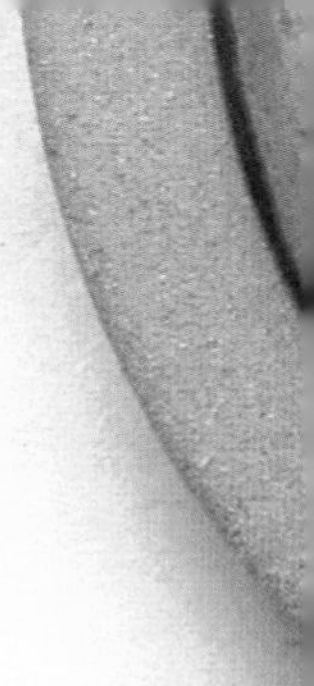

Taco Pizza (top right) and Mixed Vegetable Pizza Topping (bottom right).

Main Meals

Okra Curry

A dry vegetable curry made with okra and potato.

PREPARATION TIME: 10-15 minutes
COOKING TIME: 30 minutes
SERVES: 4 people

45ml (3 tblsp) oil
1 onion, peeled and chopped
2 medium sized potatoes, peeled and cut into 2.5cm (1 inch) pieces
450g (1lb) okra, topped and tailed, and chopped into 1cm (½ inch) pieces
Salt to taste
2.5ml (½ tsp) ground turmeric
5ml (1 tsp) chilli powder
7.5ml (1½ tsp) ground coriander
2-3 sprigs fresh green coriander leaves, chopped

Heat the oil in a wok or solid based frying pan and fry the onion for 3-4 minutes. Stir in the cubed potatoes; cover and cook for 3-4 minutes. Add the okra, and stir fry for 2 minutes. Sprinkle with salt to taste, turmeric, chilli and ground coriander. Mix gently; cover and cook for 8-10 minutes. Stir occasionally and continue cooking until the potatoes are tender. Sprinkle with the chopped coriander leaves. Mix well and serve.

Okra Fry

This is a dry "curry" – no spices are added; the okra supplies the hotness.

PREPARATION TIME: 15 minutes
COOKING TIME: 20-30 minutes
SERVES: 4 people

450-750g (1-1½lb) okra
Oil for deep frying
15ml (1 tblsp) oil
1 large onion, peeled and chopped
Salt and freshly ground black pepper to taste

Top and tail the okra; chop them into 5mm (¼ inch) even-sized pieces. Heat the oil for deep frying; add the chopped okra, a little at a time, and deep fry until brown and crisp. Drain on absorbent paper and keep warm in a dish. Heat the 15ml (1 tblsp) oil and fry the onion until tender about 4-5 minutes. Remove the onion and mix with the fried okra. Sprinkle with salt and pepper to taste. Serve with chapati, or as a side dish.

Aubergine Bake

PREPARATION TIME: 30 minutes
COOKING TIME: 30-40 minutes
SERVES: 6 people

3 large Dutch aubergines
10ml (2 tsp) salt
Malt vinegar
30ml (2 tblsp) oil
2 large onions, peeled and sliced
2 green chillies, chopped
425g (15oz) can peeled tomatoes, chopped
2.5ml (½ tsp) chilli powder
5ml (1 tsp) crushed garlic
2.5ml (½ tsp) ground turmeric
Oil for deep frying
60ml (4 tblsp) natural yogurt
5ml (1 tsp) freshly ground black pepper
4 tomatoes, sliced
225g (½lb) Cheddar cheese, grated

Cut the aubergines into 5mm (¼ inch) thick slices. Lay in a shallow dish. Sprinkle with 5ml (1 tsp) salt and add sufficient malt vinegar to cover. Allow to marinate for 20-30 minutes. Drain well. Heat 30ml (2 tblsp) oil in a frying pan and fry the onions until golden brown. Add the chillies, chopped tomatoes, remaining salt, chilli powder, garlic and turmeric. Mix well and simmer for 5-7 minutes. Remove from the heat. Cool and blend to a smooth sauce in the liquidiser. Keep the sauce on one side. Heat the oil for deep frying and deep fry the drained, marinated aubergine until brown on both sides (2-3 minutes each side). Drain well on kitchen paper. Grease a large deep baking tray. Arrange half the fried aubergine rounds closely together in the tray. Spoon over half the tomato sauce and beaten yogurt. Season with pepper. Add the remaining aubergine rounds and the rest of the tomato sauce and yogurt. Cover with slices of tomatoes and grated cheese. Bake at 180°C, 350°F, Gas Mark 4, for 10-15 minutes, or until the cheese melts and turns brown. Serve hot as a side dish, or as a main course with brown bread or pitta bread.

Stuffed Courgettes

This is a delightful dish from Southern Italy.

PREPARATION TIME: 30 minutes
COOKING TIME: 30-40 minutes
SERVES: 4 people

50g (2oz) fresh coarse breadcrumbs
60ml (4 tblsp) milk
8 medium sized courgettes, trimmed
1 onion, peeled and finely chopped
2 tomatoes, chopped
6-8 mushrooms, sliced
1 clove garlic, peeled and chopped
60ml (4 tblsp) olive oil
10ml (2 tsp) dried oregano
Salt and freshly ground black pepper to taste
1 egg, beaten
75g (3oz) Mozzarella cheese (or Cheddar), cut into thin slivers
75g (3oz) grated Parmesan cheese

Soak the breadcrumbs in the milk for 15-20 minutes. Cook the courgettes in boiling water for 5 minutes. Drain and cool. Slice them in half lengthways and scoop out the flesh, leaving a thick shell at least 5mm (¼ inch). Take care not to break or crack the courgettes.

This page: Aubergine Bake (top left), Okra Curry (centre right) and Okra Fry (right).

Overleaf: Courgette Bake (left), Stuffed Courgettes (centre) and Spicy Corn (right).

Keep the scooped flesh on one side. Squeeze out the excess milk from the breadcrumbs and put them into a bowl. Fry the scooped courgette flesh, chopped onion, tomatoes, mushrooms and chopped garlic in half the olive oil for 5 minutes. Mix with the breadcrumbs, oregano, salt and pepper to taste, the beaten egg and half the cheeses. Spoon the mixture evenly into all the courgette shells. Arrange the stuffed courgettes on a lightly greased baking tray. Sprinkle the remaining cheese over them and brush with the rest of the oil. Bake for 18-20 minutes at 200°C, 400°F, Gas Mark 6, or until the cheese has melted and turned golden brown. Serve at once.

Spicy Corn

This dish originates from East Africa, it makes a tasty hot snack or supper dish.

PREPARATION TIME: 15 minutes
COOKING TIME: 35-40 minutes
SERVES: 6 people

45ml (3 tblsp) oil
1 large onion, peeled and chopped
2 medium potatoes, peeled and cubed
8 fresh curry leaves (optional)
2.5ml (½ tsp) cumin seed
2.5ml (½ tsp) mustard seed
5ml (1 tsp) crushed fresh root ginger
5ml (1 tsp) crushed garlic
750g (1½lb) frozen sweetcorn kernels
5ml (1 tsp) salt
5ml (1 tsp) chilli powder
5ml (1 tsp) ground coriander
2.5ml (½ tsp) ground turmeric
425g (15oz) can peeled tomatoes, chopped
15ml (1 tblsp) tomato puree
1-2 green chillies, chopped
2 green peppers, seeded and cut into 2.5cm (1 inch) pieces
3 sprigs fresh green coriander, chopped
15ml (1 tblsp) thick tamarind pulp, or
30ml (2 tblsp) lemon juice

Heat the oil and fry the onion for 3 minutes; add the potatoes and fry for 5 minutes. Add the curry leaves, cumin and mustard seed and stir fry for 1-2 minutes. Add ginger and garlic and stir fry for 1-2 minutes. Add the sweetcorn, salt, chilli powder, ground coriander and turmeric. Mix well and cook for 2-3 minutes. Add the chopped tomatoes, tomato puree, chopped chillies, green peppers and coriander leaves. Stir in the tamarind pulp and mix well adding a little water if the mixture seems too dry. Cover and cook over a low heat until the potatoes are tender about 10-15 minutes. The spicy corn should be thick but moist. Serve hot or cold.

Spiced Peas

PREPARATION TIME: 10 minutes
COOKING TIME: 15 minutes
SERVES: 6 people

30ml (2 tblsp) oil
1 large onion, peeled and chopped
2 green chillies, sliced in half lengthways
1kg (2lb) shelled peas (fresh or frozen)
Salt and freshly ground black pepper to taste
15ml (1 tblsp) lemon juice
Lemon wedges

Heat the oil in a wok or solid based frying pan and fry the onion until tender. Add the chillies and fry for 1 minute. Add the peas and salt and pepper to taste; stir fry for 5-10 minutes, or until well coloured and "dry". Put into a serving dish and sprinkle with lemon juice. Garnish with lemon wedges. Serve as a side dish, or as a snack.

Spinach with Paneer

Paneer is a home-made cheese; it is made by separating milk into curds and whey by means of a souring agent such as lemon juice. It is eaten extensively in northern parts of India and is a good source of protein.

PREPARATION TIME: 15 minutes, plus time for making paneer
COOKING TIME: 20-30 minutes
SERVES: 4 people

To make paneer: (This is an overnight process)
1.2 litres (2 pints) milk
30ml (2 tblsp) lemon juice

Bring the milk to the boil. Reduce the heat and sprinkle with the lemon juice. The milk will separate into pale watery whey and thick white paneer (or curds). Remove from the heat and allow the paneer to coagulate (if the milk has not separated properly, add a few more drops of lemon juice. The whey should be a clear, pale, yellow liquid. Pour the paneer and liquid through a muslin-lined sieve. Discard the liquid whey and tie the muslin over the paneer. Flatten the paneer to 1cm (½ inch) thick; place it on a tray and rest it in a tilted position. Place more muslin over the top and weight it down. The pressure will drag out the remaining moisture and the tilted position will channel the liquid away from the paneer. Leave to drain overnight. Next day, cut the firm paneer into 2.5cm (1 inch) cubes.

75g (3oz) butter
1 medium onion, peeled and finely chopped
2.5cm (1 inch) piece cinnamon stick
1 bayleaf
450g (1lb) frozen spinach puree, or fresh leaf spinach, cooked and pureed
5ml (1 tsp) chilli powder
2.5ml (½ tsp) salt
120g (4½oz) natural yogurt
3 sprigs fresh green coriander leaves, chopped
5ml (1 tsp) garam masala powder
Oil for deep frying

Heat the butter in a pan and fry the onion until golden brown. Add the cinnamon and bayleaf and fry for 1 minute. Add the spinach and stir to mix. Sprinkle with the chilli powder and salt and stir in the yogurt, coriander leaves and garam masala. Cover and cook for 2-3 minutes. Simmer gently. Meanwhile, deep-fry the drained paneer cubes until golden. Add the paneer cubes to the spinach and simmer together for 4-5 minutes. Serve hot with chapati or pulao rice.

New Potato Fry

This Oriental dish is very versatile; it can be served as a side dish, as a snack, or as a main curry. It is also a wonderful way of serving potatoes with traditional roast meats.

PREPARATION TIME: 20 minutes
COOKING TIME: 10-12 minutes
SERVES: 3-4 people

45ml (3 tblsp) oil
5ml (1 tsp) mustard seed
450g (1lb) small, even sized new potatoes, boiled in their skins and peeled
5ml (1 tsp) red chilli powder
7.5ml (1½ tsp) ground coriander
1.25ml (¼ tsp) ground turmeric
2.5ml (½ tsp) salt
3 sprigs fresh green coriander leave[s] chopped (optional)
Lemon juice to taste

Heat the oil in a wok or solid bas[ed] frying pan and add the mustard seed and the whole, peeled potatoes. Stir fry over a low heat until they are lightly browned. Sprinkle with the spices, salt and chopped coriander leaves. Stir fr[y] over a low heat for 5-6 minutes until golden brown. Remove fro[m] heat. Put into a dish and sprinkle with the lemon juice. Serve hot o[r] cold.

Courgette Bake

Serve this dish as a main course with fried rice, or as a side dish.

PREPARATION TIME: 20-30 minutes
COOKING TIME: 35 minutes
SERVES: 4-6 people

1kg (2lbs) courgettes, trimmed and coarsely grated
5ml (1 tsp) salt
30ml (2 tblsp) melted unsalted but[ter] (or oil)
3-4 eggs, well beaten
175-200g (6-7oz) grated mild che[ese] (Edam, Samso, etc)
1 medium onion, peeled and finely chopped
2 cloves garlic, peeled and finely chopped
30ml (2 tblsp) chopped parsley
5ml (1 tsp) dried basil
2.5ml (½ tsp) freshly ground black pepper
30-40g (1-1½oz) grated Parmesan cheese

Put the grated courgettes into a colander and sprinkle with salt. Leave to drain for 10 minutes. Squeeze the moisture out of the

Facing page: Spiced Peas (top), Spinach with Paneer (centre right) and New Potat[o] Fry (bottom).

courgettes until quite dry. Lightly grease a baking dish (size approx. 25cm x 18cm (10 inches x 7 inches). Heat the butter in a non-stick frying pan and fry the courgettes for 3-4 minutes until tender. Mix the beaten eggs, grated cheese, chopped onion, garlic, parsley, basil and pepper. Place the sauteed courgettes in the baking dish and pour egg mixture over the top. Sprinkle with the Parmesan cheese and bake at 180°C, 350°F, Gas mark 4, for 25-30 minutes until set. Serve cut into squares or diamond shapes. Can be eaten hot or cold.

Vegetable Stir Fry with Tofu

This is a Chinese stir fry dish with Tofu which makes a filling main course.

PREPARATION TIME: 30 minutes

COOKING TIME: 10 minutes

SERVES: 4 people

10ml (2 tsp) soya sauce
10ml (2 tsp) Worcestershire sauce
2.5cm (1 inch) fresh root ginger, peeled and thinly sliced
3 cloves garlic, peeled and crushed
225g (8oz) Tofu, cut into 1cm (½ inch) pieces
10ml (2 tsp) cornflour
200ml (⅓ pint) water
45ml (3 tblsp) oil
3 stems celery, sliced thinly
2 carrots, peeled and cut into thin diagonal slices
2-3 courgettes, trimmed, and cut into thin diagonal slices
1 green pepper, quartered, seeded and sliced thinly
8 mushrooms, thinly sliced
1-2 tomatoes, cut into wedges
50g (2oz) mange tout, or thinly sliced green beans

Mix the soya sauce with the Worcestershire sauce, ginger and garlic. Add the Tofu cubes and marinate for 8 minutes. Pick out the Tofu and keep on a plate. Stir the cornflour into the soya sauce mixture and blend in the water. Heat the oil in a wok over a medium heat. Add the celery and carrots and stir fry for 2 minutes. Add the courgettes and green pepper and stir fry for 2 minutes. Add the tomatoes and mange tout or green beans. Stir fry for 2 minutes. Add the mushrooms and stir fry for 1 minute. Stir in the water and soya sauce mixture. Cook until thickened, stirring for 1-2 minutes. Add the Tofu. Heat through and serve immediately.

Cheese Bourag

PREPARATION TIME: 30-40 minutes

COOKING TIME: 20-25 minutes

SERVES: 4 people

225g (8oz) plain flour
Salt
7.5ml (3 tsp) baking powder
40g (1½oz) unsalted butter
120-150ml (4-5 fl oz) milk
225g (8oz) strong Cheddar cheese, grated
45ml (3 tblsp) chopped parsley
Oil for deep frying

Sieve the flour, 1.25ml (¼ tsp) salt and baking powder into a bowl; rub in the butter. Add the milk, a little at a time, and mix to a dough with a palette knife. Cover the dough and leave in a cool place to relax. Mix the grated cheese with the chopped parsley and a little salt to taste. Roll the dough out very thinly on a floured board and cut into 5cm (2 inch) squares. Brush the edges of half the squares with a dampened pastry brush. Place a little filling in the centre of each one and cover with the remaining squares. Seal the edges well by pinching with the fingers or notching with the prongs of a fork. Heat the oil for deep frying. Fry the bourags a few at a time in hot oil until golden and crisp. Drain on kitchen paper and serve hot with sweet and sour sauce.

Avial

This is a mixed vegetable dish made with coconut.

PREPARATION TIME: 30 minutes

COOKING TIME: 20 minutes

SERVES: 4 people

2 medium sized potatoes, peeled and cut into 2.5cm (1 inch) cubes
175g (6oz) lobia beans, trimmed and cut into 5cm (2 inch) pieces
50g (2oz) green beans, trimmed and sliced
4 drumstick or yard long beans, strung and cut into 2.5cm (1 inch) pieces
175g (6oz) squash, peeled and cut into 2.5cm (1 inch) cubes
1 green unripe banana, peeled and cut into 2.5cm (1 inch) pieces
1 aubergine, trimmed and cut into 2.5cm (1 inch) chunks
100g (4oz) shelled peas
½ fresh coconut, shelled, skin removed and thinly sliced
7.5ml (1½ tsp) cumin seeds
2 green chillies, chopped
120ml (4 fl oz) water
150ml (5oz) natural yogurt
45ml (3 tblsp) coconut oil for cooking

Steam all the vegetables for 10-15 minutes until almost tender, but still slightly crisp. Grind the spices with the water in a liquidiser until smooth. Mix the spice liquid with the coconut. Heat the coconut oil in a saucepan and add the vegetables, spice mixture and yogurt. Bring to the boil and simmer with the lid on for 5 minutes. Serve with rice.

Garlic Hash Brown

This is a favourite dish in America, where it is eaten with steak and burgers.

PREPARATION TIME: 20 minutes

COOKING TIME: 30 minutes

SERVES: 4 people

60ml (4 tblsp) oil
4 cloves of garlic, peeled and quartered lengthways
3 whole red chillies
Salt
450-750g (1-1½lb) potatoes, peeled and coarsely grated

Heat the oil in a wok or a large non-stick frying pan. Fry the garlic until lightly browned. Add the red chillies and fry for 30 seconds. Sprinkle with salt to taste and add the grated potato. Stir fry for 5 minutes. Cover and cook for a further 8-10 minutes. The potatoes should be crisp and golden brown. Cook until the potatoes are tender. Serve as a side dish or for breakfast.

Vegetable Stir Fry with Tofu (top), Avial (centre left) and Cheese Bourag (bottom right).

Spiced Chick Peas

This dryish curry is a "must" on any Punjabi menu. It is usually served with milk bread or pitta bread and an onion salad.

PREPARATION TIME: overnight overnight for soaking, plus 15 minutes

COOKING TIME: 40-50 minutes

SERVES: 4-6 people

450g (1lb) chick peas
5ml (1 tsp) baking powder
4 cloves
5ml (1 tsp) cumin seed
4 large black cardamoms, ground
4 small cardamoms, ground
1 large onion, peeled and chopped
45ml (3 tblsp) oil
2 bayleaves
2.5cm (1 inch) piece cinnamon stick
2 green chillies, sliced in half lengthways
2.5cm (1 inch) fresh root ginger, peeled and finely chopped
4 cloves garlic, peeled and crushed
7.5ml (1½ tsp) ground coriander
250-300ml (8-10 fl oz) canned tomatoes, chopped
2.5ml (½ tp) freshly ground black pepper
2.5ml (½ tsp) salt
5-6 sprigs fresh green coriander leaves, chopped

Wash the chick peas and soak them overnight in 1.2 litres (2 pints) water and the baking powder. The following day, cook the chick peas in their soaking liquid in a pressure cooker for 10-15 minutes. If a lot of liquid has been absorbed during soaking, add a little more. Dry roast the cloves and cumin seed in a frying pan. Grind the cloves, cumin, large and small cardamons into a fine powder. Fry the onion in the oil for 2-3 minutes. Add the bayleaves, cinnamon, chillies, ginger and garlic. Fry for 1 minute, add the ground coriander and tomatoes. Fry for 2-3 minutes. Strain the chick peas, retaining any liquid. Add the chick peas to the tomato mixture and add black pepper, salt and the dry roasted spices. Mix well and add 250ml (8 fl oz) of the strained chick pea liquid. Sprinkle with chopped coriander; cover and cook for 8-10 minutes. Add a little extra liquid if necessary. Serve with bread or rice.

Vegetable Pancakes (far left) and Spiced Chick Peas (left).

Vegetable Pancakes

A combination of shredded vegetables makes a delicious pancake, when added to the batter before cooking.

PREPARATION TIME: 15 minutes
COOKING TIME: 15 minutes
SERVES: 4-6 people

100g (4oz) butter
225g (8oz) shredded or coarsely grated carrots
225g (8oz) shredded or coarsely grated courgettes
450g (1lb) shredded or coarsely grated potatoes
1 medium onion, thinly sliced
3 eggs, well beaten
200ml (⅓ pint) soured cream
60ml (4 tblsp) cornflour
2.5ml (½ tsp) salt
2.5ml (½ tsp) freshly ground black pepper
Oil for frying
Wedges of lemon

Melt the butter in a frying pan; add the carrots, courgettes, potatoes and onion. Saute for 3-4 minutes, stirring continuously. Beat the eggs together with the soured cream, cornflour and salt and pepper. Mix well. Stir in the semi-cooked vegetables. Mix together gently. Heat a large non-stick frying pan and brush with 10ml (2 tsp) oil; add 15ml (1 tblsp) batter. Cook until light brown; turn the small pancake over and cook until the other side is also brown. Make 3 or 4 at a time. The size of the pancakes can be increased by using more batter for each pancake. Serve with salads or with tomato sauce as a light meal or snack.

Green Beans with Coconut

PREPARATION TIME: 10 minutes
COOKING TIME: 20 minutes
SERVES: 3-4 people

30ml (2 tblsp) oil
2 cloves garlic, peeled and crushed
2 green or red dried chillies
450g (1lb) green beans, sliced
1.25ml (¼ tsp) salt
30ml (2 tblsp) desiccated coconut, or grated fresh coconut

Heat the oil in a wok or frying pan. Add the garlic and fry until golden brown. Add the chillies and stir fry for 30 seconds. Add the green beans and sprinkle with salt. Stir fry for 8-10 minutes until the beans are tender but still crisp. Sprinkle with the coconut and stir fry for a further 2-3 minutes. Serve as a side dish.

Mixed Vegetable Raita

Raitas are yogurt-based Indian dishes served as accompaniments to curries etc. Natural yogurt is usually mixed with fruits, vegetables, and herbs such as coriander or mint.

PREPARATION TIME: 10 minutes
SERVES: 4-6 people

300ml (½ pint) natural yogurt
½ cucumber, chopped
1 small onion, peeled and chopped
2 tomatoes, chopped
2 stems celery, chopped
1 small apple, cored and chopped
2 boiled potatoes, peeled and chopped
1.25ml (¼ tsp) salt
1.25ml (¼ tsp) freshly ground black pepper
1 sprig fresh green coriander, chopped

Beat the yogurt in a bowl. Add all the remaining ingredients, seasoning well with salt and pepper. Chill before serving.

Cannelloni with Spinach and Ricotta

PREPARATION TIME: 20 minutes
COOKING TIME: 1 hour 20 minutes
SERVES: 4 people

30ml (2 tblsp) olive oil or melted butter
1 large onion, peeled and finely chopped
2 large cloves garlic, peeled and crushed
425g (15oz) can peeled tomatoes, chopped
15ml (1 tblsp) tomato puree
Salt and freshly ground black pepper to taste
7.5ml (1½ tsp) dried basil
2.5ml (½ tsp) dried oregano
350g (12oz) cannelloni tubes
60ml (4 tblsp) thick spinach puree
225g (8oz) Ricotta cheese
30ml (2 tblsp) grated Parmesan cheese

To make the sauce: heat the oil or butter and fry the onion and garlic for 2-3 minutes. Add the tomatoes and tomato puree and mix well. Simmer for 2 minutes. Add the salt and pepper, basil and oregano. Cover and simmer for 10-15 minutes until thick.

Bring a large pan of salted water to the boil; cook the cannelloni tubes for 10 minutes until just tender. Do not overboil. Lift out the cannelloni tubes and put them into a bowl of cold water to cool quickly. Drain well. Mix together the spinach, ricotta and salt and pepper to taste. Fill the cannelloni tubes with the spinach mixture and arrange them in a greased shallow ovenproof dish. Pour the tomato sauce over the cannelloni; sprinkle with the Parmesan cheese. Bake for 20-30 minutes at 180°C, 350°F, Gas Mark 4 or until the top is browned and bubbling. Serve at once.

Ginger Cauliflower

This is a very simple and extremely subtle vegetable dish spiced with ginger.

PREPARATION TIME: 15 minutes
COOKING TIME: 15 minutes
SERVES: 4 people

45ml (3 tblsp) oil
1 medium onion, peeled and chopped
2.5cm (1 inch) fresh root ginger, peeled and sliced
1-2 green chillies, cut in half lengthways
1 medium cauliflower, cut into 2.5cm (1 inch) florets, along with tender leaves and stalk
Salt to taste
2-3 sprigs fresh green coriander leaves, chopped
Juice of 1 lemon

Heat the oil in a wok or solid based saucepan; fry the onion, ginger and chillies for 2-3 minutes. Add the cauliflower and salt to taste. Stir to

Noodles with Vegetables (top left), Green Beans with Coconut (centre right) and Garlic Hash Brown (bottom).

mix well. Cover and cook over a low heat for 5-6 minutes. Add the coriander leaves and cook for a further 2-3 minutes, or until the florets of cauliflower are tender. Sprinkle with lemon juice, mix well and serve immediately. Serve with pitta bread.

Mung Fritters

These tiny marble-sized fritters are made with mung pulse. They can be eaten as a cocktail snack or made into a curry with a well-flavoured sauce.

PREPARATION TIME: 1 hour 30 minutes

COOKING TIME: 30 minutes

SERVES: 4 people

225g (8oz) split mung pulse
1 small onion, peeled and chopped
5ml (1 tsp) chilli powder
7.5ml (1½ tsp) garam masala powder
2.5ml (½ tsp) cumin seed
4-5 sprigs fresh green coriander leaves, chopped
2.5ml (½ tsp) salt
Oil for deep frying

Wash and soak the mung pulse for 1 hour in sufficient cold water to cover. Drain and then grind into a thick coarse paste, adding 120-250ml (4-8 fl oz) water as you go. It should be the consistency of peanut butter. Mix the mung paste with the onion, chilli powder, garam masala, cumin seed, coriander leaves and salt. Mix well and adjust seasoning if necessary. Heat the oil for deep frying. Using a teaspoon, shape the paste into small "marbles" and fry in the hot oil until golden brown. Drain on kitchen paper and serve piping hot with chutney, a chilli sauce or a dip. To turn into a curry, add the Mung Fritters to the following curry sauce.

Sauce
10ml (2 tsp) oil
1 small onion, finely chopped
2.5ml (½ tsp) chilli powder
5ml (1 tsp) ground coriander
5ml (1 tsp) ground cumin
4-6 canned tomatoes, chopped
Salt to taste
3-4 sprigs fresh green coriander leaves, chopped

Heat the oil in a saucepan and fry the onion for 3 minutes. Stir in all the above ingredients; cover and simmer for 5-8 minutes. Add a little water to make a thickish sauce. Add ready-fried Mung Fritters and simmer for 3-5 minutes.

Noodles with Vegetables

This exotic noodle dish can be served hot or cold, as a main course, as a side dish or as a snack.

PREPARATION TIME: 20 minutes

COOKING TIME: 30 minutes

SERVES: 4 people

Salt to taste
450g (1lb) egg noodles, or broken spaghetti
45ml (3 tblsp) oil
2.5cm (1 inch) fresh root ginger, peeled and thinly sliced
1 large or 2 medium onions, peeled and sliced
75g (3oz) green beans, sliced
75g (3oz) carrots, peeled and cut into matchstick strips
100g (4oz) white cabbage, or Chinese leaves, shredded
50g (2oz) shelled peas
75g (3oz) sprouting mung beans
1 green pepper, seeded and cut into 2.5cm (1 inch) pieces
1-2 stems celery, chopped
1-2 green chillies, split lengthways
2.5ml (½ tsp) monosodium glutamate (optional)
30ml (2 tblsp) soya sauce
15ml (1 tblsp) lemon juice
5-10ml (1-2 tsp) Chinese red pepper sauce
60ml (4 tblsp) vegetable stock

Bring a large pan of water to the boil and add 5ml (1 tsp) salt. Add the noodles or spaghetti and boil gently for 5-6 minutes. Drain the noodles. Rinse the noodles in cold water and drain once again. Heat the oil in a wok or large frying pan. Fry the ginger for 1-2 minutes. Add the onions and fry for 2-3 minutes. Add the beans and carrots and for 2 minutes. Add the remain vegetables and the chillies and fry for 3-4 minutes. Add salt to taste and the noodles. Stir ligh with two forks. Dissolve the monosodium glutamate in the sauce and sprinkle over the no mixture; stir in the lemon juic Chinese sauce and stock. Hea through for 2-3 minutes. Serv

This page: Mung Fritters.

Facing page: Ginger Cauliflower (top left), Mix Vegetable Raita (top right) and Cannelloni with Spin and Ricotta (bottom).

Sauces, Dips and Chutney

Plum Chutney

Any variety of plum can be used; either singly or in a mixture of one or more varieties.

PREPARATION TIME: 10 minutes
COOKING TIME: 40 minutes
MAKES: about 3kg (6lbs)

2kg (4½lb) plums, pitted
2.5cm (1 inch) fresh root ginger, peeled and finely chopped
10ml (2 tsp) salt
1.5kg (3lb) brown sugar
5ml (1 tsp) cumin seed
5ml (1 tsp) coriander seed
4 dried red chillies
5ml (1 tsp) onion seed
30ml (2 tblsp) malt vinegar
50g (2oz) chopped blanched almonds
50g (2oz) chopped cashew nuts or hazelnuts
100g (4oz) raisins
100g (4oz) sultanas

Put the plums, ginger, salt and sugar into a saucepan, preferably a non-stick pan. Cover and cook gently until the plums are soft (about 15-20 minutes). Dry roast the cumin seed, coriander seed and red chillies in a frying pan for 1-2 minutes. Remove the red chillies and coarsely grind the cumin and coriander seeds. Add the roasted red chillies, ground spices and onion seed to the cooked plums. Add the malt vinegar, nuts, raisins and sultanas and simmer gently for 5-6 minutes. Allow to cool slightly. Pour into clean, warm glass jars and seal.

Guacamole
(AVOCADO DIP)

This is a popular Mexican dip, usually eaten with crisps, salty biscuits or sticks of raw vegetable, such as cucumber, celery etc.

PREPARATION TIME: 5 minutes
SERVES: 6-8 people

1 avocado, peeled, stoned and mashed
1 large clove garlic, peeled and crushed
5ml (1 tsp) salt
1.25ml (¼ tsp) freshly ground black pepper
1 large tomato, skinned and chopped
5ml (1 tsp) olive oil
15ml (1 tblsp) lemon juice
2-3 sprigs fresh green coriander leaves, finely chopped
1 small onion, peeled and grated

Blend the avocado pulp in the liquidiser with the salt, pepper, tomato, olive oil, lemon juice and coriander leaves. Put into a small bowl and mix with the onion. Serve with savoury biscuits, crisps or sticks of raw vegetables.

Tamarind Dip

PREPARATION TIME: 20 minutes
MAKES: about 400ml (⅔ pint)

75g (3oz) tamarind pods
250ml (8 fl oz) boiling water
2.5ml (½ tsp) salt
75-90g (3-3½oz) brown sugar
1 green chilli, chopped
1.25ml (¼ tsp) chilli powder

Soak the tamarind pods in boiling water for 5-6 minutes, or until soft. Rub the pods in the water to separate the dried pulp around the seeds. Squeeze out the seeds and skins of the pods. (Do not discard as a second extract can be obtained for future use). Add the salt and sugar to the tamarind pulp. Mix in the chilli and chilli powder and leave to stand for 5 minutes before using. Salt and sugar can be adjusted according to personal taste.

Savoury Coconut Chutney

PREPARATION TIME: 15 minutes
MAKES: about 450ml (¾ pint)

1-2 fresh coconuts, shell removed, outer skin peeled and cut into pieces
1cm (½ inch) fresh root ginger, peeled and chopped
2 green chillies, chopped
5ml (1 tsp) cumin seed
1-2 bunches fresh green coriander leaves, chopped
45ml (3 tblsp) thick tamarind pulp or
60ml (4 tblsp) lemon juice
5ml (1 tsp) sugar
2.5ml (½ tsp) salt

Put all the ingredients into the liquidiser and blend until smooth and creamy. If the mixture is too thick, add a little water. Serve with hot snacks, such as toasted chicken sandwiches.

Mixed Fruit Chutney

This sweet-sour chutney goes particularly well with pork dishes, such as spareribs.

PREPARATION TIME: 30 minutes
COOKING TIME: 40 minutes
MAKES: about 2¼kg (5¼lb)

3 firm pears, cored and sliced
4 apples, cored and chopped
4 peaches, skinned, stoned and sliced or
425g (15oz) can peach slices, drained
450g (1lb) plums, halved and stoned
6 rings canned pineapple, cut into cubes
100g (4oz) dates, stoned and chopped
225g (8oz) dried prunes, soaked overnight
100g (4oz) dried apricots, soaked overnight
1kg (2¼lb) brown sugar
10ml (2 tsp) salt
2.5cm (1 inch) fresh root ginger, peeled and thinly sliced
100g (4oz) chopped blanched almonds
100g (4oz) cashew nuts, chopped
60ml (4 tblsp) malt vinegar
8 cloves, coarsely ground
5ml (1 tsp) chilli powder
5cm (2 inch) piece cinnamon stick
2 bananas, peeled and sliced

Put all the fruit into a saucepan (apart from the bananas) with the sugar, salt and ginger. Cover and cook for 15-20 minutes. Add the nuts, vinegar, cloves, chilli powder and cinnamon stick. Stir well and cook for 6-8 minutes. Simmer gently, stirring occasionally, until most of the liquid has evaporated. The chutney should be thick and sticky. Add the sliced bananas and stir over the heat for 1 minute. Cool slightly. Pour into clean, warm glass jars and seal.

Green Tomato Relish

Use the last crop of tomatoes to make this relish. Serve with any grilled meat, barbecued chicken, etc.

PREPARATION TIME: 4 hours
COOKING TIME: about 20 minutes
MAKES: about 1½kg (3lb)

1kg (2lb) green tomatoes, seeded and chopped
75g (6oz) shredded white cabbage
2 red peppers, seeded and chopped
1 onion, peeled and chopped
15ml (1 tblsp) salt
225g (8oz) brown sugar
300ml (½ pint) distilled white vinegar
10ml (2 tsp) mustard seed
10ml (2 tsp) celery seed
15ml (1 tblsp) prepared horseradish sauce

Mix the tomatoes, cabbage, peppers and onion together. Sprinkle with the salt and mix well. Leave to stand for 2-3 hours. Drain well and then rinse under cold running water. Drain and gently squeeze out the excess moisture. Mix the sugar, vinegar, mustard seed, celery seed and horseradish

Facing page: Plum Chutney (top right), Mixed Fruit Chutney (centre) and Green Tomato Relish (bottom).

Tamarind Dip (far left), Savoury Coconut Chutney (centre) and Guacamole (Avocado Dip) (above).

sauce together in a large solid based pan. Bring to the boil over a medium heat. Add the vegetables, cover and simmer gently for another 16-18 minutes until the relish is sticky. Remove from the heat and cool slightly. Pour into clean, warm glass jars and seal. Will keep for up to 2 months.

Mexican Salsa

This is a beautiful fresh sauce which goes well with barbecued meats, curries and, of course, burritos and tacos.

PREPARATION TIME: 10 minutes

MAKES: about 150ml (1/4 pint)

5 tomatoes, skinned and chopped
1 small onion, chopped
1-2 pickled or canned Mexican chillies, chopped
2 cloves garlic, peeled and crushed
10ml (2 tsp) malt vinegar
2.5ml (1/2 tsp) salt
2.5ml (1/2 tsp) sugar
2-3 sprigs fresh green coriander, chopped
5ml (1 tsp) bottled chilli sauce

Mix all the ingredients together in a bowl. Chill for 2 to 3 hours before serving.

Salsa Verde

A perfect Italian sauce to serve with any pasta, or with veal.

PREPARATION TIME: 15 minutes

MAKES: about 200ml (1/3 pint)

75ml (5 tblsp) chopped fresh parsley
30ml (2 tblsp) white wine vinegar
3 cloves garlic, peeled and sliced
30ml (2 tblsp) capers, finely chopped
30ml (2 tblsp) olive oil
2-3 spring onions, chopped
Salt and freshly ground black pepper to taste

Blend the parsley, garlic and vinegar in the liquidiser. Pour the parsley sauce into a small bowl and mix with the capers, olive oil, spring onions and salt and pepper. Mix well. Cover and chill for 10-15 minutes. The sauce can be thinned to the desired consistency with a little olive oil or chicken stock.

Chilli Sauce

This classic piquant sauce is perfec for those who love hot, spicy food.

PREPARATION TIME: 20 minutes

COOKING TIME: 2 hours 30 minutes

MAKES: about 600ml (1 pint)

8 large ripe tomatoes, skinned and chopped
2-3 small green peppers, seeded and chopped
2 medium onions, peeled and finely chopped
4 stems celery, chopped
10-15ml (2-3 tsp) salt
250g (9oz) granulated sugar
350ml (12 fl oz) cider vinegar
2-3 bay leaves
5ml (1 tsp) coriander seeds
5ml (1 tsp) freshly ground black pepper
1.25ml (1/4 tsp) ground cloves
2.5ml (1/2 tsp) ground cinnamon
5ml (1 tsp) ground ginger
5ml (1 tsp) mustard seed

Mix all the ingredients together i a pan and bring to the boil. Cove and simmer for about 2 hours ov a low heat, until thick. Stir once mix and simmer again for 10 minutes. Remove from the heat and cool slightly. Pour into clean warm glass jars and seal.

This page: Chilli Sauce (top left), Salsa Verdi (centre) an Mexican Salsa (bottom).

Facing page: Rice Pudding (top), Potato Pudding (cent and Cabbage Pudding (bottom).

Sweets

Carrotella

PREPARATION TIME: 15 minutes
COOKING TIME: 35-40 minutes
SERVES: 4-6 people

1.2 litre (2 pints) milk
450g (1lb) carrots, peeled and shredded
200ml (⅓ pint) canned evaporated milk
100g (4oz) granulated sugar
50g (2oz) raisins
Seeds of 8 small cardamoms, crushed
2 drops rose-water or vanilla essence
50g (2oz) chopped blanched almonds
50g (2oz) pistachio nuts, chopped

Put the milk into a pan and simmer over a low heat until reduced to 900ml (1½ pints). Add the carrots; cover and cook over a medium heat for 15 minutes. Add the evaporated milk, sugar and raisins. Cover and simmer gently for another 5 minutes. Remove from the heat. Stir in the crushed cardamom seeds and essence and pour into a serving dish. Allow to cool slightly. Sprinkle nuts on the top and serve. On hot summer days, the Carrotella is best chilled.

Carrot Cake

PREPARATION TIME: 30 minutes
COOKING TIME: 45-50 minutes
MAKES: 25cm (10 inch) loaf

175g (6oz) butter or margarine
175g (6oz) brown sugar
100g (4oz) granulated sugar
2 eggs, well beaten
225g (8oz) plain flour
7.5ml (1½ tsp) bicarbonate of soda
2.5ml (½ tsp) baking powder
1.25ml (¼ tsp) ground cinnamon
2.5ml (½ tsp) salt
225g (8oz) peeled carrots, shredded
75g (3oz) raisins
50g (2oz) chopped walnuts
1.25ml (¼ tsp) small cardamom seeds, crushed
Icing sugar for dredging

Cream the butter and sugars together. Add the eggs, a little at a time, beating well after each addition. Sieve the flour, bicarbonate of soda, baking powder, cinnamon and salt together. Fold the dry ingredients into the egg mixture. Add the carrots, raisins, nuts and crushed cardamom. Mix well and pour the mixture into a well buttered 25cm (10 inch) loaf tin. Bake at 180°C, 350°F, Gas Mark 4, for 45-50 minutes, or until a fine metal skewer comes out clean when inserted into the centre of the cake. Cool in the tin for 10-15 minutes, before turning out. Dredge with icing sugar before serving.

Rice Pudding

There are many ways of making a rice pudding, but this is definitely one of the best. It is suitable for serving on any occasion, from everyday meals to smart dinner parties.

PREPARATION TIME: 10 minutes
COOKING TIME: 1 hour 30 minutes
SERVES: 6 people

50g (2oz) unsalted butter
1 bayleaf, crumbled
2.5cm (1 inch) piece cinnamon stick, crushed
175g (6oz) pudding rice, washed and drained
1.2 litre (2 pints) milk
400ml (⅔ pint) canned evaporated milk
175g (6oz) granulated sugar
50g (2oz) raisins
50g (2oz) chopped blanched almonds
50g (2oz) pistachio nuts, chopped or cut into slivers
Seeds of 8 small cardamoms, crushed

Melt the butter in a saucepan and fry the bayleaf and cinnamon for 1 minute. Add the rice and stir well. Add the milk and bring to the boil. Reduce the heat and simmer for 40-50 minutes, stirring occasionally to prevent the rice from sticking to the pan. Add the sugar and evaporated milk, and simmer for a further 20-30 minutes, stirring frequently. Thin layers of light brown skin form on the base of the pan, this is what gives the pudding its rich reddish tinge and flavour. Add the raisins and half the chopped almonds. Mix well and simmer for a further 5-10 minutes, or until the pudding is really thick. Mix in the crushed cardamom seeds and pour into a serving dish. Decorate with the remaining chopped almonds and pistachio nuts. Serve hot or cold.

Carrot Halva

A delightful sweet from the mysterious East. Serve it hot or cold, with or without cream.

PREPARATION TIME: 20 minutes
COOKING TIME: 50 minutes
SERVES: 8-10 people

2kg (4lb) large sweet carrots, peeled and shredded
900ml (1½ pints) canned evaporated milk
750g (1½lbs) granulated sugar
175g (6oz) unsalted butter
75g (3oz) raisins
Seeds of 10 small cardamoms, crushed
100g (4oz) chopped mixed nuts (blanched and chopped almonds, cashews, pistachios etc.)
Single cream

Put the carrots, evaporated milk and sugar into a large solid based pan and bring to the boil. Reduce the heat and cook the carrots gently for 30-40 minutes, or until the milk has evaporated. Add the butter and raisins and stir over a gentle heat for 8-10 minutes, until the Halva is dark and leaves the sides of the pan clean. Add the cardamom seeds and mix well. Pour into a flat shallow dish about 2.5cm (1 inch) deep. Flatten the Halva evenly with a spatula. Sprinkle with the chopped nuts. Serve hot or cold, cut into squares, with single cream.

Potato Pudding

This old-fashioned Oriental pudding has a rich and lovely flavour. It keeps for weeks and can be frozen.

PREPARATION TIME: 15 minutes
COOKING TIME: 1 hour 15 minutes
SERVES: 6 people

1kg (2lb) potatoes, peeled and shredded
225g (8oz) unsalted butter
750ml (1¼ pints) canned evaporated milk
350g (12oz) granulated sugar
100g (4oz) ground almonds
1.25ml (¼ tsp) saffron
50g (2oz) chopped almonds and pistachios

Wash the potatoes thoroughly drain them well. Squeeze the potatoes to remove all excess moisture. Put the potatoes, but and evaporated milk into a larg solid based saucepan and cook slowly until mushy. The potatc will disintegrate into a mashed state as they cook. Add the sug and stir to dissolve. The mixtu will bubble and splatter like bubbling mud from hot springs Wrap a damp tea towel around your hand and stir the mixture 20-30 minutes over a gentle he Add the ground almonds and saffron. Continue stirring over heat until the pudding become thick, sticky and oily on the surface. Pour the pudding into shallow dish and decorate with chopped nuts.

Cabbage Pudding

PREPARATION TIME: 10 min
COOKING TIME: 40 minutes
SERVES: 4-6 people

175g (6oz) finely shredded white cabbage
30ml (2 tblsp) pudding rice
1.2 litre (2 pints) milk

Facing page: Carrot Cake (top), Carrot Halva (centre and Carrotella (bottom).

200ml (⅓ pint) canned evaporated milk
2.5cm (1 inch) piece cinnamon stick
1 bayleaf
100-175g (4-6 oz) granulated sugar
50g (2oz) raisins
50g (2oz) chopped blanched almonds
50g (2oz) pistachio nuts, chopped
Seeds of 6 small cardamoms, crushed

Put the cabbage, rice, both milks, cinnamon and bayleaf into a pan. Bring to the boil and simmer gently for 15-20 minutes, stirring occasionally to prevent the mixture from sticking to the pan. Add the sugar and simmer gently until the mixture is thick. Add the raisins and nuts. Remove from the heat when the rice is tender and the milk has been reduced to approx. 600ml (1 pint). Pour into a serving dish and sprinkle with the crushed cardamom seeds. Mix well and serve.

Frozen Lemon Yogurt Souffle

PREPARATION TIME: 20 minutes
SERVES: 4-6 people

900ml (1½ pints) natural yogurt
225g (8oz) caster sugar
Juice and finely grated rind of 2 lemons
5ml (1 tsp) vanilla essence
2 egg whites
1.25ml (¼ tsp) salt
1.25ml (¼ tsp) cream of tartar
120ml (4 fl oz) double cream, whipped
Few thin lemon slices for decoration

Mix the yogurt, sugar, lemon juice, lemon rind and vanilla essence together. Whisk the egg whites, salt and cream of tartar until stiff but not dry. Fold the egg whites gently into the yogurt mixture, and then fold in the whipped cream. Pour the mixture into a souffle dish and freeze overnight. Garnish with lemon slices before serving. Serve either frozen or partially thawed.

Mango Fool

This delicious sweet can be made with fresh or canned mangoes; crushed cardamom seeds give it a characteristic flavour.

PREPARATION TIME: 10 minutes
SERVES: 4-6 people

450g (1lb) canned mango slices or the equivalent amount of fresh mango, stoned and peeled
200ml (⅓ pint) canned evaporated milk
Seeds of 6 cardamoms, crushed
Sugar to taste
Whipped cream

Put the mango, evaporated milk and cardamoms into a liquidiser and blend until smooth. Add a little sugar if necessary. Pour into a serving bowl and chill for 20 minutes before serving. Serve with whipped cream.

Tropical Fruit Dessert

An exotic sweet dish to finish any special meal. A delightful dessert from nature's fruit garden.

PREPARATION TIME: 30 minutes
SERVES: 8-10 people

4 bananas, cut into 5mm (¼ inch) thick slices
5 rings pineapple, cut into chunks (fresh or canned)
2 semi-ripe pears, peeled, cored and cut into chunks
2 medium red-skinned apples, cored and cut into chunks
8 peach slices, chopped
225g (8oz) red cherries, pitted
45ml (3 tblsp) grated fresh coconut
1 honeydew melon, peeled and cut into chunks
450g (1lb) marshmallows
6-8 slices mango, cut into chunks (fresh or canned)
2 kiwi fruit, peeled and cut into chunks
20-25 strawberries, halved
Few seedless white and black grapes, halved
15ml (1 tblsp) icing sugar
100g (4oz) cottage cheese
Few drops vanilla essence

Mix all the ingredients together in a large bowl. Cover and chill for 1 hour.

Tropical Fruit Salad

This medley of fruits is very colourful and it offers a variety of tastes and textures.

PREPARATION TIME: 40 minutes

2 bananas, sliced
4 kiwi fruit, peeled and sliced
10 dates, stoned and sliced in half
2 guavas, halved and then sliced into wedges
1 pawpaw, cut into thin crescent shapes
450g (1lb) canned lychees, drained
225g (8oz) canned pineapple chunks, drained (or pieces of fresh pineapple)
2 fresh mangoes, peeled and sliced
Few seedless grapes, white and black, halved
1 small melon, cut into chunks
¼ water-melon, cut into chunks
4 fresh figs, halved

Dressing
30ml (2 tblsp) lemon juice
Pinch salt
50g (2oz) chopped toasted walnut or pine kernels

Prepare the fruits as suggested and arrange in a large glass bowl, in layers. Spoon over the lemon juice and sprinkle with salt. Sprinkle over the chopped nuts.

Semolina and Coconut Slices

PREPARATION TIME: 10 minutes
COOKING TIME: 30 minutes
SERVES: 6 people

175g (6oz) unsalted butter
175g (6oz) coarse semolina
225g (8oz) desiccated coconut
350g (12oz) granulated sugar
250ml (8 fl oz) canned evaporated milk
250ml (8 fl oz) water
100g (4oz) chopped mixed nuts: blanched almonds, cashews, walnuts, hazelnuts and pistachios
75g (3oz) raisins
Seeds of 6 cardamoms, crushed

Melt the butter in a frying pan and add the semolina. Dry roast the semolina by stirring it until it turns lightly golden. Spoon onto a plate. Dry roast the coconut in the same pan until lightly golden. Add the

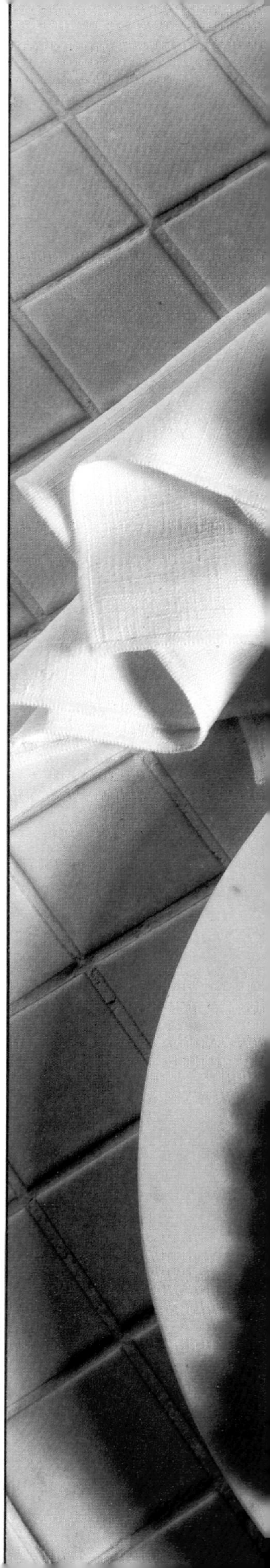

Tropical Fruit Dessert (top right), Frozen Lemon Yogurt Souffle (top left) and Tropical Fruit Salad (bottom).

semolina, sugar, milk and water to the coconut. Stir the mixture over the heat for 5-8 minutes. Add the chopped nuts, raisins and crushed cardamom seeds. Mix well and stir over a gentle heat for 5-6 minutes, until the mixture is thick and the oil begins to separate. Pour into a shallow dish, smooth with a spatula and allow to cool. Cut into diamond shapes or squares.

Mint Barley Sherbet

PREPARATION TIME: 10 minutes
COOKING TIME: 20 minutes
SERVES: 4-6 people

100g (4oz) whole barley
900ml (1½ pints) water
25g (1oz) mint leaves, minced
Pinch salt
75g (3oz) granulated sugar
Juice of 3 lemons
1-2 drops green food colouring
Grated rind of 1 lemon
Few mint leaves and lemon slices to decorate

Wash the barley in 2-3 changes of water. Soak the barley in the measured water for a few minutes; add the minced mint leaves and

This page: Yogurt, Almond and Saffron Sherbet (top centre), Mango Sherbet (left), Maori Shake (centre) and Tropical Blizzard (right).

Facing page: Mint Barley Sherbet (top left), Spiced Tea (top right) and Rich Coffee (bottom).

bring to the boil. Simmer gently for 10-15 minutes. Remove from the heat and strain; discard the barley grains. Dissolve the salt and sugar in the barley liquid; add the lemon juice, colouring and lemon rind. Mix well and make up to 900ml (1½ pints) with water. Pour into glasses and add crushed ice. To make clear sherbet; allow the barley water to stand for 10 minutes, so that the starch settles. Pour off the clear liquid and serve with a twist of lemon and mint leaves floating on the top.

Yogurt Dessert

This yogurt dessert is a light, delicious way of ending a rich meal; it is also simple and easy to make.

PREPARATION TIME: 15 minutes, plus setting time

COOKING TIME: 15 minutes

SERVES: 4-6 people

2¼ litres (4 pints) milk
100-125g (4-5oz) granulated sugar or to taste
50g (2oz) finely chopped blanched almonds
50g (2oz) raisins
Seeds of 8 small cardamoms, crushed
2-3 drops rose water or vanilla essence
30ml (2 tblsp) natural yogurt
25g (1oz) pistachio nuts, chopped

Simmer the milk in a large pan until it is reduced by half. Add the sugar to the milk and stir until dissolved. Add half the almonds, the raisins and cardamom seeds. Allow to cool until the milk is just tepid. Add the essence and beaten yogurt to the milk and stir well. Pour into a large, shallow serving dish. Cover and leave in a warm place, such as an airing cupboard, until the yogurt has set (about 5-6 hours). Sprinkle with the chopped pistachio nuts and remaining chopped almonds. Chill for 1 hour before serving. Will keep for up to 15 days in the refrigerator.

Tropical Blizzard

PREPARATION TIME: 3-4 minutes

SERVES: 4 people

250ml (8 fl oz) pineapple juice or orange juice
300ml (10 fl oz) natural yogurt
6 slices mango (canned or fresh)
15ml (1 tblsp) sugar
Soda water
Ice cubes

Put the fruit juice, yogurt, mango and sugar into the liquidiser; blend for ½ minute. Pour into 4 glasses and dilute with soda water. Serve with ice cubes.

Maori Shake

A new taste experience; kiwi fruit blended with lemon yogurt.

PREPARATION TIME: 5 minutes

SERVES: 4-6 people

250ml (8 fl oz) pineapple juice
2 kiwi fruits, peeled and chopped
300ml (10 fl oz) lemon yogurt
Ice cubes
Lemonade
1 kiwi fruit, peeled and thinly sliced for decoration

Put the pineapple juice, chopped kiwi fruit and lemon yogurt into the liquidiser; blend for 30 seconds-1 minute, until smooth. Pour into 4-6 tall glasses; add ice cubes and top up with lemonade. Stir to mix. Serve with slices of kiwi fruit on top.

Mango Sherbet

This is a pretty green mango sherbet made from unripe mangoes. Windfallen mangoes are usually used for making this refreshing drink in India.

PREPARATION TIME: 20 minutes

COOKING TIME: 5-6 minutes

SERVES: 6 people

2 medium size unripe mangoes
1.25ml (¼ tsp) salt
1 litre (1¾ pints) water
Sugar to taste
Crushed ice

Boil the mangoes in sufficient water to cover for 5-6 minutes. Remove and allow to cool under cold running water. Peel off the skins. Put the water and salt into a punch bowl. Scrape all the mango flesh away from the stones and add to the punch bowl. Discard the stones. Whisk the sherbet until well blended. Pour into tall glasses; add sugar to taste and crushed ice.

Yogurt, Almond and Saffron Sherbet

A good healthy drink, which can be given a sweet or salty flavour.

PREPARATION TIME: 5 minutes

SERVES: 5-6 people

1 litre (1¾ pints) water
450ml (¾ pint) natural yogurt
10ml (2 tsp) lemon juice
12 blanched almonds
1.25ml (¼ tsp) saffron
2 drops vanilla essence or rose water
Salt or sugar to taste

Put 400ml (2/3 pint) water into the liquidiser with the yogurt, lemon juice, almonds, saffron and essence; blend until smooth. Mix in the remaining water. Pour into tall glasses over crushed ice. To make sweet sherbet, stir 10-15ml (2-3 tsp) sugar into each glass; and to make a salty sherbet, sprinkle on a pinch of salt.

Rich Coffee

This is an old and traditional method of making coffee from the Orient.

PREPARATION TIME: 8 minutes

SERVES: 6-8 people

1 litre (1¾ pints) water
450ml (¾ pint) milk
30ml (2 tblsp) freshly ground medium roast coffee
Seeds of 4 small cardamoms, crushed
Sugar to taste

Put the water and milk into a stainless steel pan and bring to the boil. Add the coffee and crushed cardamoms. Cover the pan and remove from the heat. Allow to brew for 2-3 minutes. Stir once. When the coffee grains settle to the bottom, strain off the coffee into cups and add sugar to taste.

Spiced Tea

This is a very different and interesting way of serving tea; it is refreshing served hot or cold.

PREPARATION TIME: 5 minutes

SERVES: 6 people

1 litre (1¾ pints) water
450ml (¾ pint) milk
1.25cm (½ inch) piece cinnamon stick
4 cloves
Seeds of 4 small cardamoms, crushed
6 teabags
or 30ml (2 tblsp) tea leaves
Sugar to taste

Put the water, milk, cinnamon, cloves and cardamom seeds into a stainless steel pan. Bring to the boil and add the tea. Cover the pan and remove from the heat. Allow to brew for 2 minutes. Stir well. Add sugar to taste. Strain into cups and serve. Alternatively, allow the tea to cool and then chill and serve with ice.

Yogurt Dessert (top left), Mango Fool (left) and Semolina and Coconut Slices (bottom left).

HOME FARE

Smoked Haddock in French Mustard Sauce (top), Chicken Curry (left) and Poussin in White Sauce (right).

Meals for Two

Poussin in White Sauce

1 pkt sage and onion stuffing
2 poussins
Fat
300ml (½ pint) milk
25g (1oz) plain flour
25g (1oz) soft margarine
Salt and pepper

Make the stuffing as directed on the packet and use to stuff the poussins. Place the poussins in a roasting tin with melted fat, and cook in the oven for 30-40 minutes at 180°C, 350°F, Gas Mark 4, until tender. Put the milk, flour, margarine and seasoning into a pan and bring gradually to the boil, whisking all the time. Cook gently for 3 minutes, stirring. Serve with baked potatoes and sweet corn with red peppers.
Serves two.

Smoked Haddock in French Mustard Sauce

350g (¾lb) smoked haddock fillet, skinned and cut into two
A little milk
Salt and pepper
15g (½oz) butter
15g (½oz) flour
150ml (¼ pint) milk
15ml (1 tblsp) French mustard
Chopped chives (optional)

Place the fish in an ovenproof serving dish. Pour a little milk over the fish and season. Cover and

cook in the oven for 15-20 minutes at 160°C, 325°F, Gas Mark 3. Heat the butter in a pan, stir in the flour and cook for 2 minutes. Allow to cool, then pour in the milk gradually. Bring to the boil, stirring. Season and stir in the French mustard. Spoon the sauce over the fish and garnish with chopped chives if desired. Serve with potato croquettes and broccoli.
Serves two.

Mixed Grill

2 sausages
Liver
2 pork chops
Tomatoes
Mushrooms, sliced if flat

Grill the sausages, liver, pork chop and tomatoes until tender. Boil mushrooms until soft. Serve with baby new potatoes.
Serves two.

Chicken Curry

25g (1oz) butter
1 small chicken, jointed
1 small onion, peeled and chopped
1 small apple, peeled and chopped
5ml (1 tsp) curry powder
10g (¼oz) flour
2.5ml (½ tsp) curry paste
300ml (½ pint) chicken stock
1 chilli (optional)
Pinch of powdered ginger
Pinch of powdered turmeric
5ml (1 tsp) chutney
Squeeze of lemon juice
Salt and pepper
25g (1oz) desiccated coconut
15g (½oz) sultanas

Garnish
Thin onion rings, lightly fried
Thin green pepper rings, lightly fried
Lemon rind, lightly fried

Heat the butter and fry the chicken pieces. Remove and drain on paper towels. Fry the onion and apple for 2-3 minutes, then add the curry powder, flour and curry paste. Cook briefly, then carefully blend in most of the stock, reserving 50ml (2 fl oz). Bring to the boil and cook for a few minutes until a thin sauce. Add the remaining spices, chutney, lemon juice and seasoning. Return the chicken pieces to the pan. Pour the remaining stock over the coconut and allow to stand for a few minutes, then add the strained liquid to the curry. If preferred, fresh coconut or coconut milk can be used instead. Add the sultanas then cover and simmer for 2-3 hours. Garnish with onion, pepper and lemon rind to serve.
Serves two.

Plaited Lamb

450g (1lb) minced lamb
2 onions, peeled and chopped
25g (1oz) breadcrumbs
15g (1 tsp) dried rosemary
15ml (1 tblsp) tomato purée
15ml (1 tblsp) Worcestershire sauce
2 eggs, beaten
Salt and pepper
225g (8oz) puff pastry

Mix together the minced lamb, onions, breadcrumbs, rosemary, tomato purée, Worcestershire sauce and one of the eggs. Add salt and pepper. Roll out the pastry on a floured surface into an oblong. Place the lamb mixture in the centre, cut diagonal strips from the centre to the edges along both sides. Brush all four sides with a little beaten egg. Fold the pastry at each end and then fold the strips over alternately so they meet in the centre. Place the plaited lamb on a greased baking tray and brush with the remaining beaten egg. Cook in the oven for 15-20 minutes at 220°C, 425°F, Gas Mark 7. Then reduce the heat to 180°C, 350°F, Gas Mark 4 and cook for a further 30 minutes. Serve with new potatoes and a green vegetable.
Serves two.

Pasta Fish Pie

40g (1½oz) macaroni
Salt
225g (8oz) white fish

Cheese Sauce
15g (½oz) butter or margarine
15g (½oz) flour
150ml (¼ pint) milk
Salt and pepper
Pinch of dry mustard
40g (1½oz) Cheddar cheese, grated

Break the macaroni into small pieces (if using long macaroni) and cook in 2 pints of boiling, salted water until tender. Meanwhile, simmer the fish in a little salted water until tender. Lift the fish out and flake with a fork. Heat the butter or margarine in a pan, stir in the flour, and cook the 'roux' for 2-3 minutes over a low heat. Remove the pan from the heat and gradually add the milk, seasoning and mustard. Bring to the boil, cook until thickened, then add the grated cheese. Put the drained macaroni and fish into a hot dish and top with the cheese sauce. Place for 2-3 minutes under a hot grill until the cheese topping bubbles. Serve with runner beans and sweet corn.
Serves two.

Braised Beef

15g (½oz) fat
350g (12oz) of brisket or topside of beef cut into pieces
1 carrot, peeled and sliced
1 onion, peeled and sliced
1 turnip, peeled and sliced
1 leek, trimmed and sliced
2 sticks celery, trimmed and sliced
25g (1oz) fat bacon, diced
Bouquet garni (mixture of fresh herbs, i.e. parsley, thyme, sage, in muslin bag)
Salt and pepper
150ml (¼ pint) beef stock
60ml (2 fl oz) red wine

Heat the fat in a flameproof casserole or large saucepan and brown the meat for 3 minutes. Lift the meat onto a plate. Brown the vegetables in the fat together with the diced bacon. Add the bouquet garni, seasoning, stock and wine then return the meat on top of the mixture. Cover tightly and cook very slowly for about 1 hour. Lift the lid from time to time and add more stock if the mixture appears to be running dry. Remove the bouquet garni. Sieve the vegetables and stock to make a sauce or use a blender and reheat with the meat. Serve with boiled potatoes.
Serves two.

Stuffed Mushrooms

Two large, flat mushrooms
15g (½oz) butter
1 rasher of streaky bacon, rinded and chopped
15g (½oz) fresh breadcrumbs
5ml (1 tsp) chopped parsley
Grated rind of ¼ lemon
2.5ml (½ tsp) lemon juice
25g (1oz) Cheddar cheese, grated
Salt and pepper
Cress

Remove the stalks from the mushrooms and chop finely. Heat the butter and fry the mushroom stalks and the bacon for a few minutes. Remove from the heat and stir in the breadcrumbs, parsley, lemon rind and juice, and cheese. Season well. Place the mushroom caps on a greased baking sheet, divide the filling between each cap and cook for 15-20 minutes at 170°C, 325°F, Gas Mark 3. Sprinkle with cress. Serve with sweet corn and sauté potatoes.
Serves two.

Veal Cutlets Bonne Femme

2x225g (two 8oz) veal cutlets
Salt and pepper
25g (1oz) flour
50g (2oz) clarified butter or butter and oil mixed
100g (4oz) boiled, cold potatoes, thinly sliced
50g (2oz) button onions
50ml (2 fl oz) sherry
150ml (¼ pint) demi-glacé sauce
15ml (1 tblsp) chopped parsley

Sprinkle the veal cutlets with salt and pepper and dredge with flour Heat the butter or butter and oil, in a frying pan and gently fry the cutlets on both sides for a few minutes. Place the cutlets in an ovenproof dish and cook in the oven for 15-20 minutes at 180°C 350°F, Gas Mark 4 until tender. F the potatoes in the same pan unt golden brown, remove and keep warm. Fry the onions for two minutes. Transfer the onions to a saucepan of water and boil until soft. Drain off the butter and pou the sherry into the pan. Add the demi-glacé sauce and bring to th boil, stirring continuously. Arran the cutlets on a serving dish, surrounded by the fried potatoe and onions. Cover with the dem glacé sauce and decorate with chopped parsley.
Serves two.

Facing page: Plaited Lamb (t left), Pasta Fish Pie (top right and Veal Cutlets Bonne Fem (bottom).

Bacon and Chestnuts

450g (1lb) joint of bacon, boned and rolled
25g (1oz) butter
1 small onion, peeled and chopped
50g (2oz) chestnut purée
1.25ml (¼ tsp) mixed herbs
1.25ml (¼ tsp) mixed spice
5ml (1 tsp) soft brown sugar
1 beaten egg
450g (1lb) puff pastry

Place the bacon in a saucepan, cover with cold water, bring to the boil then simmer for 1 hour. Remove the bacon from the pan and trim off any excess fat, leave until cold. Melt the butter and fry the onion until soft. Mix with the chestnut purée, herbs, spice and sugar, and half the beaten egg to bind the mixture. Roll out the pastry to a circle large enough to wrap around the bacon joint. Spread the mixture over the top of the bacon. Fold the pastry up over the joint and seal with a little of the beaten egg. Place on a baking sheet. Brush with beaten egg. Cook in the oven for 30-35 minutes at 220°C, 425°F, Gas Mark 7. Serve with carrots and broad beans.
Serves two.

Demi-Glacé Sauce

25g (1oz) dripping or butter
25g (1oz) peeled and chopped onion
25g (1oz) peeled and chopped carrot
25g (1oz) flour
1 rasher bacon, rinded and diced
600ml (1 pint) brown stock
5ml (1 tsp) tomato purée
5ml (1 tsp) mixed herbs
Salt and pepper

Heat the dripping or butter, fry the onion, bacon and carrot until very lightly browned. Do not overcook at this stage as burnt onion gives a bitter taste to the sauce. Add the flour and continue cooking slowly until a rich chestnut colour. Draw

Pork Fillets and Apricots

225g (8oz) pork fillet, cut into small pieces
15ml (1 tblsp) seasoned flour
25g (1oz) butter
200g (7oz) can of apricot halves
15ml (1 tblsp) Worcestershire sauce
15ml (1 tblsp) soft brown sugar
10ml (2 tsp) wine vinegar
5ml (1 tsp) lemon juice
2.5ml (½ tsp) powdered cinnamon
60ml (4 tblsp) water
100g (4oz) long grain rice

Toss the pork pieces in the seasoned flour. Heat the butter in a flameproof casserole and fry the pork until lightly browned. Chop all but three of the apricot halves. Mix 4 tablespoons of the apricot syrup with the Worcestershire sauce, sugar, vinegar, lemon juice, cinnamon and water. Pour the apricot sauce and chopped fruit over the pork. Bring to the boil, stirring continuously. Reduce the heat, cover and simmer for 15 minutes. Meanwhile, cook the rice in boiling, salted water. Spoon the pork and sauce onto a serving dish and spoon the drained rice around the meat. Decorate with the reserved apricots. If required serve with a green vegetable.
Serves two.

This page: Braised Beef (top left), Mixed Grill (centre) and Stuffed Mushrooms (bottom).

Facing page: Filled Jacket Potatoes (top left), Sausage and Mushroom Pie (top right), Bacon and Chestnuts (bottom right) and Stuffed Aubergines (bottom left).

the pan aside, add the stock and when all the liquid has been incorporated, add the purée, herbs and seasoning to taste. Bring to the boil, skim thoroughly and simmer, covered, for 30 minutes. Strain through a fine-meshed strainer, pressing as much as possible of the vegetables through.
Makes 1 pint.

Sausage and Mushroom Pie

225g (8oz) pork sausages
25g (1oz) butter
1 onion, peeled and sliced
20g (¾oz) flour
150ml (¼ pint) milk
150ml (¼ pint) brown stock
Salt and pepper
Pinch of mixed herbs
100g (4oz) sliced button mushrooms
225g (8oz) puff pastry
1 egg, beaten

Prick the sausages and grill them until golden. Heat the butter in a pan and fry the onion for 5 minutes. Stir in the flour and cook for a further minute. Gradually add the milk and stock and bring to boil. Stir until thickened then add the seasoning, herbs and mushrooms. Place the sausages in a pie dish and pour over the mushroom sauce. Roll out the puff pastry, and use to cover the dish. Trim off any excess pastry. Glaze the top of the pie with the beaten egg and cook in the oven for 40 minutes at 200°C, 390°F, Gas Mark 6. Serve with new or boiled potatoes and a green vegetable.
Serves two.

Stuffed Aubergines

3 medium aubergines, washed and stalks removed
Salt
275g (10oz) butter
1 medium onion, peeled and finely chopped
1 clove garlic, peeled and crushed
175g (6oz) minced beef
400g (14oz) can of tomatoes
15ml (1 tblsp) chopped parsley
5ml (1 tsp) dried marjoram
10ml (2 tsp) tomato purée
Pepper
10ml (2 tsp) cornflour
100g (4oz) Cheddar cheese, grated

Slice the aubergines in half lengthways. Scoop out the flesh carefully and chop finely. Put the flesh on a large plate, sprinkle with salt and leave for 30 minutes. Blanch the aubergine skins in boiling water for 5 minutes. Remove and place on a serving dish. Heat the butter, add the onion and garlic and cook until soft. Stir in the minced beef and cook until brown. Add the tomatoes, parsley, marjoram and tomato purée. Season with pepper and bring to the boil. Blend the cornflour with a little cold water and add to the beef and tomato mixture. Return to the boil, then remove from the heat. Drain the aubergine flesh in a sieve and rinse in cold water. Stir half the flesh into the beef and tomato mixture and use to stuff the aubergine halves. Top each one with grated cheese and cook in the oven for about 30 minutes at 180°C, 350°F, Gas Mark 4. (Use the left-over aubergine flesh in a bolognese sauce or as a vegetable covered with a cheese sauce.) Serve the stuffed aubergines hot with a tossed green salad.
Serves two.

Hearts and Stuffing

2 lambs' hearts
Seasoned flour
20g (¾oz) unsalted butter
300ml (½ pint) brown stock
1 small onion
100g (4oz) carrots
1 celery heart

Stuffing
2 shallots
1 stick celery
25g (1oz) belly pork
25g (1oz) fresh breadcrumbs
1 rounded tblsp parsley
5ml (1 tsp) curry powder
Salt and pepper
20g (¾oz) melted butter

First make the stuffing. Peel and chop the shallots. Scrub and dice the celery stick. Mince or finely chop the pork. Place these ingredients in a bowl with the breadcrumbs, parsley, curry powder and seasoning. Bind together with the melted butter. Rinse the hearts. Cut out any tubes and discard, and fill the hearts with the stuffing. Sew up the openings and coat the hearts with seasoned flour. Melt the butter in a heavy pan and fry the hearts over a high heat until brown. Lift the hearts into a casserole dish. Stir in enough seasoned flour to absorb the fat. Cook for 2-3 minutes then add the stock and bring to the boil. Pour over the hearts. Cover the casserole and cook in the oven at 170°C, 325°F, Gas Mark 3 for 2 hours. After 2 hours peel and chop the onion, carrot and celery heart. Add to the casserole and continue to cook for a further 1 hour. Serve with boiled potatoes and green vegetables.
Serves two.

Filled Jacket Potatoes

2 medium-sized potatoes
25g (1oz) butter
Salt and pepper

Cheddar Cheese Filling
75g (3oz) Cheddar cheese, grated
25g (1oz) butter
A little milk
Salt and pepper
15ml (1 tblsp) Parmesan cheese

Bacon Filling
75g (3oz) bacon, rind removed, chopped and fried
25g (1oz) butter
A little milk
Salt and pepper
1 small green pepper, cored, seeded and finely chopped

Sausage and Onion Filling
2 small pork sausages, chopped and grilled
25g (1oz) butter
A little milk
Salt and pepper
1 small onion, peeled, chopped and fried

Liver and Courgette Filling
75g (3oz) lamb's liver, chopped and fried
25g (1oz) butter
A little milk
Salt and pepper
2 small courgettes, diced and fried

Scrub the potatoes well. Prick them and dot their skins with butter. Sprinkle lightly with salt and pepper. Cook in the oven for 1-1¼ hours at 200°C, 400°F, Gas Mark 6. When cooked, cut in half lengthways and scoop out the centres, keeping the skins intact. Mash the potato in a basin, adding one of the filling mixtures. Return the mixture to the potato skins. Cook for a further 15-20 minutes.
Serves two.

Lasagne

150g (5oz) margarine
1 small onion, peeled and sliced
100g (4oz) minced beef
200g (7oz) can of tomatoes
5ml (1 tsp) tomato purée
150ml (¼ pint) beef stock
5ml (1 tsp) dried marjoram
5ml (1 tsp) mixed herbs
Pinch garlic salt
Salt and pepper
5ml (1 tsp) cornflour
75g (3oz) lasagne
10g (¼oz) butter
100g (4oz) margarine
150g (5oz) flour
150ml (¼ pint) milk
75g (3oz) Cheddar cheese, grated

Heat the margarine and fry the onion until soft. Stir in the minc beef and cook until browned. A the tomatoes, tomato purée, sto herbs and garlic. Season well, co and simmer for 30 minutes. Meanwhile, mix the cornflour t paste with a little cold water, stir into the meat sauce and bring to the boil, stirring continuously. Cook the lasagne in boiling, salt water, adding the 10g (¼oz) but for 10-15 minutes. Drain careful Heat the margarine, stir in the fl and cook for a few minutes. All to cool and gradually add the mi Return to the heat and bring to boil, stirring continuously. Stir in two-thirds of the cheese. Cover base of a greased ovenproof dish with half the lasagne. Spoon ove half the meat and tomato sauce. Cover with the remaining lasagn and spoon over remaining toma sauce. Pour on the cheese sauce, sprinkle the Cheddar cheese on and cook in the oven at 190°C, Gas Mark 5 for 30-35 minutes.
Serves two.

Facing page: Lasagne (top left Hearts and Stuffing (top right and Pork Fillets and Apricots (bottom).

The Family Roast

Turkey

ROASTING TIME: For a 2.75-3.5kg (6-8lb) turkey cook for 15 minutes at 200°C, 400°F, Gas Mark 6, then reduce temperature to 180°C, 350°F, Gas Mark 4 and allow 15 minutes per 450g (1lb) + 15 minutes.

If the bird is frozen it must be allowed to thaw out completely before cooking. Stuff the bird, sprinkle with salt and place in a roasting tin. Brush the bird with melted dripping, butter or oil. The bird may be wrapped in foil, but the cover should be removed for the last 20-30 minutes to brown the skin. If left unwrapped, the bird should be basted frequently. Transfer to a large carving dish when cooked. As accompaniments: sausages, chestnut, sausage meat or veal forcemeat stuffing, bacon rolls, cranberry or celery sauce, thickened gravy. Serve with roast, fried or boiled potatoes, onions, peas or Brussels sprouts.

Lamb

ROASTING TIME: 25 minutes p 450g (1lb) + 25 minutes, at 160°C, 325°F, Gas Mark 3.

Place in the centre of a preheate oven. If a covered roasting tin is used basting is not necessary, b the joint is uncovered or pot-roasted, the meat should be bas every 20-30 minutes. The meat should be turned over, using 2 metal spoons, halfway through cooking. Transfer the meat from the tin to a hot, flat dish large enough to allow for carving. Ke hot. As accompaniments: medi brown, thickened gravy, mint o cranberry sauce. Serve with nev potatoes, peas, French or runne beans.

Veal

ROASTING TIME: 25 minutes p 450g (1lb) + 25 minutes at 16C 325°F, Gas Mark 3.

Place in the centre of a preheate oven. If a covered roasting tin is used basting is not necessary, b the joint is uncovered or pot-roasted, the meat should be bas every 20-30 minutes. The meat should be turned over, using 2 metal spoons, halfway through cooking. Transfer the meat from the tin onto a large, flat carving dish. Keep hot. As accompaniments: medium brown, thicken gravy, veal forcemeat stuffing, squeeze of lemon, bacon rolls. Serve with green vegetables, onions, tomatoes, baked or boil potatoes.

This page: Turkey (top), Pork (centre right) and Lamb (bottom).

Facing page: Mutton (top), Steak (centre left), Veal (centr right) and Duck (bottom).

Beef

ROASTING TIME: 15 minutes per 450g (1lb) + 15 minutes, at 180°C, 350°F, Gas Mark 4.

Place in the centre of a preheated oven. If a covered roasting tin is used basting is not necessary, but if the joint is uncovered or pot-roasted, the meat should be basted every 20-30 minutes. The meat should be turned over, using 2 metal spoons, halfway through the cooking. Transfer the meat from the tin to a hot, flat dish large enough to allow for carving. Keep hot. As accompaniments: thin, dark brown gravy, Yorkshire pudding, horseradish sauce, roast parsnips. Serve with baked or boiled potatoes and any vegetable.

Baked Whole Gammon

ROASTING TIME: 30 minutes per 450g (1lb) + 30 minutes at 180°C, 350°F, Gas Mark 4.

Spread gammon with a little melted butter or margarine and wrap in foil. Place in a roasting tin in the centre of a preheated oven. Transfer the meat from the tin when cooked, remove the foil and put the gammon onto a large, flat carving dish. Keep hot. As accompaniments: dark brown, thin gravy, sage and onion stuffing, apple sauce. Serve with baked or boiled potatoes, cabbage, celery, Brussels sprouts or cauliflower.

Pork

ROASTING TIME: 30 minutes per 450g (1lb) + 30 minutes, at 180°C, 350°F, Gas Mark 4.

Place in the centre of a preheated oven. If a covered roasting tin is used basting is not necessary, but if the joint is uncovered or pot-roasted, the meat should be basted every 20-30 minutes. The meat should be turned over, using 2 metal spoons, halfway through the cooking. Transfer the meat from the tin to a hot, flat dish large enough to allow for carving. Keep hot. As accompaniments: dark brown, thin gravy, sage and onion stuffing, apple sauce. Serve with boiled potatoes, cabbage, cauliflower, celery, onion, spinach or Brussels sprouts.

Duck

ROASTING TIME: For a 1-1.5kg (2-3lb) duck cook for 15 minutes per 450g (1lb) + 15 minutes at 180-190°C, 350-375°F, Gas Mark 4-5.

If the bird is frozen it must be thawed out completely before cooking. Stuff the bird with sage and onion stuffing, and place in a roasting tin. Brush the bird with melted dripping, butter or oil. Duck must be well pricked all over the breast to allow the fat to run out and leave the breast skin crisp and succulent. Transfer to a large carving dish when cooked. As accompaniments: apple sauce; thin gravy, flavoured with orange juice if liked. Serve with roast potatoes, peas, carrots and any green vegetable.

Steak

Season steak before cooking. Steak can be grilled, fried or roasted until tender and cooked to one's liking. Serve with baked or boiled potatoes and any vegetable.

Mutton

ROASTING TIME: 25 minutes per 450g (1lb) + 25 minutes, at 160°C, 325°F, Gas Mark 3.

Place in the centre of a preheated oven. If a covered roasting tin is used basting is not necessary, but if the joint is uncovered or pot-roasted, the meat should be basted every 20-30 minutes. The meat should be turned over, using 2 metal spoons, halfway through the cooking. Transfer the meat from the tin onto a large, flat carving dish. Keep hot. As accompaniments: medium brown, thickened gravy, redcurrant, cranberry or mint sauce. Serve with baked or boiled potatoes and any vegetable.

Chicken

ROASTING TIME: 15 minutes per 450g (1lb) + 15 minutes at 200°C, 400°F, Gas Mark 6.

If the bird is frozen it must be allowed to thaw out completely before cooking. Stuff the bird, sprinkle with salt and place in a roasting tin. Brush the bird with melted dripping, butter or oil. The bird may be wrapped in foil, but the cover should be removed for the last 20-30 minutes to brown the skin. If left unwrapped, the bird should be basted frequently. Transfer the bird to a large carving dish. As accompaniments: veal forcemeat, bread sauce, bacon rolls and thin gravy. Serve with baked, fried or boiled new potatoes, and green vegetables.

Beef (top), Chicken (far left) and Baked Whole Gammon (left).

Meals for Special Occasions

Turkey and Apricot Loaf

675g (1½lb) uncooked turkey meat, minced
175g (6oz) fresh white breadcrumbs
1 onion, peeled and finely chopped
15ml (1 tblsp) Worcestershire sauce
1 egg, beaten
Pinch of mixed herbs
Pinch of allspice
Salt and pepper
425g (15oz) can apricot halves
100g (4oz) stuffed, green olives, sliced
10ml (2 tsp) cornflour
150ml (¼ pint) dry white wine

Grease a 450g (1lb) loaf tin and set aside. In a large bowl, mix together the turkey, breadcrumbs, onion, Worcestershire sauce, egg, herbs, allspice and seasoning, and combine well. Spoon the mixture into the loaf tin, making sure the corners are well filled, smooth over the top and bang the tin on a flat surface to release any air bubbles. Cook in the oven for about 90 minutes at 180°C, 350°F, Gas Mark 4, or until the meat loaf is cooked through. The juices will run clear when a skewer is inserted. Remove from the oven, allow t cool in the tin for 30 minutes, t turn out and leave to cool completely. Drain the apricots, reserving the juice. Garnish the with apricot halves and the stu olives. Mix the cornflour with a little of the apricot juice, then a the rest of the juice and the wi Heat, stirring, until thickened. Cool, then brush over the mea loaf and serve the rest separate a jug. Serve the meat loaf on a l of lettuce leaves, with potato croquettes and vegetables. Serves eight-ten.

Boeuf en Croûte

15ml (1 tblsp) oil
1.5kg (3lb) beef topside
25g (1oz) butter
1 onion, peeled and chopped
100g (4oz) button mushrooms, chopped
30ml (2 tblsp) freshly chopped parsley
Salt and pepper
275g (10oz) bought or home-ma rough puff pastry
A little milk
Few sprigs of watercress to garnish

Heat the oil in a large pan and fr the meat quickly on all sides to the juices. Transfer the oil and t meat to a roasting dish. Cook in the oven for 45 minutes at 200° 400°F, Gas Mark 6. Leave to co Melt the butter in a pan and fry onions until soft. Add the mushrooms, parsley and season Cover and fry for 5 minutes. Ro out the pastry to make a rectan large enough to cover the meat. Spread ⅓ of the stuffing over th

This page: Sweet and Spicy Noisettes (top), Veal in Oran (centre left) and Peppered Ste (bottom right).

Facing Page: Boeuf en Croûte (top), Turkey and Apricot Loa (centre left) and Stuffed Trou with Almonds (bottom).

S
P

centre of the pastry and place the meat on top. Spread the rest of the stuffing over the meat. Dampen the edges of the pastry and fold them over the meat like a parcel. Trim as necessary. Place the meat, joins downwards, in a roasting pan. Roll out any pastry trimmings and cut into leaf shapes, to decorate the top. Brush the top with a little milk. Increase the oven temperature to 220°C, 425°F, Gas Mark 7, and cook the beef for about 40-45 minutes until the pastry is golden. Place the meat on a serving dish and garnish with watercress. Serve with baked potatoes, Brussels sprouts and carrots.
Serves six-eight.

Veal in Orange

750g-1kg (1½-2lb) veal fillet
1 onion
600ml (1 pint) white stock
Salt and pepper
2 oranges
4 small, young carrots
225g (8oz) long grain rice
50g (2oz) butter
40g (1½oz) flour
Pinch of powdered saffron
150ml (¼ pint) double cream
Parsley to garnish

Dice the veal. Peel the onion and keep it whole. Put the veal, onion, stock and seasoning into a pan. Bring to the boil. Lower the heat and simmer for 40 minutes until the meat is tender. Remove the onion. Cut away the peel from 1 orange, remove the white pith, then cut the orange flesh into narrow strips. Soak in 150ml (¼ pint) water for 30 minutes. Peel the carrots, cut into neat matchsticks, put with the orange rind and a little seasoning and simmer in a covered pan for 20 minutes. Remove the carrots and orange rind and cook the rice in remaining salted water. Heat the butter in a pan, stir in the flour and cook for several minutes. Add the strained veal stock and bring to the boil. Cook until thickened. Add the orange rind, carrots, cooked rice and any liquid left, together with the pinch of saffron powder and the cream. Stir over a low heat until smooth. Add the cooked veal and mix thoroughly. Arrange a border of rice with the remaining orange cut into slices on a serving dish. Spoon the veal mixture in the centre of the dish and sprinkle with parsley. Serve with potatoes and vegetables of your own choice.
Serves six.

Veal with Cucumber

225-350g (8-12oz) fillet veal, cubed
Salt and pepper
15ml (1 tblsp) cornflour
50g (2oz) butter
100g (4oz) button mushrooms
2 eating apples, peeled, cored and sliced
1 cucumber, peeled and diced
1 green pepper, cored, deseeded and sliced
1 red pepper, cored, deseeded and sliced
100g (4oz) cooked rice

Sweet and Sour Sauce
15ml (1 tblsp) cornflour
30ml (2 tblsp) sugar
10ml (2 tsp) soy sauce
45ml (3 tblsp) vinegar
150ml (¼ pint) chicken stock

Toss the veal in seasoned cornflour and fry in the butter until golden. Remove and keep warm. Fry the mushrooms, apple slices and cucumber. Fry the peppers. Return the meat to the pan. Cover and cook for 10 minutes until the meat is tender. Stir in the cooked rice. Transfer to a serving dish and keep hot. Mix the sweet and sour sauce ingredients together, add to the pan and, stirring gently, boil for 2-3 minutes, until the sauce is transparent. Pour the sauce over the veal and cucumber mixture. This can be served as a meal in its own right, or served with a vegetable if required.
Serves four.

Sweet and Spicy Noisettes

5ml (1 tsp) honey
5ml (1 tsp) dry mustard
Salt and pepper
1 garlic clove, peeled and crushed
10ml (2 tsp) lemon juice
6 noisettes of lamb
3 canned pineapple rings with juice
15g (1oz) butter
20ml (1½ tblsp) chopped mint
1 tomato, quartered
3 glacé cherries

Combine the honey, mustard, seasoning, garlic and lemon juice and spread the noisettes with the mixture. Leave to stand for 20 minutes. Place 50ml (2 fl oz) of the pineapple juice in a pan, add the butter and bring to the boil. Boil until reduced by half and add the mint. Keep warm. Grill the noisettes, basting them occasionally with the pineapple mixture. When the meat is cooked, arrange it on a warmed serving dish and decorate with the tomatoes and the pineapple rings. Garnish with the glacé cherries. Serve with fried mushroom rings and bird's nest potatoes.
Serves three.

Stuffed Trout with Almonds

Salt and pepper
2 medium trout, filleted
100-150g (4-5oz) butter
50g (2oz) blanched almonds

Stuffing
175g (6oz) fresh, white breadcrumbs
30ml (2 tblsp) chopped fresh parsley
1 medium onion, peeled and finely chopped
Salt and pepper
10ml (2 tsp) mixed dried herbs
1 cooking apple, peeled and finely chopped
1 small egg, beaten
A little water

Season the fish lightly and fry for about 10 minutes in the butter, until tender. Transfer to a hot dish. For the stuffing mix together the breadcrumbs, parsley, onion, seasoning, herbs and apple. Stir in the beaten egg, and water if necessary, to give a soft consistency. Stuff the fish with this mixture. Fry the almonds for about 5 minutes, adding extra butter if necessary. Scatter the almonds over the fish. Garnish with parsley, and serve with sauté potatoes and a vegetable.

Three Ring Rice

1 red pepper
100g (4oz) butter or margarine
225g (8oz) cooked rice
2 medium onions, peeled and chopped
½ green pepper, cored, deseeded and chopped
1 small garlic clove, peeled and crushed
225g (8oz) minced beef
175g (6oz) can of concentrated tomato purée
5ml (1 tsp) salt
2.5ml (½ tsp) chilli powder
100g (4oz) packet of frozen peas

Core, deseed and cut the red pepper into strips. Arrange at intervals in the bottom of a ring mould. Melt half the butter or margarine. Stir in the rice and spoon into the mould over the pepper. Fry the onion and green pepper together with the garlic in the remaining butter until soft. Add the minced beef and cook until brown. Stir in the tomato purée, salt and chilli powder. Cook the peas, strain, put on top of the rice, then cover with the beef mixture. Press down each layer firmly. Place the mould in a shallow pan of hot water. Cook in the oven for about 20 minutes at 180°C, 350°F, Gas Mark 4, or until firm to the touch. Turn out onto a hot dish. Serve with sweet corn or a side salad.

Veal with Cucumber (above right) and Three Ring Rice (below right).

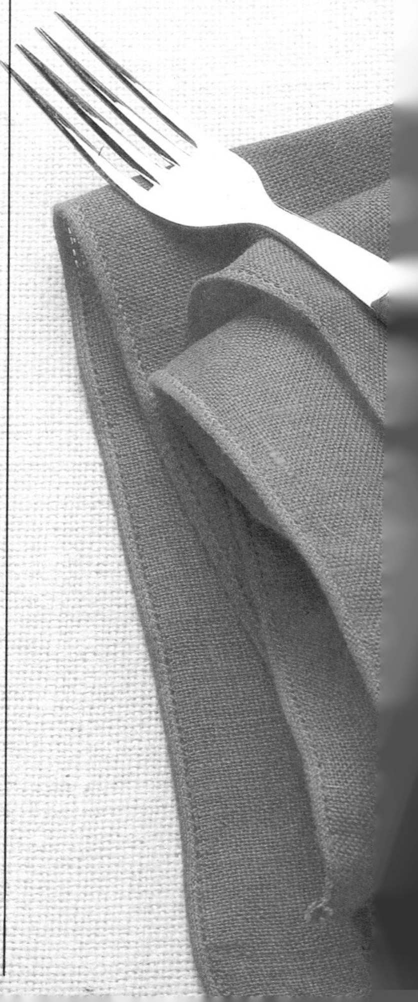

S
P

Crown Roast of Lamb

2 best ends of lamb, chined
10ml (2 tsp) butter
1 cooking apple, peeled, cored and chopped
225g (8oz) pork sausage meat
30ml (2 tblsp) fresh breadcrumbs
15ml (1 tblsp) chopped fresh parsley
15ml (1 tblsp) finely chopped mint
Glacé cherries

Trim the skin and fat from the ends of the rib bones so that 2.5cm (1 inch) of the bone protrudes. Place the two joints back-to-back with the bones curving upwards and outwards. Secure with kitchen thread. Heat the butter and sauté the apple, add the sausage meat, cook for 2-3 minutes then stir in the rest of the ingredients. Place the stuffing in the cavity of the crown. Cover the tips of the bones with foil and roast in the oven for 30 minutes per 450g (1lb) plus 30 minutes at 180°C, 350°F, Gas Mark 4. Decorate the bone ends with cutlet frills and glacé cherries and serve with roast potatoes and a green vegetable.
Serves six-eight.

Pork Provençal

1kg (2lb) pork fillets
425g (15oz) can tomatoes
750g (1½lb) potatoes, peeled and thinly sliced
350g (12oz) onions, peeled and thinly sliced
Salt and pepper
1.25ml (¼ tsp) dried mixed herbs
25g (1oz) butter

Slice the meat and trim off any surplus fat. Butter an ovenproof dish then arrange the tomatoes, meat, onions and potatoes in layers. Season each layer and ad herbs. Pour over the juice from tomatoes and finish with a layer potato slices. Pour water in to c halfway up the dish and dot the butter over the top. Cover tigh and cook in oven for 90 minute 180°C, 350°F, Gas Mark 4. Remove the lid and cook for a further 30 minutes to brown th potatoes. Serve with boiled car tossed in butter and chopped parsley.
Serves six.

Gammon with Mixed Fruit

1.75-2.25kg (4-5lb) gammon ho
30ml (2 tblsp) apricot jam
30ml (2 tblsp) made mustard
Cloves for decoration
1 small, fresh pineapple, peeled
15ml (1 tblsp) chutney
60ml (2¼ fl oz) unsweetened pineapple juice
1kg (2lb) canned apricot halves, drained

Cover the gammon with cold water and soak for 4 hours. Dr the gammon and wrap in foil. P in a roasting pan and cook in th oven for 2 hours at 190°C, 375 Gas Mark 5. Remove the rind the gammon and score the surf of the meat. Mix half the aprico jam with the mustard and spre the mixture over the gammon. Stud the meat with the cloves i decorative pattern and return t meat to the oven for about 30 minutes. Cut the pineapple int slices and remove the core fron each slice. Heat the remaining apricot jam with the chutney a pineapple juice in a wide pan. C the pineapple slices and the apr halves in this mixture. Place the finished gammon joint in a serv dish and garnish with the glaze pineapple slices and apricot hal Serve with an exotic salad.
Serves ten.

This page: Pork Provençal (t and Turkey Roast with Fruit Sauce (bottom).

Facing page: Crown Roast o Lamb (top), Egg and Melon Salad (bottom left) and Gammon with Mixed Fruit (bottom right).

Egg and Melon Salad

1 small cabbage
1 firm, ripe melon
1 orange
Salt and pepper
2 carrots, peeled and grated
4 hard-boiled eggs
Few sprigs of watercress
Few leaves of chicory
8 radishes

Cooked Salad Dressing
5ml (1 tsp) flour
15ml (1 tblsp) sugar
Salt and pepper
2.5ml (½ tsp) mustard powder
1 large egg, beaten
30ml (2 tblsp) water
30ml (2 tblsp) vinegar
5ml (1 tsp) butter

To prepare the dressing, combine the flour, sugar, mustard and seasoning in a heavy-based saucepan. Mix in the egg to form a smooth paste. Add the water, vinegar and butter and stir over a low heat until the sauce begins to thicken. Remove from the heat, stir thoroughly and, if necessary, strain to remove any lumps. Cool in the refrigerator. Chop the cabbage very finely. Cube the melon. Peel the orange and cut the segments into pieces. Combine these ingredients with the grated carrots in a mixing bowl. Season as required. Pour over the cooled dressing and spoon the salad mixture onto a large salad dish. Shell and slice the hard-boiled eggs and arrange them with the watercress and chicory leaves round the salad. Cut the radishes into floral shapes and garnish the salad and serve.
Serves four.

Barbados Turkey

25g (1oz) flour
5ml (1 tsp) powdered ginger
5ml (1 tsp) curry powder
100g (4oz) turkey escalopes
75g (3oz) butter
50ml (2 fl oz) rum
50g (2oz) desiccated coconut
45ml (3 tblsp) pineapple juice
70ml (2½ fl oz) chicken stock
50ml (2 fl oz) double cream
Salt and pepper
Few sprigs of parsley
6-8 slices canned pineapple

Mix together the flour, ginger and curry powder and use to coat the turkey. Heat the butter and fry the escalopes for about 10 minutes each side until cooked and golden. Add the rum and set alight. When the flames subside, remove the escalopes and keep hot. Add the coconut to the pan and brown quickly. Then stir in the pineapple juice and stock. Boil for 5 minutes, reduce the heat and stir in the cream and seasoning. Arrange the escalopes in a serving dish and cover with the sauce. Garnish with the parsley and pineapple. Serve with boiled rice and green vegetables.
Serves four.

Crown of Chicken

Salt and pepper
25g (1oz) flour
1kg (2lb) potatoes
45ml (3 tblsp) milk
25-50g (1-2oz) butter
6 or 8 chicken legs
60ml (4 tblsp) olive oil
1 can cherry fruit pie filling
Watercress to garnish

Coat the chicken legs in seasoned flour. Peel the potatoes and cook in boiling, salted water. Drain and mash the potatoes with the milk and butter and keep hot. Meanwhile, fry the chicken in the olive oil until cooked and golden brown. Drain on paper towels and keep hot. Drain excess oil from the frying pan, add the cherry pie filling and heat gently. Place the creamed potatoes in centre of a hot serving dish, stand the chicken legs round the edges. Pour over the hot cherry sauce. Garnish with watercress and serve with a green salad.

Duck with Orange Sauce

1 large duck, e.g. 1.5kg (3lb)
1 orange
300ml (½ pint) bought Espagnole sauce
15ml (1 tblsp) lemon juice
30ml (2 tblsp) white wine
150ml (¼ pint) water
Orange segments to garnish

Place the duck in an open roasting tin. No fat is necessary. Cook in the oven at 150°C, 300°F, Gas Mark 2. Cook for 25 minutes for every 450g (1lb) in weight and 30 minutes over. Prick the breast skin after 30 minutes with a fine skewer. Pare the rind from the orange, cut into wafer-thin strips and simmer in water for about 10 minutes. Strain the Espagnole sauce carefully, reheat with the orange rind, orange juice, lemon juice and wine. Garnish the duck with orange segments and serve with the orange sauce. Serve with potato croquettes, broccoli and roast turnips.
Serves four.

Peppered Steak

Steak, as required
A little oil or butter
Peppercorns

Brush the steak with oil or melted butter and grill until tender, or as required. When the steak is cooked, place on a serving dish and sprinkle with the peppercorns. Tap with a steak hammer to crush the peppercorns into the steak. Serve with French fries, potato croquettes, onion rings or broccoli, or a mixed side salad.

Turkey Roast with Fruit Sauce

25g (1oz) butter
2.5kg (5½lb) white turkey roast
1 red pepper
1 small green pepper
1 onion
225g (8oz) can mandarin oranges
225g (8oz) canned sweet corn

For the Sauce
10ml (2 tsp) cornflour
15ml (1 tblsp) vinegar
5ml (1 tsp) sugar
5ml (1 tsp) Worcestershire sauce
15-30ml (1-2 tblsp) sherry

Spread the butter over the turkey roast then wrap in foil to make a parcel. Place in a roasting pan and roast in the oven for 90 minutes at 190°C, 375°F, Gas Mark 5. Core, deseed and chop the peppers. Peel and chop the onion. Drain the mandarins and sweet corn, reserving the juices. Mix the mandarins, sweet corn, peppers and onion together. To make the sauce, mix the cornflour with a little water to make a smooth paste. Blend the juices from the mandarins and sweet corn with the vinegar, sugar, Worcestershire sauce, sherry and cornflour and heat until thickened, stirring well. Add the fruit and vegetables. Remove the turkey roast from the oven and unwrap the foil. Pour a little of the sauce all over and round the turkey and cover agai with the foil. Cook the turkey fo further 1-1½ hours or until the turkey is tender and cooked through. Unwrap the turkey and place on a serving dish. Surroun with fruit sauce and serve the re of the sauce separately. Serve wi roast potatoes and vegetables of your own choice.
Serves six-eight.

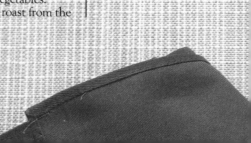

own of Chicken (right),
ck and Orange Sauce
low) and Barbados
rkey (bottom).

MICROWAVE COOKING

ntroducing the Microwave

: microwave oven is one of the most exciting kitchen appliances ilable. It may be used to defrost, reheat, and cook foods, and is refore more versatile than a conventional oven; in fact it can cope 1 75% of your normal cooking chores.

: theory behind microwave cooking must be learned and fully lerstood before a microwave oven can be used to its full extent. It very different method of cooking, which is clean, quick, efficient, our saving and economical.

e Principles of Microwave Cookery

: oven is plugged in by means of a 13 amp plug to a normal trical socket and it is usually positioned on the kitchen work top. ctricity is converted into microwave energy inside the oven by the gnetron. The 'microwaves' are transferred into the oven cavity re they bounce off the metal interior and penetrate the outer 2- 1 (1"-1½") of the food. They pass through non-metal containers hough they were not there, and simply cause the molecules in the food to vibrate very fast indeed. The heat that is created passes by conduction through to the centre of the food and the food is cooked by friction heat. As a rough guide, cooking times by the microwave method are about ⅓ to ¼ of the conventional times.

Different Types of Microwave Ovens

A microwave oven may be either free standing or built-in. If built-in, it is placed in a housing unit, with a conventional oven situated above or below the microwave.

Convected Hot Air and Microwave Combined

These ovens are now widely available. They are more expensive than an ordinary microwave oven as they combine two units in one. The most common criticism of food cooked in a microwave is that it does not appear 'brown'. This is because there is no dry heat available to caramelise or 'brown' the food. Some people prefer to buy the combination ovens, which use traditional cooking methods and

microwave cooking combined. In some models both cooking methods may be used simultaneously, whilst in others the microwave and the hot air ovens are used one after the other.

Grills
Some microwave ovens offer a browning grill.

Safety
All microwave ovens offered for sale in this country pass rigorous safety tests. Choose one which has the British Standard kite mark.

The Output of the Microwave
The cooking time for each dish/recipe is governed by the electrical output of the microwave oven, and the output also controls the running costs of the appliance. The output is measured in watts. A 700w microwave oven (the most powerful available on the domestic market) consumes about 1.3k per hour and is, therefore, a most economical method of cooking. Microwave ovens are available with maximum power ratings of 700w, 650w, 600w and 500w. The cooking, re-heating and defrosting times vary according to the output. A 1.5kg (3lb) chicken takes 21 minutes in a 700w microwave and 28 minutes in a 500w. There is no pre-heating before use, and no cooling down after cooking.

Versatility
A microwave oven may be used to defrost, cook and reheat food. It is also well suited to the many different methods of cooking – a microwave oven can poach, shallow fat fry, braise, roast, boil and bake. It will even dry herbs for winter use, and may be used to sterilise jam jars. The oven and cooking containers stay cool, and microwave ovens are, therefore, perfectly safe for elderly people to use, and for households where there are children.

leaning

s the oven cabinet does not get very hot, all that is necessary is a pe with a clean dish cloth. Should smells cling e.g. curry or fish, nply squeeze a lemon into 450ml (¾ pint) water and bring to the oil. Wipe the oven with the acidulated water. Food does not bake nto the containers so they are easier to wash up.

urntables

anufacturers choose different methods of ensuring that the food ooks evenly. Go by personal recommendation wherever possible. idden turntables are popular as they do not restrict the shape of sh used. Some ovens offer stirrer fans and turntables.

tanding Times

anding, or equalising, time is simply the time that the food takes to nish cooking. The heat is passed from the outside to the centre by nduction. The standing time will vary according to the size and ensity of the food. Standing time may take place either inside or utside the microwave oven; it is an important part of microwave ookery which must be used. It is just as important after defrosting.

Containers for Use in the Microwave Oven

Special containers are available for microwave cookery, but they are not essential. The heat is localised in the food, and not in the container, so the dish itself does not usually become hot. Some plastics, Pyrex, china, glass, and even paper and basketware, may be used. Be guided by the length of time the food is to be in the microwave, and by the temperature that it will reach.

Plastic cling film is a boon to the microwave owner, as it may be used in place of a lid to cover foods and prevent splashing. Do remember to pierce cling film and roasta bags to allow steam to escape.

Metal – including tin foil – may damage the heart of the microwave oven, the magnetron, and should not be used unless specifically directed by the manufacturer.

Browning Dish or Skillet

A browning dish is a special dish which, when preheated in the microwave oven, will become very hot over the base. Several shapes and sizes are available, either with a lid or without. The dish is used to brown such foods as chops, sausages, hamburgers, bacon, eggs etc. The food must be turned to brown on the other side. The deep

erby Roast Chicken (left), evilled Pork Chops (below) nd Chicken Breasts in Garlic ream Sauce (right).

Variable Power Chart

MICROWAVE POWER LEVEL	DESCRIPTION AND SUGGESTED USE
10 or Full–High	Microwave energy constant at full wattage. For cooking vegetables, poultry, fish and some sauces, start joints.
8 or Roast	Power on for 13 seconds, auto cut-out for 2 seconds. Repeated continually for time selected, for reheating some joints.
7 and 6 – Medium	Power is on for about 10 seconds, off for 5 seconds, for chops, meat balls, chicken pieces, cakes.
4 and 5 – Simmer	Power is on for 6 seconds, off for 9 seconds, for completing casseroles, defrosting large joints, egg and cheese dishes.
3 – Defrost	Generally for defrosting (allow a standing time afterwards), for melting chocolate, and for delicate sauces.
2 – Very Low	Power is on for 3 seconds, off for 12 seconds. Keep cooked food warm for up to ½ hour. Soften butter and cream cheese from refrigerator.

Please note that this chart is gi[ven] only as a guide. The variable power dial differs slightly from manufacturer to manufacturer.

Cooked food reheats remarka[bly] quickly without drying out. A [chart] is provided to give some of the most common foods. Allow a f[ew] minutes standing time, after reheating, and before serving.

GENERAL RULES FOR REHEATING.

1. Cover food, allowing steam [to] escape, unless told specifically to cover.

2. Stir foods such as casseroles, baked beans, stewed fruits, hal[f] through reheating.

3. Allow a short standing time [of] 5 minutes before removing covering and serving.

4. Reheat small items, such as sausage rolls or sausages, arra[nged] in ring fashion on outside edge [of] plate. Reheat on Power 4, or Simmer.

Re-heating Chart

TYPE OF FOOD & WEIGHT	COVER	STIRRING	POWER LEVEL	TIME
1 Plated Meal	Cling Film	–	Full	3-4 minutes
1 Large Macaroni Cheese	Cling Film	Yes, once	Power 7 or Roast	10 minutes
2 Bowls Soup	–	Yes, once	Full	5 minutes
Baked Beans 100g (4ozs)	–	–	Power 7 or Roast	2 minutes
Baked Beans 450g (16ozs)	Yes	Yes, twice	Power 7 or Roast	7 minutes
Chicken Pieces 2 x 225g (8ozs)	Yes	–	Full	3-4 minutes
Beef Casserole for 4	Yes	Yes, twice	Full	10-12 minutes
Cooked Vegetables 100g (4ozs)	Yes	–	Full	45 seconds
Cooked Vegetables 450g (1lb)	Yes	Yes, once	Full	2 minutes
1 Family Meat Pie	No	No	4 or Simmer	7-8 minutes
6 Mince Pies	No	No	4 or Simmer	4 minutes
4 Bread Rolls	Kitchen Roll	No	4 or Simmer	2 minutes
Christmas Pudding 750g (1½lb)	Cling Film	No	Power 7 or Roast	3 minutes
Sauce 300ml (½ pt)	Cling Film	Yes, twice	Full	2 minutes
Fish 350g (12ozs)	Cling Film	–	Full	2 minutes

Defrosting Chart

FOOD TO BE DEFROSTED AND WEIGHT	POWER LEVEL	MICROWAVE TIME	STANDING TIME
Mince 450g (1lb)	4 or Defrost	6 minutes	15 minutes
Chicken 1½kg (3lb)	4 or Defrost	30 minutes	30 minutes
Joint of Beef 1½kg (3lb)	4 or Defrost	20 minutes	30 minutes
Shepherd's Pie 450g (1lb)	4 or Defrost	8 minutes	10 minutes
Large Lasagne	6 or Simmer	20 minutes	15 minutes
Chops 450g (1lb)	4 or Defrost	6 minutes	10 minutes
Sausages 450g (1lb)	4 or Defrost	6 minutes	10 minutes
Cod 225g (8ozs)	4 or Defrost	6 minutes	10 minutes
Raspberries 225g (8ozs)	4 or Defrost	4 minutes	15 minutes
1 Victoria Sandwich (2 egg)	4 or Defrost	2-3 minutes	15 minutes
Large Sliced Loaf	4 or Defrost	7 minutes	10 minutes
Cheese Sauce 300ml (½ Pint)	4 or Defrost	7 minutes	7 minutes
Chicken in Sauce for 4	Simmer	12 minutes	10 minutes
Family Apple Pie	4 or Defrost	8 minutes	5 minutes
Family Meat Pie or Quiche Lorraine	4 or Defrost	6-7 minutes	10 minutes

The microwave oven makes a perfect partner for your freezer as it enables you to defrost frozen foods in a fraction of the time that it would normally take. Remember to turn or stir the foods, for more even defrosting, and remember that a standing time is very important.

ALTERING TIMINGS

The recipes given in this book can be cooked in any model of variable power microwave oven that is available today. Each of these recipes was tested in a 700W microwave oven. Convert the timings in the following way, if the output of your oven is other than 700W:–

If using an oven of 500W, add 40 seconds for each minute stated in the recipe.

If using an oven of 600W, add 20 seconds for each minute stated in the recipe.

If using an oven of 650W plus, you will only need to allow a slight increase in the overall time.

wning dishes with lids are also used as casserole dishes. **These ntainers must not be used in conventional ovens.**

rring and Turning

ring and turning are methods used to equalise the heat in the d, i.e. the cooking of the food. The amount of stirring or turning be governed by the type of food to be cooked, the cooking time the even distribution of energy in the microwave oven. The pes in this section give you a guide as to when to stir and turn. ust, if necessary, according to your own particular oven. Arrange ds such as baked apples or jacket potatoes in a ring fashion, ving a space in the centre.

rting Temperature of Food

e starting temperature of food will alter the cooking time. It may at average room temperature, at cold room temperature or taken n the refrigerator or cold larder. Please note that the timings in section are calculated for food at average room temperature, ess otherwise stated.

Can You Cook a Complete Meal by Microwave?

The easiest way to use a microwave oven is to employ stage cookery. The microwave oven cooks according to weight and time, not by temperature, and different types of food require different cooking times. During the standing time of the denser foods, such as joints and jacket potatoes, the less dense items, such as vegetables and sauces, are completely cooked. Foods of similar density may be cooked together, e.g. potatoes and carrots, but remember that the total energy available in the microwave oven must be shared between the foods introduced. If carrots and potatoes are cooked simultaneously, the resulting weight must be checked, and the cooking time calculated accordingly.

Some Things Cannot be Done

Do not try to cook Yorkshire puddings or other batter recipes, boil eggs, deep fat fry, or produce really crisp foods such as roast potatoes, as none of these will be successful. **Pastry** – baking blind, suet crust and some puff pastry recipes work beautifully, but do not try to cook the top of an apple pie. Baked pies may be reheated successfully on Simmer, or Power 4 – see chart.

Soups and Starters

Vegetable Soup

PREPARATION TIME: 10 minutes
MICROWAVE TIME: 21-26 minutes
SERVES: 4 people

25g (1oz) butter
450g (1lb) young leeks, cleaned and sliced
1 medium onion, peeled and sliced
175g (6oz) potato, peeled and diced
1 carrot, peeled and diced
Salt and freshly ground black pepper to taste
15ml (1 tblsp) chopped fresh parsley
450ml (¾ pint) homemade chicken stock
300ml (½ pint) milk

Melt the butter in a 2¼ litre (4 pint) casserole dish. Microwave on Full Power for 1 minute. Stir in all the prepared vegetables, salt and pepper, parsley and 45ml (3 tblsp) of the stock. Cover the dish, piercing the cling film if used. Microwave on Full Power for 12 minutes. Stir. Set aside, covered, for 5 minutes. Transfer the vegetables into the food processor bowl or liquidizer goblet; add the milk and liquidize or process until smooth. Return to the casserole and stir in the remaining stock. Microwave on Full Power, covered, for 3-5 minutes. Stir well before serving.

Asparagus with Mayonnaise

PREPARATION TIME: 10 minutes
MICROWAVE TIME: 10-12 minutes
SERVES: 4 people

450g (1lb) frozen asparagus spears
250ml (8 fl oz) corn oil
25g (1oz) butter
1 egg
1 egg yolk
150ml (¼ pint) olive oil
Salt and freshly ground black pepper to taste
30ml (2 tblsp) lemon juice
Chopped fresh parsley

Arrange the asparagus in a roasta bag in a suitable dish. Add 45ml (3 tblsp) water to the bag, with the butter. Seal the bag with a rubber band. Pierce the bag once at the base. Microwave on Full Power for 10-12 minutes, turning the bag over once halfway through cooking time. Set aside. Put the egg and egg yolk into the goblet of a food processor or liquidizer with the salt and pepper. Blend on maximum. Add the oil, in a steady trickle, blending to a smooth mayonnaise. Add the lemon juice. Carefully drain the asparagus and arrange on a heated serving dish. Sprinkle with the parsley and serve accompanied by the mayonnaise. Serve immediately.

Soured Cream Prawns

PREPARATION TIME: 5 minutes
MICROWAVE TIME: 7-8 minutes
SERVES: 4 people

50g (2oz) butter
225g (8oz) peeled shrimps
Freshly ground black pepper to taste
1 egg yolk
150ml (¼ pint) soured cream
Paprika

Butter 4 ramekin dishes and divide the shrimps amongst them. Season well with black pepper. Combine the egg yolk and soured cream and spoon over the shrimps. Dot with the remaining butter. Microwave all 4 ramekins together on Power 4, or Simmer, for 7-8 minutes. (The dishes should be arranged in a ring, leaving a space in the centre.) Serve immediately sprinkled with paprika.

Sweetcorn Starter

PREPARATION TIME: 5 minutes
MICROWAVE TIME: 15 minutes
SERVES: 4 people

4 corn cobs
Sprigs of fresh savory
Salt and freshly ground black pepper to taste
100g (4oz) butter

Arrange the cobs in a suitable dish. Add 2-3 tblsp cold water and a few sprigs of savory. Season. Cover with cling film and pierce. Microwave on Full Power for 6 minutes. Turn each cob over. Re-cover and microwave on Full Power for 6 minutes. Set aside. Put the butter into a 600ml (1 pint) jug and microwave on Power 4 or Simmer for about 3 minutes or until melted. Transfer the cooked cobs to a serving dish. Pour over the butter and sprinkle with extra chopped savory before serving.

Individual Frozen Pizzas

PREPARATION TIME: 2 minutes
MICROWAVE TIME: 6½-8½ minutes
SERVES: 1 person

Preheat a browning dish, without the lid, for 5-7 minutes. Put 15ml (1 tblsp) of oil and 1 individual pizza onto the dish. Microwave uncovered for approximately 1½ minutes on Full Power. Allow to stand for 1 minute before serving. As many pizzas as will fit onto your dish may be microwaved at the same time; increase the microwave time accordingly. Pizzas may be heated directly from the freezer, without the browning dish, on an ordinary non-metallic plate but the base will not be as crisp.

Chestnut Soup

PREPARATION TIME: 15 minutes
MICROWAVE TIME: 34 minutes
SERVES: 4 people

25g (1oz) butter
1 stem celery, chopped
2 large onions, chopped
900ml (1½ pint) homemade chicken stock (hot)
225g (8oz) unsweetened chestnut puree
Salt and freshly ground black pepper to taste
4 rashers streaky bacon, de-rinded

Put the butter, celery and onions into a 2¼ litre (4 pint) casserole dish; cover with a lid and microwave on Full Power for 4 minutes. Stir. Mix 300ml (½ pint) stock with the chestnut puree, in a 1.2 litre (2 pint) mixing bowl. Stir into the onion mixture. Seas with salt and black pepper; c and microwave on Full Powe minutes. Stir in the remainin stock and microwave on Full for 20 minutes. Allow to star whilst preparing the bacon. Arrange the bacon on a micr roasting rack, or on 2 sheets absorbent kitchen paper. Microwave, uncovered, on F Power, for about 3 minutes. S the soup sprinkled with the crumbled crispy bacon.

Tomato Baskets

PREPARATION TIME: 5 min
MICROWAVE TIME: 5½-6½ minutes
SERVES: 6 people

6 large firm tomatoes
225g (8oz) packet frozen mixe vegetables
50g (2oz) butter
Salt and freshly ground black p to taste
Few sprigs of fresh mint

Cut the top off each tomato a reserve. Using a grapefruit kn a teaspoon, carefully scoop ou centre flesh. (Use in a soup o sauce recipe). Pierce the pouc frozen vegetables once and pl a dish. Microwave on Full Pov for 3½ minutes, turning the b once halfway through the coc time. Set aside. Stand the pre tomatoes upright on a serving

Asparagus with Mayonnais (top), Vegetable Soup (centr and Soured Cream Prawns (bottom).

in a ring. Dot with half the butter. Microwave on Full Power for about 2-3 minutes until very hot. Mix the drained, cooked vegetables with the remaining butter and salt and pepper and spoon into the tomato shells. Top with the reserved lids, and garnish with sprigs of mint. Serve immediately.

Quick Bap Pizzas

PREPARATION TIME: 10 minutes

MICROWAVE TIME: 6½-7½ minutes

SERVES: 4 as a main meal, 8 as a snack

4 baps
1 medium onion, finely chopped
5ml (1 tsp) tomato puree
5ml (1 tsp) dried oregano
225g (8oz) can tomatoes, chopped
5ml (1 tsp) French mustard
Salt and freshly ground black pepper to taste
150g (5oz) Cheddar cheese, thinly sliced or grated
Stuffed olives, sliced

Tomato Baskets (right), Quick Bap Pizzas (below) and Individual Frozen Pizza (far right).

Cut the baps in half and arrange in a ring on a suitable baking sheet. Place the onion in a 1.2 litre (2 pint) mixing bowl; cover and microwave for 1½ minutes on Full Power. Stir in the tomato puree, oregano, chopped tomatoes and the mustard. Season with salt and pepper. Divide amongst the baps, and cover with the cheese. Decorate with the sliced olives. Microwave on Power 4 for 5-6 minutes, until the cheese has melted. Serve immediately.

Garlic Prawn Starter

PREPARATION TIME: 30 minutes

MICROWAVE TIME: 20 minutes

SERVES: 4 people

750g (1½lb) courgettes, cleaned, topped and tailed
Salt and freshly ground black pepper to taste
350g (12oz) peeled prawns
15ml (1 tblsp) chopped chives
30ml (2 tblsp) dry white wine
2 cloves garlic, crushed
15ml (1 tblsp) lemon juice
50g (2oz) butter

Garnish
Unpeeled prawns

Slice the courgettes thinly into a colander, sprinkling them generously with salt. Cover with a plate and weigh down; leave to stand for 20 minutes. Rinse well under cold running water. Drain thoroughly. Arrange the courgettes

in a vegetable dish. Season with salt and pepper. Cover and microwave on Full Power for 12 minutes. Stir. Set aside, covered. Put the peeled prawns, chives, wine, garlic, lemon juice and butter into a 1.2 litre (2 pint) casserole. Cover with a lid. Microwave on Power 4, or Simmer, for 8 minutes. Stir once halfway through cooking time. Drain the excess liquid from the courgettes. Top with the heated prawns and their juices. Garnish with the unpeeled prawns and serve immediately.

Egg and Tuna Starter

PREPARATION TIME: 10 minutes

MICROWAVE TIME: 10 minutes

SERVES: 4 people

200g (7oz) can tuna fish in oil, drained
2 hard boiled eggs, cooked conventionally and chopped
300ml (½ pint) milk
25g (1oz) butter
Salt and freshly ground black pepper to taste
25g (1oz) plain flour
5ml (1 tsp) made mustard
50g (2oz) grated Cheddar cheese

Garnish
Stuffed olives, sliced

Flake the tuna fish and divide between 4 ramekin dishes. Top with the egg. Melt the butter in a 1 litre (1¾ pint) jug for 1 minute on Full Power, or until very hot. Stir in the flour and gradually stir in the milk. Microwave on Full Power for 2 minutes. Beat well with a balloon whisk. Microwave on Full Power for 2 minutes. Beat well with a balloon whisk. Beat in salt and pepper and cheese. Divide the sauce amongst the ramekins. Garnish with sliced olives. Microwave all 4 ramekins together for 5 minutes on Power 4 or Simmer. Serve immediately.

This page: Sweetcorn Starter (top), Garlic Prawn Starter (bottom).

Mackerel Pate

PREPARATION TIME: 10 minutes plus chilling

MICROWAVE TIME: 3 minutes

SERVES: 6 people

1 onion, finely chopped
50g (2oz) butter
225g (8oz) cream cheese
30ml (2 tblsp) lemon juice
30ml (2 tblsp) chopped fresh parsley
350g (12oz) smoked mackerel fillets
5ml (1 tsp) coarse French mustard
Freshly ground black pepper to taste
45ml (3 tblsp) soured cream
10ml (2 tsp) tomato puree

Garnish
Lemon wedges
Fresh parsley and cucumber slices

Put the onion into a soup bowl. Cover with cling film and pierce. Microwave on Full Power for 1 minute. Set aside. Flake the fish into the food processor or liquidizer goblet, discarding skin and bones. Add the onion. Place the butter in the bowl used for the onion and microwave on Power 4, or Simmer, for 2 minutes. Add to the processor or liquidizer with all the remaining ingredients. Process or liquidize until smooth. Pour into a dampened loaf tin; smooth the surface. Chill until firm. Turn out onto a serving dish and garnish with wedges of lemon, crimped cucumber slices and parsley.

Vegetables

All types of vegetables, both frozen and fresh, microwave exceptionally well. They keep their colour, flavour and shape. Follow a few simple rules and use the charts to help you.

Helpful Hints
1. If you want to add salt, dissolve it in a little water beforehand. Adding salt can cause some vegetables to dry; to be on the safe side season with salt after cooking.
2. Always cover vegetables – roasta or freezer bags are very useful, but remember to pierce them.
3. Stir at least once during the cooking time or, if using a bag, turn it over.
4. Add only the amount of water necessary.
5. Cut the vegetables into even sized pieces.
6. Allow a standing time after cooking and before serving.
7. Cook frozen vegetables from frozen, do not defrost them first.

Fresh Vegetable Chart

VEGETABLE AND WEIGHT	ADDITION	MICROWAVE TIME	STANDING TIME
Sliced Green Beans 450g (1lb)	45ml (3 tblsp) water	8 minutes	5 minutes
Broad Beans 450g (1lb)	45ml (3 tblsp) water	8 minutes	5 minutes
Broccoli Spears 225g (8ozs)	45ml (3 tblsp) water	7 minutes	4 minutes
Sliced Carrots 450g (1lb)	30ml (2 tblsp) water	7-8 minutes	4 minutes
Cauliflower Florets 450g (1lb)	45ml (3 tblsp) water	7-8 minutes	5 minutes
Chopped Celery 225g (8ozs)	45ml (3 tblsp) water	7 minutes	4 minutes
Courgettes 450g (1lb)	25g (1oz) butter	10 minutes	3 minutes
Leeks 450g (1lb)	30ml (2 tblsp) water	7-8 minutes	3 minutes
Mushrooms (Sliced) 225g (8ozs)	25g (1oz) butter	2 minutes	2 minutes
Sliced Marrow 450g (1lb)	25g (1oz) butter	7 minutes	3 minutes
New Potatoes 450g (1lb)	30ml (2 tblsp) water	7 minutes	4 minutes
Old Potatoes 450g (1lb)	45ml (3 tblsp) water	9 minutes	5 minutes
Sliced Onions 450g (1lb)	30ml (2 tblsp) water	8-9 minutes	4 minutes
Brussels Sprouts 450g (1lb)	30ml (2 tblsp) water	6-7 minutes	4 minutes
Diced Swede 450g (1lb)	30ml (2 tblsp) water	13 minutes	6 minutes

Baked Stuffed Marrow

PREPARATION TIME: 20 minutes
MICROWAVE TIME: 22 minutes
SERVES: 4 people

1 medium size marrow
25g (1oz) butter
1 onion, peeled and finely chopped
450g (1lb) raw, lean minced beef
15g (½oz) plain flour
5ml (1 tsp) dried basil or oregano
1 egg, beaten
1 beef stock cube, crumbled
Salt and freshly ground black pepper to taste
15ml (1 tblsp) tomato puree

Wipe the marrow with a damp cloth. Cut both ends off the marrow and keep on one side. Scoop out the seeds with a spoon and discard. Melt the butter in a 1.75 litre (3 pint) mixing bowl for 1 minute on Full Power. Stir in the onion. Microwave on Full Power for 1 minute. Stir in all the remaining ingredients. Mix well. Secure one end of the marrow with wooden cocktail sticks. Stuff the marrow with the mince mixture. Secure the remaining end in place with wooden cocktail sticks. Place the marrow on a meat roasting rack and cover with cling film. Pierce. Microwave on Full Power for about 20 minutes, turning the marrow once halfway through cooking time. Allow to stand, covered with foil, for 5 minutes before serving. Cut into rings, and serve piping hot.

Brussels Sprouts with Chestnut and Bacon

PREPARATION TIME: 15 minutes
MICROWAVE TIME: 8 minutes
SERVES: 4 people

450g (1lb) fresh Brussels sprouts
15ml (1 tblsp) lemon juice
5ml (1 tsp) dried mixed herbs
30ml (2 tblsp) cold water
Salt and freshly ground black pepper to taste
75g (3oz) butter
225g (8oz) canned whole chestnuts, drained
3 rashers streaky bacon, de-rinded, cooked and chopped (see Garlic Mushrooms recipe)

Peel the sprouts and make a cross in the base of each one. Put the sprouts into a 1.2 litre (2 pint) casserole dish, or into a roasta bag. Add the lemon juice, herbs, water, and salt and pepper. Cover with a lid, or pierce the bag if used. Microwave on Full Power for 5 minutes. Stir or turn once, halfway through cooking time. Set aside for 5 minutes. Put the butter into a 300ml (½ pint) Pyrex jug and microwave on Power 4 or Simmer until melted (about 3 minutes). If using a roasta bag, tip the sprou into serving dish. Add the ches to the Brussels sprouts, stirring gently. Cover with a lid. Microv on Full Power for 1 minute. Co with melted butter, sprinkle wit chopped bacon, and serve.

Brussels Sprouts with Chest and Bacon (top), Carrot and Parsnip Puree (centre) and Baked Stuffed Marrow (bottom).

Frozen Vegetable Chart

VEGETABLE AND WEIGHT	AMOUNT OF WATER	COOKING TIME	STANDING TIME
Asparagus 225g (8ozs)	30ml (2 tblsp)	7 minutes	5 minutes
Broccoli 225g (8ozs)	45ml (3 tblsp)	10 minutes	5 minutes
Brussels Sprouts 225g (8ozs)	30ml (2 tblsp)	4 minutes	3 minutes
Carrots 225g (8ozs)	30ml (2 tblsp)	6 minutes	3 minutes
Cauliflower Florets 225g (8ozs)	30ml (2 tblsp)	3 minutes	2 minutes
Courgettes 225g (8ozs)	Nil	4 minutes	2 minutes
Leeks 225g (8ozs)	30ml (2 tblsp)	6-7 minutes	2 minutes
Mixed Vegetables 225g (8ozs)	30ml (2 tblsp)	4 minutes	3 minutes
Mushrooms 225g (8ozs)	25g (1oz) butter and herbs	4 minutes	2 minutes
Baby Onions 225g (8ozs)	25g (1oz) butter	5 minutes	4 minutes
Peas 225g (8ozs)	Nil	4 minutes	2 minutes
Spinach 225g (8ozs)	Nil	5 minutes	3 minutes
Sweetcorn 225g (8ozs)	Nil	4 minutes	2 minutes

Carrot and Parsnip Puree

PREPARATION TIME: 15 minutes
MICROWAVE TIME: 13 minutes
SERVES: 4 people

225g (8oz) carrots, peeled
225g (8oz) parsnips, peeled
2.5ml (½ tsp) dried basil
45ml (3 tblsp) well-flavoured stock
30ml (2 tblsp) double cream
Salt and freshly ground black pepper to taste
Pinch grated nutmeg

Garnish
Carrot curls

Dice the peeled carrots and parsnips and place in a roasta bag in a 1.2 litre (2 pint) casserole. Add 30ml (2 tblsp) water and the basil. Snip the bag once at the base. Microwave on Full Power for 8 minutes, turning the bag over once halfway through cooking time. Set aside for 5 minutes. Empty the contents of the roasta bag into the goblet of a food processor or liquidizer. Add the stock and process until smooth. Add cream, salt and pepper, and nutmeg. Process just to blend. Return to the casserole and cover with a lid. Microwave on Power 4, or Simmer, for 5 minutes. Garnish with carrot curls and serve.

Courgette Choice

PREPARATION TIME: 40-45 minutes
COOKING TIME: 10 minutes
SERVES: 4 people

450g (1lb) young courgettes, topped, tailed and washed
Salt and freshly ground black pepper to taste
450g (1lb) large firm tomatoes, skinned and sliced
2.5ml (½ tsp) dried tarragon
1 clove garlic, crushed
25g (1oz) butter

Arrange the sliced courgettes in a colander. Sprinkle generously with salt and leave to stand for 30 minutes. (This draws out the bitter juices.) Rinse well under cold running water. Drain. Layer the courgettes and tomatoes in a 1.2 litre (2 pint) casserole dish, starting and finishing with courgettes. Season each layer with salt, pepper, tarragon and garlic. Dot the top with small knobs of butter. Cover tightly with a lid. Microwave on Full Power for 10 minutes. Allow to stand for 3 minutes before serving.

Cauliflower Cheese

PREPARATION TIME: 10 minutes
MICROWAVE TIME: 12 minutes
SERVES: 4 people

1 cauliflower, trimmed and divided into florets
15g (½oz) cornflour
300ml (½ pint) milk
5ml (1 tsp) made mustard
Salt and freshly ground black pepper to taste
75g (3oz) grated Cheddar cheese
25g (1oz) butter
½ red pepper, de-seeded and chopped

Arrange the florets of cauliflower in a roasta bag. Add 30ml (2 tblsp) water. Pierce the bag, and place in a 1.2 litre (2 pint) casserole. Microwave on Full Power for 7-8 minutes, turning the bag over once halfway through cooking time. S aside, covered. Cream the cornflour with a little of the mil a smooth paste. Stir in the must and salt and pepper to taste. He the remaining milk in a 1 litre (1 pint) jug for 2 minutes on Full Power. Pour the heated milk ont the cornflour mixture, stirring continuously. Return to the jug and microwave on Full Power fo minutes or until boiling. Beat in cheese and butter, and any liqui from the cauliflower. Transfer cauliflower florets to a warmed serving dish. Pour the sauce ove evenly. Sprinkle with the red pepper and serve immediately. T red pepper may be heated in a c in the microwave for 1 minute o Full Power, if liked.

Ratatouille

PREPARATION TIME: 40 minu
MICROWAVE TIME: 22-24 min
SERVES: 4 people

225g (½lb) courgettes
450g (1lb) aubergines
Salt and freshly ground black pep to taste
50g (2oz) butter
1 medium onion, peeled and slice
1 large clove garlic, crushed
A little oil
1 red pepper, de-seeded and slice
425g (15oz) can tomatoes, chopp
2.5ml (½ tsp) dried oregano
50g (2oz) crumbled Danish Blue cheese

Wash the courgettes and aubergines. Cut off the ends an discard. Slice into ½ cm (¼ inc slices and layer with a generous sprinkling of salt in a colander. with a plate and a weight and se aside to drain for 15 minutes. Rinse well under cold running water and drain. Put the butter 600ml (1 pint) measuring jug. Microwave on Full Power for 1- minutes until melted. Stir in th onion and garlic. Grease the sid and base of a 1.75-2.25 litre (3- pint) casserole or souffle dish w

Ratatouille (top), Courgette Choice (centre left) and Cauliflower Cheese (bottom

oil. Layer the aubergines, courgettes and red pepper in the dish with the tomatoes, oregano, onion and garlic. Season each layer with salt and pepper. Cover with a lid. Microwave on Full Power for 20-22 minutes, removing the lid for the last 8 minutes. Turn the dish ¼ turn twice during the cooking time, if necessary. Top with the crumbled cheese and serve immediately.

Buttery Mashed Potato

PREPARATION TIME: 10 minutes
MICROWAVE TIME: 17 minutes
SERVES: 4-5 people

1kg (2lb) old potatoes, peeled
45ml (3 tblsp) milk
50g (2oz) butter
Salt and freshly ground black pepper to taste
50ml (2 tblsp) single cream
Chopped fresh parsley

Cut the potatoes into small, even sized pieces and put into a roasta bag with the milk and butter. Season. Secure the bag with an elastic band and stand in a 1.75 litre (3 pint) mixing bowl. Pierce the bag once at the base. Microwave on Full Power for 17 minutes, turning the bag over once halfway through the cooking time. Allow to stand for 5 minutes. Turn the potatoes and their liquid into the bowl and mash with a fork. Beat with a wooden spoon adding the cream. Turn into a serving dish. Fork up and sprinkle with the parsley. Serve.

Potatoes Gratinee

PREPARATION TIME: 20 minutes
MICROWAVE TIME: 26 minutes
SERVES: 4 people

750g (1½lb) old white potatoes, peeled and thinly sliced
300ml (½ pint) pouring white sauce
50g (2oz) grated cheese
45ml (3 tblsp) milk
Salt and freshly ground black pepper to taste
25g (1oz) butter
1 Recipe quantity of Crispy Topping (see recipe)

Soak the potato slices in cold water for a few minutes. Heat the sauce in a large jug for 1 minute on Full Power. Beat in the grated cheese, milk, and salt and pepper to taste. Grease a shallow dish with the butter. Arrange the drained potato slices, overlapping slightly, in the

Spinach Fiesta (top), Buttery Mashed Potato (far left) and Potatoes Gratinee (left).

base of the dish. Pour the sauce evenly over the top. Cover with cling film and pierce. Microwave on Power 7, or Roast, for 25 minutes. Stir once, gently, halfway through cooking time. Serve after 5 minutes standing time, sprinkled with the crispy topping.

Stuffed Baked Peppers

PREPARATION TIME: 10 minutes
MICROWAVE TIME: 14½-15½ minutes
SERVES: 4 people

4 large, even-sized peppers, about 225g (8oz) each
30ml (2 tblsp) water
350g (12oz) cooked chicken, pork or turkey
30ml (2 tblsp) drained, canned sweetcorn kernels
60ml (4 tblsp) soured cream
75g (3oz) chopped button mushrooms
Salt and freshly ground black pepper to taste

Cut the tops off the peppers and reserve. Scoop out the seeds and discard them. Stand the peppers upright in an oblong or round casserole dish. Add the water; cover and microwave on Full Power for 3½ minutes. Set aside. Combine all the remaining ingredients to make the filling and mix well. Drain the water from the peppers and divide the filling amongst them. Replace the tops. Cover with cling film and pierce. Microwave on Full Power for 11-12 minutes. Stand for 3 minutes before serving.

Garlic Mushrooms

PREPARATION TIME: 20 minutes
MICROWAVE TIME: 12½-14½
SERVES: 4 people

75g (3oz) butter
2 cloves garlic, crushed
350g (12oz) button mushrooms, stalks removed
4 rashers streaky bacon, de-rinded
100g (4oz) cream cheese
Salt and freshly ground black pepper to taste
15ml (1 tblsp) natural yogurt or soured cream
2.5ml (½ tsp) dried parsley

Garnish
Chopped fresh parsley

Place the butter and garlic into a small bowl and microwave on Power 4, or Simmer, for 3 minutes, or until melted. Using a pastry brush, brush the mushrooms all over, inside and out, with the melted butter. Arrange on a dinner plate, or baking sheet, in a circular fashion, leaving a space in the centre. Arrange the bacon on 2 sheets of absorbent kitchen paper, on a dinner plate, fat to outside. Cover with 1 piece absorbent kitchen paper. Microwave the bacon on Full Power for 2½-3 minutes. Set aside. Transfer the cream cheese to a 1.2 litre (2 pint) mixing bowl. Microwave, uncovered, on Defrost for 2 minutes. Stir in salt and pepper to taste, yogurt, dried parsley and chopped bacon. Soften the chopped onion in a cup for 45 seconds on Full Power. Stir into the cream cheese mixture. Fill the mushrooms with the cheese mixture. Microwave, uncovered on Roast, or Power 7, for 4-6 minutes. Serve immediately garnished with chopped parsley, on croutons of fried bread.

Spinach Fiesta

PREPARATION TIME: 20 minutes
MICROWAVE TIME: 22 minutes
SERVES: 4 people

225g (8oz) long grain rice
Salt and freshly ground black pepper to taste
3 frozen cod steaks
225g (8oz) frozen spinach
25g (1oz) butter
50ml (2 tblsp) milk
30ml (2 tblsp) canned tuna fish, drained
50g (2oz) Cheddar cheese, cubed
Chopped fresh parsley

Put the rice into a 1.75-2.25 litre (3-4 pint) mixing bowl. Pour on 600ml (1 pint) boiling water. Add 2.5ml (½ tsp) salt. Cover lightly with cling film and pierce once in the centre. Microwave on Full Power for 12 minutes. Set aside. Snip the fish packets open and microwave all 3 together, arranged on a dinner plate in a ring, for 6 minutes on Defrost. Turn each packet over, halfway through cooking. Set aside. Pierce the packet of spinach and place in a vegetable dish. Microwave on Full Power for 6 minutes. Set aside. Slip the cod steaks out of their packets and arrange on a pie plate in a ring. Dot with butter. Season and spoon over the milk. Cover with cling film and pierce. Microwave on Full Power for 4 minutes. Drain the spinach. Chop and fork into the cooked rice. Add the tuna fish to the rice with the cheese. Drain the cooked cod and flake into the rice. Pile onto a warmed dish and serve, sprinkled with plenty of chopped parsley.

JACKET POTATOES WITH FILLINGS

Plain Jacket Potatoes

PREPARATION TIME: 15-20 minutes
MICROWAVE TIME: 15 minutes
SERVES: 4 people

4 x 200g (7oz) potatoes, scrubbed clean

Prick the potatoes with a fork and arrange in a ring on a dinner plate. Microwave uncovered, on Full Power, for 15 minutes. Wrap in a clean tea towel and set aside for 10-15 minutes. (The potatoes will continue to cook). Meanwhile prepare one of the fillings (all fillings serve 4 people).

Cottage Cheese with Prawns and Chives

Instead of pricking the potatoes, make a cross in the top of each one before baking.

225g (8oz) cottage cheese
15ml (1 tblsp) chopped chives
100g (4oz) peeled prawns
15ml (1 tblsp) soured cream
5ml (1 tsp) tomato puree
Sliced cucumber and whole prawns to garnish

Blend all the ingredients together, apart from the cucumber and prawns. Using a cloth, carefully push up each hot potato from the base, to form a water lily. Divide the filling between the potatoes. Garnish with the cucumber and whole prawns before serving.

Pilchards with Corn

30ml (2 tblsp) natural yogurt or mayonnaise
Salt and freshly ground black pepper to taste
350g (12oz) pilchards in tomato sauce
45ml (3 tblsp) drained canned sweetcorn kernels
4 spring onions, chopped

Cut the potatoes in half and carefully scoop out the flesh, leaving the skin intact. Put the potato flesh into a 1.75 litre (3 pint) mixing bowl. Mash well wi a fork, adding the yogurt or mayonnaise and salt and pepper taste. Open each pilchard and remove the backbone. Flake the pilchards into the potato; mix w adding the sweetcorn and chopp spring onion. Pile the mixture ba into the potato shells. Arrange i serving dish. Cover with cling fil Microwave on Full Power for 4 minutes.

Baked Beans with Edam Cheese

425g (15.9oz) can baked beans i tomato sauce
225g (8oz) Edam cheese, cubed
Salt and freshly ground black pep to taste

Garnish
Watercress

Empty the beans into a 900ml (1½pint) casserole dish. Add th cheese and salt and pepper to ta Cover with a lid and microwave Power 7, or Roast, for 2½ minut Stir gently. Microwave on Power or Roast, for 2½ minutes. Halve the potatoes after their standing time. Spoon the beans and chee onto the potatoes. Garnish with watercress and serve.

Stuffed Baked Peppers (top), Jacket Potatoes with Fillings (centre) and Garlic Mushroon (bottom).

Supper Dishes

Shish Kebabs

PREPARATION TIME: 10 minutes
MICROWAVE TIME: 8 minutes
SERVES: 3-4 people

350g (12oz) raw minced lamb
1 onion, finely chopped
10ml (2 tsp) lemon juice
5-10ml (1-2 tsp) mild curry powder
15ml (1 tblsp) soured cream
½ egg, beaten
25g (1oz) plain flour
30ml (2 tblsp) finely chopped fresh parsley
2.5ml (½ tsp) salt
15ml (1 tblsp) tomato sauce

Mix all the ingredients together. Form the mixture into small balls. Arrange the meatballs on a microwave roasting rack in a ring. Microwave, uncovered, on Power 7, or Roast, for 8 minutes. Serve hot with yogurt sauce.

Yogurt Sauce

PREPARATION TIME: 5 minutes
SERVES: 4 people

150ml (5 fl oz) natural yogurt
5ml (1 tsp) granular mustard
10ml (2 tsp) tomato puree
5ml (1 tsp) concentrated mint sauce
5ml (1 tsp) lemon juice
5ml (1 tsp) caster sugar
30ml (2 tblsp) soured cream

Mix all the ingredients together until well blended. Refrigerate until required. Serve with Shish Kebabs.

Pasta Shells with Cheese and Bacon

PREPARATION TIME: 15 minutes
MICROWAVE TIME: 24 minutes
SERVES: 4 people

175g (6oz) dried pasta shapes
2.5ml (½ tsp) salt
15ml (1 tblsp) oil
225g (8oz) packet frozen mixed vegetables
5ml (1 tsp) cornflour
300ml (½ pint) milk
5ml (1 tsp) made mustard
Salt and freshly ground black pepper to taste
75g (3oz) grated Red Leicester cheese
2 bacon chops
1 Recipe Crispy Topping (see recipe)

Place the pasta in a 2.25-2.75 litre (4-5 pint) mixing bowl. Add the salt and the oil. Pour on 1.75 litres (3 pints) boiling water. Cover tightly with cling film and pierce once in the centre. Microwave on Full Power for 8 minutes. Set aside, covered. Microwave the pierced packet of vegetables in a suitable dish, for 4 minutes on Full Power, turning the packet over once halfway through the cooking time. Blend the cornflour with 15ml (1 tblsp) milk until smooth. Put the remaining milk into a 1 litre (1¾ pint) jug and microwave on Full Power for 3 minutes. Beat the blended cornflour into the hot milk together with the mustard and salt and pepper to taste. Microwave on Full Power for 2 minutes. Beat well adding the cheese Microwave the bacon chops on 2 sheets of absorbent kitchen paper (with the fat facing outwards). Microwave on Roast for 4 minutes. To assemble the dish: drain the pasta and pile onto a serving dish; drain the vegetables and add to the pasta; chop the bacon and mix into the pasta and vegetables. Pour the cheese sauce evenly over the top and top with crispy crumbs. Microwave on Power 5, or Roast, for 3 minutes. Serve immediately.

Fish Fingers

PREPARATION TIME: 5 minutes
MICROWAVE TIME: 14 minutes
SERVES: 3-4 people

30ml (2 tblsp) cooking oil
8 frozen cod fish fingers

Preheat a large browning dish, without a lid, for 7 minutes, on Full Power. Put the oil into the heated dish. Microwave on Full Power for 1 minute. Carefully press the fish fingers into the oil. Microwave, uncovered, on Full Power for 3 minutes. Turn each fish finger over and microwave on Full Power for 3-4 minutes. Drain on absorbent kitchen paper and serve immediately (brown side uppermost).

Crispy Topping

PREPARATION TIME: 10 minutes
MICROWAVE TIME: 8 minutes

65g (2½oz) butter
100g (4oz) fresh brown breadcrumbs
50g (2oz) oatmeal

Put the butter into a 1.75 litre (3 pint) mixing bowl and microwave on Full Power for 1½ minutes. Stir in the breadcrumbs and oatmeal. Microwave on Full Power for 2½ minutes. Stir with a fork. Microwave on Full Power for 2 minutes. Stir. Microwave on Full Power for 2 minutes. Allow to stand for 5 minutes before using. Alternatively, the topping may be cooled and stored in an airtight container. Serve as a crispy finish for sweet and savoury dishes.

Kidney and Sausage Supper Dish

PREPARATION TIME: 20 minutes
MICROWAVE TIME: 18 minutes
SERVES: 4 people

450g (1lb) chipolata sausages
30ml (2 tblsp) oil
225g (8oz) lambs' kidneys, skinned, halved and cored
30ml (2 tblsp) tomato sauce
15ml (1 tblsp) Worcestershire sauce
Salt and freshly ground black pepper to taste
4 large, ripe tomatoes, skinned and chopped
225g (8oz) frozen peas
10ml (2 tsp) cornflour

Preheat the deep browning dish, without the lid, for 4-7 minutes according to size. Prick the sausages and cut into 2.5cm (1 inch) pieces. Add the oil and the pieces of sausage to the preheated dish, pressing the sausage against the sides of the browning dish. Microwave on Full Power for 2 minutes. Stir in the kidneys, tomato sauce and Worcestershi sauce. Cover with the lid and microwave on Power 7, or on Roast, for 5 minutes. Season wi salt and pepper and stir in the tomatoes and peas. Mix the cornflour to a smooth paste wit 60ml (4 tblsp) water and stir in. Microwave on Full Power for 2 minutes. Stir. Microwave on Fu Power for a further 2 minutes. S and serve immediately.

Cowboy Supper

PREPARATION TIME: 15 minu
MICROWAVE TIME: 13 minute
SERVES: 4 people

425g (15.9oz) can baked beans
200g (7oz) can corned beef, chille
Freshly ground black pepper to ta
½ beef stock cube, crumbled
50g (2oz) Cheddar cheese, cubed
1 French loaf

Empty the baked beans into a 1 litre (3 pint) casserole dish. Cov with a lid. Microwave on Power for 5 minutes. Gently stir in the corned beef and season with pepper. Add the stock cube. Co and microwave on Power 6 for 5 minutes. Add the cheese just before serving.
To warm the bread, cut the brea into pieces and arrange in a brea basket, between absorbent pape napkins. Microwave on Power 4 Simmer, for 3 minutes. Serve immediately.

Shish Kebabs with Yogurt Sauce (top), Pasta Shells with Cheese and Bacon (centre right) and Kidney and Sausa Supper Dish (bottom).

Fish Fingers (top right), Poached Eggs on Cheese on Toast (far left) and Chicken with Ham (left).

Poached Eggs on Cheese on Toast

PREPARATION TIME: 10 minutes
MICROWAVE TIME: about 10 minutes
SERVES: 4 people

4 eggs
Salt and freshly ground black pepper to taste
Softened butter
4 slices toast
150g (5oz) grated cheese
Chopped chives

Put 15ml (1 tblsp) cold water into each of the 4 hollows of a microwave muffin pan or into 4 ramekin dishes. If using ramekins, arrange them in a ring on a dinner plate. Microwave on Full Power until the water boils. Carefully crack 1 egg into each hollow or dish. Prick each yolk once with a cocktail stick. Season with salt and pepper. Microwave on Simmer for about 4 minutes until the whites are just set. Leave aside. Butter the toast and top with the grated cheese. Microwave on Power 5, or Simmer, for about 4 minutes until melted. Slide the toasted cheese onto a serving dish and place an egg on top of each one. Sprinkle with chopped chives and serve immediately.

Cod and Prawn Supper Dish

PREPARATION TIME: 15 minutes
MICROWAVE TIME: 15½ minutes
SERVES: 4 people

4 x 75g (3oz) frozen cod steaks, thawed
50g (2oz) butter
Salt and freshly ground black pepper to taste
25g (1oz) flour
300ml (½ pint) milk
75g (3oz) grated Cheddar cheese
100g (4oz) peeled prawns
1 Recipe Crispy Topping (see recipe)

Garnish
Tomato wedges
Parsley

Arrange the fish steaks in a ring on a dinner plate. Divide half the butter into 4; put a small knob onto each fish steak. Season with salt and pepper and cover with cling film. Microwave on Full Power for 3½ minutes. Set aside. Microwave the remaining butter in a 1 litre (1¾ pint) jug for 1 minute on Full Power. Stir in the flour and then gradually stir in the milk; season to taste. Microwave on Full Power for 2 minutes. Beat well. Microwave on Full Power for a further 2 minutes. Beat in the cheese. Cut the fish into bite-size pieces and arrange in a suitable dish with the prawns. Pour the sauce evenly over the fish. Sprinkle with the crispy crumbs. Microwave on Power 4 for 7 minutes. Serve immediately, garnished with tomato and parsley.

Chicken with Ham

PREPARATION TIME: 15 minutes
MICROWAVE TIME: 13 minutes
SERVES: 4 people

350g (12oz) cooked chicken, roughly chopped
100g (4oz) cooked ham, chopped
60ml (4 tblsp) drained canned sweetcorn kernels with peppers
25g (1oz) butter
25g (1oz) flour
Salt and freshly ground black pepper to taste
300ml (½ pint) well flavoured chicken stock
75g (3oz) grated cheese
45ml (3 tblsp) single cream

Garnish
Sliced tomato and parsley

Arrange the chicken, ham and sweetcorn in a suitable dish. Melt the butter in a large jug for about 1 minute on Full Power. Stir in the flour and salt and pepper to taste. Stir in a little of the stock, blending it in well. Add the remaining stock. Microwave on Full Power for 2 minutes. Beat well with a balloon whisk. Microwave on Full Power for 2 minutes. Beat well. Beat in the cheese and the cream. Pour the sauce evenly over the meat. Microwave on Power 4, or Simmer, for about 8 minutes. Serve immediately, garnished with the tomato and parsley.

Sweet and Sour Pork

PREPARATION TIME: 25 minutes
MICROWAVE TIME: 29 minutes
SERVES: 4 people

15ml (1 tblsp) oil
½ red pepper, de-seeded and chopped
1 carrot, peeled and cut into strips
1 large onion, sliced
10cm (4 inch) cucumber, seeded and cut into strips
1 stem celery, chopped
450g (1lb) pork fillet, cubed
400g (14oz) can pineapple pieces in natural juice

30ml (2 tblsp) soya sauce
10ml (2 tsp) tomato puree
15ml (1 tblsp) wine vinegar
Salt and freshly ground black pepper to taste
10ml (2 tsp) cornflour

Preheat the deep browning dish without the lid for 4-7 minutes according to size on Full Power. Put the oil, pepper, carrot, onion, cucumber and celery into the dish. Stir well. Cover and Microwave on Full Power for 4 minutes. Stir in all remaining ingredients, apart from the cornflour. Cover and microwave on Full Power for 3 minutes and then on Power 4, or Simmer, for 20 minutes. Cream the cornflour with a little water and stir into the pork mixture. Microwave on Full Power for 2 minutes. Stir and then serve immediately on a bed of rice.

Cowboy Supper (top) and Sweet and Sour Pork (bottom)

Fish Dishes

Plaice with Lemon

PREPARATION TIME: 12-15 minutes

MICROWAVE TIME: 9 minutes

SERVES: 4 people

4 plaice fillets (about 90g (3½oz) each), skinned
Salt and freshly ground black pepper to taste
Juice of ½ a lemon
30ml (2 tblsp) milk
100g (4oz) button mushrooms, sliced
25g (1oz) butter
120ml (4 fl oz) soured cream

Lay the plaice fillets out flat; season with salt and pepper and sprinkle with lemon juice. Roll up and secure with wooden cocktail sticks. Arrange the fillets close together in a dish and spoon over the milk; cover and microwave on Full Power for 5 minutes. Set aside. Put the mushrooms and butter into a small dish. Cover and microwave on Full Power for 2 minutes. Add the soured cream and stir in the juices from the fish. Microwave on Full Power for 2 minutes. Arrange the fish on a warmed serving dish. Pour over the sauce and serve immediately.

Curried Prawns with Chicken

PREPARATION TIME: 15 minutes

MICROWAVE TIME: about 22 minutes

SERVES: 4 people

g (2oz) butter
medium onion, finely chopped
ml (4 tsp) flour
ml (4 tsp) mild curry powder
ml (2 tsp) tomato puree
0ml (1½ pints) boiling chicken stock
ml (1 tblsp) apple chutney
banana, thinly sliced
g (1oz) raisins
lt and freshly ground black pepper to taste
5g (8oz) peeled prawns
5g (8oz) cooked chicken, chopped
ml (2 tblsp) lemon juice

Place the butter in a 2.25 litre (4 pint) casserole. Microwave on Full Power for 1-2 minutes. Stir in the onion. Microwave on Full Power for 1½ minutes. Stir in the flour and curry powder. Microwave on Full Power for 2 minutes. Stir in the tomato puree and gradually add the stock. Add the apple chutney, banana, raisins and salt and pepper to taste. Cover and microwave on Full Power for 12 minutes. Stir in the peeled prawns, chicken and lemon juice. Microwave on Full Power for 3-4 minutes.

Curried Prawns with Chicken (top left), Scampi Italienne (top right) and Plaice with Lemon (bottom).

Scampi Italienne

PREPARATION TIME: 10 minutes
MICROWAVE TIME: 10 minutes
SERVES: 4 people

½ red pepper, de-seeded and sliced
½ green pepper, de-seeded and sliced
50g (2oz) butter
1 small onion, finely chopped
1 clove garlic, crushed
150ml (¼ pint) dry white wine
15ml (1 tblsp) lemon juice
Salt and freshly ground black pepper to taste
450g (1lb) frozen shelled scampi, thawed

Garnish
Lemon butterflies
Savory

Put the red and green peppers, butter, onion and the garlic into a 1.75 litre (3 pint) casserole. Cover with the lid. Microwave on Full Power for 3 minutes. Stir in the white wine, lemon juice, salt and pepper to taste and the scampi. Cover and microwave on Full Power for 6-7 minutes, stirring once halfway through. Serve immediately, garnished with lemon butterflies and savory.

Special Fish Pie

PREPARATION TIME: 15 minutes
MICROWAVE TIME: 15 minutes
SERVES: 4 people

450g (1lb) young leeks, washed and cut into 4cm (1½ inch) lengths
4 large, firm tomatoes, skinned and sliced
10ml (2 tsp) mixed dried herbs
25g (1oz) butter
Salt and freshly ground black pepper to taste
350g (12oz) cod, skinned and filleted
30ml (2 tblsp) frozen sweetcorn kernels, thawed
50g (2oz) grated Cheddar cheese
15ml (1 tblsp) tomato sauce
450g (1lb) potatoes, peeled, cooked and mashed

Arrange the leeks and tomatoes in the base of a casserole dish; sprinkle with half the herbs. Dot the butter over the surface and season well with salt and pepper. Cover and microwave on Full Power for 5 minutes. Cut the fish into 2.5cm (1 inch) pieces. Arrange evenly over the vegetables and season once again. Cover and microwave on Full Power for 7 minutes. Drain off excess liquid and add the sweetcorn. Add the cheese, tomato sauce and remaining herbs to the potato; beat well. Pile or pipe the potato on top of the fish and vegetables. Microwave, uncovered, on Full Power for about 3 minutes. Brown under a pre-heated grill, if desired, and serve immediately.

Mackerel with Apple Sauce

PREPARATION TIME: 30 minutes
MICROWAVE TIME: 15 minutes
SERVES: 4 people

4 fresh mackerel, heads and fins removed, and filleted (approx. 175g (6oz) per fish)
100g (4oz) fresh brown breadcrumbs
1 eating apple, peeled, cored and chopped
50g (2oz) shredded suet
5ml (1 tsp) lemon juice
10ml (2 tsp) finely chopped fresh parsley
1 onion, peeled and finely chopped
Salt and freshly ground black pepper to taste
1 egg, beaten
30ml (2 tblsp) apple juice

Sauce
750g (1½lb) cooking and eating apples (mixed), peeled, cored and sliced
10ml (2 tsp) lemon juice
10ml (2 tsp) caster sugar
15g (½oz) butter

Put the breadcrumbs, apple, suet, lemon juice, parsley and onion into a mixing bowl. Season to taste with salt and pepper. Mix with the beaten egg to bind. Divide the stuffing amongst the fish, pressing it well into each cavity. Make an incision with a sharp knife in the thickest side of each fish. Arrange the fish, nose to tail, in a shallow dish. Pour over the apple juice. Cover tightly with cling film and pierce. Microwave on Full Power for 8 minutes. Stand on one side while preparing the sauce. Put the apples into a 1.75 litre (3 pint) Pyrex mixing bowl with the lemon juice and sugar. Cover. Microwave on Full Power for 6-7 minutes. Allow to stand for 3 minutes. Beat together with the butter and the juices from the cooked fish. Serve immediately with the fish.

Trout with Almonds

PREPARATION TIME: 10 minutes
MICROWAVE TIME: about 19 minutes
SERVES: 4 people

4 rainbow trout, cleaned and gutted (approx 225g (8oz) per fish)
65g (2½oz) butter
1 clove garlic, crushed
Salt and freshly ground black pepper to taste
250ml (8 fl oz) double cream
50g (2oz) flaked almonds

Garnish
Fresh parsley

Use a very small amount of foil to mask the tail of each fish. Make 2 incisions in the thick side of each fish. Put 50g (2oz) of the butter into a suitable shallow dish and microwave on Full Power for 1½ minutes. Stir the garlic and salt and pepper into the butter. Arrange the fish, nose to tail, in the flavoured butter. Cover with cling film and pierce. Microwave on Full Power for 8 minutes. Turn each fish over once during cooking. Stand aside, covered. Put the almonds and the remaining butter into a soup bowl. Microwave on Full Power for 2 minutes. Stir. Microwave on Full Power for a further 2 minutes. Pour the cream over the fish, and microwave on Power 4 or, Simmer, for 5 minutes. Serve immediately sprinkled with the toasted nuts and garnished with parsley.

Devilled Herrings

PREPARATION TIME: 15-20 minutes
MICROWAVE TIME: 6-7 minutes
SERVES: 4 people

30ml (2 tblsp) dry mustard
15ml (1 tblsp) brown sugar
15ml (1 tblsp) malt vinegar
4 fresh herrings, about 225g (8oz) each
75ml (⅛ pint) white wine
1 medium onion, finely chopped
15ml (1 tblsp) finely chopped fresh parsley
Salt and freshly ground black pepper to taste
25g (1oz) butter

Blend together the mustard, sugar and vinegar. Cut the heads and the tails off the fish and remove the back-bones; flatten each fish. Spread the mustard mixture ins[ide] the herrings and roll up. Secure with cocktail sticks. Arrange the fish in a suitable dish. Add the wine, parsley and salt and pepp[er] to taste. Dot with butter. Cover tightly with cling film or a lid. Pierce if using cling film. Microwave on Full Power for 6- minutes. Stand for 3 minutes before serving.

Smoked Haddock wit[h] Scrambled Eggs

PREPARATION TIME: 5-10 minutes
MICROWAVE TIME: 11 minute[s]
SERVES: 3-4 people

450g (1lb) smoked haddock fille[t]
Salt and freshly ground black pe[pper] to taste
150ml (¼ pint) milk
50g (2oz) butter
4 eggs
15ml (1 tblsp) finely chopped fre[sh] parsley

Arrange the fish in a shallow container. Season with salt an[d] pepper and add 30ml (2 tblsp) the milk. Dot the fish with hal[f] butter. Cover with cling film a[nd] pierce. Microwave on Full Pow[er] for 7 minutes. Set aside, cover[ed]. Make the scrambled egg: beat eggs with the remaining milk i[n] 1.75 litre (3 pint) mixing bowl season to taste and add the remaining butter. Microwave [on] Full Power for 2 minutes; beat using a balloon whisk. Microw[ave] on Full Power for 2 minutes u[ntil] light and fluffy. Carefully arra[nge] the fish on a serving dish. Sp[oon] the scrambled eggs either side [of] the fish. Sprinkle with the ch[opped] parsley and serve immediately.

Special Fish Pie (top), Mac[kerel] with Apple Sauce (centre) [and] Trout with Almonds (botto[m])

Prawns Creole

PREPARATION TIME: 15 minutes
MICROWAVE TIME: 18 minutes
SERVES: 4 people

225g (8oz) long grain rice
600ml (1 pint) boiling chicken stock
2 medium size onions, chopped
½ red pepper, de-seeded and chopped
½ green pepper, de-seeded and chopped
225g (8oz) peeled prawns
425g (15oz) can pineapple segments in natural juice, drained
25g (1oz) seedless raisins
Salt and freshly ground black pepper to taste

Put the rice into a 1.75-2.25 litre (3-4 pint) mixing bowl. Pour on the boiling stock. Cover tightly with cling film and pierce once in the centre. Microwave on Full Power for 12 minutes. Set aside, covered with a clean tea towel. Put the onion and red and green pepper into a 1.2 litre (2 pint) mixing bowl. Cover with cling film and pierce. Microwave on Full Power for 3 minutes. Stir. Fork up the rice after 10 minutes standing time, and add the onions, peppers, prawns, pineapple, raisins and salt and pepper. Cover with cling film and pierce. Microwave on Full Power for 3 minutes to reheat. Serve immediately.

Smoked Haddock with Scrambled Eggs (below left), Prawns Creole (below) and Devilled Herrings (below right).

Meat Dishes

Sausagemeat Stuffing

PREPARATION TIME: 15 minutes
MICROWAVE TIME: 10 minutes
SERVES: 4 people

450g (1lb) pork sausagemeat
85g (3¼oz) packet parsley and thyme stuffing mix
15ml (1 tblsp) tomato sauce
5ml (1 tsp) made mustard
1 small onion, finely chopped
Salt and freshly ground black pepper to taste
150ml (¼ pint) boiling water

Put the sausagemeat into a 1.75 litre (3 pint) mixing bowl. Add all the remaining ingredients. Leave to stand for 3 minutes. Knead together until well mixed. Using dampened hands, form the sausagemeat mixture into 20 balls. Arrange on a large roasting rack, or in a ring on a large circular dish, on 2 sheets of absorbent kitchen paper. Microwave on Power 7, or Roast, for 10 minutes.

Savoury Mince with Dumplings

PREPARATION TIME: 20 minutes
MICROWAVE TIME: 23 minutes
SERVES: 4 people

2 rashers streaky bacon, de-rinded and chopped
1 medium onion, chopped
½ green pepper, de-seeded and chopped
750g (1½lb) raw minced beef or pork
1 beef stock cube, crumbled
2.5ml (½ tsp) mixed dried herbs
150ml (¼ pint) water
5ml (1 tsp) chive mustard
Salt and freshly ground black pepper to taste
425g (15.9oz) can butter beans, drained

Dumplings
100g (4oz) self-raising flour
50g (2oz) suet
2.5ml (½ tsp) dried tarragon

Put the bacon, onion and pepper into a soup bowl. Cover with cling film and pierce. Microwave on Full Power for 2 minutes. Put the mince into a 1.75 litre (3 pint) casserole dish. Microwave on Full Power for 4 minutes. Break down with a fork and stir in the onion mixture, stock cube, herbs, water and mustard. Season well with salt and pepper. Microwave on Power 6, or Roast, for 12 minutes. Stir in the butter beans. Set aside. To prepare the dumplings: mix together the flour, suet and tarragon. Bind with sufficient cold water to make an elastic dough. Divide into 6 dumplings and arrange on top of the mince. Cover with a lid and microwave on Power 7 for 4-5 minutes. Stand for 3 minutes before serving.

Mixed Meat Loaf

PREPARATION TIME: 30 minutes
MICROWAVE TIME: 27 minutes
SERVES: 6-8 people

1 clove garlic
175g (6oz) lean streaky bacon, de-rinded
450g (1lb) raw minced beef
225g (8oz) raw minced pork
175g (6oz) lambs' liver, finely chopped
175g (6oz) back bacon, de-rinded and finely chopped
50g (2oz) shredded suet
50g (2oz) fresh brown breadcrumbs
2.5ml (½ tsp) dried oregano
2.5ml (½ tsp) mixed dried herbs
Salt and freshly ground black pepper to taste
45ml (3 tblsp) sherry
1 egg, beaten

Glaze
30ml (2 tblsp) apricot jam or marmalade, sieved
5ml (1 tsp) French mustard
2.5ml (½ tsp) Bovril

Rub a 1.75 litre (3 pint) plastic bread baker with the clove of garlic. Lay the streaky bacon in the bread baker to line the base and the sides. In a large mixing bowl, mix the minced beef with the pork, liver, back bacon, suet, breadcrumbs and herbs. Season to taste. Beat together the sherry and the egg; add to the mixture and bind together. Transfer to the prepared bread baker. Smooth the top. Cover and microwave on Power 6, or Roast, for 27 minutes. Turn the dish ½ a turn twice during this time. Allow to stand for 10 minutes. Pour off the excess fat and carefully unmould the loaf. Mix all ingredients together for the glaze and brush over the top and sides of the meat loaf. Delicious hot or cold.

Cheesey Beef Cobbler

PREPARATION TIME: 30 minutes
MICROWAVE TIME: 20 minutes
SERVES: 4 people

450g (1lb) raw minced beef
1 onion, chopped
225g (8oz) can tomatoes, chopped
1 beef stock cube, crumbled
15ml (1 tblsp) bottled brown sauce
Celery salt and freshly ground black pepper to taste
30ml (2 tblsp) frozen peas

Scone Topping
225g (8oz) self-raising flour, sieved with 2.5ml (½ tsp) baking powder
50g (2oz) margarine or butter, chilled
50g (2oz) grated Cheddar cheese
2.5ml (½ tsp) mixed dried herbs
1 egg, mixed with 90ml (6 tblsp) milk
5ml (1 tsp) Bovril

Put the minced meat and onion into an 18cm (7 inch) souffle dish. Cover and microwave on Full Power for 4 minutes. Stir well with a fork. Stir in the tomatoes, stock cube, brown sauce and celery salt and pepper. Cover and microwave on Power 7, or Roast, for 10 minutes. Stir in the peas and set aside. Put the flour and baking powder into a 1.75 litre (3 pint) mixing bowl. Rub in the margarine or butter. Mix in the cheese and herbs. Add the beaten egg and milk and mix to a soft dough. Knead lightly. Roll the dough out to a thickness of 1cm (½ inch). Using a 5cm (2 inch) pastry cutter, cut the dough into scones. Arrange the scones on top of the mince. Cook, uncovered, on Full Power for 6 minutes. Serve immediately.

Note: to improve the colour scones mix the Bovril with a water and use to brush the sc prior to cooking.

Lamb Curry

PREPARATION TIME: 20 mi
MICROWAVE TIME: about 45 minu
SERVES: 4 people

2 carrots, peeled and chopped
1 medium onion, chopped
25g (1oz) butter
25g (1oz) plain flour
15-20ml (3-4 tsp) mild curry p
450g (1lb) lamb fillet, cubed
450ml (¾ pint) boiling chicke
15ml (1 tblsp) desiccated coco
25g (1oz) sultanas
1 medium sized eating apple, p cored and chopped
1 peach, peeled, stoned and rou chopped
15ml (1 tblsp) tomato puree
30ml (2 tblsp) lemon juice
Salt and freshly ground black p to taste

Preheat a large browning dish without the lid, for 3 minutes Full Power. Put the carrots, on and butter into the preheated Microwave on Full Power for minutes, covered. Stir in the curry powder and meat. Microwave on Full Power for minutes. Gradually add the st stirring all the time. Stir in the coconut, sultanas, apple, peac tomato puree, lemon juice an seasoning to taste. Cover and

Lamb Curry (top left), Savo Mince with Dumplings (top right) and Mixed Meat Loa (bottom).

microwave on Full Power for 7 minutes. Stir. Microwave on Power 4, Simmer or Defrost, for 30-35 minutes. Stir twice during this time. Serve immediately.

Pasta with Pork and Liver

PREPARATION TIME: 15 minutes

MICROWAVE TIME: 25 minutes

SERVES: 4 people

30ml (2 tblsp) oil
1 medium onion, sliced
350g (12oz) raw minced pork
100g (4oz) chicken livers, minced
100g (4oz) mushrooms, chopped
225g (8oz) can tomatoes, chopped
45ml (3 tblsp) sherry
Salt and freshly ground black pepper to taste
1 beef stock cube, crumbled
175g (6oz) dried pasta shells
Chopped fresh parsley

Heat the browning dish, without the lid, for 4-6 minutes on Full Power, according to size. Put half the oil, the onion and minced meats into the preheated dish. Stir well. Microwave on Full Power for 4 minutes. Stir in all the remaining ingredients, apart from the pa and the parsley. Cover with th and microwave on Full Power minutes. Stir. Microwave, cov on Power 5, or Simmer, for 10 minutes. Allow to stand whils preparing the pasta. To cook t pasta, place the remaining oil the pasta into a 2.25-2.75 litre pint) bowl. Add 1.75 litres (3 pints) water and 2.5ml (½ tsp to the pasta. Cover and micro on Full Power for 8 minutes. A to stand for 5 minutes. Drain pasta and arrange on a serving Spoon the meat sauce evenly the pasta, and garnish with ch parsley. Serve immediately.

Pasta with Pork and Liver (far left), Cheesey Beef Cobbler (below) and Sausagemeat Stuffing (below right).

Chicken Breasts in Garlic Cream Sauce

PREPARATION TIME: 10 minutes
MICROWAVE TIME: 17 minutes
SERVES: 4 people

50g (2oz) butter
1 clove garlic, crushed
1 medium onion, sliced
2 rashers bacon, de-rinded and chopped
50g (2oz) button mushrooms, sliced
2.5ml (½ tsp) dried basil
Salt and freshly ground black pepper to taste
4 chicken breasts, skinned and boned (about 150g (5oz) each)
300ml (½ pint) double cream

Garnish
Savory
Toasted flaked almonds

Melt the butter in a 1.75 litre (3 pint) casserole dish for 1-2 minutes on Full Power. Stir in the garlic, onion, bacon, mushrooms, basil and salt and pepper to taste. Cover and microwave on Full Power for 2 minutes. Arrange the chicken breasts on top of the vegetables. Cover and microwave on Power 7, or Roast, for 10 minutes. Season the cream and pour evenly over the top to coat. Microwave on Roast, or Power 7, for 3 minutes. Garnish with savory and almonds. Serve immediately.

Chicken Casserole

PREPARATION TIME: 15 minutes
MICROWAVE TIME: about 40 minutes
SERVES: 4 people

4 chicken portions, skinned (about 225g (8oz) each)
25g (1oz) butter
1 onion, finely chopped
2 stems celery, chopped
2 carrots, chopped
30ml (2 tblsp) drained canned sweetcorn kernels
10ml (2 tsp) cornflour
300ml (½ pint) chicken stock
Salt and paprika to taste

Put the butter into a 2.25 litre (4 pint) casserole dish. Microwave on Full Power for 1 minute. Stir in the onion, celery and carrots. Cover with a lid and microwave on Full Power for 3 minutes. Pour the stock into the casserole, and add salt to taste. Arrange the chicken pieces on top of the vegetables, keeping the thickest part to the outside of the dish. Sprinkle each chicken piece with a little paprika. Microwave, covered, on Full Power for 4 minutes. Stir. Microwave on Power 4, Simmer or Defrost, for a further 30 minutes. Using a draining spoon, transfer the chicken to a warmed serving dish. Cover with a piece of foil and set aside. Cream the cornflour with a little water and stir into the casserole dish. Microwave on Full Power for 2-3 minutes, until boiling and thickened. Stir in the sweetcorn. Serve the chicken pieces with the vegetable sauce spooned over the top.

Sausage Suet Pudding

PREPARATION TIME: 30 minutes
MICROWAVE TIME: 21 minutes
SERVES: 4 people

Filling
225g (8oz) pork sausages, cut into 2.5cm (1 inch) pieces
225g (8oz) chicken livers, roughly chopped
25g (1oz) seasoned flour
15ml (1 tblsp) oil
1 medium onion, chopped
½ green pepper, de-seeded and chopped
300ml (½ pint) well flavoured boiling stock
Salt and freshly ground black pepper to taste

Suet Pastry
225g (8oz) self-raising flour
2.5ml (½ tsp) salt
5ml (1 tsp) baking powder
100g (4oz) finely grated (or shredded) suet
150ml (¼ pint) water

Toss the sausages and chicken livers in the seasoned flour. Put the oil into a 1.75 litre (3 pint) mixing bowl. Microwave on Full Power for 2 minutes. Stir in the onion and green pepper. Microwave on Full Power for 2 minutes. Stir the chicken livers and sausage into the onion. Cover and microwave on Power 8, or Roast, for 5 minutes. Carefully stir in the boiling stock and salt and pepper to taste. Microwave on Full Power for 2-3 minutes, until thickened. Stir and set aside while preparing the pastry. Sieve the flour, salt and baking powder into a bowl. Stir in the suet and mix to a soft dough with the water. Knead lightly. Roll out ⅔ of the pastry and use to line a greased 900ml (1½ pint) boilable plastic pudding basin. Roll the remaining pastry into a circle. Fill the pastry-lined basin with the filling mixture. Dampen the pastry rim with cold water and top with the circle of pastry. Seal edges. Cut a small slit in the top to allow the steam to escape. Cover loosely with absorbent kitchen paper or cling film. Microwave on Power 7, or Roast, for 9 minutes. Stand for 5 minutes before serving.

Herby Roast Chicken

PREPARATION TIME: about 35 minutes
MICROWAVE TIME: about 36 minutes
SERVES: 6 people

75g (3oz) fresh brown breadcrumbs
50g (2oz) shredded suet
5ml (1 tsp) finely chopped fresh parsley
5ml (1 tsp) finely chopped fresh tarragon
1 eating apple, peeled, cored and chopped
5ml (1 tsp) lemon juice
Salt and freshly ground black pepper to taste
1 small onion, finely chopped
1 egg, beaten
1¾kg (4lb) chicken, giblets removed

Coating
50g (2oz) butter
10ml (2 tsp) chicken seasoning
5ml (1 tsp) paprika
2.5ml (½ tsp) mixed dried herbs

Garnish
Watercress

To make the stuffing, combine the breadcrumbs, suet, parsley, tarragon, apple, lemon juice and seasoning to taste. Put the onion into a small bowl and microwave on Full Power for 1 minute. Add the onion to the other ingredients. Bind together with the beaten egg.

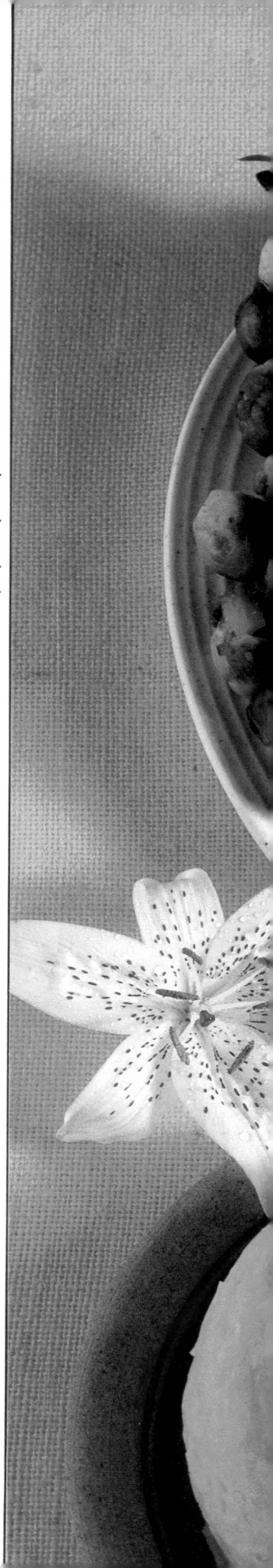

Chicken Casserole (top right), Herby Roast Chicken (top left), Chicken Breasts in Garlic Cream Sauce (bottom right) and Sausage Suet Pudding (bottom left).

Roasting Meats

TYPE OF MEAT	MICROWAVE POWER LEVEL	TIME PER 450g (1lb)	INTERNAL TEMPERATURE AFTER MICROWAVING	INTERNAL TEMPERATURE AFTER STANDING
Chops 1. Lamb	Power 7 or Roast Use pre-heated browning dish)	7-8 minutes	Turn the chops over once during cooking time.	
2. Pork	Power 7 or Roast (Use pre-heated browning dish)	9-10 minutes	Allow to stand for 5-10 minutes before serving.	
Beef (Boned & Rolled)	Power 7 or Roast	5-6 minutes *Rare* 7-8 minutes *Medium* 8-10 minutes *Well done*	57°C/130°F 65°C/150°F 70°C/160°F	62°C/140°F 70°C/160°F 78°C/170°F
Beef on the Bone	Power 7 or Roast	5 minutes *Rare* 6 minutes *Medium* 8 minutes *Well done*	57°C/130°F 65°C/150°F 70°C/160°F	62°C/140°F 70°C/160°F 78°C/170°F
Poultry (Unboned)	Full Power	7 minutes	85°C/185°F	94°C/190°F
Pork	Power 7 or Roast	10-11 minutes	82°C/180°F	85°C/185°F
Lamb	Power 7 or Roast	8-9 minutes	78°C/170°F	82°C/180°F

1. Have joints boned and rolled for best results.
2. Use a microwave meat thermostat to gauge when the meat should be removed from the microwave oven.
3. Any joint which is 1½kg (3lbs) or over will brown in the microwave oven, to increase the colouring, use a browning agent before cooking, or flash the meat under a pre-heated hot grill after standing time.
4. Turn the joint over once during the cooking time.
5. Use a microwave roasting rack, or an upturned saucer, placed in a suitable dish so as to allow the juices to drain.

Stuff the neck end of the bird with the stuffing. Truss. Weigh the stuffed bird and calculate the cooking time accordingly (7 minutes per 450g (1lb)). Use small amounts of foil to mask the wings and the stuffed area, to prevent overcooking. Arrange the chicken in a suitable roasting dish, on two upturned saucers, or on a microwave roasting rack. Melt the butter in the microwave for 1 minute on Full Power. Brush the butter all over the chicken. Combine the chicken seasoning, paprika and herbs together and sprinkle all over the chicken. Cover with a split roasta bag. Microwave on Full Power for the calculated time. Allow the chicken to stand, covered with a tent of foil, before serving. Garnish with watercress.

Devilled Pork Chops

PREPARATION TIME: 10 minutes
MICROWAVE TIME: 16 minutes
SERVES: 4 people

30ml (2 tblsp) oil
4 chump pork chops (about 175g (6oz) each)
100g (4oz) butter
15ml (1 tblsp) dry mustard
30ml (2 tblsp) fresh breadcrumbs
15ml (1 tblsp) soya sauce
10ml (2 tsp) Worcestershire sauce
15ml (1 tblsp) tomato chutney
Salt and paprika to taste

Preheat the browning dish (without the lid) for 4-7 minutes, according to size, on Full Power. Put the oil into the heated dish and microwave on Full Power for 1 minute. Put the 4 chops into the dish, pressing them down well. Microwave on Full Power for 2 minutes. Turn the chops over and microwave on Power 7, or Roast, for 10 minutes. Combine all the remaining ingredients in a mixing bowl. Spread over the partly cooked chops. Microwave on Power 7, or Roast, for a further 3 minutes.

Beef or Pork Burgers

PREPARATION TIME: 20 minutes
MICROWAVE TIME: 6-7 minutes
SERVES: 4 people

450g (1lb) raw minced beef or pork
1 small onion, finely chopped
50g (2oz) fresh breadcrumbs
1 stock cube, crumbled
2.5ml (½ tsp) dried parsley
Salt and freshly ground black pepper to taste
15ml (1 tblsp) tomato sauce
5ml (1 tsp) made mustard
1 egg, beaten
4 baps

Mix the mince, onion and breadcrumbs together. Add the stock cube and all the other ingredients, apart from the baps. Mix well. Divide the mixture in and form into burgers. Arrange a microwave roasting rack, or o suitable dish, in a ring. Microw on Full Power for 6-7 minutes, turning each burger over once halfway through cooking time. the baps and fill with the burge

Glazed Leg of Lamb

PREPARATION TIME: 25 min
MICROWAVE TIME: about 50 minutes
SERVES: 6 people

1¾kg (4lb) leg of lamb
2-3 cloves peeled garlic, cut into strips
Salt and freshly ground black pep to taste
30ml (2 tblsp) tomato sauce
5ml (1 tsp) dry mustard
5ml (1 tsp) brown sugar
2.5ml (½ tsp) mixed dried herbs

Devilled Pork Chops (top right), Beef or Pork Burgers (centre left) and Glazed Leg Lamb (bottom).

Make incisions all over the joint with a sharp knife; push a strip of garlic into each one. Season with salt and pepper. Combine the tomato sauce, mustard, brown sugar and herbs, and spread evenly over the joint. Arrange the joint on a roasting rack. Cover with a roasta bag. Microwave for 12 minutes on Full Power. Turn the joint over and microwave on Power 4, or Simmer, for 30-40 minutes or until the meat thermometer registers 70°C (160°F). Remove the joint. Cover with a tent of foil and allow to stand for 15 minutes before serving.

Rolled Roast Rib of Beef

PREPARATION TIME: 18 minutes

MICROWAVE TIME: 30 minutes

SERVES: 6-8 people

1¾kg (4lb) piece rib of beef, boned and rolled
Salt and freshly ground black pepper to taste
15ml (1 tblsp) tomato sauce
5ml (1 tsp) soft brown sugar

Stand the joint on the microwave roasting rack, in a suitable dish, keeping the fat side of the meat underneath. Season with salt and pepper. Microwave for 7 minutes, on Full Power. Turn the joint over and microwave on Roast, or Power 7, for 21 minutes. Remove from the microwave. Cover loosely with a tent of foil and allow to stand for 15 minutes. Spread the tomato sauce and brown sugar all over the fat. Microwave on Full Power for 2 minutes. (Check temperatures with a microwave thermometer. See chart).

Barbecue Lamb Chops

PREPARATION TIME: 10 minutes, plus marinating time

MICROWAVE TIME: 16 minutes

SERVES: 6 people

Marinade
30ml (2 tblsp) wine vinegar
60ml (4 tblsp) pure orange juice
15ml (1 tblsp) tomato sauce
5ml (1 tsp) soft brown sugar
5ml (1 tsp) French mustard
2.5ml (½ tsp) dried tarragon
5ml (1 tsp) mild curry powder
Salt and freshly ground black pepper to taste
5ml (1 tsp) oil
6 chump chops, each about 150g (5oz)

Blend all the ingredients together for the marinade, apart from the oil. Lay the chops in a large shallow dish and pour over the marinade. Cover and chill for at least two hours. Turn the chops over in the marinade, once or twice. Preheat a large browning dish for 7 minutes on Full Power. Put the oil and the drained chops into the dish, pressing the chops against the hot dish. Microwave, uncovered, on Full Power for 5 minutes. Turn the chops over. Microwave on Roast, or Power 7, for 3-4 minutes. Serve immediately.

Shepherd's Pie

PREPARATION TIME: 30 minutes

MICROWAVE TIME: 38 minutes

SERVES: 4 people

15ml (1 tblsp) cooking oil
2 courgettes, thinly sliced
1 small onion, finely chopped
450g (1lb) raw lean minced beef
15ml (1 tblsp) plain flour
Salt and freshly ground black pepper to taste
15ml (1 tblsp) tomato puree
60ml (4 tblsp) water
1 beef stock cube, crumbled
900g (2lb) potatoes
90ml (6 tblsp) milk
1 egg
15g (½oz) butter
30ml (2 tblsp) Red Leicester cheese, grated

Preheat a small browning dish on Full Power for 3½ minutes (if using a large browning dish preheat on Full Power for 5 minutes). Add the oil, courgettes and onion, and stir. Cover with a lid and microwave on Full Power for 2 minutes. Add the meat and microwave on Full Power for 3 minutes, stirring once. Add the flour, salt and pepper to taste, tomato puree, water and stock cube. Stir well and cover. Microwave on Power 7, or Roast, for 12 minutes, stirring after the first 4 minutes. Remove from the microwave oven and leave to stand. Meanwhile prepare the potatoes. Peel and dice the potatoes. Put them into a roasta bag with 60ml (4 tblsp) of the milk. Put the bag into a 1.75 litre (3 pint) bowl. Secure with a rubber band and pierce once at the base. Microwave on Full Power for 17 minutes (turn the bag over once during this time). Stand, covered, for 5 minutes. Drain the potatoes and mash them together with the egg, remaining milk and the butter. Pile the potato onto the meat mixture and sprinkle with the

Rolled Roast Rib of Beef (top) and Barbecue Lamb Chops (left).

cheese. Microwave on Full Power for 3-4 minutes, until the cheese has melted and the pie is very hot. To speed this recipe up you can use reconstituted powdered potato.

Pork with Leeks and Grapes

PREPARATION TIME: 20 minutes
MICROWAVE TIME: 53 minutes
SERVES: 4-5 people

30ml (2 tblsp) oil
1 carrot, peeled and sliced
1 stick celery, chopped
225g (8oz) potato, peeled and diced
450g (1lb) young leeks, washed and sliced
750g (1½lb) boned shoulder of pork, cut into 2.5cm (1 inch) cubes
25g (1oz) plain flour
Salt and freshly ground black pepper to taste
½ pint well flavoured chicken stock
100g (4oz) seedless white grapes

Preheat the browning dish for 4 or 7 minutes, according to size. Add the oil, carrot, celery, potato and leeks to the heated dish. Cover with the lid. Microwave on Full Power for 4 minutes. Using a perforated spoon, transfer the vegetables to a dinner plate. Return the browning dish to the microwave, without the lid, for 1 minute on Full Power. Toss the meat in the flour and seasoning; stir into the dish, turning so that all sides come in contact with the hot skillet. Microwave, uncovered, for 3 minutes on Full Power. Stir in the drained vegetables, stock and extra seasoning to taste. Cover with the lid. Microwave, covered, on Power 5, or Simmer, for 40 minutes. Stir in the grapes and serve after a standing time of 5 minutes.

Turkey Fricassee

PREPARATION TIME: 20 minutes
MICROWAVE TIME: 12 minutes
SERVES: 4 people

25g (1oz) butter
25g (1oz) plain flour
300ml (½ pint) chicken or turkey stock
Salt and freshly ground black pepper to taste
100g (4oz) button mushrooms, sliced
½ red pepper, de-seeded and chopped

This page: Pork with Leeks Grapes.

Facing page: Stewed Steak Garlic (top), Shepherd's Pie (centre right) and Turkey Fricassee (bottom).

4 rashers streaky bacon, de-rinded and chopped
1 medium onion, chopped
350g (12oz) cooked turkey, chopped
100g (4oz) stuffed olives, halved
30ml (2 tblsp) single cream
1 egg yolk

To make the sauce: melt the butter in a 1 litre (1¾ pint) jug for 1 minute on Full Power. Stir in the flour to make a smooth paste. Gradually stir in the stock, mixing well. Season with salt and pepper. Microwave on Full Power for 2 minutes. Beat well with a balloon whisk. Microwave on Full Power for 2 minutes. Beat in the sliced mushrooms. Put the red pepper, bacon and onion into a 1.2 litre (2 pint) mixing bowl. Cover and microwave on Full Power for 2 minutes. Stir. Arrange the cooked turkey in a serving dish. Add the pepper mixture and most of the halved olives (reserve a few for decoration). Beat the cream and egg yolk into the sauce. Pour the sauce evenly over the vegetables and turkey. Cover with cling film and pierce. Microwave on Power 5 for 5 minutes. Allow to stand for 5 minutes before serving. Garnish with the remaining olives.

Stewed Steak with Garlic

PREPARATION TIME: 25 minutes
MICROWAVE TIME: about 1 hour 40 minutes
SERVES: 4 people

750g (1½lb) chuck steak, cubed
15ml (1 tblsp) seasoned flour
2 leeks, washed and sliced
1 medium onion, sliced
1 carrot, peeled and chopped
2 cloves garlic, crushed
30ml (2 tblsp) cooking oil
2 rashers streaky bacon, de-rinded and chopped
425g (15oz) can tomatoes, chopped
15ml (1 tblsp) tomato puree
Salt and freshly ground black pepper to taste
300ml (½ pint) well flavoured beef stock
2.5ml (½ tsp) dried parsley

Toss the meat in the seasoned flour. Put the leeks, onions, carrot and the garlic into a 1.2 litre (2 pint) dish. Cover and microwave on Full Power for 3 minutes. Stir and set aside. Preheat the large browning dish, without the lid, for 7 minutes on Full Power. Pour oil into the dish and quickly st the bacon and the meat. Press meat against the sides of the di Cover and microwave on Full Power for 4 minutes. Stir, and all the remaining ingredients. Cover. Microwave on Full Pow for 4 minutes, and then on Pow 4, or Simmer, for 70 minutes. S once after the first 30 minutes. and allow to stand for 10 minu before serving.

Sauces and Preserves

Basic Savoury White Sauce

PREPARATION TIME: 5 minutes
MICROWAVE TIME: 5 minutes
MAKES: 300ml (½ pint)

25g (1oz) butter
25g (1oz) plain flour
300ml (½ pint) milk or chicken stock
Salt and freshly ground black pepper to taste

Melt the butter in a 1 litre (1¾ pint) jug. Microwave on Full Power for 1 minute until very hot. Stir in the flour to form a roux. Gradually stir in all the milk or stock. Season to taste with salt and pepper. Microwave on Full Power for 2 minutes. Beat well with a balloon whisk. Microwave on Full Power for 2 minutes. Beat with a balloon whisk and serve.

Variations on Basic White Sauce

Cheese Sauce
Beat 50g (2oz) finely grated chees and 5ml (1 tsp) made mustard in

Mushroom Sauce (above right), Basic Savoury White Sauce (far right) and Cheese Sauce (right).

e finished sauce. The heat of the
uce will melt the cheese.

ushroom Sauce
at 50g (2oz) finely chopped
ıshrooms into the prepared
sauce. The heat of the sauce will
cook the mushrooms.

Egg Sauce
Chop 1 hard-boiled egg (cooked conventionally). Beat into the prepared sauce.

Parsley Sauce
Beat 15ml (1 tblsp) chopped fresh parsley into the finished sauce.

Onion Sauce
Finely chop 1 medium sized peeled onion and put it into a bowl. Cover with cling film and pierce. Microwave on Full Power for 1-1½ minutes to soften. Beat the softened onion into the prepared sauce (the onion should be softened before the sauce is made).

Cranberry Sauce

PREPARATION TIME: 10 minutes
MICROWAVE TIME: 4 minutes
MAKES: about 400ml (⅔ pint)

1 orange
225g (8oz) frozen cranberries, defrosted
100g (4oz) granulated sugar

Finely grate the rind from the orange into a 1.2 litre (2 pint) mixing bowl. Squeeze the juice from the orange and make up to 150ml (¼ pint) with cold water. Put the cranberries, sugar, orange juice and water into the mixing bowl. Microwave on Full Power for 4 minutes. Stir once, halfway through cooking time. Stir and serve.

Custard Sauce

PREPARATION TIME: 5 minutes
MICROWAVE TIME: 4 minutes
MAKES: 600ml (1 pint)

30ml (2 tblsp) custard powder
50g (2oz) granulated sugar
600ml (1 pint) milk
30ml (2 tblsp) single cream

Put the custard powder and the sugar into a 1.2 litre (2 pint) mixing bowl. Mix to a smooth cream with a little of the milk. Put the remaining milk into a 1 litre (1¾ pint) jug and microwave on Full Power for 2 minutes. Pour the hot milk onto the blended custard powder, stirring well. Pour the custard back into the jug and microwave on Full Power for 2 minutes. Beat well with a balloon whisk. Allow to cool slightly before beating in the cream. Serve hot or cold.

Chocolate Sauce

PREPARATION TIME: 5 minutes
MICROWAVE TIME: 5 minutes
MAKES: about 300ml (½ pint)

25g (1oz) butter
15ml (1 tblsp) cocoa powder
300ml (½ pint) milk
15ml (1 tblsp) golden syrup

Melt the butter in a 1 litre (1¾ pint) jug for 1 minute on Full Power. Stir in the cocoa, mixing well. Gradually add the milk, stirring. Microwave on Full Power for 2 minutes. Beat well with a balloon whisk. Microwave on Full Power for 2 minutes. beat in the golden syrup. Serve immediately.

Beefy Tomato Sauce

PREPARATION TIME: 10 minutes
COOKING TIME: 20 minutes
MAKES: about 600ml (1 pint)

50g (2oz) butter
2 medium sized onions, finely chopped
50g (2oz) plain flour
750ml (1¼ pint) hot beef stock
30ml (2 tblsp) tomato puree
15ml (1 tblsp) vinegar
5ml (1 tsp) French mustard
5ml (1 tsp) soft brown sugar
5ml (1 tsp) Worcestershire sauce
15ml (1 tblsp) tomato sauce
Salt and freshly ground black pepper to taste

Melt the butter in a really large jug or mixing bowl for 1-2 minutes on Full Power. Stir in the onion and microwave, uncovered, for 3 minutes on Full Power. Stir in the flour, mixing well. Gradually add the stock, stirring continuously. Mix the puree with the vinegar and add to the sauce together with the French mustard, sugar, Worcestershire sauce, tomato sauce and salt and pepper to taste. Microwave on Full Power for 10 minutes. Beat well twice during this time. Turn on to Power 4, or Simmer, and microwave for a further 5 minutes. Beat well. Serve with meat balls, meat loaf, etc.

St Clement's Sauce

PREPARATION TIME: 10 minutes
MICROWAVE TIME: 3½ minutes
MAKES: about 200ml (⅓ pint)

45ml (3 tblsp) fine cut marmalade
Juice of 1 lemon
Juice of 1 orange
5ml (1 tsp) arrowroot

Put the marmalade and lemon and orange juices into a 1 litre (1¾ pint) jug. Microwave on Full Power for 1½ minutes. Stir well. Microwave on Full Power for 1 minute. Blend the arrowroot to a smooth paste with a little cold water. Stir into the jug. Microwave on Full Power for 30 seconds. Stir. Microwave on Full Power for a further 30 seconds. Stir and serve.

Plum Jam

PREPARATION TIME: 20 minutes
MICROWAVE TIME: 1 hour
MAKES: 1¼kg (2½lb)

Juice of 1 orange
900g (2lb) plums, halved and stoned
900g (2lb) granulated sugar

Put the juice and the plums into a large microwave container. Cover and microwave on Full Power for 10 minutes. Stir in the sugar to dissolve. Cover and microwave on Power 6 for about 40 minutes, or until setting point is reached. Test for setting. Pot and label in the usual way.

Strawberry Jam

PREPARATION TIME: 20 minutes, plus chilling overnight
COOKING TIME: 31 minutes
MAKES: about 1¼kg (2½lb)

900g (2lb) freshly picked strawberries, hulled
900g (2lb) granulated sugar

Place the hulled strawberries in a 2.75 litre (5 pint) microwave dish. Add the sugar and stir. Cover and leave overnight in the refrigerator. Stir well. Cover and microwave on Full Power for 7 minutes, until boiling point is reached. Microwave on Power 5, or Simmer, for 24 minutes, until setting point is reached. Test for setting. Pot and label in the usual way.

Green Tomato Chutney

PREPARATION TIME: 40 minutes
MICROWAVE TIME: 1¾-2 hours
MAKES: about 2¾kg (6lbs)

2 medium onions, finely chopped
350ml (12 fl oz) malt vinegar
250ml (8 fl oz) wine vinegar
1 small stem celery, chopped
2.5ml (½ tsp) mustard seed
1¾kg (4lb) green tomatoes, washed and chopped
2 large Bramley cooking apples, peeled, cored and chopped
175g (6oz) seedless raisins
1 clove garlic, crushed
4 peppercorns, 2 cloves and 2 chillies (tied in muslin)
450g (1lb) soft brown sugar
Salt and freshly ground black pepper to taste

Put the onions into a 750g (1½lb) pudding basin. Microwave on Full Power for 2 minutes. Put half the vinegar, the celery, mustard seed, tomatoes, apples, raisins, garlic and onions into a very large bowl.

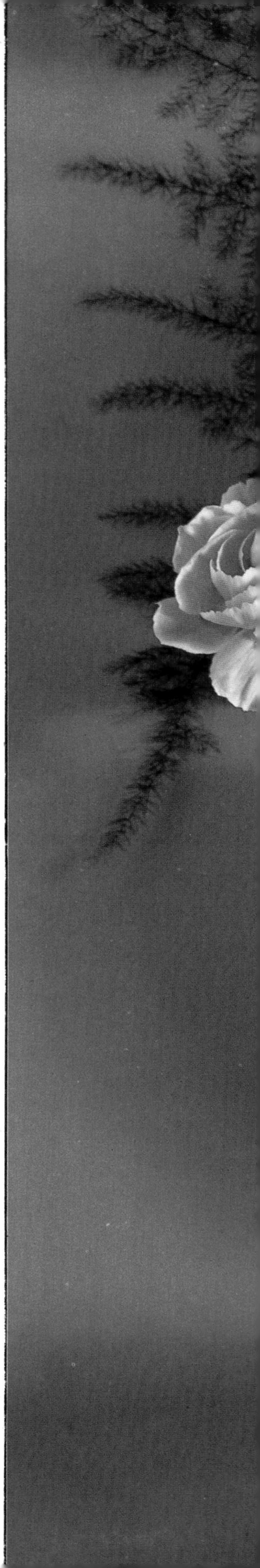

Parsley Sauce (top), Cranberry Sauce (centre left), Onion Sauce (centre right) and Egg Sauce (bottom).

Crush the muslin bag with a rolling pin and add to the bowl. Stir. Cover and microwave on Full Power for 10 minutes. Stir in the sugar to dissolve. Add the remaining vinegar and season with salt and pepper to taste. Microwave on Full Power for 20-30 minutes. Remove the lid and stir well. Microwave on Full Power, uncovered, for about 75 minutes until the mixture reduces and thickens. Stir twice during this time. Ladle into clean jam jars. Seal and label when cool. The chutney should be kept in a cool dark place for 2 months to mature, before using.

This page: Strawberry Jam (top), Plum Jam (centre right) and Green Tomato Chutney (bottom).

Facing page: Chocolate Sauc (top), St Clement's Sauce (centre left), Beefy Tomato Sauce (centre right) and Custard Sauce (bottom).

Sweets

Pear Upside Down Pudding

PREPARATION TIME: 25 minutes
MICROWAVE TIME: 9 minutes
SERVES: 6 people

Oil and caster sugar
45ml (3 tblsp) golden syrup
425g (15oz) can pear halves, drained
5 glace cherries, halved and rinsed
Recipe quantity Victoria Sandwich mixture (see recipe)

Grease an 18cm (7 inch) souffle dish with oil and sprinkle the base and sides lightly with caster sugar. Spread the golden syrup over the bottom. Make an attractive pattern over the base with the pears and the glace cherries. Spoon the Victoria Sandwich mixture into the prepared dish. Smooth the top. Microwave on Full Power for 9 minutes. Allow to stand for 7 minutes in the dish before carefully turning out. Serve warm with custard or cream.

Apple and Blackcurrant Flan

PREPARATION TIME: 30 minutes
MICROWAVE TIME: 37 minutes
SERVES: 6 people

Base
150g (5oz) plain flour
150g (5oz) wholemeal flour
Pinch of salt
50g (2oz) margarine
50g (2oz) lard
1 egg and 30ml (2 tblsp) cold water, beaten together

Filling
450g (1lb) Bramley cooking apples, peeled, cored and sliced
225g (8oz) blackcurrants
50g (2oz) caster sugar
75g (3oz) ground almonds
25g (1oz) butter
2 egg yolks

Meringue
3 egg whites
175g (6oz) caster sugar
Glace cherries and angelica for decoration

To make the pastry, sieve the flours and salt into a mixing bowl. Rub in the margarine and lard until the mixture resembles fine breadcrumbs. Mix to a dough with the egg and cold water. Knead the dough lightly. Roll out and use to line a 25cm (10 inch) fluted flan dish. Press up pastry to come ½cm (¼ inch) above the rim of the dish. Prick the sides and base with a fork. Refrigerate for 15 minutes. Using a single strip of foil, about 2.5cm (1 inch) wide, line the inside edge of the flan case. Place 2 sheets of absorbent kitchen paper in the base. Weigh down with a few baking beans. Microwave on Full Power for 6 minutes. Remove the foil, beans and absorbent paper.

This page: Mille Feuille (top), Apple Mousse (centre right) and Pear Upside Down Pudding (bottom).

Facing page: Chocolate Rice Krispie (top), Rhubarb Sunburst (centre right) and Creme Caramel (bottom).

Microwave on Full Power for 2-3 minutes. Set aside. Put the fruits into a 1.75 litre (3 pint) mixing bowl. Cover and microwave on Full Power for about 7-8 minutes, stirring once halfway through. Stir in sugar to dissolve and beat to a puree. Cool. Beat in the ground almonds, butter and egg yolk. Put the egg whites into a large, clean bowl and whisk until stiff and dry. Beat in the sugar, a little at a time, until a thick glossy meringue results. Spread the fruit mixture into the flan case. Pipe or spread the meringue mixture on top to cover completely. Put the flan into a pre-heated moderate oven, 180°C, 350°F, Gas Mark 4, for 15-20 minutes, until pale golden. Serve sprinkled with tiny pieces of cherry and angelica.

Mille Feuille

PREPARATION TIME: 15-20 minutes, plus cooling time

MICROWAVE TIME: 6 minutes

SERVES: 6 people

225g (8oz) puff pastry (you can use a small packet of frozen puff pastry)
225g (8oz) fresh strawberries
300ml (½ pint) double cream, whipped
25g (1oz) caster sugar
100g (4oz) icing sugar, sieved
Pink food colouring
25g (1oz) toasted flaked almonds

Roll the pastry out into a circle 20cm (8 inch) in diameter. Place on a large dinner plate and chill for 10 minutes. Microwave, uncovered, for 5-6 minutes, on Full Power. Turn the plate once halfway through the cooking time. Brown the top under a pre-heated hot grill for a few seconds, if required. Allow to cool completely. Hull strawberries and roughly chop them. Fold the strawberries into the cream with the caster sugar. Split the pastry horizontally into 3 layers and place the first layer on a serving dish. Spread thickly with strawberries and cream. Top with the second pastry layer and spread with more strawberries and cream. Add the final layer of pastry, browned side uppermost. Put the icing sugar into a basin. Add a few drops of pink food colouring and just enough boiling water to produce a smooth glace icing. Ice the Mille Feuille using a teaspoon – see picture. Sprinkle with the cold, toasted almonds and serve immediately.

Creme Caramel

PREPARATION TIME: 15 minutes, plus chilling time

MICROWAVE TIME: 28 minutes

SERVES: 4 people

Caramel
175g (6oz) granulated sugar
120ml (4 fl oz) cold water

Custard
450ml (¾ pint) milk
4 eggs, lightly beaten
50g (2oz) caster sugar

To make the caramel, place the granulated sugar and water into a large Pyrex jug. Microwave on Full Power for 9-11 minutes, or until a golden caramel results. Swirl the caramel evenly around the inside of a suitable, lightly-greased 900ml (1½ pint) dish. Leave to set. Put the milk into a large, clean jug and microwave on Full Power for 2 minutes. Add the beaten eggs and caster sugar. Strain onto the set caramel. Cover with cling film and pierce. Stand the dish in a larger container, which will act as a water bath. Pour in sufficient boiling water to come halfway up the sides of the dish containing the creme caramel. Microwave on Power 5, or Simmer, for about 15 minutes or until the custard has set. Remove from the water bath. Carefully peel away the cling film and allow to cool. Chill until ready to serve. Turn out and serve very cold with whipped cream.

Apple Mousse

PREPARATION TIME: 20 minutes

MICROWAVE TIME: 7 minutes

SERVES: 6 people

750g (1½lb) Bramley cooking apples, peeled, cored and sliced
Juice of 1 lemon
3 cubes of lime jelly (from a packet jelly)
45ml (3 tblsp) caster sugar
200ml (⅓ pint) whipping cream
2 egg whites
1 red-skinned eating apple

Put the prepared cooking apples into a 1.75 litre (3 pint) casserole dish with half the lemon juice and the lime jelly. Cover with a lid and microwave on Full Power for about 7 minutes until the apples are pulpy (stir once during this time). Beat with a fork, beating in the sugar until melted. Set aside and allow to cool. Blend the cooled apple in a food processor or liquidizer until smooth. Add the half-whipped cream and process together for a few seconds. Whisk the egg whites in a clean bowl until they stand in soft peaks. Transfer the apple mixture to a large, clean bowl and fold in the beaten egg whites gently. Turn into a serving dish. Decorate with slices of eating apple, which have been brushed with the remaining lemon juice to prevent discolouration.

Rhubarb Sunburst

PREPARATION TIME: 10 minutes, plus chilling time

MICROWAVE TIME: 6 minutes

SERVES: 4 people

450g (1lb) fresh young rhubarb, cut into 2.5cm (1 inch) pieces
Finely grated rind and juice of 1 orange
15ml (1 tblsp) apricot jam
6 canned apricot halves, chopped

Place the rhubarb, orange rind and juice, and the jam into a 900ml (1½ pint) mixing bowl. Cover and microwave on Full Power for 6 minutes. Stir. Set aside to cool, and then chill. Stir in the chopped apricots. Serve with natural yogurt, ice cream or whipped double cream.

Chocolate Pudding with Cherries

PREPARATION TIME: 10 minutes

MICROWAVE TIME: 8½ minutes

SERVES: 4-6 people

75g (3oz) softened butter
75g (3oz) soft brown sugar
75g (3oz) self-raising flour
25g (1oz) cocoa powder
2 eggs
30ml (2 tblsp) milk
425g (15oz) can cherry pie filling

Put all ingredients, apart from the cherry pie filling, into a mixing bowl. Beat with a wooden spoon for 1 minute. Spoon into a lightly greased 900ml (1½ pint) plastic pudding basin. Microwave on Full Power for 3½-4 minutes, until well risen and springy to the touch. Set aside. Empty the cherry pie filling into a bowl and microwave on Full Power for 3 minutes, stirring after 1½ minutes. Turn the sponge pudding into a dinner plate. Spoon the hot cherry sauce over the top and serve immediately.

Chocolate Rice Krispie

PREPARATION TIME: 15 minut plus chilli time

COOKING TIME: 5 minutes

MAKES: 16-20 wedges

100g (4oz) margarine
50g (2oz) caster sugar
25g (1oz) cocoa powder
50g (2oz) golden syrup
100g (4oz) Rice Krispies

Lightly grease 2 x 20cm (8 inch) sandwich tins with a little of the margarine (these are not to be us in the microwave). Put the remaining margarine, cut into pieces, into a 1.75 litre (3 pint) mixing bowl with the caster suga cocoa powder and golden syrup. Microwave on Power 5 or Simm for 4 minutes. Stir halfway throu and again at the end. Microwave on Full Power for a further 1 minute. Stir in the Rice Krispies, making sure that they are all coat with the chocolate mixture. Divi between the prepared tins and smooth level with a knife. Cool and then chill until set. Cut into finger wedges to serve. As an alternative, 50g (2oz) washed, seedless raisins may be stirred in with the Rice Krispies.

Apple Ginger Crisp

PREPARATION TIME: 15 minut

MICROWAVE TIME: 9 minutes

SERVES: 4-6 people

450g (1lb) Bramley cooking apples peeled, cored and sliced
50g (2oz) demerara sugar
15ml (1 tblsp) orange juice
65g (2½oz) butter
225g (8oz) plain ginger biscuits, crushed
50g (2oz) flaked almonds

Place the apples, sugar and orang juice into a 1.5 litre (2½ pint) casserole dish. Cover and microwave on Full Power for 4-5 minutes. Stir and set aside. Put th butter into a 1.75 litre (3 pint) mixing bowl. Microwave on Powe 7, or Roast, for about 2 minutes, until melted. Stir the biscuits and almonds into the melted butter. Mix well. Microwave on Full Pow for 2 minutes. Stir well with a for after 1 minute. Carefully spoon th biscuit crumble over the apples. Serve immediately with whipped cream or ice cream. This pudding can also be served cold.

Chocolate Pudding with Cherries (left), Apple Ginger Crisp (below left) and Apple and Blackcurrant Flan (bottom).

Tea Time Treats

Celebration Gateau

PREPARATION TIME: 40 minutes
MICROWAVE TIME: 14 minutes
MAKES: 1 gateau

Cake
Caster sugar and oil for preparing the dish
3 eggs
150g (5oz) self-raising flour
25g (1oz) cocoa powder
2.5ml (½ tsp) baking powder
175g (6oz) soft margarine
175g (6oz) caster sugar

Icing
225g (8oz) icing sugar, sieved
75g (3oz) butter
10ml (2 tsp) boiling water
5ml (1 tsp) liquid coffee essence
Few drops of vanilla essence

Decoration
1 packet sponge finger biscuits
175g (6oz) plain chocolate
1m 40cm (1½ yards) brown nylon ribbon, 2.5cm (1 inch) wide

Lightly grease a deep, 18cm (7 inch) diameter souffle dish with oil. Line the base with a circle of greaseproof paper and use a little caster sugar to dust the sides. Knock out any surplus. Put all the ingredients for the cake into a mixing bowl. Beat for 1 minute. Spoon into the prepared souffle dish and smooth the top. Microwave on Power 7, or Roast, for about 7 minutes, and then on Full Power for 2-3 minutes until the sponge has risen to the top of the souffle dish and is set. Allow to stand in the container for 10 minutes before turning out onto a clean tea towel which has been sprinkled with a little caster sugar. Cool completely.

To make the icing: gradually beat the sieved icing sugar into the butter, adding the boiling water. Take 15ml (1 tblsp) buttercream out of the bowl and beat the coffee essence into it. Beat the vanilla essence into the remaining butter cream. Cut the cake in half horizontally and sandwich together with some of the vanilla buttercream. Spread the vanilla buttercream around the sides and across the top of the cake. Pipe half the cake with vanilla butter cream and the other half with the coffee buttercream. Arrange the prepared sponge fingers, like soldiers, around the edge of the cake – see picture. Tie brown ribbon around to finish the gateau.
To prepare the sponge fingers: measure 1 sponge finger against the cooked cake. Trim all the sponge fingers to the same size. Break the chocolate into a large mixing bowl and microwave on Power 4 for 3-4 minutes. Stir. Dip the rounded end of the sponge fingers into the melted chocolate to coat the top half of each one. Arrange on a tray and leave in a cool plac for 10-15 minutes to set.

Chocolate Icing

PREPARATION TIME: 5 minutes
MICROWAVE TIME: 2½ minutes

25g (1oz) soft margarine, chilled
22ml (1½ tblsp) cocoa powder, sieved
150g (5oz) icing sugar, sieved
30ml (2 tblsp) milk

Put the margarine and cocoa into a 1.2 litre (2 pint) bowl. Microwave on Power 5, or Simmer, for 2½ minutes, until the margarine has melted and is very hot. Stir once, halfway through. Beat in the icing sugar and the milk. Beat with a wooden spoon until thick and glossy. Use to coat the top and sides of the cake.

Collettes

PREPARATION TIME: 30 minutes
MICROWAVE TIME: 7½ minutes
MAKES: 12

175g (6oz) plain chocolate
50g (2oz) milk chocolate
60ml (tblspk double cream
15g (½oz) butter
10ml (2 tsp) brandy or coffee essence
36 paper sweet cases, separated into twelve groups of three cases

Break the plain chocolate into pieces and put into a 900ml (1½ pint) bowl. Microwave on Power 3, or Defrost, for 4-5 minutes. Stir. Using a small paint brush or teaspoon, coat the base and sides of each group of paper cases with the melted chocolate. Leave to set. Put the milk chocolate and the butter into a clean bowl. Microwave on Power 3, or Defrost, for 2-2½ minutes. Beat well for a few minutes. Beat in the brandy or coffee essence. Half whip the cream and fold into the milk chocolate mixture using a metal spoon. Chill until firm enough to pipe. Peel the paper cases away from the set chocolate and discard. Pipe rosettes of chocolate filling into the chocolate case. Serve immediately in new paper sweet cases.

Fruit and Almond Cake

PREPARATION TIME: 20 minutes
MICROWAVE TIME: 13-16 minutes
MAKES: 1 cake

Use the large Anchor Hocking ring mould, which should be lightly greased and coated with caster sugar.

175g (6oz) soft margarine
175g (6oz) soft brown sugar
2.5ml (½ tsp) liquid gravy browning
3 eggs, beaten
175g (6oz) self-raising flour
2-3 drops almond essence
25g (1oz) ground almonds
50g (2oz) seedless raisins
50g (2oz) glace cherries, washed and roughly chopped
30ml (2 tblsp) milk

Cream margarine and sugar until light and fluffy. Beat in the gravy browning and beaten eggs, a little at a time (add 15ml (1 tblsp) flour with each addition of egg to prevent curdling). Beat in the almond essence, ground almonds and milk. Fold in the remaining flour, and then the raisins and cherries. Place in the prepared ring mould and smooth the top. Microwave on Power 6, or Roast, for 12-14 minutes, and then on Full Power for 1-2 minutes until just set. Stand for 15 minutes, before turning out. When quite cold, the top may be sprinkled with a little sieved icing sugar.

Cheese and Paprika Scones

PREPARATION TIME: 20 mi
MICROWAVE TIME: 5-6 min
MAKES: about 10

225g (8oz) self-raising flour
Pinch salt
Pinch paprika
50g (2oz) firm margarine
50g (2oz) Red Leicester cheese, grated
5ml (1 tsp) made mustard
1 egg
45ml (3 tblsp) milk
5ml (1 tsp) Bovril

Sieve the flour, salt and papr into a 1.75 litre (3 pint) mixi bowl. Rub in the margarine fork in the cheese. Beat the mustard and egg together an with the milk. Mix into the ingredients, using a round b knife, to form a soft dough. on a lightly floured board. R to a thickness of 1cm (½ inc Cut into 6cm (2½ inch) rou Arrange the shaped scones on a non-metallic tray, leavi in the centre. Mix 5ml (1 ts Bovril with a little boiling w and brush over the surface scones (do not cover). Mic immediately on Power 7, or for 5-6 minutes. Transfer to cooling rack and allow to st 2-3 minutes. Serve hot wit or cold if preferred. As an alternative to the Bovril gla cooked scones may be flash under a pre-heated hot grill brown and crisp them.

Celebration Gateau (to Collettes (centre left) a and Almond Cake (bot

Microwave Meringues (right), Victoria Sandwich (below) and Porridge (bottom right).

Porridge

PREPARATION TIME: 5 minutes
MICROWAVE TIME: 9 minutes
SERVES: 3 people

2 cups milk and water, mixed
2.5ml (½ tsp) salt
1 cup porridge oats
75g (3oz) demerara sugar
75g (3oz) butter

Put the milk, water and salt into a 1.75 litre (3 pint) mixing bowl. Stir in the porridge oats. Microwave on Full Power for 3 minutes. Stir. Microwave on Full Power for 3 minutes. Stir. Microwave on Full Power for 3 minutes. Turn into individual serving dishes. Sprinkle with the brown sugar and top with the butter. Serve immediately.

Microwave Meringues

PREPARATION TIME: 20 minutes
MICROWAVE TIME: about 8 minutes
MAKES: 10 sandwiched meringues

1 egg white
180ml (12 tblsp) icing sugar, sieved
Pink food colouring
175g (6oz) chocolate buttercream
Chocolate Vermicelli

Put the egg white into a 1.75 litre (3 pint) mixing bowl and beat until frothy. Gradually work in the icing sugar and mix to give a really stiff fondant. Divide the fondant into two portions. Knead a few drops pink food colouring into one portion of fondant. Roll both the fondants separately into small balls, each about the size of a marble. Arrange 4 balls of fondant in a ring on a large dinner plate. Microwave on Full Power for 1½ minutes. Allow to stand for 2 minutes before removing to a cooling tray. Repeat until all the mixture has been cooked. Fill the cooled meringue halves with the chocolat buttercream. Sprinkle with a little vermicelli and serve in paper cake cases.

Victoria Sandwich

PREPARATION TIME: 15 minutes
MICROWAVE TIME: 7 minutes
MAKES: 1 cake

Oil
Caster sugar for dusting
3 eggs
175g (6oz) self-raising flour
175g (6oz) soft margarine
175g (6oz) caster sugar
2 drops liquid gravy browning
30ml (2 tblsp) milk
45ml (3 tblsp) strawberry jam

Lightly grease an 18cm (7 inch) souffle dish with oil; dust the sides with a little caster sugar. Place a circle of greaseproof paper in the base. Put the eggs, flour, margarine, caster sugar, gravy browning and milk into a mixing bowl. Beat for 1 minute. spoon into the prepared dish and smooth the top. Microwave on Full Power for about 7 minutes. Test by putting a wooden cocktail stick into the centre of the sponge after a 3 minute standing time. The cocktail stick should come out clean. Stand for 10 minutes. turn out into a wire cooling rack. When quite cold, split in half horizontally. Sandwich together with the jam. Serve with a little caster sugar sprinkled over the top.

Cream Slices

PREPARATION TIME: 15-20 minutes, plus cooling time
MICROWAVE TIME: 6-8 minutes
MAKES: about 6 slices

225g (8oz) puff pastry (small packet frozen puff pastry can be used)
Black cherry jam
45ml (3 tblsp) icing sugar, sieved
A few drops of pink food colouring

Roll the pastry into an oblong about 10cm (4 inch) wide and 30-35cm (12-14 inches) long. Cut in half, crossways. Dampen the surface of a suitable container. Lift one half of the pastry onto the prepared tray and microwave on Full Power for 3-4 minutes, until well puffed up (when the door is

This page: Mr Hedgehog Ca (top), Cream Slice (centre lef and Rich Fruit Cake (bottom

Facing page: Pineapple Gate (top right), Chocolate Pear Sponge (centre left) and Cheese and Paprika Scones (bottom).

opened, the pastry should hold its shape). Allow to stand for 2-3 minutes and then remove to a cooling tray. Repeat the process with the remaining half of the pastry. Allow to cool. Using a sharp knife, divide each layer into 3 slices. Sandwich each group of three layers together with the jam. Mix the icing sugar with a little boiling water to make a smooth, glossy icing. beat in a few drops pink food colouring. Quickly spread the icing over the top of each layered slice. Cut each one into 3 slices.

Mr Hedgehog Cake

PREPARATION TIME: 40 minutes
MICROWAVE TIME: 3½-7 minutes
MAKES: 1 cake

75g (3oz) softened margarine
75g (3oz) caster sugar
100g (4oz) self-raising flour
2 eggs
15ml (1 tblsp) milk
15ml (1 tblsp) cocoa powder
100g (4oz) butter
225g (8oz) icing sugar, sieved
1 packet chocolate buttons
2 raisins
Green coloured coconut for grass

To make the sponge, put the margarine, the caster sugar, flour, eggs and milk into a mixing bowl. Beat with a wooden spoon for 1 minute. Lightly grease the base and sides of a 900ml (1½ pint) Pyrex or plastic pudding basin. Fill with the sponge mixture and smooth the top. Microwave on Full Power for 3½ minutes, or on Power 6, or Roast, for 6-7 minutes. The spo should be well risen and just 'se Remove from the microwave ov and allow to stand for 5 minute before turning out. Allow to become quite cold. To make the buttercream, mix the cocoa wit 30ml (2 tblsp) boiling water to form a smooth paste. Beat with butter and icing sugar until ligh and creamy. Split the cooled ca in half horizontally. Sandwich together with a little of the butt cream and arrange on a cake bo Use the remaining buttercream completely coat the 'hedgehog'. Form a 'snout' for his nose. For over. Cut most of the chocolate buttons in half and stud the hedgehog with these to represe the prickles. Use 1 whole choc button for his nose and 2 raisin for his eyes. Spread some green coconut around the base for gra

Rich Fruit Cake

PREPARATION TIME: 30 minu
MICROWAVE TIME: 40 minute
MAKES: 1 cake

100g (4oz) soft margarine
100g (4oz) dark soft brown sugar
30ml (2 tblsp) black treacle
5ml (1 tsp) gravy browning
3 eggs
45ml (3 tblsp) milk
225g (8oz) self-raising flour, sieve with 5ml (1 tsp) mixed spice a pinch of salt
500g (1lb 2oz) mixed dried fruit (sultanas, raisins, currants and peel)
25g (1oz) chopped blanched alm
50g (2oz) glace cherries, washed quartered
45ml (3 tblsp) sherry or brandy

Lightly grease a deep, 23cm (9 inch) diameter souffle dish. Lin the base with a circle of ungreas greaseproof paper and dust the

sides with a little caster sugar (knocking out any surplus). Beat the margarine, sugar, treacle and gravy browning in a large mixing bowl until light and fluffy. Gradually beat in the eggs and the milk. Add 15ml (1 tblsp) flour with each addition of egg, to prevent it curdling. Fold in the remaining flour using a metal spoon. Fold in the fruits, nuts and glace cherries, together with the sherry or brandy. Spoon the mixture into the prepared container. Microwave on Power 4, Simmer or Defrost, for 40 minutes. Remove from the microwave oven and allow to stand in its dish for 20 minutes before turning out. When quite cold, the cake may be marzipanned and iced, or finished with glace fruits, and glazed. Allow the cake to mature for at least 1 month before using.

Date and Walnut Loaf Cake (below) and Crepes Suzette (bottom).

Date and Walnut Loaf Cake

PREPARATION TIME: 15 minutes

COOKING TIME: 6 minutes

MAKES: 1 loaf

2 eggs
60ml (4 tblsp) milk
15ml (1 tblsp) golden syrup
5ml (1 tsp) gravy browning
100g (4oz) soft margarine
175g (6oz) self-raising flour
75g (3oz) soft brown sugar
75g (3oz) chopped stoned dates
1 small banana, sliced
50g (2oz) walnuts, chopped

Put the eggs, milk, syrup, gravy browning, margarine, flour and brown sugar into a large mixing bowl. Beat with a wooden spoon. Using a metal spoon, fold in the dates, banana and walnuts. Turn into a lightly greased 1.75 litre (3 pint) microwave bread baker. Microwave on Full Power for about 6 minutes, turning the dish a half turn, halfway through cooking time. Allow to stand in the bread baker for 10 minutes before turning out. Serve sprinkled with caster sugar

Crepes Suzette

PREPARATION TIME: 25 minutes

MICROWAVE TIME: about 24 minutes

SERVES: 4-6 people

Pancakes
120g (4oz) plain flour
Pinch salt
1 egg
150ml (¼ pint) milk
150ml (¼ pint) water
Cooking oil

Sauce
75g (3oz) butter
50g (2oz) caster sugar
Grated rind of 1 orange
Grated rind and juice of ½ a lemon
60ml (4 tblsp) brandy or Cointreau

Sieve the flour and salt into a bowl. Make a well in the centre. Add the egg and half of the milk. Beat well. Gradually beat in the remaining milk and the water. Beat in 5ml (1 tsp) oil. Allow to stand for 10 minutes. Fry the pancakes in the usual way, making 12 pancakes in all. Fold the 12 cooked pancakes in half and then in half again, to form triangles. Arrange in a shallow dish. To make the sauce, put the butter into a 1 litre (1¾ pint) jug and microwave on Defrost for 5 minutes, or until melted and hot. Stir in the sugar to dissolve. Add the fruit rinds, lemon juice, and the brandy or Cointreau. Microwave on Full Power for 2 minutes. Stir. Pour over the pancakes. Cover with cling film and microwave on Power 5, or Simmer, for 5 minutes. Turn each pancake over in the sauce before serving. Serve piping hot.

Pineapple Gateau

PREPARATION TIME: 30 minutes

MICROWAVE TIME: 7 minutes

MAKES: 1 gateau

Oil and caster sugar
1 recipe quantity Victoria Sandwich mixture (see recipe)
225g (8oz) can pineapple slices, drained
300ml (½ pint) whipping cream, whipped
100g (4oz) chopped blanched almonds, toasted
Angelica for decoration

Lightly grease an 18cm (7 inch) souffle dish or plastic pan with oil. Put a circle of greaseproof paper into the base of the dish; dust the base and sides with caster sugar (knock out any surplus). Spoon the prepared Victoria Sandwich mixture into the dish, and smooth the surface. Microwave on Full Power for about 7 minutes. Allow to stand for 10 minutes before turning out onto a wire cooling rack. Once the cake is quite cold, remove the greaseproof paper. Split the cake in half horizontally. Chop 1 slice of pineapple and mix with 45ml (3 tblsp) of the whipped cream; use to sandwich the cake layers together. Spread some of the cream round the sides of the cake and roll it in nuts to coat evenly. Arrange on a serving dish. Spread the top with the remaining cream, piping it if liked. Decorate the top with pineapple and angelica – see picture.

Chocolate Pear Sponge

PREPARATION TIME: 15 minutes

MICROWAVE TIME: 6 minutes

MAKES: 1 sponge cake

120g (4oz) sugar
90g (3½oz) self-raising flour
15g (½oz) cocoa powder
2.5ml (½ tsp) baking powder
100g (4oz) soft margarine
15ml (1 tblsp) milk
5ml (1 tsp) mixed spice
100g (4oz) ripe pear, peeled, cored and chopped
Oil and caster sugar for preparing the souffle dish

Put all the ingredients, apart from the pear, into a 1.75 litre (3 pint) mixing bowl. Mix with a wooden spoon and then beat for 1 minute. Fold in the pear, using a metal spoon. Lightly grease an 18cm (7 inch) souffle dish; line the base with a circle of greaseproof paper and coat the sides with a little caster sugar. Turn the mixture into the prepared souffle dish and smooth the top. Microwave on Power 6, or Roast, for 4 minutes, and them on Full Power for 2 minutes. Allow to stand for 10 minutes before turning out onto a cooling rack. The cooling rack should be covered with a clean tea towel, sprinkled with a little caster sugar. When quite cold, ice the cake with chocolate icing.

Bread and Rice

Ubley Chawal
(BOILED RICE) 1

This method of cooking rice in a large quantity of water is very safe and ideal for all grades of rice, especially for starchy short and medium grades. Also for cooking large quantities as the fluffiness can be controlled.Use a few drops of lemon juice to whiten the rice.

COOKING TIME: 10-15 minutes

450g (1lb) Basmati rice
Pinch of salt
Few drops lemon juice

Wash rice in 4-5 changes of water until water is clear. Drain rice and put into a large pan. Fill pan with cold or tepid water 5-10cm (2-4 inches) above the rice level. Add pinch of salt and bring to boil gradually. When boiling, add drops of lemon juice, which bleaches the rice as well as cuts the starch formation. Boil for 7-10 minutes covered, or until the rice is almost cooked and has a hard core in the centre. Test by pressing a few grains of rice between thumb and forefinger. Drain well and cover the top of the pan with a clean cloth or foil and put the lid on lightly. Replace on a very low heat. The moisture around the rice is enough to form steam and cook the core in 2-4 minutes. Serve with or without butter/ghee, with daal or curry.

Ubley Chawal
(BOILED RICE) 2

PREPARATION TIME: 5 minutes

COOKING TIME: 15 minutes

This method is good for long grain rice only, like Basmati, American, Deradun or Pahari rice. In cooking, the rice absorbs twice its dry measure of liquid. Bearing this in mind always measure rice with a cup or some such container and note. Then measure twice this amount of water.

450g (1lb) Basmati rice
Pinch of salt
Lemon juice

Wash rice in 4-5 changes of wa until water is clear. Drain rice a put into a large pan. Fill the par with measured quantity of wat and let the rice soak for 10-15 minutes. The longer it stands t better the result. Add salt and lemon juice and gently bring to boil. Stir once or twice when boiling and cook covered until is almost cooked with a hard centre; about 7-10 minutes. W should be totally absorbed. Do stir rice during cooking. Keep o low heat for a further 1-2 minu to evaporate any remaining moisture and complete the coo of the rice. Serve.

Sada Pulao (left), Meat Pulao (below, far left) and Ubley Chawal (below left).

Meat Pulao

PREPARATION TIME: 15 minutes

COOKING TIME: 1 hour

1 small onion, peeled and sliced
75g (3oz) ghee or butter
2.5cm (1 inch) stick cinnamon
6 green cardamoms
3 large cardamoms
6 cloves
1 bayleaf
5ml (1 tsp) whole black cumin seeds
5ml (1 tsp) ginger paste
5ml (1 tsp) garlic paste
225g (8oz) lean meat, cut into cubes
5ml (1 tsp) ground coriander
5ml (1 tsp) ground cumin
150ml (¼ pint) natural yogurt
5ml (1 tsp) salt
450g (1lb) Basmati rice

Fry onion until golden brown in ghee. Add cinnamon, cardamoms, cloves, bayleaf and cumin seed. Fry for 1 minute. Add ginger and garlic pastes and fry for ½ minute. Add meat and sprinkle with ground coriander and cumin. Stir and add yogurt and salt. Mix well, cover and cook for 10-12 minutes until yogurt is dry and oil separates. Add 300ml (½ pint) of water and cook until meat is tender, 20-25 minutes. Remove from heat. Strain meat from its liquid. Take a large saucepan and add washed rice. Add gravy from the meat by measuring with the same cup. Use twice as much gravy as rice. If short, make up with water. Add the meat and the spices. Check for salt and adjust. Bring to the boil and then lower the heat, give a stir and cover and cook on low heat without stirring for 10-15 minutes until water is totally absorbed by the rice. Serve with a curry.

Sada Pulao
(CUMIN FRIED RICE)

PREPARATION TIME: 5 minutes plus 15 minutes to soak the rice.

COOKING TIME: 15 minutes

450g (1lb) Basmati or American long grain rice
Water
75g (3oz) ghee or butter
5ml (1 tsp) cumin seed
1.25ml (¼ tsp) turmeric powder
5ml (1 tsp) salt

Measure rice with a cup and note. Wash rice in 4-5 changes of water. Drain well and add twice as much water as rice. Cover and set aside for 10-15 minutes. Heat ghee or butter and add cumin seed. Fry for a few seconds, do not allow to burn. Add strained rice, retaining water. Add turmeric and salt. Mix well and add strained water. Bring to the boil, cover and lower the temperature. Do not stir rice. Cook for 10-12 minutes until water is absorbed by the rice.
Serve with any curry.

Biryani

There are two methods of making biryani; one with uncooked meat and the other with cooked meat. Both styles give equally good results but have slightly different flavours.

Method 1

In this method meat is marinated and cooked with semi-cooked rice.

PREPARATION TIME: 15-20 minutes and at least 1 hour for meat to marinate.

COOKING TIME: 60-70 minutes

275g (10oz) meat cut into cubes (leg or shoulder of lamb)
150ml (¼ pint) natural yogurt
5ml (1 tsp) salt
5ml (1 tsp) ground coriander
5ml (1 tsp) ground cumin
5ml (1 tsp) chilli powder
2.5ml (½ tsp) turmeric powder
5ml (1 tsp) ginger paste
5ml (1 tsp) garlic paste
2 onions, peeled and sliced
Oil for frying
3-4 green chillis, chopped
2 sprigs fresh coriander leaves, chopped
450g (1lb) Basmati rice
2.5cm (1 inch) cinnamon stick
6 small cardamoms
6 cloves
2 bayleaves
5ml (1 tsp) black cumin seed
10ml (2 tsp) salt
50g (2oz) ghee, melted
5-10ml (1-2 tsp) saffron dissolved in 90ml (6 tblsp) milk

In a small bowl, mix meat, yogurt, salt, coriander, cumin, chilli and turmeric powder, ginger and garlic pastes. Cover and set aside to marinate for at least 1 hour. For best results marinate overnight.

For boiling rice

Fry onions until brown and crisp in plenty of oil. Drain on kitchen paper. Put the meat and marianade into a large saucepan with lid. Add half of the fried onions, half of the chopped chillis and coriander. Mix well. In a separate saucepan, wash rice in 3-4 changes of water, add lots of water together with the cinnamon, cardamom, cloves, bayleaves, black cumin and salt. Bring to the boil. Cook for 3-4 minutes until rice is half cooked. Drain well and put the steaming rice over the meat. Sprinkle with the remaining fried onions, chillis and coriander leaves. Make 5-6 holes with the handle of a wooden spoon for steam to escape and pour saffron milk all over the rice. Sprinkle with lemon juice and melted ghee. Cover with the lid and place the pan on the stove to cook over a moderate heat. As soon as steam is visible, lower the temperature. Cook for 45-50 minutes rotating the pan, so that all areas receive even heat. The rice will cook with the steam formed by the milk and yogurt and moisture from the meat. Lower heat to minimum and cook for another 10 minutes. Serve biryani from one end of the saucepan, mixing meat with rice with the aid of a spoon. Serve with a mixed vegetable raita.

Method 2

This method is the layering method. It involves two stages:

Stage 1
Cooking the meat

Stage 2
Layering the meat with rice

1 onion, peeled and chopped
100g (4oz) ghee or
75-90ml (5-6 tblsp) oil
5ml (1 tsp) ginger paste
5ml (1 tsp) garlic paste
275g (10oz) meat (leg or shoulder of lamb), cubed
5ml (1 tsp) ground coriander
5ml (1 tsp) chilli powder
1.25ml (¼ tsp) turmeric powder
5ml (1 tsp) ground cumin
150ml (¼ pint) natural yogurt
5ml (1 tsp) salt
2.5ml (½ tsp) saffron
15ml (1 tblsp) milk
1 onion, peeled and thinly sliced
Oil for deep frying
450g (1lb) Basmati rice
2.5cm (1 inch) cinnamon stick
6 cloves
5ml (1 tsp) black cumin seed
1 bayleaf
6 small cardamoms
10ml (2 tsp) salt
2 sprigs fresh green coriander, chopped
2-3 green chillis, chopped
Juice of 1 lemon

Fry chopped onion in ghee or oil until light brown in a large pan. Add ginger and garlic pastes and fry for another ½ minute. Add meat and coriander, chilli, turmeric and cumin powder. Add yogurt and salt. Mix well and cook with lid on for 10-15 minutes until dry. Add 350ml (12 fl oz) water. Cover and cook for 8-10 minutes on low heat until meat is tender and there is approx. 120ml (4 fl oz) gravy left.

For rice

Dissolve saffron in milk. Deep fry sliced onion in oil until crisp and brown and drain on kitchen paper. Wash rice in 4-5 changes of water. Add plenty of water and add cinnamon, cloves, black cumin, bayleaf and cardamom. Add salt and bring to boil. Cook until rice is nearly done. The rice should increase in size but have a hard centre. Drain well, leaving whole spices in the rice. Divide rice in two. Line the saucepan base with half the rice, and top with the cooked meat, saving the sauce. Sprinkle with half the fried onion, half the fresh coriander and chilli. Cover with the remaining rice. Sprinkle top with the remaining fried onion, chilli and coriander. Sprinkle with lemon juice and saffron milk. Pour the meat gravy all round. Make a few holes with the handle of the spoon for steam to rise. Cover and put on gentle heat for 4-5 minutes. Mix from one end before serving. Serve with mixed vegetable raita.

Tahiri

PREPARATION TIME: 10 minutes

COOKING TIME: 20 minutes

1 onion, peeled and sliced
75g (3oz) ghee or butter
2.5cm (1 inch) cinnamon stick
6 cloves
6 cardamoms
5ml (1 tsp) black cumin seed
5ml (1 tsp) whole black pepper
1-2 bayleaves
100-125g (4-5oz) shelled or frozen peas
450g (1lb) Basmati rice washed in 4-5 changes of water
460ml (16 fl oz) water
15-20ml (3-4 tsp) salt

Fry onion in ghee until light brown. Add cinnamon, cloves, cardamom, black cumin, pepper and bayleaf. Fry for ½ minute. Add peas and cook for 2 minutes. Add rice and 460ml (16 fl oz) water and salt. Bring to boil. Cover and lower heat to simmer. Cook for 10-12 minutes until rice is cooked and water is absorbed. Serve with vegetable or meat curry.

Vegetable Pulao

PREPARATION TIME: 15 min

COOKING TIME: 15 minutes

450g (1lb) Basmati or any long rice
75g (3oz) ghee or butter
1 onion, peeled and chopped
2.5cm (1 inch) cinnamon stick
1-2 bayleaves
6 small cardamoms
4 large cardamoms
6 cloves
3-4ml (3-4 tsp) salt
Water
225-275g (8-10oz) mixed vegetables, sliced
5ml (1 tsp) ground coriander
5ml (1 tsp) garam masala powd
1-4ml (1-4 tsp) turmeric powder
5ml (1 tsp) chilli powder
Salt to taste

Measure rice with a cup and n Wash rice in 4-5 changes of wa drain well. Heat ghee and fry o until light brown. Add cinnam bayleaf, cardamoms, and clove for 1 minute. Add mixed vegetables and fry for 4-5 min Add rice and sprinkle with coriander, garam masala, turm and chilli powder. Mix well. A twice the measure of water. A salt to taste. Bring to boil. Red heat, cover and gently cook fo 15 minutes, without stirring, u water is completely absorbed. by itself, with a raita or with a curry.

Recommended vegetables:- C used in any combination.

1-2 aubergines, cut in 1cm (½ inch) chunks
1-2 potatoes, diced
1-2oz shelled or frozen peas
1-2 carrots, peeled and diced
2oz sliced green beans
1-2oz corn kernels
2-3 cauliflower florets, cut into smaller pieces
1-2oz broad beans, frozen or shelled

Facing page: Vegetable Pula (top), Khichri (left) and Sha Pulao (bottom).

No leafy vegetables or pithy vegetables like marrow, courgettes, gourd etc. are advisable as they will make the pulao soggy. To colour the rice at random, do not use turmeric powder, but use food colouring, adding a few drops of any colour, at random, after the rice is semi-cooked and water is more-or-less absorbed.

Khichri
(KEDGEREE)

PREPARATION TIME: 6 minutes
COOKING TIME: 10-15 minutes

225g (8oz) Basmati rice
225g (8oz) red lentils
3-4ml (3/4 tsp) salt, or to taste
2.5ml (1/2 tsp) turmeric
5ml (1 tsp) ground coriander
75g (3oz) butter
1 large onion, peeled and chopped
1-2 green chillis, chopped

Mix rice and lentils, measure with a cup and note. Wash in 4-5 changes of water. Drain and add twice the measure of water with the same cup. Add salt, turmeric and coriander. Bring to boil. Mix well by stirring gently. Lower the temperature, cover and cook over a gentle heat for 10-12 minutes until water is absorbed. In a frying pan, melt butter and fry onions golden brown. Add chopped chillis and pour over cooked khichri. Serve with poppadums and chutney.

Shahi Pulao
(NUT AND RAISIN PULAO)

PREPARATION TIME: 5-6 minutes.
COOKING TIME: 10-15 minutes.

450g (1lb) Basmati or long grain rice
75g (3oz) ghee or butter
2.5cm (1 inch) cinnamon stick
6 small cardamoms
2 large cardamoms
2 bayleaves
6 cloves
5ml (1 tsp) salt
Water
50-75g (2-3oz) raisins
50-75g (2-3oz) mixed nuts (almonds, cashew, pistachio)

Measure rice with a cup. Wash rice in 4-5 changes of water, drain. Heat ghee and fry cinnamon, cardamoms, bayleaves and cloves for half minute. Add washed rice, salt and twice the quantity of water. Bring to boil gently. Stir once or twice. Reduce heat, add raisins and nuts, cover and cook for 10-12 minutes or until water is totally absorbed. Serve with meat or vegetable curry.

Jhinga Pulao
(PRAWN PULAO)

PREPARATION TIME: 6 minutes
COOKING TIME: 10-15 minutes

225g (8oz) long grain or Basmati rice
1 onion, peeled and chopped
75g (3oz) ghee or butter
2.5cm (1 inch) cinnamon stick
1 bayleaf
6 small cardamoms
6 cloves
5-10ml (1-2 tsp) ginger paste
5-10ml (1-2 tsp) garlic paste
225g (8oz) peeled and cooked prawns
15ml (1 tblsp) chopped fresh coriander
5ml (1 tsp) garam masala powder
1-2 green chillis
3-4ml (3/4 tsp) salt

Measure rice and note. Wash in 3-4 changes of water. Drain and soak in twice the measure of water. Keep aside. Fry onion in ghee or butter until golden brown. Add cinnamon, bayleaf, cardamom and cloves, fry for 1 minute. Add ginger and garlic paste. Cook for 1/2-1 minute. Add prawns and sprinkle with coriander and garam masala. Add green chillis and salt. Stir in soaked rice and water. Mix well and bring to boil. Reduce heat, cover and cook until water is absorbed, about 10-15 minutes. Do not stir during cooking. Serve with curry. To colour pulao, add a few drops of red or orange food colour, 2-3 minutes before removing from heat. A pinch of saffron may be added along with the spices.

Pita

PREPARATION TIME: 10 minutes and 1 hour for dough to rest.
COOKING TIME: 30 minutes

10ml (2 tsp) dried yeast
5ml (1 tsp) sugar
Water
450g (1lb) refined or wholemeal flour
Pinch of salt
25g (1oz) butter or margarine

Mix yeast and sugar and add 30ml (2 tblsp) tepid water. Cover and let it rise. When it becomes frothy it is ready for use. Sift flour and salt, add butter and yeast mixture. Knead with water to make a pliable dough, cover and rest for 1 hour. Knead again and divide into 16 even-sized balls. Preheat oven to Gas Mark 5 (190°C-375°F). Roll each one out on lightly floured surface to a 15cm (6 inch) oblong or a circle. Bake in the oven on a tray for 7-10 minutes.

Saag Paratha
Paratha made with a leafy vegetable.

PREPARATION TIME: 10 minutes
COOKING TIME: 20 minutes

450g (1lb) wholemeal flour (atta)
Pinch of salt
75-100g (3-4oz) drained cooked spinach or
50g (2oz) boiled methi leaves
25g (1oz) butter
Vegetable ghee or butter ghee
Water

Sift flour and salt, add boiled spinach or methi and butter. Knead with water to make a soft, pliable dough. Knead well and rest for 5 minutes. Heat a non-stick frying pan or a Tawa. Make 16-18 even-sized balls. Roll each ball out onto a lightly floured surface into a 15-18cm (6-7 inch) circle. Place in Tawa. Cook for 1-3 minutes on low heat. Turn over and cook the other side. Apply vegetable ghee on both sides and shallow fry to light brown. Serve hot or cold.

Kulcha
Kulcha is yeast bread, deep fried.

PREPARATION TIME: 5-6 minutes and 5-6 hours for yeast to rise.
COOKING TIME: 3 minutes

5ml (1 tsp) dried yeast
5ml (1 tsp) sugar
Water
450g (1lb) rice flour
Pinch of salt
50g (2oz) ghee or butter
30ml (2 tblsp) natural yogurt
Oil

Take yeast and sugar and add 15ml (1 tblsp) tepid water. Cover and let it stand. When it becomes frothy it is ready for use. Sift flour and s Add ghee or butter and yogur Knead with water to form a medium-hard dough. Make a w in the centre, add yeast mixtur and knead. Let it rest for 5-6 h in a warm place to rise. Knead again and make a soft, pliable dough. Make 20-25 even-sizec balls. Heat oil and roll each ba into a 5-6cm (2-2½ inch) circl until lightly golden brown, abo 3 minutes. Serve hot or cold w curry.

Stuffed Paratha

PREPARATION TIME: 10 min
COOKING TIME: 30 minutes

450g (1lb) wholemeal flour or chupati atta
Pinch of salt
25g (1oz) ghee or butter
Water
Ghee or oil for frying

Filling
A few florets of cauliflower, chop
Pinch of salt
5ml (1 tsp) cumin seed
1.25ml (1/4 tsp) chilli powder
5ml (1 tsp) ground coriander
Mix the above ingredients togeth

Sift flour and salt. Add ghee or butter and knead with water t make a soft, pliable dough. Ma 16-18 even-sized balls. Take a of dough, make a slight depres in the centre. Fill the centre wi 5ml (1 tsp) of cauliflower mixt Pull the surrounding dough fr around the filling to gather at t top. Roll gently into a complet ball. On a lightly floured floor, each paratha into a 15-18cm (6 inch) round. On a preheated T or frying pan, place the paratha it cook for 2 minutes, until litt brown specs appear. Flip over the other side and cook for 2 minutes. Take a little ghee or o and shallow fry parathas on bo sides. Cook each side on low h – until golden brown. Serve hc cold with a curry.

Facing page: Biryani (top), Jhinga Pulao (centre left) an Tahiri (bottom right).

Nan

The actual taste of nan comes by baking the bread in a clay oven. Nan baked in gas or electric ovens does not have the same charcoal flavour.

PREPARATION TIME: 10-15 minutes and 2-3 hours for dough to rest.

COOKING TIME: 30-40 minutes

10ml (2 tsp) dried yeast
5ml (1 tsp) sugar
7.5ml (1½ tsp) bicarbonate of soda
Water
15ml (1 tblsp) sesame or onion seeds
450g (1lb) refined plain flour
Pinch of salt
25-35g (1-1½oz) butter, melted
60g (2½oz) natural yogurt

Mix yeast and sugar and add 15ml (1 tblsp) tepid water. When mixture becomes frothy it is ready for use. Sift flour and salt, add bicarbonate of soda. Make a well and add melted butter, yogurt and yeast mixture. Knead with sufficient water to give a smooth dough. Cover and rest to rise for 2-3 hours. Knead again and make 16-17 balls. Roll each ball into either an elongated flat bread – 15x25cm (6 x 10 ins) or a 15-18cm (6-7 inch) circle on a lightly floured surface. Coat with butter and sprinkle with a few onion or sesame seeds. Bake in oven, preheated to Gas Mark 6 (200°C or 400°F), for 5-6 minutes. When ready the bread will have brown spots on it. Serve hot.

Sheermaal

PREPARATION TIME: 10 minutes and time for yeast to rise.

COOKING TIME: 30-40 minutes

450g (1lb) self-raising flour
Pinch of salt
40ml (8 tsp) sugar
75g (3oz) butter or margarine
15ml (1 tblsp) dried yeast
1 cup tepid water
Milk
Sesame seed

Sift flour and salt, add 35ml (7 tsp) sugar. Add butter or margarine. Mix yeast with 1 cup water and add 5ml (1 tsp) sugar, mix and leave to rise. When frothy, add to flour. Knead with water to make a soft dough. Let it rest. When risen to twice its volume, knead again for 4-5 minutes. Divide into 10 equal portions. Roll each one out into a round or oblong shape of 5mm (¼ inch) thick. Brush with milk and sprinkle with sesame seeds. Preheat oven to Gas Mark 5 (190°C - 375°F) and bake for 5 minutes. Turn over and bake for a further 5 minutes until light brown and cooked.

Below: Saag Paratha (top left), Stuffed Paratha (top right) and Kulcha (botto

Paratha

Parathas are shallow-fried breads.

PREPARATION TIME: 10 minutes

COOKING TIME: 25 minutes

450g (1lb) wholemeal flour (atta)
Pinch of salt
Water
Ghee for frying
Butter

Sift flour and salt. Add water and knead into a soft dough. Knead well and keep aside to rest for 5 minutes. Make 16-18 even-sized balls. Roll each ball out into a 5cm (2 inch) circle. Apply 1.25ml (¼ tsp) butter. Fold in half and apply a little butter and fold in half again to make a triangular shape. On a floured surface roll each into a 15cm (6 inch) triangle. Heat a frying pan or a Tawa. Place the paratha on it. Cook for 1-2 minutes. Flip over and cook fo[r] minutes. Apply a little ghee on surface and flip over and fry firs[t] side again. Repeat for second si[de]. Both sides should be browned [and] pressed with a spatula to cook corners. Make the remaining parathas up as above and stack them. Serve hot or cold with c[u]

Facing page: Sheermal (top), Nan (centre) and Pita (botto[m])

Roti/Chapati/Phulka

PREPARATION TIME: 6 minutes
COOKING TIME: 20 minutes

450g (1lb) plain wholemeal flour (Atta)
Pinch of salt
130-175ml (4-6 fl oz) water

Sift flour and salt into a mixing bowl. Knead to a soft, pliable dough with water and leave to rest for 5 minutes. Make 16-20 even-sized balls and roll one ball out on lightly floured surface to a circle of 18cm (7ins). Heat a non-stick frying pan or Indian bread griddle known as 'Tawa'. Place the rolled circle on it. When little bubbles appear, turn over and cook for ½ minute. Place under preheated grill. The roti will swell, turn over to the other side. Make the rest in the same way and stack them. A little butter may be applied to keep the rotis soft on one side. Keep them well wrapped in a clean tea cloth or baking foil.

Alternative method:
The roti can be cooked for 1-1½ minutes on each side in the frying pan until little brown specs appear. Make them puff up by pressing with tea cloth to rotate the steam.

Puri

These are deep-fried, little, round breads.

PREPARATION TIME: 6 minutes
COOKING TIME: 10 minutes

450g (1lb) wholemeal flour or chupati atta
Pinch of salt
50g (2oz) ghee or 45ml (3 tblsp) oil
Water
Oil for deep frying

Sift flour and salt and add ghee or oil. Knead with water to make a soft, pliable dough. Knead well and allow to stand for 5 minutes. Make 25-30 small balls. Roll each ball out into a small circle 5-6cm (2-2½ inches) in diameter. Heat oil, drop in a tiny bit of dough. When the dough surfaces immediately, the oil is ready. If not then wait for oil to heat to right temperature. Slide one puri into the oil. Press gently with a straining spoon. Turn over and the puri will swell. It may need a little pressing. Cook for 1-2 minutes until it is light brown. The side of the puri which goes in first, always has a thin crust, the other side will always have a thick side. When this thick side is light brown the puri is cooked. Fry all the puri and serve hot or cold with a curry or chutney, or both.

Roti/Chapati/Phulka (left), Paratha (top left) and Puri (above).

Sherbets and Snacks

Green Mango Sherbet

PREPARATION TIME: 10-12 minutes

2 green, unripened mangoes
1 litre (1¾ pints) water
Pinch of salt
Sugar to taste
Crushed ice

Boil mangoes for 10 minutes. Remove from water and cool. Remove skin gently. Scrape all the pulp from around the stone and skin. Dissolve pulp in water. Add salt and sugar. Stir well to mix. Serve on a bed of ice.

Mint Barley

PREPARATION TIME: 15 minutes

600-750ml (1-1¼ pints) water
75g or 3oz broken barley
6-8 mint leaves, finely chopped
Pinch of salt
Sugar to taste
Fresh lemon juice

Boil 300ml (½ pint) water and add barley. Simmer for 5 minutes. Strain and discard barley. Add remaining water and finely chopped mint leaves. Add salt and sugar to taste. Chill and serve on ice with lemon juice.

Lemon Sherbet

PREPARATION TIME: 5 minutes

Sugar to taste
Pinch of salt
1.2 litres (2 pints) water
Juice of 2 lemons
5ml (1 tsp) grated lemon rind
Few mint leaves, bruised
Ice cubes

Dissolve sugar and salt in water. Add lemon juice and lemon rind. Add mint leaves and stir well. Serve in tall glasses with ice. 120ml (4 fl oz) of gin or vodka may be added.

Lassi
(YOGURT SHERBET)

PREPARATION TIME: 5-7 mi

300ml (½ pint) natural yogurt
50g (2oz) sugar
Pinch of salt
1 litre (1¾ pints) water
Pinch of saffron
10ml (2 tsp) lemon juice
Ice cubes

In a mixing bowl beat yogurt w add sugar and salt, beat again a add water. Dissolve sugar by stirring well. Add saffron and lemon juice and serve with ice cubes.

Tandi Masala Chaa
(SPICED ICED TEA)

PREPARATION TIME: 10 min

600ml (1 pint) water
1 teabag or
10ml or 2 tsp orange peko tea le
Sugar to taste
4 cloves
2.5cm (1 inch) cinnamon stick
4 small cardamoms, seeds remo and ground
Crushed ice
Fresh lemon juice

Boil 150ml (¼ pint) of water. P tea, sugar, cloves, cinnamon sti and crushed cardamom seeds i teapot. Pour in boiling water a allow to stand for 2-4 minutes. well, strain and mix with remai cold water. Allow to cool. Mix serve in tall glasses with crushe and lemon juice to taste.

This page: Lassi (left), Mint Barley (centre) and Tandi Masala Chaaey (right).

Facing page: Badam Ka She (left), Lemon Sherbet (centr and Spiced Grape Sherbet (right).

(Normally served before the meal)

Spiced Grape Sherbet

PREPARATION TIME: 10 minutes

225g (8oz) white seedless grapes
100g (4oz) black grapes, seeded
2 cloves
1 litre (1¾ pints) water
Pinch of salt
6 small cardamoms, seeds removed and crushed
Sugar to taste
10ml (2 tsp) lemon juice
Pinch of freshly ground pepper
Pinch of ground cinnamon
Crushed ice

Wash grapes and liquidise with cloves, strain through a sieve to collect juice. Add 1 cup/8 fl oz water to grapes and strain once again to collect the juice. Mix grape juice with remaining water and dissolve salt, crushed cardamom seeds and sugar. Add lemon juice, pepper and cinnamon. Mix well. Serve on crushed ice.

Passion Fruit Sherbet

PREPARATION TIME: 10 minutes

8-10 passion fruits
750ml (1¼ pints) water
Sugar
Pinch of salt
1-2 drops of red food colouring (optional)
Ice cubes

Cut passion fruits in half. Remove the pulp and blend with the water. Strain and dissolve sugar; add salt. Add red food colouring, if desired, this will make the sherbet pink. Serve with ice cubes.

Blackcurrant Sherbet

PREPARATION TIME: 10 minutes

100-175g or 4-6oz fresh or frozen blackcurrants
750ml (1¼ pints) water
50-60g or 2-3oz sugar
Pinch of salt
15ml (1 tblsp) lemon juice
Ice cubes

Mash blackcurrants in a bowl or blend them in a liquidiser. Add water and mix well, then strain. Dissolve sugar and salt and add lemon juice. Serve with ice cubes.

Badam Ka Sherbet
(ALMOND SHERBET)

PREPARATION TIME: 10 minutes

450ml (¾ pint) milk
150ml (¼ pint) water
60g (2½oz) sugar
15g (½oz) blanched almonds, soaked in water
15g (½oz) pistachio nuts, soaked and skins removed
Pinch of saffron
6 small cardamoms, seeds removed and crushed
3-4 drops rosewater
Ice cubes

Mix milk and water and dissolve sugar. Liquidise almonds and pistachio nuts with a little diluted milk. Dissolve saffron, add crushed seeds of cardamom and add rose essence. Serve with ice cubes or well chilled.

Dahi - Wada
(DAAL DUMPLINGS IN YOGURT)

PREPARATION TIME: 5 minutes and 1 hour for soaking

COOKING TIME: 30 minutes

100g (4oz) urid daal, washed and soaked for 1 hour
50g (2oz) moong daal, washed and soaked for 1 hour
2.5ml (½ tsp) salt
2.5cm (1 inch) ginger root, peeled and finely chopped
1.25ml (¼ tsp) chilli powder or
2 green chillis, finely chopped
50g (2oz) mixed sultanas and raisins
Oil for deep frying

For Yogurt Sauce:
450-600ml (¾-1 pint) natural yogurt
1.25ml (¼ tsp) salt
2.5ml (½ tsp) cumin seed
Water to dip fried wada
2 sprigs coriander, chopped for garnish

Blend drained urid daal and moong daal with sufficient water in a liquidiser to make a very thick purée. Put liquidized urid and moong daal into mixing bowl, add salt, ginger, chillis and mixed fruits. Mix well. Heat oil for deep frying. Add small spoonfuls of the mixture to the hot oil to make small dumplings. To make more uniform wadas, you could wet your hands in water and form a little mixture into a flat, round shape before gently lowering the mixture into the oil. Fry both sides for 3-4 minutes or until golden brown. Drain on kitchen paper. Make all the wadas in this way. Mix yogurt and salt together. Soak fried wadas in water for 2-3 minutes. Gently squeeze out any excess water, arrange in a flat serving dish. Pour the yogurt evenly over them. In a hot frying pan, dry roast cumin and coriander seeds for 1-2 minutes. Place the roasted spices in folded kitchen paper and, with a rolling pin, coarsely grind to a powder. Sprinkle ground spice mixture o the yogurt. Garnish with chopp fresh green coriander. Alternativ sprinkle with a pinch of paprika powder.

Pakoras or Bhajias
(DEEP FRIED CHICK PEA FLOUR FRITTERS)

PREPARATION TIME: 15 minut

COOKING TIME: 10 minutes

100g (4oz) baisen flour (chick pea flour)
Pinch of salt
2.5ml (½ tsp) chilli powder
2.5ml (½ tsp) bicarbonate of soda
Water to make batter
Oil for deep frying

Vegetables and Fruits
1 small potato, peeled and sliced i ⅛ inch thick wafers
1 small aubergine, cut into thin sl
1 small onion, sliced
1 green pepper, seeded and sliced rings
3-4 florets of cauliflower, separate into smaller pieces

Mix baisen flour, salt, chilli pow and soda and make a medium consistency batter with water. M well and allow to stand for 3-4 minutes. Heat oil for deep frying Dip prepared vegetables one by one into the batter, coat well an fry them a few at a time for 4-5 minutes in hot oil until golden brown on both sides. Drain well Serve hot or cold with chutney.

Other suggestions:
Pineapple rings, apples, tomatoe spinach leaves, green chillis, bre slices cut in quarter, semi-ripe bananas, sweet potatoes, swede, parsnips, chicken and fish pieces

This page: Blackcurrant Sher (centre) and Passion Fruit Sherbet (right).

Facing page: Pakoras (top), Ghoogni (centre left) and Da Wada (bottom).

Crispy Rolls or Curry Patties

PREPARATION TIME: 1 hour

COOKING TIME: 30 minutes

225-275g (8-10oz) plain flour
Salt
15ml (1 tblsp) cornflour
1.25ml (¼ tsp) bicarbonate of soda
25g (1oz) butter or margarine
Water
Paste

Take 2 tsp (10ml) flour and a little water to make a thick paste. Crispy rolls can be made with either a vegetable or meat filling. The rolls themselves are made in the same way for either filling. Sift flour, salt, cornflour and soda. Rub in butter. Make dough with water. Knead well and leave to stand for 10 minutes. Knead once again and divide into 4-6 portions. Roll each portion as thinly as possible on a lightly floured surface. Then cut 10cm (4 inch) squares. Heat frying pan and cook on both sides for ½ minute each. Make the rest similarly. Take a square wrapper and place a little filling slightly above one corner and fold corner over the filling. Bring the two side corners over as if to make the folds of an envelope. Secure with a little water and flour paste and press to seal. Roll over the folded edge to make a neat roll. Seal the flap with water and flour paste. Make all the rolls. Heat oil and fry a few at a time until golden brown. Drain on kitchen paper and serve hot with either chutney or tomato ketchup.

Vegetable Filling
1 onion
30ml (2 tblsp) oil
450g (1lb) potatoes, peeled and cubed
100g (4oz) shelled or frozen peas
Salt
5ml (1 tsp) ground black pepper
Oil for deep frying

Fry onion, in 30ml (2 tblsp) oil for 3-4 minutes. Add cubed boiled potatoes, peas and sprinkle with salt and pepper. Mix well and cook for 3-4 minutes. Cover and allow to cool.

Meat Filling
15ml (1 tblsp) oil
1 onion, peeled and sliced thinly
50g (2oz) grated cabbage
50g (2oz) grated carrots
50g (2oz) sliced green beans
50g (2oz) frozen peas
Salt
2.5ml (½ tsp) ground black pepper
50g (2oz) sprouted beans
225g (8oz) cooked meat (any kind) shredded
10-15ml (2-3 tsp) lemon juice

Heat oil and fry onions for 2 minutes. Add cabbage and carrots and fry for 3 minutes. Add green beans, peas and sprinkle with salt and black pepper. Cover and cook for 4-5 minutes. Add sprouted beans and stir fry for 2 minutes. Add shredded meat. Mix well, add lemon juice and stir the mixture. Cook for 2-3 minutes. Remove from heat, cool and use for filling.

Aloo-Bonda
(POTATO BALLS IN BATTER)

PREPARATION TIME: 20 minutes

COOKING TIME: 15 minutes

Batter
100g (4oz) baisen flour (chick pea flour)
Salt
Pinch of baking powder
1.25ml (¼ tsp) chilli powder
150ml (¼ pint) water
Oil for deep frying

Filling
450g (1lb) potatoes, boiled, peeled and cubed
1 onion, peeled and chopped
2 sprigs fresh green coriander, chopped
2.5cm (1 inch) ginger root, peeled and finely chopped
1-2 green chillis, chopped
15ml (1 tbsp) lemon juice or freshly ground black pepper to taste
Salt
10ml (2 tsp) dry mango powder

Sift flour and salt together with baking powder and chilli powder. Add water and mix well to make a smooth batter. If the batter is too thick add a little extra water; if thin add extra sifted baisen flour. Put aside to rest. In a large bowl, put cubed potatoes, chopped onions, coriander, ginger, chillis and lemon juice, mix well and sprinkle with pepper, salt and mango powder. Mix well and take a small lump to form a smooth ball, the size of a golf ball. Mould remaining mixture in the same way. Heat oil and dip potato bonda in baisen batter, coat well and slide them into the oil. Fry a few at a time until the bonda are golden brown. Drain on kitchen paper and serve hot with chutney. Aloo-bondas can be eaten cold, but they do not freeze well.

Dokhala

PREPARATION TIME: Overnight for soaking and 10-12 hours for fermenting.

COOKING TIME: 30-40 minutes

450g (1lb) channa daal (split chick pea), washed
1-2 green chillis
2.5cm (1 inch) ginger root, peeled and sliced
Salt to taste
Pinch of asafoetida
5ml (1 tsp) bicarbonate of soda
60ml (3½ fl oz) oil
6-8 curry leaves
2.5ml (½ tsp) mustard seed
45ml (3 tblsp) fresh grated coconut
2 sprigs coriander leaves, chopped

Soak channa daal overnight. Drain and grind with a little water, the green chillis and ginger to a coarse paste. Beat with a circular motion to incorporate air and leave to ferment for 10-12 hours (use a warm place like an airing cupboard and cover the pan). After it has fermented add salt, asafoetida, soda and half the oil. If too thick, add 30ml (2 tblsp) water. Beat again. Grease a flat 5-6cm (2-2½ inch) deep pie dish with oil. Spread the mixture on it about 2.5cm (1 inch) thick. Steam over a large saucepan for 15-20 minutes. Allow to cool slightly. Heat remaining oil, add curry leaves and mustard seeds and pour over dokhala evenly. Serve garnished with grated coconut and chopped coriander leaves, cut dokhala into 2.5cm (1 inch) square pieces. Dokhala can be frozen for future use.

Khari Sevian
(SAVOURY MINCE VERMICELLI)

PREPARATION TIME: 10 minutes

COOKING TIME: 20 minutes for mince and 10 minutes for sevian

1 onion, peeled and finely chopped
25g (1oz) ghee or
22ml (1½ tblsp) oil
2.5ml (½ tsp) ginger paste
1.25ml (¼ tsp) garlic paste
225g (8oz) lamb or beef mince

Salt
5ml (1 tsp) ground black pepper
50g (2oz) butter
225g (8oz) vermicelli, broken into smaller pieces
Juice of 1 lemon

Fry onion in ghee or oil for 3-4 minutes. Add ginger, garlic, mince and salt. Fry for 6-7 minutes. Add ground black pepper. Mix well. Cover and cook until mince is dry. Remove from heat and put aside. In a non-stick pan, heat butter and fry vermicelli for 1-2 minutes. Add cooked mince and stir fry for 1 minute. Add 300ml (½ pint) water. Cook until dry. Sprinkle with lemon juice and serve hot.

Khari Sevian (far left), Aloo Bonda (below), Crispy Rolls (centre) and Dokhala (bottom).

Ghoogni
(GREEN PEA FRY OR SPICED GREEN PEAS)

PREPARATION TIME: 5 minutes
COOKING TIME: 10 minutes

1 onion, peeled and chopped
25g (1oz) ghee or
15ml (1 tblsp) oil
2 green chillis, cut in half
2.5cm (1 inch) ginger root, peeled and chopped
450g (1lb) shelled or frozen peas
1.25ml (¼ tsp) black ground pepper
2 sprigs fresh green coriander, chopped
1.25ml (¼ tsp) salt
Juice of 1 lemon

Fry onion in ghee or oil until tender (2-3 minutes), add green chillis and ginger. Fry for 1 minute and add green peas. Stir and cook for 5-6 minutes. Add black pepper, chopped coriander and salt. Cook for a further 2 minutes. Pour into a serving dish and sprinkle with lemon juice. Serve hot with tea.

Samosa
(DEEP FRIED STUFFED SAVOURY PASTRIES)

PREPARATION TIME: 30 minutes
COOKING TIME: 15 minutes

100-150g (4-5oz) plain flour
Pinch of salt
2.5ml (½ tsp) baking powder
25g (1oz) ghee or
22ml (1½ tblsp) oil
Water to mix

Flour paste
15ml (1 tblsp) flour mixed with little water to form thick paste
Oil for deep frying

Samosas may be made with either a vegetable or meat filling. The samosas are made in the same way for either filling. Sift flour and salt and add baking powder. Rub in ghee or oil and add the water, a little at a time, to form a dough. Knead well and set aside. When the filling has been made, knead dough again and make 16-20 even-sized balls. On lightly floured surface roll each ball into a thin circle 10-13cm (4-5 inch) round. Cut across the centre and apply the flour paste along the straight edge and bring the two corners together, overlapping slightly to make a cone. Secure by pressing the pasted edges together. Fill the cone with the filling, apply paste to the open mouth and seal the edge. Prepare the rest of the samosas in the same way. Heat oil. When it is moderately hot, fry samosas, a few at a time, until golden brown. Drain on kitchen paper and serve hot or cold with a sweet chutney or plain tomato ketchup.

For Vegetable Filling
15ml (1 tblsp) oil
1 onion, peeled and chopped
10ml (2 tsp) garam masala powder
2.5ml (½ tsp) salt
2.5ml (½ tsp) chilli powder
450g (1lb) potatoes, boiled, peeled, cubed and boiled for 4 to 5 minutes
50g (2oz) frozen or shelled peas
10ml (2 tsp) dry mango powder
Lemon juice

To make filling, heat oil and fry onion until just tender. Sprinkle with garam masala, salt and chilli powder. Fry for one minute and add drained potatoes and peas. Mix well and fry for 2-3 minutes until potatoes are tender. Sprinkle with mango powder or lemon juice. Allow to cool.

Meat Filling
1 onion, peeled and chopped
50g (2oz) ghee or
30ml (2 tblsp) oil
450g (1lb) mince (lamb or beef)
5ml (1 tsp) ginger paste
5ml (1 tsp) garlic paste
10ml (2 tsp) ground black pepper
2.5ml (½ tsp) salt

Fry onion until golden brown in ghee or oil. Add mince, ginger and garlic paste, black ground pepper and salt. Fry the mixture for 8-10 minutes until dry. Remove from pan and allow to cool. Samosas made with mince can be frozen either half fried or unfried. Fry straight from the freezer when required. They can also be thawed before frying without any damage or alteration to taste.

Tikia
(POTATO-MINCE PATTIES)

PREPARATION TIME: 20 minutes
COOKING TIME: 20-30 minutes

1 onion, peeled and chopped
25g (1oz) ghee or
15ml (1tblsp) oil
225g (8oz) minced lamb or beef
100g (4oz) frozen or shelled peas
2 sprigs fresh green coriander leaves, chopped
2-3 small green chillis, chopped (optional)
5ml (1 tsp) ground black pepper
450g (1lb) boiled potatoes, peeled and mashed
5-10ml (1-2 tsp) salt
1-2 beaten eggs
Oil for frying

Fry onion in ghee or oil until just tender (2-3 minutes). Add mince, peas, coriander leaves, chillis and black pepper. Fry for 4-5 minutes. Cool and mix with mashed potatoes and salt. Make 20-25 small, flat burger shapes. Heat the oil in a frying pan and dip tikias in beaten egg to coat. Shallow fry in hot oil. Fry on each side for 2-3 minutes. Serve hot or cold with chutney.

Khageea
(SPICED SCRAMBLED EGG)

PREPARATION TIME: 6 minutes
COOKING TIME: 10 minutes

1 onion, peeled and chopped
30ml (2 tblsp) oil
2.5ml (½ tsp) chilli powder
1.25ml (¼ tsp) turmeric powder
1 green chilli, chopped
2 sprigs fresh coriander leaves, chopped
2 fresh tomatoes, chopped
Salt to taste
15ml (1 tblsp) water
4 well-beaten eggs

Fry onion in oil for 2 minutes. Add spices and green chilli and coriander leaves, stir fry for 1 minute. Add chopped, fresh tomatoes. Season with salt and sprinkle in the water. Add beaten eggs. Cover and cook on gentle heat for 6-7 minutes. Stir and mix egg over gentle heat. Khageea should look like spiced scrambled eggs. Serve with parathas for any meal, including a hearty breakfast.

Wada
(DAAL FRITTERS)

PREPARATION TIME: 2-3 hours
COOKING TIME: 20 minutes

100g (4oz) urid daal, washed an[d] soaked for 2-3 hours
100g (4oz) yellow, dehusked moo[ng] daal, washed and soaked for 2 hours
Little water to grind
1 onion, peeled and finely choppe[d]
5-10ml (1-2 tsp) salt
2-3 sprigs fresh coriander leaves, chopped
1 small green chilli finely chopped
2.5ml (½ tsp) chilli powder
2.5cm (1 inch) ginger root, peeled and finely chopped
1.25ml (¼ tsp) bicarbonate of so[da]
Oil for deep frying

Grind drained urid and moong daal with a little water to a coar[se] thick paste. Pour into a mixing bowl and add onion, salt, coria[nder] leaves, chilli powder or green chillis, ginger and soda. Mix wel[l] and set aside for 4-5 minutes. Fry small spoonfuls of the mixt[ure] a few at a time, for 3-4 minutes until golden brown. Drain and serve hot with chutney.

Omelette

PREPARATION TIME: 5 minut[es]
COOKING TIME: 5 minutes

2 eggs per person, white and yolk separated
1 small onion, finely chopped
1 fresh tomato, thinly sliced
1 green chilli, finely chopped
1 sprig coriander leaves, finely chopped
5ml (1 tsp) water
Salt to taste
15ml (1 tblsp) oil

Beat egg white until stiff. Add e[gg] yolk and beat well. Mix in chop[ped] onion, tomato, chilli, coriander [and] water. Grease a frying pan well w[ith] oil. Heat the pan and pour the e[gg] mixture into it. Sprinkle with sal[t] to taste. Cover and cook the omelette for 2-3 minutes until th[e] sides leave the pan. With a flat

Facing page: Tikia (top left), Samosa (top right) and Wada (bottom).

spoon or spatula ease the base of the omelette and turn it over to cook the other side. Cover and cook for another 2-3 minutes. Serve hot with tomato ketchup or chutney, along with rotis or parathas.

Ganthia
(BAISEN STICKS)

PREPARATION TIME: 10 minutes
COOKING TIME: 10-15 minutes

225g (8oz) baisen flour (chick pea flour)
1.25-2.5ml (¼-½ tsp) salt
2.5ml (½ tsp) bicarbonate of soda
2.5ml (½ tsp) omum (ajwain)
20 whole peppercorns, crushed
Pinch of asafoetida
50ml (2½ fl oz) oil
Oil for frying
Water

Sift flour, salt, bicarbonate of soda and omum together. Add crushed peppercorns, asafoetida and 30ml (1½ fl oz) warm oil. Rub in well and knead with water to make a stiff dough. Take 5ml (1 tsp) oil, rub over dough and knead. Repeat 3-4 times until dough is quiet smooth. Pass lumps of dough, through sev mould or spaghetti machine, with a large hole setting. Fry baisen sticks in hot oil until golden brown and crisp over a low heat. Drain on kitchen paper and store in airtight containers. Serve with tea or drinks.

Egg Curry

PREPARATION TIME: 10 minutes
COOKING TIME: 20 minutes

1 large onion, peeled and chopped
25g (1oz) ghee or
15ml (1 tblsp) oil
2.5cm (1 inch) cinnamon stick
1 bayleaf
4 small cardamoms
6 cloves
5ml (1 tsp) garlic paste
5ml (1 tsp) ginger paste
5ml (1 tsp) ground coriander
5ml (1 tsp) ground cumin
1.25ml (¼ tsp) turmeric powder
5ml (1 tsp) garam masala powder
5ml (1 tsp) chilli powder
200-225g (7-8oz) canned tomatoes, crushed
Salt to taste
175ml (6 fl oz) water
4-6 eggs, hard boiled and shelled
2 sprigs fresh green coriander leaves, chopped
2 green chillis, chopped

Fry onion in oil for 2-3 minutes. Add cinnamon, bayleaf, cardamoms, cloves. Fry for 1 minute. Add ginger and garlic paste. Stir the mixture, add coriander, cumin, turmeric, garam masala and chilli powder. Add canned tomatoes and salt to taste. Cook the spices for 5 minutes. Add water, cover and bring to boil. Add eggs and cook for 10-12 minutes. Garnish with green chillis and fresh coriander leaves. The gravy can be increased or reduced as required. Serve with plain boiled rice.

Nimki and Papadi

PREPARATION TIME: 10 minutes
COOKING TIME: 15-20 minutes

225g (8oz) plain flour
1.25g (¼ tsp) salt
2.5ml (½ tsp) bicarbonate of soda
5ml (1 tsp) onion seed (kalongi)
2.5ml (½ tsp) omum
Pinch of asafoetida
50g (2oz) ghee or
45ml (3 tblsp) oil
Water
Oil for deep frying

Sift flour, salt, bicarbonate of soda, and add onion seed and omum. Add asafoetida and rub in ghee or oil. Knead with water to make a stiff dough. Knead for 3-4 minutes until smooth. Make 2 equal portions. Roll out each portion as thinly as possible, to about 3mm (⅛ inch) thickness. Then cut the first piece of dough diagonally into strips both ways to make small bite size diamond shapes and prick with fork. Roll out the other dough to a similar thickness and cut neat, round shapes with a clean, sharp jar lid or a biscuit cutter. Heat the oil and fry the shapes until golden brown and crisp. Drain on kitchen paper and allow to cool before storing them in jars or tins. These can be stored for up to 2 months. Serve with tea or drinks. The diamond shapes are called nimki and the round shapes are called papadi.

Ganthia (top) and Nimki and Papadi (bottom).

HEALTHY EATING

Introduction

For most of us, eating is one of life's great pleasures, with delectable flavours and aromas, and bright colours and textures, all stimulating our appetites. Unfortunately, these pleasurable aspects of food and eating often lead us to eat more than we need, and to crave for the wrong sorts of food. Wise decisions for healthy eating need to be made with some basic knowledge of nutrition.

What is Healthy Eating?

For optimum health we need a diet that regularly contains carbohydrates, proteins, fat, vitamins and minerals. Some foods are particularly rich in one nutrient, whereas others contain three or more. Each of the following nutrients is essential to the body.

Protein: for body growth and cell replacement.
Carbohydrate: for energy.
Fibre: aids digestion, and helps to prevent digestive-associated complaints.
Fat: concentrated source of energy; also provides vitamins A, D, E and K.
Vitamin A: for healthy eyes and strong bones and teeth.
Vitamin B: necessary for healthy skin, as well as the digestive and nervous system and blood formation.
Vitamin C: increases resistance to infection; aids healing of wounds.
Vitamin D: helps strengthen teeth and bones.
Calcium: strengthens teeth and bones; essential to the nervous system, muscles, heart and blood.
Iron: maintains haemoglobin in the blood.

Generally speaking, we all eat a diet which is too rich in fat (espec animal fat), too high in refined sugar, too high in salt, and too lo natural fibre.

General Guidelines for a Healthy Eating Pattern.

Eat white fish, chicken, turkey and veal as the main protein m
Eat low fat cheeses, such as curd and cottage cheese, rather thar high fat cheeses such as Cheddar.
Use skimmed milk in place of full fat milk, both for drinks anc cooking.
Use the minimum amount of margarine or butter for spreadin bread and toast, and use olive oil for cooking wherever possib
If dishes need sweetening, use an unrefined sugar or honey – pe who are also trying to lose weight can use an artificial sweet instead (choose a good one).
Choose breads and cereals which are rich in fibre – wholemeal br brown rice, wholewheat pasta, etc.
Eat plenty of fresh fruits and vegetables, raw whenever possib
Choose healthy cooking methods – poaching, baking, cassero etc. If frying is a necessary stage in a recipe, use the minimum amc of fat.

Recipes

All the recipes in this section have been put together in such a that they not only offer a good balance of nutrients, but also fol the healthy eating guidelines listed above. They also taste delici

Facing page: Noodles with Kidney Beans and Pesto (top) and Cucumber with Yogurt, Dill and Burghul (bottom).

Soups and Starters

Houmus with Lime and Pine Kernels

PREPARATION TIME: 15 minutes, plus soaking and chilling time
COOKING TIME: 1 hour
SERVES: 4 people

100g (4oz) dried chick peas
Salt and freshly ground black pepper to taste
Juice of 2 limes
2 large cloves garlic, peeled and crushed
30ml (2 tblsp) natural yogurt
15ml (1 tblsp) tahina (sesame seed paste)
15ml (1 tblsp) pine kernels, lightly toasted and chopped

Garnish
Wedges of fresh lime

To Serve
Warm wholemeal pitta bread, or fingers of hot wholemeal toast

Soak the chick peas in cold water overnight. Drain the chick peas and put them into a pan with sufficient fresh cold water to cover; add 5ml (1 tsp) salt. Bring to the boil and simmer, covered, for 1 hour, until the chick peas are tender. Drain thoroughly and allow the chick peas to cool slightly. Put the chick peas into the liquidiser with the lime juice, garlic, yogurt, tahina, and salt and pepper to taste; blend until smooth. Cover and chill for 2-3 hours. Stir in the toasted pine kernels. Spoon into a bowl, or onto small serving plates, and garnish with wedges of lime. Serve with warm pitta bread, or fingers of hot toast.
Note: this houmus also makes a delicious dip to serve with sticks of raw vegetables.

Avocado and Smoked Salmon Mousse

PREPARATION TIME: 40 minutes, plus chilling time
SERVES: 4 people

1 large ripe avocado
Juice and grated rind of ½ lemon
150ml (¼ pint) natural yogurt
Salt and freshly ground black pepper to taste
2 drops Tabasco
60ml (4 tblsp) dry white wine
10ml (2 tsp) powdered gelatine
100g (4oz) smoked salmon trimmings, finely chopped
15ml (1 tblsp) chopped chives

Garnish
Lemon peel leaves
4 small curls smoked salmon

Peel, halve and stone the avocado. Chop the avocado flesh and put it into the liquidiser with the lemon juice and rind, yogurt, salt and pepper to taste, Tabasco and half

This page: Houmus with Li and Pine Kernels (top right Avocado and Smoked Saln Mousse (top left), Leek and Cashew Nut Soup (bottom) Facing page: Spinach Rame (top), Courgette and Lemo Soup (centre left) and Chi Liver and Tarragon Pate (bottom).

the white wine. Blend until smooth. Dissolve the gelatine in the remaining white wine and blend into the avocado mixture. Leave on one side until the mixture starts to thicken. Lightly grease 4 small decorative moulds. Mix the smoked salmon and chives into the thickened avocado mixture; spoon into the prepared moulds. Chill until set. Unmould the set mousses carefully onto small plates. Garnish with lemon peel leaves and small curls of smoked salmon.

Leek and Cashew Nut Soup

PREPARATION TIME: 15-20 minutes

COOKING TIME: 30-35 minutes

SERVES: 4 people

1 medium onion, thinly sliced.
30ml (2 tblsp) olive oil
1 clove garlic, peeled and crushed
6 medium size leeks, halved, washed and shredded
300ml (½ pint) skimmed milk
450ml (¾ pint) chicken stock
Salt and freshly ground black pepper to taste
75g (3oz) shelled cashew nuts, lightly toasted

Garnish
Matchstick strips of leek
A few lightly toasted cashew nuts, finely chopped (optional)

Fry the onion gently in the olive oil for 3 minutes. Add the garlic and shredded leeks and fry together for a further 3 minutes. Add the skimmed milk, chicken stock, and salt and pepper to taste. Bring to the boil and simmer gently for 20-25 minutes. Blend the soup in the liquidiser, together with the toasted cashew nuts, until smooth. Reheat the soup gently in a clean saucepan. Serve each portion garnished with a few strips of leek and a sprinkling of toasted cashews.

Spinach Ramekins

PREPARATION TIME: 25 minutes

COOKING TIME: 35 minutes

OVEN: 180°C, 350°F, Gas Mark 4

SERVES: 4 people

450g (1lb) fresh spinach, cooked and drained thoroughly
Salt and freshly ground black pepper to taste
Pinch ground nutmeg
2 eggs
2 egg yolks
60ml (4 tblsp) fresh wholemeal breadcrumbs
30ml (2 tblsp) natural yogurt
30ml (2 tblsp) grated Parmesan cheese
8-12 small spinach leaves

Garnish
Sprigs fresh dill
Small twists of lemon

Mix the cooked spinach with the salt and pepper to taste, nutmeg, whole eggs, egg yolks, breadcrumbs, yogurt and Parmesan cheese. Line 4 lightly greased cocotte dishes or ramekins with the spinach leaves, pressing them in well to fit the shape of the dishes. Spoon in the spinach and egg mixture carefully. Stand the dishes in a roasting tin an add sufficient hot water to come halfway up the sides. Bake in the oven for 35 minutes, until just set. The Spinach Ramekins can either be served hot or cold. Unmould each one carefully onto a small serving plate. Garnish with sprigs of fresh dill and twists of lemon, and serve with fingers of lightly buttered brown bread.
Note: the mixture can be baked in a small loaf tin, if preferred, and served cut into slices.

Spicy Rice Stuffed Mushrooms

PREPARATION TIME: 20 minutes

COOKING TIME: 20-25 minutes

OVEN: 190°C, 375°F, Gas Mark 5

SERVES: 4 people

12 medium size flat mushrooms
1 small onion, finely chopped
30ml (2 tblsp) olive oil
1 clove garlic, peeled and crushed
30ml (2 tblsp) chopped parsley
120ml (8 tblsp) cooked brown rice
1 egg, beaten
30ml (2 tblsp) grated Parmesan cheese
Salt and freshly ground black pepper to taste
Generous pinch ground cinnamon

Garnish
Small radicchio leaves
Sprigs fresh parsley

Remove the stalks from the mushrooms and chop the stalks finely. Peel the mushrooms and place them dark side uppermost in a lightly greased ovenproof dish. Fry the onion gently in half the olive oil for 2-3 minutes. Add the garlic and chopped mushroom stalks and fry for a further 3 minutes. Mix with the parsley, cooked brown rice, beaten egg, half the Parmesan cheese, salt and pepper to taste and the cinnamon. Spoon the savoury mixture on top of each mushroom and dribble over the remaining olive oil. Bake in the oven for 15-20 minutes. Serve piping hot, garnished with small radicchio leaves and parsley sprigs.

Celery and Hazelnut Soup

PREPARATION TIME: 15 minutes

COOKING TIME: 30-35 minutes

SERVES: 4 people

1 medium onion, thinly sliced
30ml (2 tblsp) olive oil
6-8 stems celery, finely chopped
1 bayleaf
Salt and freshly ground black pepper to taste
30ml (2 tblsp) ground hazelnuts
300ml (½ pint) skimmed milk
450ml (¾ pint) chicken stock

Garnish
Small celery leaves
A few flaked hazelnuts

Fry the onion gently in the olive oil for 3 minutes. Add the celery and fry for a further 3 minutes. Add the bayleaf, salt and pepper to taste, ground hazelnuts, skimmed milk and chicken stock. Bring to the boil and simmer gently for 20-25 minutes. Blend the soup in the liquidiser until smooth. Reheat the soup gently in a clean saucepan. Serve each portion garnished with a celery leaf and a sprinkling of flaked hazelnuts.

Courgette and Lemon Soup

PREPARATION TIME: 20 minutes, plus chilling time

COOKING TIME: about 25 minutes

SERVES: 4 people

1 medium onion, thinly sliced
30ml (2 tblsp) olive oil
450g (1lb) courgettes, topped and tailed, and sliced
Finely grated rind of 1 lemon
450ml (¾ pint) chicken stock
Salt and freshly ground black pepper to taste
2 egg yolks
200ml (⅓ pint) natural yogurt

Garnish
Thin slices of courgette
Small sprigs of mint (optional)

Fry the onion gently in the oli
for 3 minutes. Add the courge
and fry for a further 2-3 minu
Add the lemon rind, chicken s
and salt and pepper to taste. B
to the boil and simmer, covere
20 minutes. Blend the soup in
liquidiser until smooth. If you
serving the soup hot, reheat th
soup in a clean pan with the b
egg yolks and yogurt – do not
to re-boil. To serve the soup c
cool the blended soup slightly
add the beaten egg yolks and
yogurt. Chill thoroughly. Garn
each portion of soup with a th
slice of courgette and a sprig o
mint.

Tomato and Orange Soup

PREPARATION TIME: 15 min

COOKING TIME: about 25 minutes

SERVES: 4 people

1kg (2¼lbs) ripe tomatoes, skin seeded and chopped
15ml (1 tblsp) olive oil
1 clove garlic, peeled and crushe
Finely grated rind of ½ an oran
450ml (¾ pint) chicken stock
150ml (¼ pint) fresh orange jui
Salt and freshly ground black pe to taste
5ml (1 tsp) honey

Garnish
Twists of orange peel
A little natural yogurt

Put the chopped tomatoes, oli
oil, garlic and orange rind into
pan; cover the pan and 'sweat'
gently over a moderate heat fo
minutes. Add the chicken sto
orange juice, salt and pepper t
taste, and the honey. Cover an
simmer gently for 20 minutes.
Blend the soup in the liquidise
until smooth. The prepared so
can either be served hot or chi
Serve each portion garnished
a twist or two of orange peel a
swirl of natural yogurt.

icy Rice Stuffed Mushroom ght), Tomato and Orange up (below) and Celery and zelnut Soup (bottom).

Smoked Halibut with Yogurt and Lumpfish

PREPARATION TIME: 10-15 minutes

SERVES: 4 people

225g (8oz) smoked halibut, thinly sliced
60ml (4 tblsp) natural yogurt
30ml (2 tblsp) orange lumpfish roe
Salt and freshly ground black pepper to taste
Half a lemon

Garnish
Small sprigs fennel or dill

To Serve
Small triangles lightly buttered brown bread

Arrange the slices of smoked halibut on 4 small plates. Mix the yogurt with half the lumpfish and salt and pepper to taste. Add a squeeze of lemon juice. Squeeze the remaining lemon juice over the halibut. Spoon a little yogurt sauce into the centre of each portion; top with the remaining lumpfish roe. Garnish each portion with a few sprigs of fennel. Serve with triangles of buttered brown bread. Note: if you find smoked halibut difficult to buy, you can use smoked salmon instead.

Aubergine Puree with Crudites

PREPARATION TIME: 25-30 minutes

COOKING TIME: about 10 minutes

SERVES: 4 people

2 medium size aubergines
45ml (3 tblsp) olive oil
2 cloves garlic, peeled and crushed
Juice of 1 lemon
Salt and freshly ground black pepper to taste
10ml (2 tsp) chopped fresh mint

Garnish
Sprigs fresh mint

Grill the aubergines under a moderately hot grill until the skins blister and char – when squeezed with a cloth, the aubergines should feel soft in the centre. Rub the skins off the aubergines under a cold running tap. Squeeze the peeled aubergines in a piece of clean muslin to remove as much of the bitter juices as possible. Put the aubergine flesh into a liquidiser and blend until smooth. Gradually blend in the olive oil, garlic, lemon juice and salt and pepper to taste. Stir in the chopped mint. Cover and chill briefly. Serve with vegetable crudites as dunks: sticks of carrot, cucumber, celery, pepper, small button mushrooms, strips of fennel, etc. Garnish with mint.

Chicken Liver and Tarragon Pate

PREPARATION TIME: 10-15 minutes

COOKING TIME: 7-8 minutes

SERVES: 4 people

1 small onion, finely chopped
15ml (1 tblsp) olive oil
1 clove garlic, peeled and crushed
15ml (1 tblsp) fresh tarragon, chopped
225g (8oz) chicken livers, roughly chopped
15ml (1 tblsp) brandy
30ml (2 tblsp) natural yogurt
Salt and freshly ground black pepper to taste

Garnish
Sprigs fresh tarragon or other herbs

To Serve
Hot wholemeal crusty bread, or toast

Fry the onion gently in the olive oil for 3 minutes. Add the garlic, tarragon and chicken livers and fry gently until sealed on the outside but still pink in the centre. Stir in the brandy and allow to bubble for 30 seconds. Put the chicken livers and their liquid into the liquidiser and blend until smooth. Mix in the yogurt and salt and pepper to taste. Spoon into one small terrine, or into several cocotte dishes, and chill. Garnish with fresh tarragon and serve with hot crusty bread or toast.
Note: if you are using small cocotte dishes, the surface of the pate can be smoothed level and a layer of aspic jelly spooned over the top prior to chilling.

Egg and Cheese Mousse with Watercress Sauce

PREPARATION TIME: 25-30 minutes, plus chilling time

COOKING TIME: 2-3 minutes

SERVES: 4 people

225g (8oz) curd cheese, or sieved cottage cheese
150ml (¼ pint) natural yogurt
150ml (¼ pint) chicken stock
10ml (2 tsp) powdered gelatine
Salt and freshly ground black pep[per] to taste
15ml (1 tblsp) chopped parsley
3 hard boiled eggs, shelled and fi[nely] chopped

Sauce
45ml (3 tblsp) chicken stock
1 bunch watercress
1 clove garlic, peeled and crushe[d]
15ml (1 tblsp) pine kernels
60ml (4 tblsp) natural yogurt

Garnish
1 hard boiled egg yolk, sieved
Small sprigs watercress

Lightly grease 4 individual mou[lds] or ramekin dishes. Beat the che[ese] with the yogurt and half the chicken stock until smooth. Dissolve the gelatine in the remaining chicken stock. Stir th[e] gelatine into the cheese mixtur[e] together with salt and pepper t[o] taste, parsley, and the chopped hard boiled eggs. Spoon into th[e] prepared moulds. Chill until se[t,] about 3 hours. Meanwhile, ma[ke] the sauce. Put the chicken stoc[k,] trimmed watercress and garlic i[n] a small pan. Cover and simmer 2-3 minutes. Cool slightly. Blen[d] the watercress and its liquid in liquidiser, together with the pin[e] kernels, until smooth. Stir in th[e] yogurt and chill. To serve, unm[ould] each set mousse onto a small p[late] and spoon a pool of watercress sauce around each one. Garnis[h] with a sprinkling of sieved egg y[olk] and a sprig of watercress.

This page: Aubergine Puree with Crudites (top) and Jelli[ed] Eggs en Cocotte (bottom).

Facing page: Egg and Chees[e] Mousse with Watercress Sau[ce] (top) and Smoked Halibut w[ith] Yogurt and Lumpfish (botto[m]).

Stuffed Vine Leaves

PREPARATION TIME: 40 minutes
COOKING TIME: about 1 hour
SERVES: 6 people

100g (4oz) brown or wild rice
Salt and freshly ground black pepper to taste
450g (1lb) minced chicken
1 small onion, finely chopped
1 clove garlic, peeled and crushed
15ml (1 tblsp) chopped chives
15ml (1 tblsp) chopped fresh coriander
30ml (2 tblsp) chopped parsley
30ml (2 tblsp) chopped sultanas
15ml (1 tblsp) chopped pine kernels
Finely grated rind of ½ small orange
Juice of ½ lemon
225g (8oz) prepared vine leaves (see below)
600ml (1 pint) chicken stock and dry white wine, mixed

To Serve
Thinned natural yogurt
Mixed spice (optional)
Feathery sprigs of dill or fennel

Note: vine leaves are preserved in brine, and this needs rinsing off before they can be used. Put the opened vine leaves into a large bowl and cover with boiling water; leave to stand until the vine leaves can be easily separated. Rinse the vine leaves in cold water and then drain on absorbent paper, veined sides uppermost.
Cook the rice in a pan of boiling salted water for 8 minutes. Drain thoroughly. Mix the par-cooked rice with the minced chicken, chopped onion, garlic, chives, coriander, parsley, sultanas, pine kernels, orange rind, lemon juice, and salt and pepper to taste. Line the base of a large, deep frying pan with 4 large leaves. Divide the prepared filling amongst the remaining leaves, placing each portion towards the base of the leaf. Fold the stem of the leaf over the filling and then fold in the sides; roll up to form a sausage shape. Place the prepared stuffed vine leaves close together in the pan; add salt and pepper to taste and the mixed water and wine. Cover the pan and simmer gently for 50 minutes. Allow the stuffed vine leaves to cool in their cooking liquid. Chill the vine leaves for an hour or two before serving. Serve about 5 stuffed vine leaves per person. Place a pool of yogurt onto each serving plate and top with the chilled vine leaves. Sprinkle with mixed spice and garnish with dill.
Note: the vine leaves can be marinated in a little oil and vinegar dressing, if preferred, prior to chilling.

My Gazpacho

PREPARATION TIME: 25 minutes, plus chilling time
COOKING TIME: 2-3 minutes
SERVES: 4 people

300ml (½ pint) pure tomato juice
300ml (½ pint) chicken stock
½ small cucumber, seeded and chopped
450g (1lb) ripe tomatoes, skinned, seeded and chopped
6 spring onions, chopped
1 green pepper, seeded and chopped
1 red pepper, seeded and chopped
2 cloves garlic, peeled and crushed
2 anchovy fillets, chopped
15ml (1 tblsp) chopped fresh basil
15ml (1 tblsp) dry sherry
Salt and freshly ground black pepper to taste

Garnish
Thinly sliced cucumber
Small sprigs fresh basil

Put the tomato juice and chicken stock into a pan with the chopped cucumber, tomatoes, spring onions, green and red peppers, garlic, anchovies and basil. Bring to the boil, covered, and then remove immediately from the heat. Leave to cool in the covered saucepan (this allows all the flavours to mingle). Once the vegetables and their liquid are quite cool, blend in the liquidiser until smooth, together with the sherry and salt and pepper to taste. Chill the soup thoroughly for at least 4 hours. The soup will be quite thick at this stage, which is characteristic of a 'gazpacho'; however, it can be thinned with a little extra chicken stock if preferred. Ladle the soup into bowls (usually glass ones), adding a few ice cubes to each one. Serve each portion garnished with a few slices of cucumber and a spri of fresh basil.

Jellied Eggs en Cocotte

PREPARATION TIME: 30 minutes, plus chilling time

COOKING TIME: 2 minutes

SERVES: 4 people

4 tomatoes, skinned, seeded and chopped
1 clove garlic, peeled and finely chopped
15ml (1 tblsp) chopped parsley
Salt and freshly ground black pepper to taste
4 eggs
400ml (2/3 pint) beef consomme

Garnish

Finely chopped tomato, or small tomato 'roses'
Sprigs parsley

Mix the chopped tomatoes with the garlic, parsley, and salt and pepper to taste. Divide amongst 4 cocotte dishes. Lower the eggs into a pan of boiling water and cook for 2 minutes – the eggs should be just soft boiled. Cool the eggs under cold, running water. Carefully remove the shells and sit an egg in each cocotte dish. Spoon the consomme into each dish so that it covers the eggs – if the dishes are quite deep, you will need slightly more consomme than the quantity given above. Chill until set. Garnish each dish with a small tomato rose and a sprig of parsley. To make a tomato rose, peel a thin strip of outer flesh from a firm tomato using a small sharp knife or a potato peeler. Wind the tomato strip round and round, easing it out to form the shape of a rose head.

Stuffed Vine Leaves (far left) and My Gazpacho (left).

Fish and Seafood

Smoked Haddock and Egg Quiche

PREPARATION TIME: about 25 minutes

COOKING TIME: about 40 minutes

OVEN: 190°C, 375°F, Gas Mark 5

SERVES: 6 people

225g (8oz) wholemeal pastry
350g (12oz) smoked haddock fillet
Chicken stock
2 hard boiled eggs, chopped
15ml (1 tblsp) chopped chives
75g (3oz) grated cheese
300ml (½ pint) skimmed milk
3 eggs
Salt and freshly ground black pepper to taste

Garnish
2 hard boiled eggs
Finely chopped parsley

Roll out the pastry and use to line a 23cm (9 inch), deep fluted flan case; press up the edges well. Line with greaseproof paper and baking beans and bake 'blind' for 10 minutes. Meanwhile, poach the smoked haddock fillet gently in chicken stock for about 8 minutes, until just tender. Drain the fish and flake it, discarding any skin and bone. Put the flaked smoked haddock into the pastry case with the chopped hard boiled egg, chopped chives and grated cheese. Beat the skimmed milk with the eggs and salt and pepper to taste; pour into the pastry case. Bake for 30 minutes until the filling is just set. Meanwhile, prepare the garnish. Separate the hard boiled egg whites and yolks; chop the whites finely and sieve the yolks. The quiche can either be served hot or cold. Sprinkle the top with chopped egg white, sieved egg yolk and parsley.

Provençal Fish Stew

PREPARATION TIME: about 15 minutes

COOKING TIME: about 35 minutes

SERVES: 4 people

1 medium onion, finely chopped
2 cloves garlic, peeled and crushed
45ml (3 tblsp) olive oil
750g (1½lb) tomatoes, skinned, seeded and chopped
30ml (2 tblsp) tomato puree
600ml (1 pint) dry red wine
Salt and freshly ground black pepper to taste
1¼ litres (2 pints) mussels in their shells, scrubbed
8 large Mediterranean prawns
100g (4oz) peeled prawns
4 crab claws, partly shelled

To Serve
8 small slices stale French bread, or similar crusty bread
A little olive oil
1 large clove garlic
Bruised chopped parsley

Fry the onion gently in the olive oil for 3 minutes. Add the garlic and chopped tomatoes and fry gently for a further 3 minutes. Add the tomato puree and red wine and bring to the boil; simmer for 15 minutes. Add the mussels and

This page: Fish, Courgette [and] Lemon Kebabs (top), Smok[ed] Haddock and Egg Quiche (bottom).

Facing page: Provencale Fis[h] Stew (top) and Baked Sea B[ass] with Fennel and Vegetable Julienne (bottom).

simmer, covered, for 5 minutes. Add the whole Mediterranean prawns, peeled prawns and crab claws, and simmer for a further 5 minutes. Meanwhile, prepare the bread croutes. Brush the slices of French bread with a little olive oil and rub with the crushed clove of garlic. Grill until crisp and golden and then sprinkle with chopped parsley. Spoon the fish stew into a deep serving dish and top with the bread croutes. Serve immediately.

Chilled Fish Curry

PREPARATION TIME: 20 minutes, plus chilling time

COOKING TIME: about 6 minutes

SERVES: 4 people

225g (8oz) fresh salmon
350g (12oz) white fish fillet
Chicken stock
Salt and freshly ground black pepper to taste
150ml (¼ pint) mayonnaise
300ml (½ pint) natural yogurt
10ml (2 tsp) curry powder
Juice and grated rind of ½ lemon
100g (4oz) peeled prawns

Garnish
Sliced, peeled kiwi fruit
Sprigs fresh mint
Flaked coconut

Put the fresh salmon and white fish fillet into a shallow pan and add sufficient chicken stock to just cover. Add salt and pepper to taste; cover and simmer gently until the fish is just tender. Remove the fish carefully from the cooking liquid and allow to cool slightly. Mix the mayonnaise with the yogurt, curry powder, lemon juice and rind, and salt and pepper to taste. Thin the curry sauce down a little with a small amount of the fish cooking liquid. Flake the cooked salmon and white fish and stir lightly into the prepared curry sauce, together with the peeled prawns. Arrange the chilled fish curry on a serving dish and garnish with slices of kiwi fruit, sprigs of fresh mint and a scattering of flaked coconut.

Plaice Tartare

PREPARATION TIME: 25 minutes, plus chilling time

COOKING TIME: 6 minutes

SERVES: 4 people

450g (1lb) plaice or sole fillets
Skimmed milk
Salt and freshly ground black pepper to taste
60ml (4 tblsp) olive oil
Juice of ½ lemon
2.5ml (½ tsp) soft brown sugar
4 anchovy fillets, finely chopped
1 large clove garlic, peeled and crushed
30ml (2 tblsp) chopped parsley
2 hard boiled eggs

Garnish
Small wedges of lemon
Green olives
Capers

Put the fish fillets into a large, shallow pan with sufficient skimmed milk to just cover; add salt and pepper to taste. Cover the pan and poach the fish gently until just tender – about 6 minutes. Meanwhile, make the dressing. Mix the olive oil with the lemon juice, sugar, anchovy fillets, garlic, and salt and pepper to taste. Stir in the chopped parsley. Separate the egg yolks from the whites; chop the whites finely, and sieve the yolks. Add the chopped egg white to the dressing. Drain the cooked fish and flake it; mix lightly with the prepared dressing. Cover and chill for 1 hour. Spoon the prepared plaice tartare onto serving plates; sprinkle each portion with sieved egg yolk. Garnish with wedges of lemon, green olives and capers.

Baked Sea Bass with Fennel and Vegetable Julienne

PREPARATION TIME: 30 minutes

COOKING TIME: 35-40 minutes

OVEN: 190°C, 375°F, Gas Mark 5

SERVES: 4-6 people

1 sea bass, about 1.25kg (2½lb) in weight, scaled, gutted and cleaned
Salt and freshly ground black pepper to taste
15ml (1 tblsp) chopped fresh fennel
1 large clove garlic, peeled and finely chopped
Coarsely grated rind of ½ lemon
30ml (2 tblsp) olive oil
60ml (4 tblsp) dry white wine

Vegetable Julienne
2 large carrots, peeled and cut into thin strips
3 stems celery, cut into thin strips
100g (4oz) haricots vert

Garnish
Feathery sprigs of fennel or dill

Season the sea bass inside and out; put the chopped fennel, garlic and lemon rind into the cavity of the fish. Lay the fish on a rectangle of greased foil, sitting on a baking sheet; pinch up the edges of the foil. Brush the sea bass with olive oil and spoon over the dry white wine. Pinch the foil together over the fish to completely enclose it. Bake in the oven for 35-40 minutes (the foil can be folded back for the last 10 minutes cooking time, if liked). For the vegetable julienne, steam al the vegetables over gently simmering water for about 10 minutes – they should still be slightly crunchy. Arrange the cooked sea bass on a large, oval serving platter, and surround with small 'bundles' of the steamed vegetables. Garnish with sprigs of fennel.

Cod Steaks with Asparagus Sauce and Endive

PREPARATION TIME: 25 minutes

COOKING TIME: 25-30 minutes

OVEN: 190°C, 375°F, Gas Mark 5

SERVES: 4 people

4 even size cod steaks
30ml (2 tblsp) melted butter
Salt and freshly ground black pepper to taste
5ml (1 tsp) fennel seed
450g (1lb) asparagus
150ml (¼ pint) chicken stock
1 egg yolk
45ml (3 tblsp) natural yogurt

Garnish
Curly endive
Feathery pieces of fennel
Thin lemon slices or twists

Put the cod steaks into a lightly greased ovenproof dish. Brush with melted butter; season to taste with salt and pepper and sprinkle over the fennel seed. Cover with a piece of foil and bake for 25-30 minutes, until the fish is just tender. Meanwhile, make the sauce. Trim the asparagus so that you just have nice green tips (use the remaining stems for making soup, etc.). Tie the asparagus tips together and cook upright in a little boiling water until just tender. Drain carefully and reserve 4 tips for garnish. Put the rest of the cooked asparagus tips into the liquidiser with the chicken stock, egg yolk, yogurt and salt and pepper to taste; blend until smooth. Arrange the cooked cod cutlets on a serving dish, and spoon some of the asparagus sauce over the top. Garnish with small pieces of curly endive, feathery pieces of fennel, lemon slices and the reserved asparagus tips. Serve the remaining asparagus sauce separately.

Fish, Courgette and Lemon Kebabs

PREPARATION TIME: 30 min[illegible] plus chilling time

COOKING TIME: about 8 mi[illegible]

SERVES: 4 people

16 small, thin sole fillets, or 8 la[illegible] ones, cut in half lengthways
60ml (4 tblsp) olive oil
1 clove garlic, peeled and crush[illegible]
Juice of ½ lemon
Finely grated rind of ½ lemon
Salt and freshly ground black p[illegible] to taste
3 drops Tabasco
3 medium size courgettes, cut in[illegible] ½cm (¼ inch) slices
1 medium green pepper, halved, seeded and cut into 2.5cm (1[illegible] pieces

Garnish
30ml (2 tblsp) coarsely choppe[illegible] parsley

Roll up each sole fillet, Swiss-[illegible] fashion, and secure with woo[illegible] cocktail sticks. Place them in a[illegible] shallow dish. Mix the olive oi[illegible] the garlic, lemon juice, lemon [illegible] salt and pepper to taste and t[illegible] Tabasco. Spoon evenly over t[illegible] fish. Cover and chill for 2 hou[illegible] Remove the wooden cocktail [illegible] and carefully thread the rolled[illegible] fillets onto kebab skewers tog[illegible] with the courgette slices and [illegible] of green pepper, alternating th[illegible] for colour. Brush each threade[illegible] kebab with the lemon and oil marinade. Grill for about 8 minutes, under a moderately [illegible] grill, carefully turning the keba[illegible] once during cooking. Brush th[illegible] kebabs during cooking with a[illegible] remaining marinade. Place the kebas on a serving dish and sprinkle with chopped parsley.

Plaice and Mushroo[illegible] Turnovers

PREPARATION TIME: 25 mi[illegible] plus cooling time

COOKING TIME: about 35 minutes

OVEN: 200°C, 400°F, Gas Ma[illegible]

SERVES: 4 people

4 large plaice fillets
Salt and freshly ground black p[illegible] to taste
Skimmed milk
Finely grated rind of ½ lemon
100g (4oz) button mushrooms, sliced
25g (1oz) butter
Juice of 1 lemon

Plaice Tartare (left) and Chilled Fish Curry (below).

This page: Plaice and Mushroom Turnovers (top) a Cod Steaks with Asparagus Sauce and Endive (bottom).

Facing page: Taramasalata (t and Sole with Anchovy, Cap and Mint Sauce (bottom).

45ml (3 tblsp) hazelnut stuffing mix
350g (12oz) puff pastry (preferably the vegetable oil variety)
Beaten egg
Poppy seeds

Season each plaice fillet with salt and pepper to taste. Roll up each one Swiss-roll fashion and secure with a wooden cocktail stick. Place in a shallow pan and add sufficient skimmed milk to half cover; cover the pan and poach gently for 5 minutes. Drain the fish and allow to cool. Remove the wooden cocktail sticks. Put the lemon juice, mushrooms and butter into a small pan and cook gently for 5 minutes. Allow to cool and then stir in the hazelnut stuffing mix. Roll out the pastry quite thinly and cut 6 even sized circles, each about 15cm (6 inches) in diameter. Brush the pastry edges with beaten egg. Place a fish fillet in the centre of each pastry circle and top with the mushroom and stuffing mixture; pull the pastry edges up and over the fish and pinch together to seal. Place on a lightly greased baking sheet and glaze with beaten egg. Bake in the oven for about 25 minutes, until well risen, puffed and golden. Serve piping hot.

Sole with Anchovy, Caper and Mint Sauce

PREPARATION TIME: 10-15 minutes

COOKING TIME: 10-12 minutes

SERVES: 4 people

30ml (2 tblsp) chopped fresh mint
60ml (4 tblsp) dry white wine
60ml (4 tblsp) olive oil
1 large clove garlic, peeled and finely chopped
Juice of 1 large orange
15ml (1 tblsp) capers
3 anchovy fillets, finely chopped
Salt and freshly ground black pepper to taste
8 good size sole fillets
Seasoned flour
25g (1oz) butter

Garnish
Matchstick strips orange peel
Small sprigs fresh mint

Mix half the chopped mint with the white wine, 45ml (3 tblsp) of the olive oil, the garlic, orange juice, capers, anchovy fillets and salt and pepper to taste. Dust the sole fillets very lightly in seasoned flour. Heat the remaining oil and the butter in a large, shallow pan with the remaining mint. Fry the sole fillets for 2-3 minutes on either side (you will find this easier if you fry the fillets in two batches). Remove the cooked fillets carefully to a shal serving dish and spoon over th prepared anchovy, caper and m sauce. The sole fillets can either served warm or chilled. Garnis with matchstick strips of orang peel and small sprigs of mint.

Taramasalata

PREPARATION TIME: about 20 minu

SERVES: 4 people

3 slices wholemeal bread, crusts removed
75ml (5 tblsp) water
100g (4oz) smoked cod's roe, skin
1 large clove garlic, peeled and crushed
Juice of 1 lemon
90ml (6 tblsp) olive oil
Salt and freshly ground black pep to taste

To Serve
Wholemeal pitta bread
Olives (black or green)

Note: for special occasions, serv the taramasalata in a hollowed, cooked globe artichoke. Trim ar cook the globe artichoke in the usual way. Drain thoroughly, upside-down, and brush lightly over with oil and vinegar dressi Pull out the centre leaves and remove the hairy choke. Brush inside with a little more dressin and fill with taramasalata – the outer leaves can then be pulled and dipped into the taramasalat Soak the bread in the water for minutes; squeeze the bread ligh between the fingers. Put the bre into the liquidiser with the cod' roe, garlic, lemon juice and 15m tblsp) of the olive oil. Blend unt smooth, and then gradually ble in the remaining olive oil. Seaso to taste with salt and pepper. Se with warm pitta bread and olive or as suggested above.

Meat Dishes

Stir Fried Calves' Liver with Peppers and Carrots

PREPARATION TIME: 15-20 minutes

COOKING TIME: 10-12 minutes

SERVES: 4 people

30ml (2 tblsp) olive oil
1 onion, thinly sliced
600g (1¼lb) calves' liver, cut into thin strips
Seasoned flour
60ml (4 tblsp) dry sherry
1 green pepper, seeded and cut into thin strips
3 large carrots, peeled and cut into thin strips
Salt and freshly ground black pepper to taste
1 clove garlic, peeled and cut into thin strips
100g (4oz) mung bean sprouts

Garnish
Sprigs fresh sage

Heat the olive oil in a large, shallow pan or wok; add the onion and stir fry for 3 minutes. Dust the strips of calves' liver in seasoned flour and add to the pan; stir fry until sealed on the outside but still pink in the centre. Add the sherry and bubble briskly; add 150ml (¼ pint) water or stock, green pepper, carrots, salt and pepper to taste and the garlic. Stir over a brisk heat for 3 minutes. Stir in the mung beans and heat through for 1 minute. Spoon into a serving dish and garnish with sprigs of fresh sage.

Chicken Moussaka

PREPARATION TIME: about 30 minutes

COOKING TIME: about 1 hour 5 minutes

OVEN: 190°C, 375°F, Gas Mark 5

SERVES: 6 people

60ml (4 tblsp) olive oil
1 medium onion, finely chopped
1 clove garlic, peeled and crushed
450g (1lb) minced raw chicken
30ml (2 tblsp) tomato puree
300ml (½ pint) chicken stock
30ml (2 tblsp) chopped parsley
Salt and freshly ground black pepper to taste
2 medium size aubergines, thinly sliced
150ml (¼ pint) natural yogurt
1 egg
50g (2oz) grated cheese
15ml (1 tblsp) grated Parmesan cheese

Heat half the olive oil in a pan; add the chopped onion and garlic and fry gently for 3 minutes. Add the minced chicken and fry until lightly browned. Add the tomato puree, chicken stock, parsley and salt and pepper to taste. Cover and simmer gently for 15 minutes. Lay the aubergine slices on lightly greased baking sheets and brush with the remaining olive oil; bake in the oven for 8 minutes. Arrange a layer of aubergine and then a layer of chicken in a lightly greased ovenproof dish; repeat the layers, finishing with a layer of aubergines. Beat the yogurt with the egg and grated cheese and spoon evenly over the top; sprinkle with the grated Parmesan. Bake in the oven for 35-40 minutes, until the top is bubbling and lightly golden. Serve piping hot.

Veal Casserole with Apricots and Prunes

PREPARATION TIME: 30 minutes

COOKING TIME: about 1 hour 40 minutes

OVEN: 160°C, 325°F, Gas Mark 3

SERVES: 4 people

600g (1¼lb) boned leg of veal, cubed
Seasoned flour
45ml (3 tblsp) olive oil
1 large onion, thinly sliced
450g (1lb) fresh ripe apricots, skinned, halved and stoned
300ml (½ pint) chicken stock
300ml (½ pint) dry white wine
150ml (¼ pint) fresh orange juice
Salt and freshly ground black pepper to taste
75g (3oz) dried prunes, soaked overnight
75g (3oz) dried aparicots, soaked overnight

Garnish
Matchstick strips of orange peel

Dust the cubed veal *lightly* in seasoned flour. Heat the oil in a pan; add the sliced onion and fry gently for 4 minutes. Meanwhile, put the halved and skinned fresh apricots into the liquidiser with the chicken stock and blend until smooth. Add the cubed veal to the onion and fry until evenly coloured on all sides. Gradually stir in the apricot puree, white wine and orange juice. Bring to the boil, stirring, and add salt and pepper to taste. Transfer to a casserole and add the drained prunes and apricots. Cover the casserole and cook in the oven for 1½ hours. Serve sprinkled with matchstick strips of orange peel.

Veal Paprika with Noodles

PREPARATION TIME: 10-15 minutes

COOKING TIME: about 1 hour 15 minutes

SERVES: 4 people

1 medium onion, thinly sliced
30ml (2 tblsp) olive oil
600g (1¼lb) boned leg of veal, cubed
Seasoned flour
15ml (1 tblsp) paprika
15ml (1 tblsp) tomato puree
Bayleaf
450ml (¾ pint) chicken stock
150ml (¼ pint) skimmed milk
Salt and freshly ground black pepper to taste
100g (4oz) button mushrooms, sliced

To Serve
Cooked green noodles

Facing page: Veal Casserole with Apricots and Prunes (top) and Chicken Moussaka (bottom).

Fry the onion gently in the olive oil for 3 minutes. Dust the cubed veal *lightly* in seasoned flour and add to the onion; fry until the veal is evenly coloured on all sides. Add the paprika, tomato puree and bayleaf, and gradually stir in the stock and skimmed milk. Bring to the boil, stirring, and add salt and pepper to taste. Cover and simmer gently for 55 minutes. Add the sliced mushrooms and simmer for a further 10 minutes. Serve piping hot with cooked green noodles.

Rabbit in Mustard Sauce

PREPARATION TIME: 5 minutes

COOKING TIME: about 1 hour

SERVES: 4 people

4 rabbit joints
Seasoned flour
1 medium onion, thinly sliced
30ml (2 tblsp) olive oil
450ml (¾ pint) chicken stock
150ml (¼ pint) skimmed milk
15ml (1 tblsp) coarse grain mustard
30ml (2 tblsp) coarsely chopped parsley
Salt and freshly ground black pepper to taste

Garnish

Small puff pastry leaves

Dust the rabbit joints *lightly* in seasoned flour. Fry the sliced onion gently in the oil for 4 minutes; add the rabbit joints and fry until evenly coloured on all sides. Add

This page: Tarragon Chicken Pancakes (top) and Rabbit in Mustard Sauce (bottom).

Facing page: Stir Fried Calves Liver with Peppers and Carrots (top) and Veal Paprika with Noodles (bottom).

the chicken stock, skimmed milk, mustard, parsley and salt and pepper to taste. Bring to the boil; cover and simmer gently for 40 minutes. Arrange on a serving dish or individual plates and garnish with pastry leaves.

Chicken with Blackcurrant Sauce and Mange Tout

PREPARATION TIME: 10-15 minutes

COOKING TIME: 12 minutes

SERVES: 4 people

4 chicken breasts, skinned and boned
Seasoned flour
Oil for shallow frying

Sauce
225g (8oz) fresh blackcurrants
Juice of 1 orange
150ml (¼ pint) red wine
Artificial sweetener to taste
Chicken stock

Garnish
Julienne strips orange peel
Cooked mange tout
4 lemon slices
Few whole fresh blackcurrants

Dust the chicken breasts lightly in seasoned flour; shallow fry gently in oil, for about 6 minutes on each side, until tender. Meanwhile, make the sauce. Put the blackcurrants into a pan with the orange juice, red wine, and sweetener to taste; cover and simmer gently until the blackcurrants are soft (this will only take a few minutes). Blend the sauce in the liquidiser until smooth. Reheat in a saucepan, adding sufficient stock to give a smooth coating consistency. Arrange the cooked chicken breasts on a serving dish. Spoon over the blackcurrant sauce and garnish with mange tout, strips of orange peel, and lemon slices topped with blackcurrants.

Chicken and Herb Loaf

PREPARATION TIME: 20-25 minutes

COOKING TIME: 50 minutes

OVEN: 190°C, 375°F, Gas Mark 5

SERVES: 6 people

450g (1lb) minced raw chicken
90ml (6 tblsp) wholemeal breadcrumbs
1 small onion, grated
1 clove garlic, peeled and crushed
30ml (2 tblsp) chopped parsley
15ml (1 tblsp) chopped fresh thyme
1 medium parsnip, peeled and grated
2 eggs, beaten
Salt and freshly ground black pepper to taste

Garnish
A little olive oil
15ml (1 tblsp) chopped parsley
Sprigs fresh rosemary

Mix the minced chicken with the breadcrumbs, onion, garlic, parsley, thyme, parsnip, beaten eggs and salt and pepper to taste. Spoon the mixture into a greased and lined loaf tin. Cover with a piece of greased foil. Bake in the oven for about 50 minutes, until cooked through – test with a skewer. For a brown top, remove the foil for the last 8-10 minutes. Brush the top of the loaf with the oil, while it is still hot, and sprinkle with the chopped parsley. Carefully take the loaf out of the tin, and serve either hot or cold, garnished with rosemary.

Chicken Andalusia

PREPARATION TIME: 15 minutes

COOKING TIME: 45 minutes

OVEN: 190°, 375°F, Gas Mark 5

SERVES: 4 people

4 small poussins
Salt and freshly ground black pepper to taste
Olive oil
4 small wedges of lime or lemon
4 bayleaves

Sauce
1 small onion, thinly sliced
30ml (2 tblsp) olive oil
1 clove garlic, peeled and crushed
450g (1lb) tomatoes, skinned, seeded and chopped
150ml (¼ pint) red wine
150ml (¼ pint) chicken stock
15ml (1 tblsp) tomato puree
2 green chillies, thinly sliced
1 small red pepper, seeded and cut into thin strips
1 small green pepper, seeded and cut into thin strips
30ml (2 tblsp) chopped blanched almonds
15ml (1 tblsp) pine kernels
12 small black olives
15ml (1 tblsp) raisins

Season the poussins inside and out with salt and pepper. Rub olive oil into the skin and push a wedge of lemon or lime and a bayleaf into the centre of each one. Roast the poussins in the oven for 45 minutes, until just tender (if they start to get too brown, cover them with foil during cooking). Meanwhile, make the sauce. Fry the sliced onion gently in the oil for 3 minutes; add the remaining sauce ingredients and simmer for 10 minutes. Arrange the poussins on a serving dish and spoon over the hot sauce.

Chicken Escalopes

PREPARATION TIME: 20 minutes, plus chilling time

COOKING TIME: 10 minutes

SERVES: 4 people

4 chicken escalopes
Beaten egg
Seasoned flour
60ml (4 tblsp) wholemeal breadcrumbs
15ml (1 tblsp) chopped fresh sage
25g (1oz) butter
15ml (1 tblsp) olive oil

Sauce
75ml (⅛ pint) low calorie mayonnaise
150ml (¼ pint) natural yogurt
5ml (1 tsp) grated fresh horseradish
30ml (2 tblsp) chopped walnuts

Garnish
175g (6oz) French beans, lightly cooked
4 thin slices lemon
15ml (1 tblsp) chopped walnuts

Dust the escalopes lightly in seasoned flour; dip into beaten egg and then coat with a mixture of breadcrumbs and sage. Chill for 30 minutes. Heat the butter and oil in a large, shallow pan; add the prepared escalopes and fry gently for 5 minutes on each side until lightly golden and tender. Keep warm. For the sauce: mix all the ingredients together. Arrange the cooked escalopes on a serving dish and garnish with the cooked beans and lemon slices topped with chopped walnuts. Spoon the sauce over the chicken.

Tarragon Chicken Pancakes

PREPARATION TIME: about 10 minutes

COOKING TIME: 5-10 minutes

SERVES: 4 people

8 small wholemeal pancakes (using wholemeal flour and skimmed milk in the batter)
A little melted butter
22g (¾oz) butter

Chicken with Blackcurrant Sauce and Mange Tout (left) and Chicken Escalopes (below).

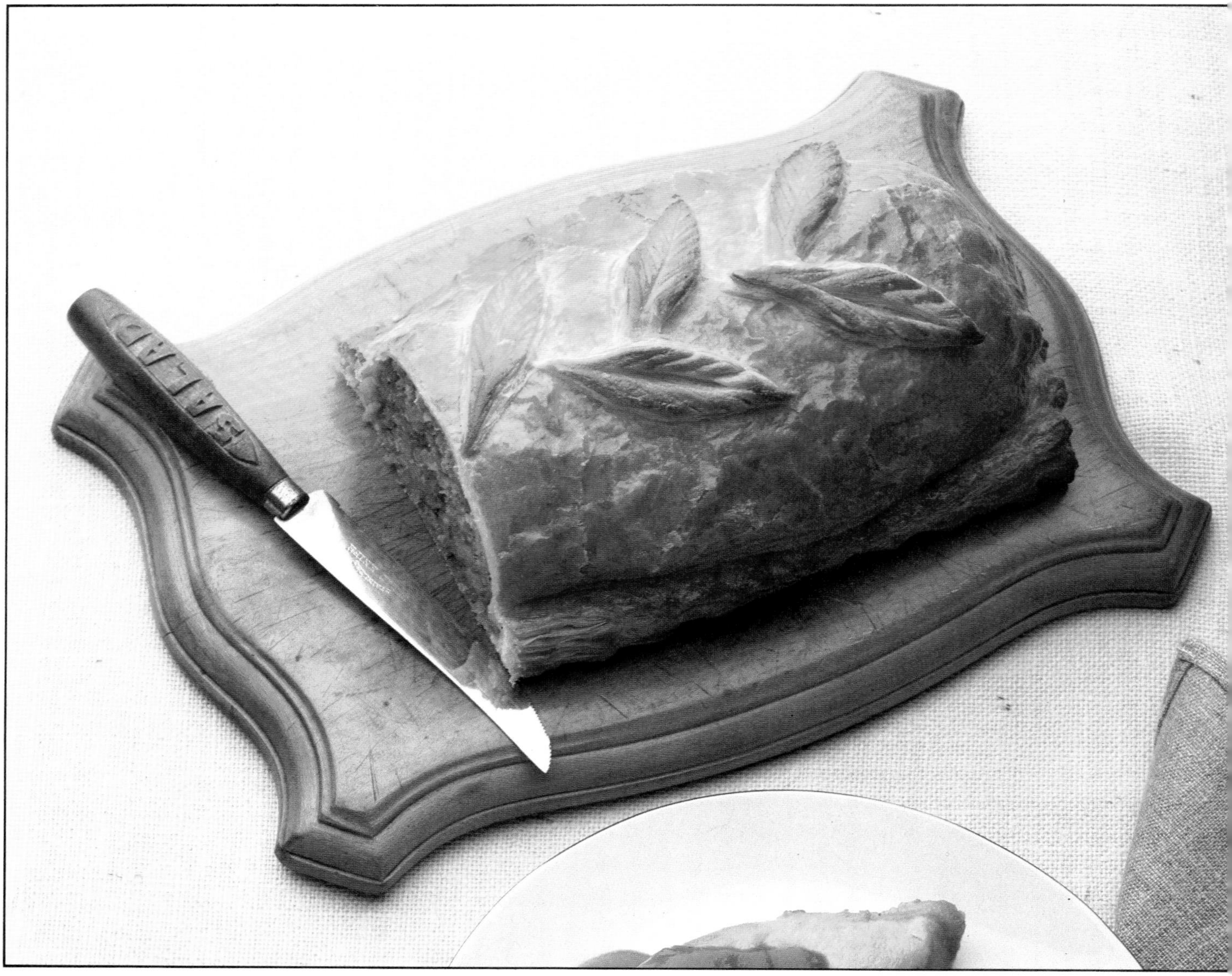

22g (¾oz) plain flour
300ml (½ pint) skimmed milk
Salt and freshly ground black pepper to taste
225g (½lb) cooked chicken, chopped
1 avocado pear (not over-ripe), peeled, halved, stoned and chopped
15ml (1 tblsp) chopped fresh tarragon

Brush the cooked pancakes lightly with melted butter and keep them warm in a parcel of foil in a moderately hot oven. Melt the butter and stir in the flour; cook, stirring, for 1 minute. Gradually stir in the skimmed milk; bring to the boil until the sauce has thickened. Add salt and pepper to taste and stir in the chopped chicken, avocado and tarragon. Fold each pancake in half, and then in half again, to form a triangle. Fill each folded pancake with the chicken and avocado mixture and serve piping hot. Garnish with sprigs of fresh tarragon, if liked.

Chicken Breasts with Plum and Cinnamon Sauce

PREPARATION TIME: 15 minutes
COOKING TIME: about 20 minutes
SERVES: 4 people

4 chicken breasts, skinned and boned
Seasoned flour
Olive oil for frying

Sauce
1 small onion, finely chopped
15g (½oz) butter
350g (12oz) ripe red plums, halved and stoned
Pinch ground cinnamon
Salt and freshly ground black pepper to taste
Artificial sweetener to taste
150ml (¼ pint) red wine

Garnish
Whole poached plums
Chopped fresh thyme
Small sprigs fresh thyme

Dust the chicken breasts lightly in seasoned flour. Shallow fry the chicken breasts in olive oil for about 6 minutes on each side, until tender. Meanwhile, prepare the sauce. Fry the chopped onion gently in the butter for 3 minutes; add the remaining sauce ingredients and simmer until the plums are soft and 'mushy'. The sauce can either be left as it is, or it can be blended in the liquidiser sieved. Reheat the sauce if necessary, thinning it to the desi consistency. Arrange the chicken breasts on a serving dish and spo over the hot plum sauce. Garnis with a few whole poached plum sprinkling of thyme, and a few small sprigs of fresh thyme.

This page: Turkey, Chestnut and Sage en Croute.

Facing page: Turkey Meatbal with Sweet and Sour Sauce (t and Sweetbreads and Courge Tarts (bottom).

Turkey, Cauliflower and Almond au Gratin

PREPARATION TIME: 20-25 minutes

COOKING TIME: about 16 minutes

SERVES: 4 people

1 medium size cauliflower
Juice of ½ lemon
Salt and freshly ground black pepper to taste
22g (¾oz) butter
22g (¾oz) flour
300ml (½ pint) skimmed milk
175g (6oz) cooked turkey, cut into thin strips
100g (4oz) grated cheese
30ml (2 tblsp) flaked almonds

Divide the cauliflower into good size florets; cook in boiling salted water to which you have added the lemon juice and salt to taste, until just tender. Meanwhile, make the sauce. Melt the butter in a pan; stir in the flour and cook for 1 minute. Gradually stir in the skimmed milk and bring to the boil; add salt and pepper to taste and stir until thickened. Add the strips of turkey and half the grated cheese to the sauce. Arrange the florets of cooked cauliflower in a greased heatproof dish and spoon over the prepared sauce; sprinkle with the almonds and remaining cheese and brown under a hot grill.

Turkey Meatballs with Sweet and Sour Sauce

PREPARATION TIME: 20-25 minutes, plus chilling time

COOKING TIME: about 35 minutes

SERVES: 4 people

1 small onion, finely chopped
30ml (2 tblsp) olive oil
450g (1lb) minced raw turkey
1 clove garlic, peeled and crushed
30ml (2 tblsp) chopped parsley
30ml (2 tblsp) finely chopped almonds
Salt and freshly ground black pepper to taste
1.25ml (¼ tsp) mixed spice
15ml (1 tblsp) chopped raisins
30ml (2 tblsp) wholemeal breadcrumbs
1 egg, beaten

Sauce
1 small onion, thinly sliced
300ml (½ pint) pure tomato juice
30ml (2 tblsp) tomato puree
Juice of ½ lemon
15ml (1 tblsp) honey
1 green chilli, thinly sliced
2 slices fresh pineapple, finely chopped
1 medium red pepper, seeded and cut into thin strips
2 carrots, peeled and coarsely grated

For the meatballs: fry the onion gently in the olive oil for 4 minutes. Mix with the minced turkey, garlic, parsley, almonds, salt and pepper to taste, mixed spice, raisins, breadcrumbs and beaten egg. Form into small balls, about the size of a table tennis ball. Chill for 30 minutes. For the sauce: put all the ingredients into a shallow pan; bring to the boil and simmer gently for 10 minutes. Add the shaped meatballs and turn them in the sauce. Cover and simmer gently for a further 20 minutes, until the meatballs are tender – if the sauce evaporates too quickly, add a little stock or water. Serve piping hot with cooked brown rice or wholewheat pasta.
Note: the shaped meatballs can be lightly fried in a little oil, before being added to the sauce, if liked.

Chicken Breasts with Plum and Tarragon Sauce (far right) and Calves' Liver Mousse with Cherry and Marsala (below).

Turkey, Chestnut and Sage en Croute

PREPARATION TIME: 35 minutes, plus chilling time

COOKING TIME: about 55 minutes

OVEN: 200°C, 400°F, Gas Mark 6, and then 180°C, 350°F, Gas Mark 4

SERVES: 6-8 people

450g (1lb) minced raw turkey
1 small onion, finely chopped
45ml (3 tblsp) chestnut puree (unsweetened)
15ml (1 tblsp) chopped fresh sage
1 clove garlic, peeled and crushed
Salt and freshly ground black pepper to taste
45ml (3 tblsp) fresh brown breadcrumbs
1 egg, beaten
450g (1lb) puff pastry (preferably vegetable oil based)
Beaten egg to glaze

Mix the minced turkey with the onion, chestnut puree, sage, garlic, salt and pepper to taste, and brown breadcrumbs. Bind with the beaten egg. Form into a fat, cylindrical sausage, and chill while you prepare the pastry coating. Divide the pastry into two portions, one slightly larger than the other; roll out thinly on a floured surface into two rectangles, one slightly larger than the other. Trim neatly, reserving the trimmings. Place the smaller rectangle of pastry into a dampened baking sheet; brush the edges with beaten egg. Place the turkey 'sausage' in the centre. Lay the larger rectangle of pastry over the top, and pinch the joining pastry edges together to seal (the pastry should fit snuggly around the filling). Trim off excess pastry. Glaze the pastry all over with beaten egg and decorate with shapes cut from the pastry trimmings; glaze the pastry decorations. Bake in the oven at the higher temperature for 20 minutes; reduce to the lower temperature and bake for a further 35 minutes, covered with a piece of foil. Serve hot or cold, cut into slices.

Calves' Liver Mousse with Cherry and Marsala

PREPARATION TIME: 25 minutes, plus chilling time

COOKING TIME: 10-12 minutes

SERVES: 6 people

450g (1lb) calves' liver
30ml (2 tblsp) marsala
300ml (½ pint) chicken stock
1 clove garlic, peeled and crushed
Salt and freshly ground black pepper to taste
300ml (½ pint) natural yogurt
20ml (4 tsp) powdered gelatine
60ml (4 tblsp) water
4 spring onions, chopped

Sauce
225g (8oz) fresh cherries, de-stalked and pitted
150ml (¼ pint) red wine
45ml (3 tblsp) marsala
Artificial sweetener to taste
5ml (1 tsp) cornflour
Juice of 1 orange

Garnish
Mint leaves
Few fresh cherries

Grease a 900ml (1½ pint) mould. Cook the calves' liver in the chicken stock and marsala until just tender – this will only take a few minutes. Put the liver and its liquid into the liquidiser and blend, until smooth, with the garlic and salt and pepper to taste. Stir in the yogurt. Dissolve the gelatine in the water and add to the liver mixture together with the chopped spring onions. Spoon into the mould and chill until set. For the sauce: put the cherries into a pan with the red wine, marsala and sweetener to taste; cover and cook until the cherries are just soft. Blend the cornflour with the orange juice and add to the cherry sauce; stir over the heat until thickened. Unmould the chilled mousse onto a serving dish and garnish with mint leaves and a few fresh cherries. Serve with the *warm* cherry sauce.

Sweetbread and Courgette Tarts

PREPARATION TIME: 40 minutes, plus chilling time

COOKING TIME: about 35 minutes

OVEN: 190°C, 375°F, Gas Mark 5

SERVES: 4 people

350g (12oz) shortcrust pastry
225g (8oz) calves' sweetbreads, soaked for 3 hours
Beaten egg
25g (1oz) butter
Finely grated rind of 1 lemon
1 clove garlic, peeled and crushed
4 courgettes, finely shredded
Salt and freshly ground black pepper to taste
Juice of ½ lemon

Divide the pastry into 4 equal portions; roll each one out to a circle and use to line an individual tartlet tin, about 10cm (4 inches) in diameter. Press up the pastry edges well. Line with greaseproof paper and baking beans, and chill for 30 minutes. Rinse the sweetbreads under cold water. Drain the sweetbreads, put them into a pan and add sufficient cold water to cover; bring to the boil slowly, covered, and simmer for 8 minutes. Drain and rinse; remove any muscly parts and skin, and chop into pieces. Bake the pastry cases for 10 minutes. Remove the paper and beans and brush the rim of each pastry case with beaten egg. Return to the oven for a further 8 minutes. Melt the butter with the lemon rind. Add the garlic and chopped sweetbreads and fry for 4 minutes. Add the shredded courgettes and salt and pepper to taste and fry together for a further 3 minutes. Spoon the hot filling into the pastry cases, squeeze over the lemon juice and serve immediately.

Chicken and Herb Loaf (top right), Chicken Andalusia (centre left) and Turkey, Cauliflower and Almond au Gratin (bottom).

Vegetables and Salads

Stir Fried Peas with Lentil Sprouts and Leeks

PREPARATION TIME: 10 minutes

COOKING TIME: about 10 minutes

SERVES: 4 people

1 medium onion, thinly sliced
2 cloves garlic, peeled and cut into thin slivers
60ml (4 tblsp) olive oil
225g (8oz) mange tout peas, topped and tailed
2 large leeks, split, washed, and cut into thin strips
100g (4oz) lentil sprouts
Salt and freshly ground black pepper to taste
15ml (1 tblsp) chopped coriander

Stir fry the onion and garlic in the olive oil for 3 minutes, either in a wok or in a large, deep frying pan. Add the mange tout and leeks and stir fry for a further 4-5 minutes. Add the lentil sprouts, salt and pepper to taste and the coriander, and stir fry for a further 3 minutes. Serve piping hot with a really good soya sauce, or a peanut sauce. For a quick peanut sauce: put 75g (3oz) shelled peanuts into the liquidiser with 1 clove garlic, peeled, 1 small onion, chopped and 200ml (⅓ pint) chicken stock; blend until smooth.

Rice and Tuna Stuffed Aubergines

PREPARATION TIME: 40 minutes

COOKING TIME: about 50 minutes

OVEN: 190°C, 375°F, Gas Mark 5

SERVES: 4 people

4 small aubergines
45ml (3 tblsp) olive oil
Salt and freshly ground black pepper to taste
1 small onion, finely chopped
1 clove garlic, peeled and crushed
90ml (6 tblsp) cooked brown or wild rice
200g (7oz) can tuna, drained and coarsely flaked
15ml (1 tblsp) mayonnaise
5ml (1 tsp) curry powder
4 tomatoes, skinned, seeded and chopped
15ml (1 tblsp) coarsely chopped parsley

Cut the aubergines in half langthways. Score the cut surfaces lightly with a sharp knife, at regular intervals. Brush lightly with oil and sprinkle with salt. Place on a greased baking sheet and bake in the oven for 15 minutes. Carefully scoop the centre flesh from each half aubergine, making sure that you do not break the skin. Fry the chopped onion gently in 30ml (2 tblsp) of the olive oil for 3 minutes. Add the garlic, scooped aubergine flesh, and salt and pepper to taste; fry gently for a further 2 minutes. Add the flaked tuna, mayonnaise,

This page: Okra in Light C Sauce (top) and Stir Fried P with Lentil Sprouts and Lee (bottom).

Facing page: Courgette, Ca and Anchovy Salad (top) an Rice and Tuna Stuffed Aubergines (bottom).

curry powder, chopped tomato and parsley, and mix together. Fill the aubergine 'shells' with the savoury rice mixture and place in a lightly greased ovenproof dish. Sprinkle with the remaining olive oil. Bake in the oven for about 25 minutes. Serve piping hot.

Courgette, Caper and Anchovy Salad

PREPARATION TIME: 15-20 minutes

SERVES: 4 people

450g (1lb) courgettes
1 small onion, thinly sliced
15ml (1 tblsp) capers
4-6 anchovy fillets, chopped
15ml (1 tblsp) anchovy oil (drained from the can of anchovy fillets)
30ml (2 tblsp) olive oil
30ml (2 tblsp) tarragon vinegar
Juice of ½ lemon
Salt and freshly ground black pepper to taste

Garnish
2 medium size heads of chicory (optional)
2 whole anchovy fillets

The secret of this salad is to slice the raw courgettes really thinly – you can do this with a sharp knife, but it is much easier if you use the slicing blade on a food processor or a mandolin. Top and tail the courgettes, and slice them very thinly. Mix the sliced courgettes with the onion, capers and chopped anchovy fillets. Mix the anchovy oil, olive oil, tarragon vinegar and lemon juice together; add salt and pepper to taste. Stir the dressing into the prepared salad ingredients. Separate the leaves from each head of chicory and use to line a salad bowl. Spoon the prepared salad into the centre and garnish with anchovy fillets.

Okra in Light Curry Sauce

PREPARATION TIME: 10 minutes

COOKING TIME: 30-35 minutes

SERVES: 4 people

1 medium onion, roughly chopped
Small piece fresh root ginger, chopped
1 large clove garlic, peeled
50g (2oz) shelled peanuts
15ml (1 tblsp) fresh coriander sprigs
15ml (1 tblsp) chopped parsley
5ml (1 tsp) ground turmeric
2.5ml (½ tsp) ground cumin
30ml (2 tblsp) olive oil
1 small onion, thinly sliced
300ml (½ pint) chicken stock
Salt and freshly ground black pepper to taste
450g (1lb) okra

Garnish
Flaked coconut (optional)
Sprigs fresh coriander

To Serve
Natural yogurt
Wedges of lime

Put the chopped onion, root ginger, garlic, peanuts, coriander, parsley, turmeric and cumin into the liquidiser; blend until smooth. Heat the olive oil in a large, shallow pan; add the sliced onion and fry gently for 3 minutes. Add the liquidised spice mixture and cook for 1 minute. Add the stock and salt and pepper to taste; bring to the boil and simmer for 5 minutes. Add the okra and cover the pan; simmer gently for 20-25 minutes, until the okra is just tender. Spoon into a serving dish and sprinkle with the flaked coconut. Garnish with fresh coriander. Serve accompanied by a bowl of well-chilled yogurt and lemon wedges for squeezing.

Radicchio and Sweetbread Salad

PREPARATION TIME: 40 minutes, plus standing time

COOKING TIME: 18-20 minutes

SERVES: 4

4 calf's sweetbreads
90ml (6 tblsp) olive oil
1 clove garlic, peeled and crushed
Salt and freshly ground black pepper to taste
2 medium size heads radicchio
4 large cooked asparagus tips
100g (4oz) firm white button mushrooms, thinly sliced
30ml (2 tblsp) white wine vinegar
15ml (1 tblsp) chopped fresh sage (optional)

Garnish
Sprig fresh basil

Soak the sweetbreads in cold water for 3 hours; change the water once or twice during this time. Rinse them under cold water. Drain the sweetbreads; put them into a pan and add sufficient cold water to cover. Bring to the boil slowly; cover and simmer for 8-10 minutes. Drain and rinse under cold water once again. Remove any muscle or fatty parts. Put the prepared sweetbreads between two plates and weight down; leave to stand in a cool place for 1 hour. Slice the pressed sweetbreads evenly. Heat half the olive oil in a large, shallow pan. Add the sweetbread slices, garlic and salt and pepper to taste and fry gently for 5 minutes; flip the sweetbread slices over and fry for a further 3-4 minutes. Meanwhile, prepare the salad ingredients. Cut the heads of radicchio into quarters and arrange on a large, flat plate. Arrange the asparagus tips and mushroom slices between the wedges of radicchio. Mix the wine vinegar with the remaining olive oil, salt and pepper to taste and the chopped sage. Spoon the dressing evenly over the salad and top with the fried sweetbread slices and their juices. Garnish with basil. Serve immediately.

Turkey Caesar Salad

PREPARATION TIME: 20 minutes

COOKING TIME: 4-5 minutes

SERVES: 4-6 people

1 Cos lettuce
Few young spinach leaves
Juice of 1 lemon
5ml (1 tsp) French mustard
90ml (6 tblsp) olive oil
2 cloves garlic, peeled and crushed
10ml (2 tsp) Worcestershire sauce
3 drops Tabasco
4 anchovy fillets, chopped
Salt and freshly ground black pepper to taste
1 egg
2 slices wholemeal bread, cut into small cubes
175g (6oz) cooked turkey, cut into thin strips

Tear the lettuce into pieces and put into a salad bowl with the young spinach leaves. Mix the lemon juice with the French mustard, 45ml (3 tblsp) of the olive oil, half the garlic, the Worcestershire sauce, Tabasco, anchovy fillets and salt and pepper to taste. Put the egg into a pan of boiling water and cook for *just 45 seconds* – the white and yolk must still be very runny. Carefully crack the egg and scoop all the centre egg into the dressing; beat well. Heat the remaining olive oil with the rest of the garlic in a large shallow pan; add the small cubes of wholemeal bread and fry until crisp and golden. Add the croutons, turkey strips and prepared dressing to the salad greens and toss well together. Serve immediately.

Brown Rice, Pineapple, Peanut and Red Pepper Salad

PREPARATION TIME: 15 minutes plus cooling time

COOKING TIME: 10-15 minutes

SERVES: 4 people

100g (4oz) brown or wild rice
Salt and freshly ground black pepper to taste
Juice of 1 orange
60ml (4 tblsp) olive oil
5ml (1 tsp) clear honey
2 slices fresh pineapple, peeled and chopped
30ml (2 tblsp) shelled peanuts
1 large red pepper, seeded and cut into thin strips
Peeled segments of 2 large oranges

Cook the rice in boiling salted water until just tender. Meanwhile prepare the orange dressing. Mix the orange juice, olive oil and

Radicchio and Sweetbread Salad (right) and Turkey Caesa Salad (below).

honey together, and season to taste with salt and pepper. Drain the cooked rice thoroughly, and stir in the prepared dressing while the rice is still warm. Allow to cool. Mix in the pineapple, peanuts, and red pepper. Spoon into a shallow salad bowl and garnish with the orange segments.

Fisherman's Wholewheat Pasta Salad

PREPARATION TIME: 20 minutes, plus cooling time

COOKING TIME: about 10 minutes

SERVES: 4 people

175g (8oz) wholewheat pasta shapes (shells, wheels, etc.)
Salt and freshly ground black pepper to taste
60ml (4 tblsp) olive oil
30ml (2 tblsp) dry white wine
15ml (1 tblsp) chopped parsley
3 spring onions, chopped
100g (4oz) shelled cooked mussels
75g (3oz) peeled prawns
100g (4oz) flaked crabmeat
12 black olives

Garnish
Large peeled prawns

Cook the wholewheat pasta in a large pan of boiling salted water until just tender – about 10 minutes. Meanwhile, prepare the dressing. Mix the olive oil with the white wine, parsley, and salt and pepper to taste. Drain the cooked pasta thoroughly and stir in the prepared dressing. Allow to cool. Mix in the chopped spring onion, and then carefully stir in the shellfish; add the black olives. Spoon into one large salad bowl, or four individual ones.

Potato and Hazelnut Nests

PREPARATION TIME: 30 minutes, plus chilling time

COOKING TIME: 35 minutes

OVEN: 190°C, 375°F, Gas Mark 5

SERVES: 6 people

750g (1½lb) potatoes, peeled
Salt and freshly ground black pepper to taste
22g (¾oz) butter
2 egg yolks
15ml (1 tblsp) natural yogurt
30ml (2 tblsp) finely chopped hazelnuts
225g (8oz) low fat cream cheese
15ml (1 tblsp) chopped chives (optional)

Garnish
A few flaked or coarsely chopped hazelnuts
Parsley

Cook the potatoes in boiling salted water until just tender. Drain them thoroughly. Mash the potatoes. Return the mashed potato to a clean saucepan and stir over a gentle heat to 'dry' them out. Remove from the heat and beat in the butter, egg yolks, salt and pepper to taste, yogurt and chopped hazelnuts. Using a large piping bag fitted with a wide star nozzle, pipe the potato mixture into 6 nest shapes on a lightly greased baking sheet. Chill for 30

This page: Potato, Lentil and Cheese Pie (top), Potato and Hazelnut Nests (centre) and Parsnip, Orange and Ginger Puree (bottom).

Facing page: Fisherman's Wholewheat Pasta Salad (top) and Brown Rice, Pineapple, Peanut and Red Pepper Salad (bottom).

minutes. Bake in the oven until pale golden – about 15 minutes (the potato nests can be glazed with beaten egg before baking, if liked). Beat the cream cheese until soft and add the chopped chives and salt and pepper to taste. As soon as the potato and hazelnut nests come out of the oven, put a spoonful of the flavoured cream cheese in the centre of each one and sprinkle with the flaked hazelnuts. Garnish with parsley. Serve immediately. They make a delicious accompanying vegetable to fish.

Mushrooms Monegasque

PREPARATION TIME: 10 minutes, plus chilling time

COOKING TIME: about 13 minutes

SERVES: 4 people

450g (1lb) tomatoes, skinned, seeded and chopped
150ml (1/4 pint) red wine
30ml (2 tblsp) tomato puree
Pinch ground ginger
Salt and freshly ground black pepper to taste
1 clove garlic, peeled and finely chopped
2 spring onions, finely chopped
30ml (2 tblsp) raisins
225g (8oz) small button mushrooms

To Serve
Crusty wholemeal bread or rolls

Put the chopped tomatoes, red wine, tomato puree, ground ginger, salt and pepper to taste, and the garlic into a shallow pan. Simmer for 6-8 minutes. Add the spring onions, raisins and button mushrooms; cover the pan and simmer for 5 minutes. Allow to cool and then chill very thoroughly. Serve in small, shallow dishes, accompanied by crusty wholemeal bread.

Fennel au Gratin

PREPARATION TIME: 15 minutes

COOKING TIME: 25-30 minutes

OVEN: 190°C, 375°F, Gas Mark 5

SERVES: 4 people

4 medium size heads of fennel
Juice of 1 lemon
Salt and freshly ground black pepper to taste
25g (1oz) butter
22g (3/4oz) flour
150ml (1/4 pint) skimmed milk
150ml (1/4 pint) dry white wine
60ml (4 tblsp) natural yogurt
2.5ml (1/2 tsp) chive mustard
75g (3oz) grated Gruyere cheese

Garnish
15ml (1 tblsp) chopped chives

Trim both ends of the fennel – reserve any feathery tops for garnish. Peel off any discoloured patches from the fennel. Cut each head in half lengthways. Put the fennel into a pan of boiling water to which you have added the lemon juice and 5ml (1 tsp) salt; simmer steadily for 5 minutes. Drain the par-cooked fennel thoroughly. Melt the butter in a pan and stir in the flour; gradually stir in the milk and white wine. Bring to the boil and stir until lightly thickened. Beat in the yogurt, chive mustard, half the grated cheese, and salt and pepper to taste. Arrange the fennel in a lightly greased ovenproof dish and spoon the sauce evenly over the top; sprinkle with the remaining grated cheese. Bake in the oven for 25-30 minutes, until the sauce is golden. Garnish with the chopped chives and any reserved pieces of feathery fennel.

Potato, Lentil and Cheese Pie

PREPARATION TIME: 25 minutes

COOKING TIME: 1 hour 15 minutes

OVEN: 190°C, 375°F, Gas Mark 5

SERVES: 4 people

225g (8oz) lentils, soaked overnight
600ml (1 pint) chicken stock
1 small onion, finely chopped
25g (1oz) butter
25g (1oz) flour
60ml (4 tblsp) natural yogurt
1 egg, beaten
Salt and freshly ground black pepper to taste
450g (1lb) medium size potatoes, peeled, par-boiled, and thinly sliced
75g (3oz) grated cheese

Garnish
A little crumbled fresh rosemary

Cook the drained, soaked lentils in three quarters of the stock, with the chopped onion, until tender – about 30 minutes. Drain thoroughly. Melt the butter in a pan and stir in the flour; add the remaining 150ml (1/4 pint) stock, and stir over the heat until thickened. Season to taste with salt and pepper and stir in half the yogurt. Stir the prepared sauce into the cooked lentils. Put the lentil mixture into a lightly greased ovenproof dish. Beat the remaining yogurt with the egg and salt and pepper to taste. Arrange the potato slices, overlapping, on top of the lentil mixture; brush all the potato slices with the egg and yogurt mixture, and sprinkle with the grated cheese. Bake in the oven for 40-45 minutes, until a rich golden brown. Sprinkle with the rosemary and serve piping hot.

Mushrooms Monegasque (top) and Fennel au Gratin (right).

Broccoli and Almond Risotto

PREPARATION TIME: 5 minutes

COOKING TIME: about 35 minutes

SERVES: 4 people

1 medium onion, finely chopped
30ml (2 tblsp) olive oil
175g (6oz) brown or wild rice
750ml (1¼ pint) chicken stock
Salt and freshly ground black pepper to taste
30ml (2 tblsp) chopped, toasted almonds
450g (1lb) broccoli, divided into small florets
50g (2oz) grated Parmesan cheese

Garnish

Lightly toasted flaked almonds

Fry the onion gently in the olive oil for 3 minutes. Add the rice and stir over the heat for 1 minute, until the rice is evenly coated with oil. Gradually stir in the chicken stock. Bring to the boil and add salt and pepper to taste and the chopped almonds; cover and simmer for 20 minutes. Add the florets of broccoli; cover and simmer for a further 8 minutes, until all the stock has been absorbed. Stir in the Parmesan cheese and spoon into a serving dish; sprinkle with the toasted almonds and serve piping hot.

Parsnip, Orange and Ginger Puree

PREPARATION TIME: 15-20 minutes

COOKING TIME: about 25 minutes

SERVES: 4 people

750g (1½lb) parsnips, peeled and roughly chopped
2 thin strips orange peel
Salt and freshly ground black pepper to taste
25g (1oz) butter
2 egg yolks
Generous pinch ground ginger
Finely grated rind of ½ orange
15ml (1 tblsp) chopped preserved stem ginger

Garnish

Finely chopped parsley
Peeled segments of orange

Put the parsnips into a pan with the strips of orange peel, salt and pepper to taste, and sufficient water to just cover. Bring to the boil and simmer, covered, until the parsnips are just tender. Drain very thoroughly, removing the strips of orange peel. Mash the cooked parsnips and return to a clean pan; stir over a gentle heat to 'dry' the parsnip puree. Beat in the butter, egg yolks, grated orange rind, salt and pepper to taste and the chopped stem ginger. Heat through and spoon into a serving dish. Garnish with chopped parsley and orange segments, and serve the puree piping hot.

Pasta, Rice and Pulses

Pasta Shells with Agliata Sauce

PREPARATION TIME: 10 minutes

COOKING TIME: about 8 minutes

SERVES: 4 people

275g (10oz) wholemeal or plain pasta shells
Salt and freshly ground black pepper to taste

Sauce
90ml (6 tblsp) olive oil
45ml (3 tblsp) coarsely chopped parsley
2 cloves garlic, peeled
15ml (1 tblsp) pine kernels
15ml (1 tblsp) blanched almonds

Cook the pasta shells in a large pan of boiling salted water until just tender. Meanwhile, make the sauce. Put all the ingredients into a liquidiser and blend until smooth; add salt and pepper to taste. Drain the hot, cooked pasta shells and toss together with the prepared sauce. Serve immediately.

Chick Pea, Mint and Orange Salad

PREPARATION TIME: 15-25 minutes

SERVES: 4 people

175g (6oz) dried chick peas, soaked overnight and cooked
30ml (2 tblsp) chopped fresh mint
1 clove garlic, peeled and crushed
Salt and freshly ground black pepper to taste
Juice of 1 orange
Rind of 1 orange, cut into matchstick strips
45ml (3 tblsp) olive oil
Segments from 2 large oranges

Garnish
Fresh mint leaves

Mix the chick peas with half the chopped mint, garlic, and salt and pepper to taste. Mix the orange juice, strips of orange rind and olive oil together; stir into the chick peas. Lightly mix in the orange segments and garnish with the remaining chopped mint.

Noodle and Ratatouille Bake

PREPARATION TIME: 25-30 minutes

COOKING TIME: 35-40 minutes

OVEN: 190°C, 375°F, Gas Mark 5

SERVES: 4 people

1 medium onion, thinly sliced
30ml (2 tblsp) olive oil
2 cloves garlic, peeled and finely chopped
1 large green pepper, seeded and cut into cubes
1 large red pepper, seeded and cut into cubes

This page: Chick Pea, Mint Orange Salad (top) and Sp and Feta Cheese Lasagne (bottom).

Facing page: Pasta Shells w Agliata Sauce (top) and No and Ratatouille Bake (bott

1 medium aubergine, cubed
6 tomatoes, skinned, seeded and chopped
15ml (1 tblsp) tomato puree
45ml (3 tblsp) red wine
Salt and freshly ground black pepper to taste
100g (4oz) green noodles, cooked
75g (3oz) grated cheese

Fry the onion gently in the olive oil for 4 minutes; add the garlic, red and green peppers, aubergine and chopped tomatoes and cook covered for 5 minutes. Add the tomato puree, wine and salt and pepper to taste; simmer gently for 10-15 minutes, until the vegetables are almost soft. Remove from the heat and stir in the cooked noodles. Spoon into a shallow flameproof dish and sprinkle with the grated cheese. Bake in the oven for 15 minutes (alternatively, the dish can be flashed under a preheated grill).

Spaghetti with Sweetbread Carbonara

PREPARATION TIME: 10-15 minutes
COOKING TIME: 10 minutes
SERVES: 4 people

1 onion, chopped
45ml (3 tblsp) olive oil
350g (12oz) wholemeal spaghetti
Salt and freshly ground black pepper to taste
225g (8oz) calves' sweetbreads, blanched, skinned and chopped
90ml (6 tblsp) dry white wine
4 eggs
50g (2oz) grated Parmesan cheese
30ml (2 tblsp) chopped fresh basil
1 clove garlic, peeled and crushed

Fry the onion gently in the olive oil for 5 minutes. Meanwhile, cook the spaghetti in a large pan of boiling salted water for about 10 minutes, until just tender. Add the chopped sweetbreads to the onion and fry gently for 4 minutes. Add the white wine and cook briskly until it has almost evaporated. Beat the eggs with the Parmesan cheese, basil, garlic, and salt and pepper to taste. Drain the hot, cooked spaghetti thoroughly; immediately stir in the beaten egg mixture and the sweetbreads, so that the heat from the spaghetti cooks the egg. Garnish with basil and serve immediately.

Wild Rice and Egg Scramble

PREPARATION TIME: 10 minutes
COOKING TIME: 7-8 minutes
SERVES: 4 people

175g (6oz) wild or brown rice, cooked
15g (½oz) butter
1 small onion, thinly sliced
30ml (2 tblsp) olive oil
3 eggs
2.5ml (½ tsp) mixed herbs
Salt and freshly ground black pepper to taste

Garnish
Chopped parsley

Heat the cooked rice through gently with the butter. Fry the onion gently in the olive oil for 3-4 minutes. Beat the eggs with the herbs, salt and pepper to taste, and 15ml (1 tblsp) water. Add the beaten egg mixture to the onion and scramble lightly. Combine the hot rice and the scrambled egg and onion and serve immediately.

Pasta Shapes with Green Mayonnaise and Crab

PREPARATION TIME: 25 minutes
COOKING TIME: 8-10 minutes
SERVES: 4 people

Green Mayonnaise
60ml (4 tblsp) mayonnaise
150ml (¼ pint) natural yogurt
45ml (3 tblsp) cooked spinach
1 clove garlic, peeled
Salt and freshly ground black pepper to taste
350g (12oz) pasta shapes – shells, wheels, twists, etc
Juice of 1 lemon
30ml (2 tblsp) olive oil
175g (6oz) flaked crabmeat, or crab flavoured sticks, shredded

Garnish
Parsley sprigs

For the green mayonnaise: put all the ingredients into the liquidiser and blend until smooth. Cook the pasta shapes in boiling salted water until tender. Drain thoroughly toss in the lemon juice and oliv oil, adding salt and pepper to ta Mix in the flaked crabmeat. Sp into a serving dish and serve w garnished with parsley.

Spinach and Feta Cheese Lasagne

PREPARATION TIME: 20-25 minutes
COOKING TIME: about 35 minutes
OVEN: 190°, 375°F, Gas Mark
SERVES: 6 people

450g (1lb) cooked and drained spinach (or thawed frozen spi
Generous pinch grated nutmeg
Salt and freshly ground black pe to taste
30ml (2 tblsp) natural yogurt
1 clove garlic, peeled and crushe
1 egg yolk
175g (6oz) Feta cheese, crumble
225g (8oz) green or wholewheat lasagne (the non pre-cook vari

Sauce
150ml (¼ pint) natural yogurt
1 egg, beaten
30ml (2 tblsp) grated Parmesan cheese
3 firm tomatoes, sliced

Mix the cooked spinach with nutmeg and salt and pepper to taste; stir in the yogurt, garlic, yolk and crumbled Feta cheese Layer the lasagne and spinach mixture in a lightly greased ovenproof dish, starting with spinach and finishing with lasa For the sauce: mix the yogurt the beaten egg and half the gra Parmesan cheese; spoon over t lasagne. Top with the sliced to and the remaining Parmesan cheese. Bake in the oven for ab 35 minutes, until golden. Serv piping hot.

This page: Wild Rice and E Scramble (top) and Pasta Sh with Green Mayonnaise an Crab (bottom).

Facing page: Chicken Liver Risotto with Red Beans (to and Spaghetti with Sweetb Carbonara (bottom).

Rice and Vegetable Loaf with Yogurt and Mint Sauce

PREPARATION TIME: 25-30 minutes

COOKING TIME: 53 minutes

OVEN: 190°C, 375°F, Gas Mark 5

SERVES: 6-8

1 small onion, finely chopped
30ml (2 tblsp) olive oil
1 clove garlic, peeled and crushed
225g (8oz) wild rice, cooked and drained (not rinsed)
3 courgettes, finely shredded
2 medium size carrots, finely shredded
30ml (2 tblsp) chopped parsley
Salt and freshly ground black pepper to taste
5ml (1 tsp) chopped fresh thyme
2-3 eggs, beaten
75g (3oz) grated cheese

Garnish
Fresh mint

Fry the onion gently in the olive oil for 3 minutes. Mix together with all the remaining ingredients, adding sufficient beaten egg to give a stiff yet moist consistency. Spoon the mixture into a deep, greased and lined loaf tin, smoothing the surface level. Cover with a piece of lightly greased foil. Bake in the oven for 50 minutes. Allow to cool slightly in the tin before turning out. Serve the rice and vegetable loaf cut into slices, and accompanied by the yogurt and mint sauce. Garnish with mint. For the sauce: mix 150ml (1/4 pint) natural yogurt with salt and freshly ground black pepper to taste and 15ml (1 tblsp) chopped mint.

Black Eye Beans with Curry Dressing (far left) and Noodles with Fresh Tomato Sauce (above left).

'oodles with Kidney eans and Pesto

'EPARATION TIME: 5 minutes

'OOKING TIME: about 10 minutes

'RVES: 4 people

'5g (8oz) wholemeal or plain noodles
'lt and freshly ground black pepper to taste
small onion, finely chopped
'ml (2 tblsp) olive oil
clove garlic, peeled and crushed
'ml (2 tsp) Pesto sauce (see recipe)
'25g (8oz) cooked red kidney beans

'arnish
'prigs fresh basil

Cook the noodles in a large pan of boiling salted water until just tender. Meanwhile, fry the onion gently in the olive oil for 3 minutes; mix in the garlic and Pesto sauce. Drain the cooked noodles thoroughly; add to the onion and pesto mixture, together with the red kidney beans. Stir over a gentle heat for 1-2 minutes and serve piping hot, garnished with basil.

Black Eye Beans with Curry Dressing

PREPARATION TIME: 10-15 minutes

COOKING TIME: 35-40 minutes

SERVES: 4 people

225g (8oz) black eye beans, soaked overnight
Salt and freshly ground black pepper to taste
1 small onion, thinly sliced
1 green pepper, seeded and finely chopped
Juice of ½ lemon
30ml (2 tblsp) cashew nuts, whole or roughly chopped

Dressing
150ml (¼ pint) natural yogurt
10ml (2 tsp) curry powder
30ml (2 tblsp) fresh pineapple juice
1 clove garlic, crushed

Garnish
Curry powder

Simmer the beans in salted water until tender. Drain. Mix the black eye beans with the onion and green pepper. Stir in the lemon juice, salt and pepper to taste and the cashew nuts. For the dressing: mix all the ingredients together, adding salt and pepper to taste. Spoon the bean salad into a bowl, and spoon the prepared dressing over the top. Sprinkle with curry powder.

Chicken Liver Risotto with Red Beans

PREPARATION TIME: 15 minutes

COOKING TIME: about 28 minutes

SERVES: 4 people

1 medium onion, finely chopped
30ml (2 tblsp) olive oil
1 clove garlic, peeled and crushed
175g (6oz) brown or wild rice
750ml (1¼ pints) chicken stock
Salt and freshly ground black pepper to taste
225g (8oz) chicken livers, chopped
25g (1oz) butter
175g (6oz) cooked red kidney beans
15ml (1 tblsp) chopped parsley

Fry the onion gently in the olive oil for 3 minutes. Add the garlic and the rice and stir over the heat for 1 minute, until the rice is evenly coated with oil. Gradually stir in the chicken stock. Bring to the boil and add salt and pepper to taste; cover and simmer for 20 minutes. Meanwhile, fry the chopped chicken livers in the butter for about 4 minutes, until sealed on the outside but still pink in the centre. Drain the chicken livers with a slotted spoon and stir into the cooked rice, together with the red kidney beans and chopped parsley. Heat through. Serve hot with grated Parmesan cheese, if liked.

Cucumber with Yogurt, Dill and Burghul

PREPARATION TIME: 25 minutes

SERVES: 4 people

90ml (6 tblsp) burghul
1 clove garlic, peeled and crushed
Juice of 1 lemon
60ml (4 tblsp) olive oil
15ml (1 tblsp) fresh dill
Salt and freshly ground black pepper to taste
½ a large cucumber, halved, seeded and chopped
30ml (2 tblsp) natural yogurt

Garnish
Coarsely grated lemon rind
Sprigs of fresh dill

Soak the burghul in sufficient warm water to cover, for 10 minutes. Squeeze the drained burghul in a clean cloth to remove excess moisture. Mix the prepared burghul with the garlic, lemon juice, oil, dill and salt and pepper to taste. Stir in the cucumber and the yogurt. Spoon into a serving dish and garnish with lemon rind and dill.

Note: instead of mixing the yogurt into the burghul, make a well in the centre of the prepared burghul and spoon the yogurt into the centre.

Noodles with Fresh Tomato Sauce

PREPARATION TIME: 10-15 minutes

COOKING TIME: 6-8 minutes

SERVES: 4 people

450g (1lb) tomatoes, skinned and roughly chopped
1 small onion, peeled and chopped
1 clove garlic, peeled and chopped
15ml (1 tblsp) chopped parsley
15ml (1 tblsp) chopped basil
200ml (⅓ pint) olive oil
Salt and freshly ground black pepper to taste
350g (12oz) noodles (green, yellow, or wholemeal)

Garnish
Sprigs fresh basil

Put the tomatoes, onion, garlic, herbs, olive oil, and salt and pepper to taste into the liquidiser and blend until smooth. Cook the noodles in boiling salted water until just tender. Drain thoroughly. Toss the cooked noodles in the prepared tomato sauce. Garnish with sprigs of fresh basil and serve immediately.

Skillet Rice Cake

PREPARATION TIME: 25 minutes
COOKING TIME: about 15 minutes
SERVES: 4 people

1 medium onion, thinly sliced or chopped
1 clove garlic, peeled and chopped
30ml (2 tblsp) olive oil
15ml (1 tblsp) chopped fresh thyme
1 red pepper, seeded and thinly sliced
1 green pepper, seeded and thinly sliced
4 eggs
Salt and freshly ground black pepper to taste
90ml (6 tblsp) cooked brown or wild rice
45ml (3 tblsp) natural yogurt
75g (3oz) grated cheese

Garnish
Chopped fresh thyme

Fry the chopped onion and garlic gently in the olive oil in a frying pan for 3 minutes. Add the thyme and sliced peppers and fry gently for a further 4-5 minutes. Beat the eggs with salt and pepper to taste. Add the cooked rice to the fried vegetables and then add the beaten egg; cook over a moderate heat, stirring from time to time, until the egg starts to set underneath. Spoon the yogurt over the top of the par-set egg and sprinkle with the cheese. Place under a moderately hot grill until puffed and golden. Serve immediately, straight from the pan.

Italian Pasta Pie

PREPARATION TIME: 35 minutes
COOKING TIME: 1 hour 5 minutes
OVEN: 190°C, 375°F, Gas Mark 5
SERVES: 6-8 people

600g (1¼lbs) puff pastry
450g (1lb) fresh spinach, cooked and drained thoroughly
175g (6oz) curd cheese
1 clove garlic, peeled and crushed
Salt and freshly ground black pepper to taste
Generous pinch ground nutmeg
100g (4oz) pasta shapes, cooked until just tender
75g (3oz) shelled mussels
15ml (1 tblsp) chopped fresh basil
1 egg, beaten

Glaze Pastry
ıten egg
ıted Parmesan cheese

ll out ⅔ of the puff pastry quite ıly and use to line the sides and e of a loose-bottomed 18cm (7 h) round cake tin; press the ıtry carefully into the shape of tin, avoiding any cracks or ıts. Roll out the remaining pastry ı circle large enough to cover top of the cake tin generously. x the spinach with the curd eese, garlic, salt, pepper and tmeg to taste, cooked pasta, mussels and the beaten egg; spoon the filling into the pastry lined tin. Brush the rim of the pastry with beaten egg; lay the rolled out portion of pastry over the filling and press the adjoining pastry edges together to seal. Trim off the excess pastry, and pinch the edges decoratively. Cut decorative shapes from the pastry trimmings and fix on top of the pie; glaze with beaten egg and sprinkle with grated Parmesan cheese. Bake in the oven for 45 minutes; cover with a piece of foil and cook for a further 20 minutes. Unmould carefully from the tin and serve the pie hot, cut into wedges.

Note: the top of the pie can be sprinkled with a few pine kernels prior to baking, if liked.

Spaghetti with Chicken Bolognese and Nuts

PREPARATION TIME: 15-20 minutes

COOKING TIME: 15 minutes

SERVES: 4 people

Sauce
1 medium onion, finely chopped
1 clove garlic, peeled and finely chopped
30ml (2 tblsp) olive oil
200ml (⅓ pint) red wine
30ml (2 tblsp) tomato puree
15ml (1 tblsp) chopped fresh thyme
Salt and freshly ground black pepper to taste
225g (8oz) finely chopped cooked chicken
6 tomatoes, skinned, seeded and chopped
5ml (1 tsp) Pesto sauce (see recipe)
15ml (1 tblsp) chopped cashew nuts
15ml (1 tblsp) chopped walnuts
350g (12oz) spaghetti, plain or wholemeal

Garnish
Chopped walnuts

Fry the onion and garlic in the olive oil for 3 minutes. Add the red wine, tomato puree, thyme and salt and pepper to taste. Bring to the boil and simmer for 10 minutes. Add the chopped chicken, chopped tomatoes, Pesto sauce, cashew nuts and walnuts; simmer the sauce for a further few minutes. Meanwhile, cook the spaghetti in boiling salted water for 8-10 minutes, until just tender. Drain the spaghetti thoroughly. If the sauce is too thick for your liking, thin it down with a little hot stock or water. Pile the cooked spaghetti into a serving dish and spoon the hot sauce over the top. Sprinkle with extra chopped walnuts and serve immediately.

Facing page: Italian Pasta Pie (top) and Spaghetti with Chicken Bolognese and Nuts (bottom).

This page: Rice and Vegetable Loaf with Yogurt and Mint Sauce (top) and Skillet Rice Cake (bottom).

Desserts and Cakes

Ricotta Pancakes with Honey and Raisin Sauce

PREPARATION TIME: 10 minutes
COOKING TIME: 2-3 minutes
SERVES: 4 people

Sauce
60ml (4 tblsp) clear honey
Juice ½ lemon
15ml (1 tblsp) raisins
15ml (1 tblsp) pine kernels

Filling
225g (8oz) curd cheese, or Ricotta
Grated rind of ½ lemon
30ml (2 tblsp) raisins
15ml (1 tblsp) chopped pine kernels

8 small, hot pancakes

To Decorate
Twists of lemon

For the sauce: put all the ingredients into a small pan and warm through gently. For the filling: beat the cheese and the lemon rind until soft; mix in the raisins and pine kernels. Divide the filling amongst the hot pancakes and either roll them up, or fold them into triangles. Arrange the pancakes on warm plates, spoon the sauce over the top and decorate with twists of lemon. Serve immediately.

Almond Stuffed Figs

PREPARATION TIME: 25 minutes
SERVES: 4 people

4 large ripe figs
60ml (4 tblsp) ground almonds
30ml (2 tblsp) orange juice
30ml (2 tblsp) finely chopped dried apricots

Sauce
60ml (4 tblsp) natural yogurt
Finely grated rind of ½ orange

Garnish
Wedges of ripe fig
Wedges of lime
Ground cinnamon

Make a cross cut in each fig, without cutting right down and through the base. Ease the four sections of each fig out, rather like a flower head. Mix the ground allmonds with the orange juice and chopped dried apricots; press into the centre of each fig. For the sauce: mix the yogurt with the orange rind, and thin down with *a little* water. Spoon a pool of orange flavoured yogurt onto each of 4 small plates; sit a stuffed fig in the centre of each one. Decorate with wedges of fig and lime and a sprinkling of ground cinnamon.

Honey and Apple Tart

PREPARATION TIME: about 45 minutes
COOKING TIME: 35-40 minutes
OVEN: 190°C, 375°F, Gas Mark 5
SERVES: 6 people

75g (33oz) wholemeal flour
75g (3oz) plain white flour
75g (3oz) butter
1 egg yolk
45ml (3 tblsp) cold water

Filling
300ml (½ pint) unsweetened apple puree
15ml (1 tblsp) honey
2 egg yolks
30ml (2 tblsp) ground almonds
3 large eating apples, quartered, cored and thinly sliced
A little pale soft brown sugar

Glaze
45ml (3 tblsp) clear honey, warmed

For the pastry: put the flours into a bowl; add the butter in small pieces and rub in. Beat the egg yolk with 30ml (2 tblsp) of the water and add to the dry ingredients; mix to a soft yet firm dough, adding a little extra water as necessary (wholemeal flour varies from batch to batch as to how much liquid it will absorb). Roll out the dough on a floured surface and use to line a 23cm (9 inch) loose-bottomed, fluted flan tin; pinch up the edges well. Prick the base. For the filling: mix the apple puree with the brandy, egg yolks, honey and ground almonds. Spread over the base of the pastry case. Arrange the apple slices in overlapping, concentric circles on top of the apple and almond filing. Dust lightly with soft brown sugar. Bake in the oven for 35-40 minutes (if the apples start to brown too much, cover the filling with a circle of foil). As soon as the flan comes out of the oven, brush the apple top with warmed honey. This flan can be served cold, but it is best served warm.

Prune, Apricot and Nut Torten

PREPARATION TIME: 30 minutes. plus 'plumping' time
COOKING TIME: 25 minutes
OVEN: 190°C, 375°F, Gas Mark 5
SERVES: 6-8 people

100g (4oz) dried apricots
100g (4oz) dried prunes
300ml (½ pint) red wine, or dry cider

Nut Shortcake
100g (4oz) butter
50g (2oz) soft brown sugar
100g (4oz) wholemeal flour
50g (2oz) ground hazelnuts
45ml (3 tblsp) finely chopped walnuts

Glaze
30ml (2 tblsp) clear honey, warmed

To Decorate
15ml (1 tblsp) pine kernels
15ml (1 tblsp) hazelnuts

Put the apricots and prunes into a bowl. Warm the wine or cider and pour it over the dried fruits; leave them to 'plump' for 4 hours. For the shortcake: work the butter, brown sugar, flour and ground hazelnuts together. Knead lightly to a smooth dough, working in the chopped walnuts. Press evenly over the base of a 23cm (9 inch) fluted, loose-bottomed flan tin. Bake in the oven for 15 minutes. Drain the plumped prunes and apricots thoroughly on absorbent paper. Remove the shortcake from the oven and arrange the plumped fruits on top. Cover with a piece of foil and return to the oven for further 10 minutes. Remove th shortcake carefully from its tin. Glaze the fruits on top with th warmed honey and sprinkle wi the nuts. This is absolutely delicious served warm from th oven, but is equally good serve cold.

Ricotta Pancakes with Hone and Raisin Sauce (right) and Almond Stuffed Figs (below

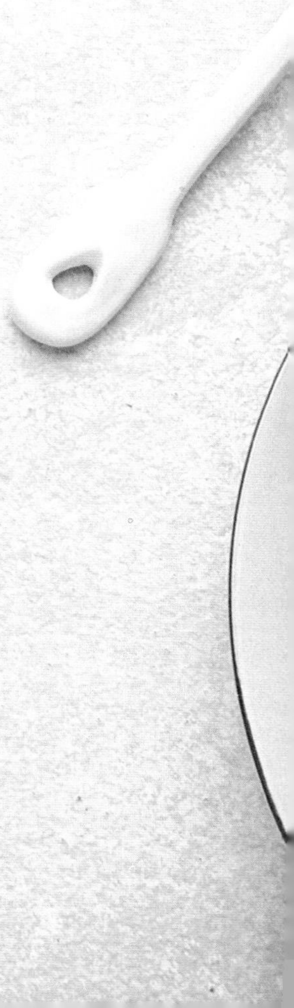

Passion Fruit Ice Crea

PREPARATION TIME: 20 minu
plus freezing time

SERVES: 4 people

6 passion fruit
300ml (½ pint) thick natural yog
2 egg yolks
10ml (2 tsp) honey

To Decorate
1-2 passion fruit, halved and scoo

For the ice cream: halve the passion fruit and scoop all the centre pulp into a bowl. Add th yogurt, egg yolks and honey, anc mix well together. Pour into a shallow container and freeze un firm. Scoop the ice cream into stemmed glasses and trickle a lit passion fruit pulp over each portion. Serve immediately. Note: this ice cream goes *very* ha and needs to be removed from t freezer several minutes before scooping.

Strawberry and Melon Salad

PREPARATION TIME: 25 minut

SERVES: 4 people

225g (8oz) large strawberries, hul
1 small Charentais or Ogen melor
Juice of 1 orange
15ml (1 tblsp) brandy

To Decorate
Small sprigs fresh mint

Slice the strawberries quite thin Halve and de-seed the melon an then scoop it into small balls (th is a special cutter for doing this, you can do it with a coffee spoor Arrange the strawberry slices anc melon balls on individual glass plates. Mix the orange juice with the brandy and dribble over the fruit. Decorate with mint.

This page: Prune, Apricot and Nut Torten (top) and Honey and Apple Tart (bottom).

Facing page: Passion Fruit Ice Cream (top) and Strawberry a Melon Salad (bottom).

Jellied Grape Shortcake

PREPARATION TIME: 45 minutes, plus cooling and chilling

COOKING TIME: about 20 minutes

OVEN: 190°C, 375°F, Gas Mark 5

SERVES: 6 people

50g (2oz) butter
25g (1oz) soft brown sugar
50g (2oz) wholemeal flour
25g (1oz) ground almonds

Jelly Topping

225g (8oz) green grapes, halved and de-pipped
600ml (1 pint) water
Thinly pared rind of 2 lemons
15ml (1 tblsp) honey
15g (½oz) powdered gelatine
30ml (2 tblsp) water
Yellow food colouring

Work the butter, brown sugar, flour and ground almonds together. Knead lightly to a smooth dough. Press evenly over the base of a 20cm (8 inch) loose-bottomed cake tin. Bake in the oven for 12-15 minutes, until the shortcake is pale golden. Remove from the oven and allow to cool completely. Lightly grease the sides of the cake tin above the baked shortcake. Arrange the halved grapes on top of the shortcake. Put the water and lemon rind into a pan; bring to the boil and allow to bubble briskly for 5 minutes. Remove the pan from the heat and allow the liquid to cool. Strain the lemon liquid and measure off 450ml (¾ pint). Stir in the honey. Dissolve the gelatine in the 30ml (2 tblsp) water and add to the lemon liquid (it can be tinted with a few drops of yellow food colouring at this stage, if liked). Leave in a cool place until it starts to set; pour the setting jelly over the grapes, making sure that the top surface is level. Chill for 2-3 hours until set. Serve cut into wedges.

Hazelnut and Apple Meringue Torten

PREPARATION TIME: 25-30 minutes

COOKING TIME: 45 minutes

OVEN: 190°C, 375°F, Gas Mark 5, then 160°C, 325°F, Gas Mark 3

SERVES: 6-8 people

100g (4oz) butter
50g (2oz) soft brown sugar
100g (4oz) wholemeal flour
50g (2oz) ground hazelnuts
30ml (2 tblsp) chopped hazelnuts
2 egg whites
75g (3oz) golden granulated sugar
300ml (½ pint) thick unsweetened apple puree

Work the butter, brown sugar, wholemeal flour and ground hazelnuts to a soft, smooth dough. Knead lightly and work in the chopped hazelnuts. Press evenly over the base of a 23cm (9 inch) fluted, loose-bottomed flan tin. Bake in the oven for 10 minutes. Meanwhile, whisk the egg whites until stiff but not 'dry'; gradually whisk in the golden granulated sugar. Remove the shortcake from the oven and pipe or swirl the meringue in a border around the edge. Return to the oven, lower the heat, and bake for a further 35 minutes, until golden. Fill immediately with the apple puree and serve while still warm.

Jellied Grape Shortcake (far right) and Chestnut Parfait (right).

hestnut Parfait

EPARATION TIME: 15 minutes
RVES: 4 people

5g (8oz) unsweetened chestnut
uree
nl (1 tblsp) honey
nl (1 tblsp) brandy
nl (4 tblsp) thick natural yogurt
nerous pinch ground cinnamon

To Decorate
Small cinnamon sticks

Beat the chestnut puree with the honey and brandy; blend in the yogurt and cinnamon. Spoon into glass custard cups or stemmed glasses. Spike each one with a cinnamon stick.
Note: this is very rich, and you may prefer to make the above quantities serve 6 small portions.

Iced Kiwi Fruit and Yogurt Pudding

PREPARATION TIME: 15 minutes, plus chilling time
SERVES: 4 people

300ml (½ pint) thick natural yogurt
Artificial sweetener to taste, or a little honey
4 kiwi fruit, peeled and chopped
2 kiwi fruit, peeled and thinly sliced

Mix the yogurt with sweetener or honey to taste, and stir in the chopped kiwi fruit. Place slices of kiwi fruit so that they stand upright against the sides of 4 stemmed glasses; spoon the yogurt and kiwi fruit mixture into the centre. Chill briefly, for about 20-30 minutes, before serving.

Glazed Cherry Rice Pudding

PREPARATION TIME: 20 minutes, plus cooling and chilling time

COOKING TIME: 45 minutes to 1 hour

SERVES: 4-6 people

60g (2oz) brown rice
25g (1oz) soft brown sugar
600ml (1 pint) skimmed milk
2.5ml (½ tsp) vanilla essence
Generous pinch ground nutmeg
30ml (2 tblsp) thick natural yogurt
225g (8oz) fresh cherries, de-stalked and pitted
150ml (¼ pint) pure red grape juice
150ml (¼ pint) water
10ml (2 tsp) powdered gelatine

Put the rice, sugar, skimmed milk, vanilla essence and nutmeg into a solid based pan; bring to the boil and simmer gently for ¾-1 hour, until the rice mixture is thick and creamy. Allow to cool and then beat in the yogurt. Spoon into a glass bowl and arrange the cherries on the top. Mix the grape juice with half the water; dissolve the gelatine in the remaining water and then add to the grape juice. Leave in a cool place until syrupy. Spoon the red glaze evenly over the cherries. Chill until set.

This page: Banana, Almond and Orange Truffles (top) and Hazelnut and Apple Meringue Torten (bottom).

Facing page: Iced Kiwi Fruit and Yogurt Pudding (top) and Glazed Cherry Rice Pudding (bottom).

Mango and Orange Mousse

PREPARATION TIME: 35-40 minutes, plus chilling time

SERVES: 4-6 people

450ml (¾ pint) fresh mango pulp
Finely grated rind of ½ orange
Artificial sweetener to taste
15g (½oz) powdered gelatine
30ml (2 tblsp) orange juice
30ml (2 tblsp) natural yogurt
2 egg whites

To Decorate
Twisted strips orange peel

Mix the mango pulp with the orange rind and artificial sweetener to taste. Dissolve the gelatine in the orange juice. Add to the mango pulp, together with the yogurt. Leave until the mixture is on the point of setting. Whisk the egg whites until stiff but not 'dry', and fold lightly but thoroughly into the thickened mango mixture. Spoon into stemmed glasses and chill until set. Decorate with twisted strips of orange peel.

No Sugar Fresh Mincemeat Tarts (top right), Lemon Yogurt Cake (above) and Muesli Biscuits (far right).

Banana, Almond and Orange Truffles

PREPARATION TIME: 25 minutes
MAKES: 10

2 bananas, peeled
Juice of ½ orange
Finely grated rind of 1 orange
100g (4oz) ground almonds
30ml (2 tblsp) finely chopped blanched almonds
15ml (1 tblsp) dark, soft brown sugar
Plain chocolate vermicelli

Mash the bananas with the orange juice and rind; mix in the ground almonds, chopped almonds and brown sugar. Chill the mixture until it is firm enough to shape. Roll into small balls, about the size of a ping pong ball. Roll each one in chocolate vermicelli so as to give an even coating. Chill once again.

No Sugar Fresh Mincemeat Tarts

PREPARATION TIME: 30 minutes
COOKING TIME: 20-25 minutes
OVEN: 190°C, 375°F, Gas Mark 5
MAKES: 4

1 eating apple, cored and finely chopped
30ml (2 tblsp) raisins
30ml (2 tblsp) currants
15ml (1 tblsp) chopped pitted dates
15ml (1 tblsp) chopped nuts (any variety)
30ml (2 tblsp) clear honey

Pastry
100g (4oz) wholemeal flour
100g (4oz) plain white flour
100g (4oz) butter
1 egg yolk
45ml (3 tblsp) water

Glaze
Beaten egg white
Caster sugar

Mix the chopped apple with the raisins, currants, chopped dates, nuts and honey. Keep covered while you make the pastry. Put the flours into a mixing bowl and rub in the butter. Mix the egg yolk with 30ml (2 tblsp) cold water; add to the sieved flours and mix to a soft, smooth dough, adding a little extra water if necessary. Roll out the dough quite thinly and use to line 4 individual tartlet tins (preferably with loose bottoms). Press up the edges well, trimming off excess pastry. Roll out the pastry trimmings and cut into thin strips. Fill the pastry cases with the fresh mincemeat, and lay a lattice of pastry strips over the top of each one. Press the strips to the side of the pastry case to seal. Glaze the strips and edges of the tarts with beaten egg white and sprinkle lightly with sugar. Bake in the oven for 20-25 minutes, until golden. Serve warm or cold.
Note: these are not little tarts, like jam tarts, and the pastry cases need to be about 10cm (4 inches) in diameter.

Lemon Yogurt Cake

PREPARATION TIME: 45 minutes
COOKING TIME: about 25 minutes
OVEN: 190°C, 375°F, Gas Mark 5
SERVES: 8-10 people

6 eggs
175g (6oz) soft brown sugar
175g (6oz) plain flour
Pinch mixed spice
Finely grated rind of 2 lemons
60ml (4 tblsp) water
30ml (2 tblsp) clear honey

Filling
225g (8oz) curd cheese
30ml (2 tblsp) clear honey
Finely grated rind and juice of ½ lemon
Few drops vanilla essence
30ml (2 tblsp) natural yogurt

Langues de chat biscuits
200ml (⅓ pint) thick natural yogurt
Matchstick strips lemon peel

Grease 3 large sandwich tins, each 23cm (9 inches) in diameter; dust each one lightly with flour. Whisk the eggs and brown sugar together until thick, light and creamy (when the whisk is lifted free from the mixture it should leave a trail on the surface). Sieve the flour and spice and fold lightly but thoroughly into the whisked mixture. Divide the mixture amongst the prepared tins, tilting them so that the mixture spreads evenly. Bake the sponge layers for 25 minutes. Allow them to shrink slightly from their tins before turning the baked sponges onto cooling racks. Put the lemon rind and water into a small pan; boil briskly until reduced by one half. Add the honey to the remaining lemon liquid and heat through together. Trickle the honey and lemon syrup over each sponge layer. For the filling: soften the curd cheese and beat with the honey, lemon rind and juice, vanilla essence and yogurt until smooth. Sandwich the three sponge layers together with the cheese filling, saving a few spoonfuls for fixing the biscuits to the sides of the cake. Fix langues de chat biscuits all around the sides of the assembled cake; attach each one with a little of the cheese filling. Spread the top of the cake with thick yogurt and decorate with matchstick strips of lemon peel.

Lemon and Ginger Cheesecake

PREPARATION TIME: 45 minutes, plus chilling time
SERVES: 6-8 people

40g (1½oz) butter, melted
25g (1oz) soft brown sugar
75g (3oz) oatmeal biscuits, crushed

Filling
175g (6oz) curd cheese
2 eggs, separated
Finely grated rind of 1 lemon
50g (2oz) light, soft brown sugar
150ml (¼ pint) natural yogurt
15g (½oz) powdered gelatine
45ml (3 tblsp) water
Juice of ½ lemon
3 pieces preserved stem ginger, rinsed in warm water and chopped

To Decorate
60ml (4 tblsp) thick natural yogurt
Fine matchstick strips lemon peel, or twists of lemon

Lightly grease an 18cm (7 inch) loose-bottomed cake tin. For the base: mix the melted butter, soft brown sugar and crushed biscuits together; press evenly over the base of the tin. Chill while you make the filling. For the filling: beat the curd cheese with the egg yolks, lemon rind, soft brown sugar and yogurt. Dissolve the gelatine in the water and add to the cheese mixture, together with the lemon juice; leave on one side until the mixture is on the point of setting. Whisk the egg whites until stiff but not 'dry', and fold lightly but thoroughly into the cheese mixture, together with the chopped ginger. Spoon the mixture into the prepared cake tin, smoothing the surface level. Chill for 3-4 hours, until the filling has set. Unmould the cheesecake carefully. Swirl natural yogurt over the top of the cheesecake and decorate with strips of lemon peel or lemon twists.

Muesli Biscuits

PREPARATION TIME: 20 minutes
COOKING TIME: 15 minutes
OVEN: 190°C, 375°F, Gas Mark 5
MAKES: about 20

100g (4oz) softened butter
100g (4oz) soft brown sugar
1 egg, beaten
100g (4oz) wholemeal flour
50g (2oz) muesli
30ml (2 tblsp) flaked almonds

Beat the margarine and sugar together until light and fluffy. Beat in the egg, adding a little flour if the mixture shows signs of curdling. Work in the remaining flour, muesli and flaked almonds. Shape the mixture into small balls, using floured hands. Place on greased baking sheets, allowing room for spreading. Flatten the balls of biscuit dough slightly. Bake in the oven for 15 minutes until crisp and golden. Allow to cool slightly before removing the baked biscuits to a cooling rack.

Date and Pistachio Shortbreads

PREPARATION TIME: 20 minutes
COOKING TIME: 12-15 minutes
OVEN: 190°C, 375°F, Gas Mark 5
MAKES: about 12

100g (4oz) butter
50g (2oz) soft brown sugar
100g (4oz) wholemeal flour
50g (2oz) ground almonds
75g (3oz) stoned dates, chopped
30ml (2 tblsp) chopped shelled pistachios

To Decorate
Chopped shelled pistachios

Work the butter, brown sugar, wholemeal flour and ground almonds to a soft, smooth dough. Knead lightly, working in the chopped dates and pistachios. Press the mixture into small boat-shaped moulds. Press a few chopped pistachios into the top of each uncooked shortbread. Bake in the oven for 12-15 minutes.

Apricot and Walnut Teabread

PREPARATION TIME: 20 minutes
COOKING TIME: 1 hour 3 minutes
OVEN: 160°C, 325°F, Gas Mark 3
MAKES: 1 loaf

175g (6oz) softened butter
175g (6oz) light soft brown sugar
3 eggs, beaten
225g (8oz) wholemeal flour
7.5ml (1½ tsp) baking powder
30ml (2 tblsp) milk
100g (4oz) dried apricots, chopped
50g (2oz) chopped walnuts

To Decorate
30ml (2 tblsp) clear honey, warmed
Extra chopped dried apricots

Lightly grease a 1kg (2lb) loaf tin, and line the base with a piece of greased greaseproof paper. Cream the butter and sugar until light and fluffy. Gradually beat in the eggs, adding a little flour if the mixture shows signs of curdling. Mix in the flour and baking powder, together with the milk, and finally stir in the chopped apricots and nuts. Put the mixture into the prepared loaf tin, smoothing the top level. Bake in the oven for 1 hour 30 minutes. If the top of the loaf starts to darken too much, cover it with a piece of foil. As soon as the loaf comes out of the oven, brush the top with the warmed honey and sprinkle with the chopped apricots. Leave to cool in the tin for a few minutes before turning out.

Golden Pistachio Meringues

PREPARATION TIME: 15-20 minutes
COOKING TIME: 1 hour
OVEN: 110°C, 225°F, Gas Mark ¼
MAKES: about 6

2 egg whites
100g (4oz) golden granulated sugar

Filling
100g (4oz) curd cheese
15ml (1 tblsp) clear honey
30ml (2 tblsp) chopped shelled pistachios

To Decorate
Chopped shelled pistachios

Whisk the egg whites until stiff but not dry and then gradually whisk in the golden granulated sugar. Pipe into 6 nest shapes on lightly greased and floured baking sheets. Bake in the oven for 1 hour. The meringues should be fairly crisp but they should not 'colour'. Allow to cool. For the filling: cream the cheese until soft; beat in the honey and chopped pistachios. Fill the meringue nests with the cheese filling. Sprinkle each one with extra pistachios.

Cinnamon and Peanut Cookies

PREPARATION TIME: 15-20 minutes
COOKING TIME: 20 minutes
OVEN: 180°C, 350°F, Gas Mark 4
MAKES: about 20

100g (4oz) softened butter
100g (4oz) soft brown sugar
1 egg, beaten
60ml (4 tblsp) clear honey
250g (9oz) wholemeal flour
2.5ml (½ tsp) ground cinnamon
5ml (1 tsp) baking powder
Pinch salt
75g (3oz) shelled peanuts

Cream the butter and sugar until well mixed (do not over-beat). M in the beaten egg and honey and then mix in the flour, cinnamon, baking powder and salt. Put heap teaspoons of the mixture onto greased baking sheets, allowing room for spreading; flatten each one slightly with the rounded si of a dampened spoon. Stud the tops with peanuts. Bake in the oven for 20 minutes.

Note: for really golden topped biscuits bake them as above for ju 15 minutes; brush each one with beaten egg and return to the ove for a further 5 minutes.

This page: (left picture) Cinnamon and Peanut Cookie (top) and Golden Pistachio Meringues (bottom). (Right picture) Mango and Orange Mousse (top) and Lemon and Ginger Cheesecake (bottom).

Facing page: Apricot and Walnut Teabread (top) and Da and Pistachio Shortbreads (bottom).

Drinks, Sauces and Dressings

Tropical Fruit Flummery

PREPARATION TIME: 10 minutes
SERVES: 4 people

3 kiwi fruit, peeled and chopped
2 ripe nectarines, halved, stoned and chopped
2 slices fresh pineapple, peeled and chopped
Juice of 1 fresh lime
300ml (½ pint) unsweetened pineapple juice

To Decorate
Slices of peeled kiwi fruit, or lime

Put the kiwi fruit, nectarines, pineapple, lime juice and pineapple juice into the liquidiser and blend until smooth. Pour into tall glasses and top up with iced water (either mineral or tap water). Decorate the rim of each glass with a slice of kiwi fruit or lime.

Mulled Apple and Honey

PREPARATION TIME: 5 minutes
COOKING TIME: 4 minutes
SERVES: 4 people

450ml (¾ pint) unsweetened apple juice
150ml (¼ pint) water
10ml (2 tsp) honey
2 cinnamon sticks, split in half
6 cloves
3 strips lemon peel

To Serve
4 cinnamon sticks

Put the apple juice into a pan with the water, honey, broken cinnamon sticks, cloves and lemon peel; simmer very gently for 4 minutes. Remove the broken cinnamon sticks and pour liquid into heat-proof glasses. Spike each drink with a whole cinnamon stick and serve.

Spicy Fresh Mango Juice

PREPARATION TIME: 15 minutes
SERVES: 4 people

300ml (½ pint) fresh mango pulp
Juice of 1 lemon
15ml (1 tblsp) clear honey
Generous pinch ground ginger
Generous pinch nutmeg
150ml (¼ pint) unsweetened orange juice
150ml (¼ pint) water
1 small piece fresh root ginger

To Decorate
4 rings of orange

Put the mango pulp, lemon juice, honey, ground ginger, nutmeg, orange juice and water into the liquidiser and blend until smooth. Pour into 4 glasses, adding two or three ice cubes to each one. Put the piece of root ginger into a garlic crusher and squeeze a few drops into each glass. Slide a ring of orange over the rim of each glass and serve.

This page: Tropical Fruit Flummery (top) and Grapefr Shrub (bottom).

Facing page: Spicy Fresh Ma Juice (right) and Mulled App and Honey (left).

Almond and Tarragon French Dressing

PREPARATION TIME: 5 minutes

MAKES: about 300ml (½ pint)

200ml (⅓ pint) good green olive oil
60ml (4 tblsp) tarragon vinegar
15ml (1 tblsp) chopped fresh tarragon
1 clove garlic, peeled and crushed
Salt and freshly ground black pepper to taste
30ml (2 tblsp) finely chopped blanched almonds

Mix all the ingredients together. Keep in a screw topped bottle or jar, in a cool place (not in the refrigerator).

Pesto Sauce

PREPARATION TIME: 5 minutes

MAKES: about 200ml (½ pint)

1 large bunch fresh basil
4 cloves garlic, peeled
45ml (3 tblsp) pine kernels
150ml (¼ pint) good green olive oil
15ml (1 tblsp) lemon juice
Salt and freshly ground black pepper to taste

Put all the ingredients into the liquidiser and blend until fairly smooth; the sauce should still have a little texture to it. Keep in a screw top jar in the refrigerator, for no more than a week. Serve with cooked pasta, with cold meats such as Italian ham, and with cooked game and poultry.

Fresh Tomato and Basil Sauce

PREPARATION TIME: 10-15 minutes

MAKES: 450ml (¾ pint)

1 small onion, finely chopped
450g (1lb) tomatoes, skinned, seeded and chopped
30ml (2 tblsp) tomato puree
5ml (1 tsp) honey
5ml (1 tsp) finely grated orange rind
2 cloves garlic, peeled
Salt and freshly ground black pepper to taste
150ml (¼ pint) red wine
150ml (¼ pint) chicken stock
30ml (2 tblsp) coarsely chopped fresh basil

Put all the sauce ingredients into the liquidiser and blend until smooth. If the sauce is too thick for your liking, thin it down a little with extra chicken stock. Can be kept in the refrigerator for up to 3 days. Serve with cooked pasta, with cooked fish, or as the base for a cold soup.

Low Fat Yogurt 'Mayonnaise'

PREPARATION TIME: 5-10 minutes

MAKES: about 300ml (½ pint)

2 egg yolks
15ml (1 tblsp) white wine vinegar
5ml (1 tsp) chive mustard
1 clove garlic, peeled and crushed
Salt and freshly ground black pepper to taste
300ml (½ pint) thick natural yogurt

Beat the egg yolks with the vinegar; beat in the remaining ingredients. This is thinner than a standard oil-based mayonnaise, but equally delicious. Serve with salads, cooked fish, over cooked vegetables, etc. Will keep in the refrigerator for up to 4 days.

Grapefruit Shrub

PREPARATION TIME: 10-15 minutes

SERVES: 4 people

Peeled segments from 2 grapefruit
300ml (½ pint) unsweetened grapefruit juice
150ml (¼ pint) water
30ml (2 tblsp) clear honey
2 egg whites

To Decorate
Small sprigs fresh mint or grated lemon rind

Put the grapefruit segments, grapefruit juice, water and hone into the liquidiser and blend un smooth. Add the egg whites an blend once again until frothy. Po into glasses, making sure that a good portion of the white 'froth goes into each one. Decorate wi mint or lemon rind.

This page: Almond and Tarragon French Dressing (t and Low Fat Yogurt 'Mayonnaise' (bottom).

Facing page: Pesto Sauce (to and Fresh Tomato and Basil Sauce (bottom).

CHINESE CUISINE

ntroduction to Chinese Cooking

in any other style of cooking, Chinese food is a symbol of life and od health, forming a central part of family and social activity for ny people. Through cooking, one demonstrates personal entiveness and creativity, as well as one's cultural background, so oking can always be seen as a pleasurable activity.

Chinese cooking, the preparation is of great importance. Many hes require very fine chopping and shredding of the various redients, and they are combined in a very orderly manner. Those redients which are not easily available in the Western world can substituted by others in the recipes. It is not necessary to use only inese utensils as these dishes can easily be prepared using basic chen equipment.

e main cooking technique used to produce good Chinese food is -frying. A wok is ideal, but a deep, non-stick skillet will serve the rpose just as well. Stir-frying requires good temperature control d this is easily learnt through practice. The wok or pan should be ated, then the temperature reduced before adding oil. If the ensil is too hot the oil will burn, giving a charred, oily taste to the od, which may burn, too! The heat should be progressively raised the addition of other ingredients. The whole process may take tween five and seven minutes. Remember, never overcook, as this will not only destroy the crispness of the food, but also its flavor and goodness.

Chinese food incorporates six basic flavors, just like Indian food. They are: sweet, sour, salty, spicy, pungent and hot. Their employment and respective proportions must be well balanced. Flavoring is always supplemented by ready-prepared sauces, the most essential of which is soy sauce. Others commonly used are oyster and plum sauces.

Finally, garnishing should not be neglected, as presentation is every bit as important as preparation. After all, what appeals to the eye also appeals to the mind and thence to heart and stomach. A slice of cleverly carved carrot, a thin sliver of tomato and carefully arranged parsley or coriander, can add that all-important dash of color.

Cooking is always a pleasure, especially Chinese cooking. It is a challenge and a way to explore one's creative talents. In any case, who does not want their efforts to be rewarded by the pleasure of an exquisite meal?

Facing page: Four Happiness Dumpling left), Steamed Shrimp Pancakes (bottor and Steamed Open Dumplings (

Snacks

Four Happiness Dumplings

PREPARATION TIME: 30-45 minutes for pastry; 20-30 minutes for filling

COOKING TIME: 20 minutes

Pastry

225g (8oz) plain flour
Pinch of salt
200ml (⅓ pint) boiling water

Put the flour and salt into a bowl. Add the boiling water and mix quickly to make a dough. Cover and allow to stand for 20-30 minutes. Knead the dough for 2-3 minutes, sprinkling the work surface with a little cornflour if needed. Divide the dough into 30-35 equal portions and roll each one to a circle 6cm (2½") in diameter.

Filling

175g (6oz) boned loin of pork, finely chopped or minced
2 black mushrooms, soaked and diced
50g (2oz) mixed vegetables, peeled and finely chopped (peas, carrots, celery, etc.)
2.5ml (½ tsp) brown sugar or maltose
10ml (2 tsp) light soya sauce
1.25ml (¼ tsp) freshly ground black pepper
1 egg
5-6 chives, finely chopped
Salt to taste
15ml (1 tblsp) oil
7.5ml (1½ tsp) cornflour
30ml (2 tblsp) flour mixed with a little cold water to a smooth paste

Mix the pork with the mushrooms, mixed vegetables, sugar, soya sauce, black pepper, egg, chives and salt to taste. Add the oil and cornflour and mix well with a fork. Divide filling into 30 to 35 equal portions. Fill each dumpling wrapper with a portion of filling and shape into crescent shape dumplings. Steam them in an ordinary steamer or a Chinese bamboo steamer for about 20 minutes. Serve with a dip and chilli sauce. To make the crescent shape, place a wrapper on a flat surface, put a little filling in the centre, spread the edges with a little flour and water paste and pinch the edges of the wrapper together to seal. Pull one corner of the filled wonton around and over the other corner. Press to seal.

Steamed Shrimp Pancakes

PREPARATION TIME: 1 hour

COOKING TIME: 10-15 minutes

175g (6oz) plain flour or high gluten flour
50g (2oz) cornflour
1.25ml (¼ tsp) salt
15ml (1 tblsp) oil
45ml (3 tblsp) beaten egg
30ml (2 tblsp) water
30ml (2 tblsp) flour mixed with cold water to a smooth paste

Filling

150g (6oz) shrimps, boiled and finely chopped
2 spring onions, bulb only, finely chopped
1.25ml (¼ tsp) salt or to taste
5ml (1 tsp) cornflour to bind

Sieve the flour, cornflour and salt into a bowl. Add the oil, beaten egg and water and mix to make a stiff dough. Leave for 30 minutes to rest. Knead well for 5-6 minutes and roll into 25-30 15cm (6") circles on greaseproof paper. Place the filling in the centre and flatten. Spread flour and water paste around the edge of each pancake and fold up from one end to make a roll. Arrange the pancakes in a greased ordinary or Chinese bamboo steamer and cook over boiling water for 10-15 minutes. Serve piping hot with chilli or soya sauce dip.

Filling

To make the filling mix all the ingredients except the cornflour together, and then bind with the cornflour.

Alternative

To make rice pancakes, soak 100g (4oz) rice for 10 minutes. Grind with water to make a very fine paste of batter consistency. Add 15ml (1 tblsp) oil and mix well. Line a steamer with fine muslin and spoon in a little batter; spread it out into a thin pancake. Steam for 5 minutes. Place a little filling on the pancake and roll up. Steam for 10 minutes and serve piping hot with a dip.

Steamed Open Dumplings

PREPARATION TIME: 1 hour

COOKING TIME: 10-15 minutes

Filling

100g (4oz) peeled prawns, finely chopped
175g (6oz) pork or beef, minced
2 black mushrooms, soaked and finely chopped
Salt to taste
2.5ml (½ tsp) brown sugar

Seasoning

2.5ml (½ tsp) monosodium glutamate (optional)
15ml (1 tblsp) cornflour
5ml (1 tsp) dark soya sauce
5ml (1 tsp) light soya sauce
1.25ml (¼ tsp) freshly ground black pepper
15ml (1 tblsp) sesame oil
24 wonton wrappers

Mix the minced pork, prawns, mushrooms, salt and sugar together. Add the seasoning ingredients and mix well. Allow to stand for 30 minutes. Take each wonton wrapper and spoon a little filling in the centre. Fold up the edges around the filling but do not completely enclose it. (An open ended dumpling is produced with the sides of the wrapper gathered around the filling.) Flatten the base by pressing it slightly so that it will stand upright in a steamer. Grease an ordinary steamer or a bamboo steamer and arrange the dumplings in it. Steam for 15-20 minutes. Serve hot with a dip.

Wontons with Pork and Shrimp Filling

PREPARATION TIME: 30 minutes

COOKING TIME: 10-15 minu

175g (6oz) lean pork, minced
Oil
175g (6oz) peeled shrimps, fine chopped
3 spring onions, finely chopped
2.5ml (½ tsp) ground white pe
15ml (1 tblsp) soya sauce
7.5ml (1½ tsp) rice wine or dry sherry
2.5ml (½ tsp) salt, or to taste
7.5ml (1½ tsp) cornflour blend with 30ml (2 tblsp) water
40-50 wonton wrappers
30ml (2 tblsp) plain flour, mixe with a little cold water to a s paste

Fry pork in 30ml (2 tblsp) oil it loses its pink colour. Add shrimps and onions and fry fo minutes. Add pepper, soya sa and wine. Season with salt an fry for 1-2 minutes. Add the blended cornflour and stir ov moderate heat until thicken Allow to cool before filling th wontons. Divide filling into 4 equal portions. Take a wonto wrapper, moisten the edges w the flour and water paste. Plac portion of filling in the centre the wonton and gather up the edges to make a neat round, c shape in such a way as to mak triangle or any other shape th you prefer. Once you have sha all the wontons, deep-fry then hot oil until crisp and golden. will need to fry them in 3 or n batches. Drain well on absorb paper before serving.

Fried Meat Dumplin

PREPARATION TIME: 10 mi

COOKING TIME: about 15 minutes

30ml (2 tblsp) cooking oil
225g (8oz) lean, minced beef o
2 spring onions, chopped
30ml (2 tblsp) light soya sauce
2.5ml (½ tsp) salt
22.5ml (1½ tblsp) rice wine or sherry
10ml (2 tsp) cornflour mixed w 30ml (2 tblsp) water

npling wrappers (see recipe)
l (2 tblsp) plain flour mixed to a
iste with cold water
for deep frying

t the 30ml (2 tblsp) oil in a pan fry the minced meat and onion 2-3 minutes. Add the soya ce, salt and wine. Cook gently 2 minutes and then stir in the nflour and water mixture. Stir the heat until the mixture kens. Put the meat mixture into sh and leave to cool. Divide equal portions – about 48. e a round dumpling wrapper place a portion of filling in the tre. Moisten the edges of the pper with a little flour and er paste, gather the edges up over the filling and pinch ther to seal. Shape neatly. ntinue to make the remaining dumplings in the same way. Deep-fry the dumplings in moderately hot oil, cooking a few dumplings at a time, until they are golden brown. Drain thoroughly on absorbent paper. Serve with chilli sauce dip.

Dumpling Wrappers

(Chiao Tze P'i)

PREPARATION TIME: 50-60 minutes

275g (10oz) plain flour
200ml (⅓ pint) cold water

Makes 40-50 wrappers

Sieve the flour into a bowl and add the cold water, a little at a time, and mix to a firm dough. Knead the dough on a flat surface for 4-5 minutes. Cover with a damp cloth or wrap in cling film. Leave to stand at room temperature for 30-40 minutes. Roll out on a well-floured surface as thinly as possible, until almost transparent. Cut into round or square pieces to suit your requirements. Use within a few hours of making otherwise they will dry out.

Wonton Wrappers

PREPARATION TIME: 5-6 hours (including standing time)

120g (4¼oz) high gluten flour
30ml (2 tblsp) beaten egg
30ml (2 tblsp) cold water
Cornflour

Makes 40-50 wrappers

Sieve flour and gradually add the beaten egg and water mixed together. Mix to a stiff dough. Knead firmly for 5-6 minutes and wrap in cling film. Leave to stand at room temperature for 4-5 hours. Roll out into a very large square on a work surface dusted with cornflour. The pastry should be almost transparent. Cut into 40-50 7.5cm (3″) round or square wrappers. Dust each wrapper with cornflour before stacking. Store the wrappers, wrapped securely in cling film, in the refrigerator, for up to 24 hours. If they are allowed to dry out they will split during cooking.

Spring Roll Wrappers

PREPARATION TIME: 20 minutes, plus chilling time

100g (4oz) strong plain flour
1 egg, beaten
A little cold water

Makes 12 wrappers

Sieve the flour into a bowl. Make a well in the centre and add the beaten egg and a little cold water. Mix to a soft yet firm dough, adding a little extra water if necessary. Knead the dough until it is really pliable. (This helps to make the gluten work.) Chill, covered, for 4 hours or overnight. Allow to come back to room temperature. Roll out the dough on a well-floured surface to about 5mm (1/4") thick. Cut into 12 equal pieces, and then roll each piece to a square about 15x15cm (6x6") – each square should be very thin.

Spring Rolls

PREPARATION TIME: 20-30 minutes

COOKING TIME: about 20 minutes

225g (8oz) lean, raw pork or beef, finely shredded
100g (4oz) prawns or shrimps (either uncooked or boiled), shelled
4 spring onions, finely chopped
Cooking oil
10ml (2 tsp) fresh root ginger, peeled and shredded
100g (4oz) white cabbage, shredded
75g (3oz) bean sprouts
15ml (1 tblsp) soya sauce
Salt to taste
12 spring roll wrappers, each 15cm (6") square (see recipe)
30ml (2 tblsp) plain flour, mixed with a little cold water to a smooth paste

Fry the shredded pork, prawns or shrimps and the spring onions in 15ml (1 tblsp) of cooking oil for 2-3 minutes. Add the ginger, cabbage and bean sprouts, and stir fry for 2-3 minutes. Add soya sauce, and season with a little salt if desired. Remove from the heat and allow to cool. Lay out the spring roll wrappers on a clean working surface, with one point of each wrapper facing you. Divide the filling mixture into 12 equal portions and place one portion of filling just above the front point of each wrapper. Fold in the opposite side points, so that they overlap slightly like an envelope – secure the side points with a little flour and water paste. Starting with the point facing you, roll each wrapper up around the filling, securing the remaining point with a little flour and water paste. Repeat in exactly the same way with the remaining spring roll wrappers. They will keep a better shape if you chill them for 1 hour before cooking. Deep fry over a medium heat until golden brown and crisp. Drain thoroughly on absorbent paper and serve hot with a selection of dips or chilli sauce. The spring rolls can be frozen, uncooked.

This page: Fried Meat Dumplings (top right), Sprin Rolls (centre left) and Wonto with Pork and Shrimp Filling (bottom). Facing page: Spice Beef (top), Steamed Beef Szechuan Style (bottom left) and Beef with Green Pepper and Chilli (bottom right).

Meat Dishes

iced Beef

PARATION TIME: 30 minutes
OKING TIME: 5-6 minutes

rinade
(1 tsp) sugar
star anise, ground
nl (½ tsp) ground fennel
ıl (1 tblsp) dark soya sauce
5ml (¼ tsp) monosodium
lutamate (optional)

g (1lb) fillet of beef, cut into
.5cm (1") strips
m (1") fresh root ginger, peeled
nd crushed
nl (½ tsp) salt
ıl (2 tblsp) oil
ring onions, sliced
nl (½ tsp) freshly ground black
epper
ıl (1 tblsp) light soya sauce

x the marinade ingredients ether. Add the beef strips, ger and salt, and marinate for 20 nutes. Heat the oil in wok and fry the onions for 1 minute. d beef, ground pepper and soya ce and stir fry for 4-5 minutes. ve with a dip.

eamed Beef Szechuan yle

EPARATION TIME: 40 minutes
OKING TIME: 15 minutes

ices fresh root ginger, minced
l (1 tsp) salt
l (1 tsp) sugar
shly ground black pepper
nl (1 tblsp) oil
nl (2 tblsp) rice wine or dry sherry
5ml (1½ tblsp) chilli bean paste
nl (2 tblsp) dark soya sauce
spring onions, finely chopped
0g (1lb) fillet of beef, cut into 5cm
2") long strips
0g (4oz) ground rice
rge lotus leaf or several cabbage
eaves

r the marinade, mix the ginger, , sugar, pepper, oil, wine, bean ste, soya sauce and half of the ing onions. Add beef strips and x well. Leave to marinate for 15-20 minutes. Heat the wok and dry-roast the ground rice for 2-4 minutes till rice changes colour from white to light brown. Roll the marinated beef in the roasted ground rice to give a thin, even coating. Line the bamboo steamer with a well-oiled lotus leaf or a few old and tough cabbage leaves. Arrange the coated beef strips in a neat pile on top. Steam fairly quickly for 10-15 minutes over boiling water. Garnish with the remaining chopped spring onions before serving. Serve hot with chilli sauce.

Beef with Green Pepper and Chilli

PREPARATION TIME: 30 minutes
COOKING TIME: 10-12 minutes

450g (1lb) fillet of beef, cut into 2.5cm (1") strips

Seasoning
30ml (2 tblsp) dark soya sauce
5ml (1 tsp) sesame oil
Pinch bicarbonate of soda
1.25ml (¼ tsp) ground black pepper
2.5ml (½ tsp) salt

Oil for cooking
2 green peppers, seeded and thinly sliced
1 onion, peeled and sliced
2 spring onions, chopped
2.5cm (1") fresh root ginger, peeled and sliced
2 garlic cloves, peeled and chopped
3 green chillis, sliced

Sauce
30ml (2 tblsp) chicken stock
2.5ml (½ tsp) monosodium glutamate (optional)
5ml (1 tsp) dark soya sauce
Salt to taste
Few drops sesame oil

Marinate beef with the seasoning ingredients for 15 minutes. Heat 30ml (2 tblsp) oil and stir fry green peppers and onions for 2 minutes. Remove to a plate. Reheat wok, add 30-45ml (2-3 tblsp) oil and fry ginger, garlic and green chillis for 1 minute. Add beef and stir fry for 4-5 minutes. Add sauce ingredients, mixed together, and the fried peppers and onions. Stir fry for a further 2 minutes and serve.

Diced Pork with Sweet Corn

PREPARATION TIME: 25 minutes
COOKING TIME: 15-20 minutes

Marinade
Pinch salt
10ml (2 tsp) dark soya sauce
1.25ml (¼ tsp) sugar
5ml (1 tsp) rice wine
15ml (1 tblsp) water

175g (6oz) pork loin, diced
Oil for deep frying
2 slices fresh root ginger, peeled and diced
1 clove garlic, peeled and chopped
250ml (8 fl oz) chicken stock

Seasoning
1.25ml (¼ tsp) salt
1.25ml (¼ tsp) freshly ground black pepper
1.25ml (¼ tsp) sugar
5ml (1 tsp) rice wine or dry sherry
Few drops sesame oil

5ml (1 tsp) cornflour mixed with 15ml (1 tblsp) water

250ml (8 fl oz) creamed sweet corn
1 egg, well beaten
4 spring onions, chopped

Mix the marinade ingredients together. Add the pork and leave to marinate for 15 minutes. Drain the pork and discard the liquid. Heat the wok and pour in the oil for deep frying. Fry the pork until light brown. Remove the pork and drain. Reserve the oil for future use. Heat 15ml (1 tblsp) oil in the wok, add the ginger and pork. Stir fry for 3 minutes. Add the stock and simmer for 3 minutes. Add the seasoning ingredients and simmer for 2-3 minutes. Add the blended cornflour and water and simmer until the sauce thickens. Add the sweet corn and beaten egg and cook for 2-3 minutes. Serve sprinkled with chopped onions. Serve this dish with plain boiled rice or noodles.

Pork Stuffed Mushroo

PREPARATION TIME: 15-20 minutes
COOKING TIME: 12 minutes

Filling
1 egg
10ml (2 tsp) cornflour
10ml (2 tsp) rice wine or dry she
1.25ml (¼ tsp) minced fresh root ginger
6 water chestnuts, finely chopped
50g (2oz) peeled shrimps, choppe
175g (6oz) lean pork, minced
1.25ml (¼ tsp) salt
1.25ml (¼ tsp) freshly ground bla pepper
2.5ml (½ tsp) sugar
10ml (2 tsp) chilli sauce

16 large, open mushrooms
600ml (1 pint) chicken stock
Oil

Mix all the filling ingredients together. Remove the mushroo stalks. Divide the filling into 16 portions. Bring the chicken stoc to the boil. Add the mushroom and leave to stand off the heat f minutes, covered. Drain the mushrooms and discard the sto Top each mushroom with a por of filling. Put the stuffed mushrooms into a well-oiled steamer. Steam for 10-12 minut over boiling water. Serve as a sn as a starter or as a side dish. Alternatively, serve with a simp sauce made from thickened chicken broth. Pour the sauce o the steamed mushrooms.

Sliced Pork in Wine Sauce

PREPARATION TIME: 30 minutes

COOKING TIME: about 16 minutes

Seasoning

15ml (1 tblsp) red vinegar
15ml (1 tblsp) light soya sauce
15ml (1 tblsp) rice wine or dry sherry
10ml (2 tsp) soya paste
5ml (1 tsp) freshly ground black pepper
5ml (1 tsp) salt
5ml (1 tsp) Shao Hsing wine

450g (1lb) pork fillet, cut into 5cm (2") long thin slices
15ml (1 tblsp) cornflour
60ml (4 tblsp) oil
2.5cm (½") fresh root ginger, finely chopped
3 spring onions (or scallions), chopped
1 green pepper, seeded and diced

Sauce

10ml (2 tsp) cornflour
60ml (4 tblsp) dry white wine
120ml (4 fl oz) chicken stock
10ml (2 tsp) dark soya sauce
5ml (1 tsp) sugar
2.5ml (½ tsp) salt

Mix the seasoning ingredients together. Add the pork slices and leave to marinate for 10-15 minutes. Drain the pork and roll in the cornflour. Leave on one side. Discard the marinade. Heat half the oil in the wok until smoking. Add the pork, reduce the heat, and

Diced Pork with Sweet Corn (far left), Sliced Pork in Wine Sauce (top left) and Pork Stuffed Mushrooms (left).

Steamed Pork with Salted Cabbage (top), Pork with Green Pepper (centre right) and Pork Chop Suey (bottom).

stir fry for 4-6 minutes until lightly browned. Remove the pork and keep on one side. Discard any oil left in the wok. Add the remaining oil to the wok and stir fry the onions, ginger and green pepper for 3-5 minutes. Return the fried pork to the wok and cook for a further 2-3 minutes with the vegetables. Remove onto a serving dish. Mix the cornflour from the sauce ingredients with 30ml (2 tblsp) water. Add the remaining sauce ingredients to the wok and bring to the boil. Add the blended cornflour. Stir and simmer until the sauce thickens, simmer for 1-2 minutes. Pour over the pork and serve.

Deep Fried Pork Meat Balls

PREPARATION TIME: 25 minutes

COOKING TIME: about 12 minutes

450g (1lb) lean pork, coarsely minced
1 small onion, finely chopped
1 green chilli, chopped
Salt and freshly ground black pepper to taste
2.5cm (½") fresh root ginger, peeled and finely chopped
1 egg, beaten
15ml (1 tblsp) cornflour
10ml (2 tsp) dark soya sauce
2 sprigs Chinese parsley, finely chopped
5ml (1 tsp) cooked oil
Oil for deep frying
2 spring onions, chopped (for garnishing)
1 green pepper, seeded and cut into rings (for garnishing) (optional)

Mix the minced pork with the chopped onion, chilli, salt and pepper to taste, chopped ginger, beaten egg, cornflour, soya sauce, parsley and cooked oil. Leave to stand for 10 minutes. Mould into 16 even-sized balls. Heat the oil in the wok for deep frying and slide a few pork balls into the oil. Fry over a gentle heat for 5-6 minutes until golden brown and tender. Rem and drain on kitchen paper. Fry the meat balls and serve with chopped spring onions and gre pepper rings sprinkled on top. Serve as a snack, as a starter or side dish.

Pork Chop Suey

PREPARATION TIME: 35 minu

COOKING TIME: 10 minutes

Marinade

15ml (1 tblsp) water
2.5ml (½ tsp) bicarbonate of sod
10ml (2 tsp) dark soya sauce

225g (½ lb) pork fillet, sliced int 5cm (2") pieces
45ml (3 tblsp) cooked oil or cooki oil
1 onion, peeled and cut into piec
1 clove of garlic, peeled and slice
25g (1oz) bamboo shoots, sliced
175g (6oz) bean sprouts

Seasoning

Pinch salt
Pinch freshly ground black peppe
Pinch monosodium glutamate (optional)
45ml (3 tblsp) light soya sauce
5ml (1 tsp) sugar
5ml (1 tsp) cornflour

Sauce

5ml (1 tsp) cornflour
15ml (1 tblsp) water

Mix the marinade ingredients together. Add the pork and leav for 15 minutes to marinate. Dra the pork and discard the marina Heat the oil in the wok and stir pork for 2-3 minutes. Remove t pork. Add the onions, garlic an bamboo shoots to the wok and fry for 1-2 minutes. Add the bean sprouts and stir fry for 2 minutes. Remove onto a dish a add the mixed seasoning ingredients. Leave for 10 minut Return the pork and the vegeta to the wok. Add the blended sa ingredients. Bring to the boil ge stirring until the sauce thickens. Serve immediately.

Facing page: Fried Pork with Vegetables (top left), Bean Sprouts with Chopped Pork (centre right) and Deep Fried Pork Meat Balls (bottom).

Braised Hong Kong Beef

PREPARATION TIME: 30 minutes
COOKING TIME: about 15-17 minutes

30ml (2 tblsp) oil
450g (1lb) fillet of beef, sliced into matchstick-size strips
1 onion, peeled and sliced
2.5cm (1") fresh root ginger, peeled and cut into thin strips
3-4 fresh tomatoes, cut into thin wedges
225g (½lb) carrots, scraped and cut into 5cm (2") sticks
10ml (2 tsp) brown sugar
2.5ml (½ tsp) five spice powder
30ml (2 tblsp) light soya sauce
15ml (1 tblsp) rice wine or dry sherry
30ml (2 tblsp) water
Salt to taste

Heat the oil in a wok and fry the beef for 3-4 minutes. Add the onion, ginger, tomatoes and carrots. Stir fry for 2-3 minutes. Add the sugar, five spice powder, soya sauce, wine and water. Season with salt to taste and cook gently for 8-10 minutes. Serve as a side dish.

Pork with Green Pepper

PREPARATION TIME: 20 minutes
COOKING TIME: 1 hour 15 minutes

450g (1lb) pork fillet, cut into 5cm (2") strips

Seasoning
1.25ml (¼ tsp) sugar
1.25ml (¼ tsp) monosodium glutamate (optional)
5ml (1 tsp) light soya sauce
10ml (2 tsp) sweet bean paste
10ml (2 tsp) Shao Hsing wine or dry sherry
60ml (4 tblsp) chicken stock

Oil for deep frying
2 cloves garlic, peeled and cut into thin strips
1 green pepper, seeded and sliced into strips
1 green chilli, sliced into strips
1 red chilli, cut in half then sliced into strips

Sauce
5ml (1 tsp) cornflour
15ml (1 tblsp) water

Boil the pork in water for ¾ hour until cooked. Drain the pork and discard the water. Mix the seasoning ingredients together and stir in the pork. Leave to stand for 10 minutes. Heat the wok and add the oil for deep frying. When oil is very hot fry the drained pork for a few minutes until golden brown. Remove and drain the pork and keep the oil for future use. Reheat the wok and add 5ml (1 tsp) oil and stir fry the garlic for 1 minute. Add the pepper and chillis and stir fry for 1 minute. Add the remaining seasoning mixture and the pork. Stir fry over a gentle heat for 1-2 minutes and then add the blended sauce ingredients. Cook until the sauce thickens. Remove from the heat and serve immediately. Serve with mixed fried rice or rice noodles.

Steamed Pork with Salted Cabbage

PREPARATION TIME: 25 minutes
COOKING TIME: 2 hours

450g (1lb) fillet pork cut into 1cm (½") thick slices
Salt
175g (6oz) cabbage, shredded (Chinese white or plain green cabbage)

Seasoning
15ml (1 tblsp) sugar
30ml (2 tblsp) cooked oil
5ml (1 tsp) monosodium glutamate (optional)
60ml (4 tblsp) stock or water
Salt and freshly ground black pepper

15ml (1 tblsp) dark soya sauce
Oil for deep frying

Sauce
5ml (1 tsp) cornflour
15ml (1 tblsp) water

Boil the pork in 450ml (¾ pint) water for ¾ hour until tender. Drain the pork and discard the water. Boil 450ml (¾ pint) fresh water with 5ml (1 tsp) salt and add the cabbage. Cook for 2 minutes. Drain, rinse in cold water and then drain again. Season the cabbage with 5ml (1 tsp) of the sugar and 15ml (1 tblsp) of the cooked oil. Mix well and keep on one side. Place the pork in a dish and mix with the dark soya sauce. Leave for 10 minutes. Drain. Mix all the seasoning ingredients together. Heat the oil for deep frying and fry the pork until it turns lightly golden. Drain and add to the seasoning mixture. Keep the oil for future use. Place the pork and the seasoning mixture into a deep dish and put the boiled cabbage on top. Cover and steam over boiling water for 1 hour. Drain off any excess liquid and retain. Heat the wok and add the cabbage liquid. Add the blended sauce thickening of cornflour and water. Stir over the heat until the sauce thickens. Pour over the cabbage and pork and serve.

Bean Sprouts with Chopped Pork

PREPARATION TIME: 15 minutes
COOKING TIME: 10 minutes

225g (½ lb) lean pork, chopped finely or coarsely minced

Marinade
2.5ml (½ tsp) salt
15ml (1 tblsp) light soya sauce
1 egg white, beaten
5ml (1 tsp) cornflour

450g (1lb) bean sprouts
Oil for cooking

Seasoning
2.5ml (½ tsp) salt
2.5ml (½ tsp) sugar
2.5ml (½ tsp) monosodium glutamate (optional)
10ml (2 tsp) soya sauce
5ml (1 tsp) rice wine or dry sherry
15ml (1 tblsp) oyster sauce

2.5cm (½") fresh root ginger, peeled and thinly sliced
2-3 spring onions, chopped
120ml (4 fl oz) chicken stock

Sauce
2.5ml (½ tsp) cornflour or arrowroot
15ml (1 tblsp) water or stock
Few drops of sesame oil

Mix the pork with the marinade ingredients and keep on one side for 10 minutes. Trim the bean sprouts and chop them coarsely. Heat the wok and 30ml (2 tblsp) oil. Stir fry the bean sprouts for 1 minute to evaporate excess water and moisture. Remove the bean sprouts and keep on a plate. Mix the seasoning ingredients together. Heat 45ml (3 tblsp) oil in the wok until it smokes. Stir fry the pork for 2 minutes and then add the ginger, onions and bean sprouts. Stir fry for 2-3 minutes. Add the seasoning ingredients and stir fry for 1 minute. Add the chicken stock and the blended sauce ingredients. Cook until the sauce thickens. Serve immediately.

Spiced Liver (top), Sliced Beef in Oyster Sauce (centre right) and Braised Hong Kong Beef (right).

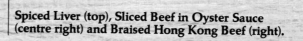

Spiced Liver

PREPARATION TIME: 10 minutes
COOKING TIME: 20 minutes

450g (1lb) lamb's liver, cut into 2.5cm (1") cubes
120ml (8 tblsp) soya sauce
3-4 spring onions, chopped
30ml (2 tblsp) rice wine or dry sherry
10ml (2 tsp) sugar
2.5cm (1") fresh root ginger, peeled and finely chopped
2.5ml (½ tsp) freshly ground black pepper
Pinch anise powder

Boil the liver in sufficient water to just cover, for 3-4 minutes. Drain well. Add soya sauce, spring onions, wine, sugar, ginger, pepper and anise powder. Simmer gently for 10-15 minutes, covered, until the liver is tender. Serve as a side dish.

Stir Fried Beef with Spring Onions

PREPARATION TIME: 30 minutes
COOKING TIME: 10 minutes

Marinade
15ml (1 tblsp) cornflour or arrowroot
1 egg white
15ml (1 tblsp) oil
5ml (1 tsp) bicarbonate of soda
450g (1lb) beef fillet, cut into 2.5cm (1") strips

Seasoning
5ml (1 tsp) Shao Hsing wine
15ml (1 tblsp) light soya sauce
5ml (1 tsp) dark soya sauce
2.5ml (½ tsp) salt
2.5ml (½ tsp) freshly ground black pepper
5ml (1 tsp) monosodium glutamate (optional)

Oil for frying
1 small onion, peeled and thickly sliced
3 spring onions, chopped lengthw
2 leeks, white part only, cut into (1½") slices
5ml (1 tsp) sesame oil

Mix the marinade ingredients w the beef strips. Leave to marina for 20 minutes. Mix all the seasoning ingredients together small bowl. Heat 30ml (2 tblsp) in a wok and when it is smokin, add the beef. Reduce the heat stir fry for 4-5 minutes. Remov the meat and keep the oil for fu use. Heat the wok, add 30ml (2 tblsp) fresh oil and stir fry the onion and leeks for 2 minutes. seasoning mixture and beef anc fry for 1-2 minutes. Sprinkle sesame oil over the top and mi well. Serve immediately. Use as main dish or a side dish.

Shredded Beef with Vegetables

PREPARATION TIME: 15 minu
COOKING TIME: 10 minutes

225g (8oz) lean beef, cut into thi strips
Pinch salt
60ml (4 tblsp) oil
2 red and green chillis, cut in hal then sliced into strips
5ml (1 tsp) black vinegar
1 stem of celery, cut into 5cm (2" thin strips
2 carrots, cut into 5cm (2") thin s
1 leek, white part only, sliced into 5cm (2") thin strips
2 cloves of garlic, peeled and fine chopped

Seasoning
5ml (1 tsp) light soya sauce
5ml (1 tsp) dark soya sauce
10ml (2 tsp) Shao Hsing wine
5ml (1 tsp) sugar
Pinch monosodium glutamate (optional)
2.5ml (½ tsp) freshly ground blac pepper

This page: Stir Fried Beef wi Spring Onions (top), Shredd Beef with Vegetables (centre left) and Sesame Beef with Dates (bottom). Facing page: Beef with Green Beans (top) Beef Steak with Ginger (cen right) and Sweet and Sour B (bottom).

Put the beef into a bowl and sprinkle with salt; rub salt into meat. Heat 5ml (1 tsp) oil in a wok until it begins to smoke. Reduce heat and add beef and chillis and stir fry for 4-5 minutes. Add remaining oil, and stir fry beef until it turns crispy. Add vinegar and mix until it evaporates then add celery, carrots, leeks and garlic. Stir fry for 2 minutes. Mix the seasoning ingredients and pour over the beef and cook for 2 minutes. Serve immediately.

Steamed Lamb with Mushroom Sauce

PREPARATION TIME: 20-25 minutes

COOKING TIME: 2 hours 10 minutes

1kg (2¼lb) boned leg of lamb, cut into 2.5cm (1") cubes
2 onions, thinly sliced
Salt and freshly ground black pepper
10ml (2 tsp) oil
2 cloves of garlic, peeled and sliced
5ml (1 tsp) cornflour
Pinch monosodium glutamate (optional)
75ml (5 tblsp) light soya sauce
45ml (3 tblsp) rice wine or dry sherry
5ml (1 tsp) crushed black pepper
2.5cm (1") fresh root ginger, peeled and thinly sliced
Few drops sesame oil

Put the lamb into a saucepan and add sufficient water to cover. Boil for 5 minutes. Drain the lamb and retain the water. Arrange the lamb cubes in a deep dish and sprinkle the onions on top. Season with pepper and salt. Heat the oil in a wok and fry the garlic until brown. Remove the garlic and discard. Mix together the cornflour, monosodium glutamate, soya sauce, wine, crushed pepper, ginger and 60ml (4 tblsp) reserved water. Stir the cornflour mixture into the oil in the wok and cook for 1-2 minutes. Pour over the lamb. Cover the lamb with overlapping foil and tie around the rim. Put the dish in a steamer and steam over boiling water for 2 hours. Serve with the sesame oil sprinkled over the lamb.

Lamb with Tomatoes

PREPARATION TIME: 20 minutes

COOKING TIME: about 10 minutes

10ml (2 tsp) cornflour
2.5ml (½ tsp) salt
15ml (1 tblsp) light soya sauce
60ml (4 tblsp) water
45ml (3 tblsp) oil
1cm (½") fresh root ginger, sliced
225g (½lb) lamb fillet, cut across the grain in thin strips of 1x5cm (½x2")
2 spring onions, chopped
1 onion, peeled and cut into 2.5cm (1") pieces
1 green pepper, seeded and cut into strips
5ml (1 tsp) curry powder
3-4 small, firm tomatoes, cut into 1cm (½") pieces

Mix the cornflour, salt, soya sauce, water and 5ml (1 tsp) of the oil together. Keep on one side. Heat the remaining oil in a wok and fry the ginger and lamb for 2-3 minutes. Add the onions, green pepper and curry powder and stir fry for 3-4 minutes. Stir in the cornflour mixture and cook for 1 minute. Add the tomatoes and cook until the sauce thickens. Serve as a side dish.

Mongolian Lamb with Onions

PREPARATION TIME: 20 minute

COOKING TIME: 8-10 minutes

450g (1lb) lean, boned lamb, cut into 5x50mm (¼x2") strips
1 egg white
2 cloves of garlic, sliced
2.5ml (½ tsp) five spice powder
1cm (½") fresh root ginger, peeled and thinly sliced
15ml (1 tblsp) cornflour
15ml (1 tblsp) light soya sauce
45ml (3 tblsp) rice wine or dry she
30ml (2 tblsp) water
45ml (3 tblsp) cooked oil
6 spring onions, chopped

Mix the lamb with the egg white garlic, five spice powder, ginger r and 5ml (1 tsp) cornflour and 5r (1 tsp) soya sauce. Keep on one side. Mix the remaining cornflou

Lamb with Tomatoes (below left), Steamed Lan with Mushroom Sauce (right) and Mongolian Lar with Onions (below righ

sauce, wine and water
ther. Heat the wok and add the
When it begins to smoke, add
beef mixture. Reduce the heat
stir fry for 3-4 minutes until
meat browns slightly. Remove
keep on one side. Add the
ons and the cornflour, soya
e and wine mixture to the wok.
until it thickens. Return the
t to the wok and simmer gently
3-4 minutes, or until the meat is
der. Serve as a main dish.

Sweet and Sour Beef

PREPARATION TIME: 15 minutes

COOKING TIME: 15 minutes

Batter

100g (4oz) plain flour
7.5ml (1½ tsp) baking powder
60ml (4 tblsp) cornflour
15ml (1 tblsp) oil
45ml (3 tblsp) oil
225g (8oz) fillet of beef, cut into 2.5cm (1") cubes
1 onion, peeled and cut into wedges
2.5cm (1") fresh root ginger, peeled and thinly sliced
1 clove garlic, peeled and thinly sliced
1 green pepper, seeded and chopped

Sweet and Sour Sauce

60ml (4 tblsp) sugar
1.25ml (¼ tsp) salt
60ml (4 tblsp) red or malt vinegar
5ml (1 tsp) fresh root ginger, peeled and minced
90ml (6 tblsp) water
15ml (1 tblsp) cornflour or arrowroot
10ml (2 tsp) cooked oil
Few drops food colouring
Oil for deep frying

For the batter: sieve the flour, baking powder and cornflour. Beat in the oil and add sufficient water to make a thick, smooth batter. Heat the 45ml (3 tblsp) oil in a wok and stir fry the beef for 2 minutes. Remove the beef. Fry the onion, ginger, garlic and green pepper for 2-3 minutes in the same oil. Remove the wok from the heat. Mix the sauce ingredients together and add to the wok. Return the wok to the heat and bring to the boil gently. Lower the heat and simmer gently for 2-3 minutes until thick and clear. Meanwhile, dip the beef cubes into the batter and deep fry in hot oil until golden brown and crisp. Drain on absorbent paper. Arrange in a deep dish and pour the hot sauce over the beef. Serve with a chow mein dish or fried rice. Thinly sliced carrots, cucumber and courgette may also be added along with the onion, ginger and green pepper.

Barbecued Pork
(Kan Hsiang Ch'a Shao or Char Siu)

PREPARATION TIME: 3 hours
COOKING TIME: 1 hour to 1 hour 30 minutes

2kg (4½lb) loin of pork

Seasoning
15ml (1 tblsp) ginger juice
Few drops red food colouring
75ml (5 tblsp) sugar
200ml (⅓ pint) light soya sauce
5ml (1 tsp) salt
15ml (1 tblsp) Mue Kwe Lo wine (or a mixture of 10ml (2 tsp) dry sherry and 5ml (1 tsp) apricot brandy)

225g (½lb) honey, melted

Remove the bones from the loin of pork. Cut pork into 4cm (1½") wide strips. With the aid of a fork scrape the surface of the pork lightly to form grooves in which the seasoning can lodge. Mix the seasoning ingredients together and rub well into the pork strips. Leave to marinate for at least 1½ hours. Thread the pork strips onto a long metal skewer and hang to dry for 1 hour. Put the pork onto a wire rack in a roasting tin. Brush with melted honey and roast in the oven 180°C, 350°F, Gas Mark 4, for 1-1½ hours, basting with honey frequently. When cooked, brush the pork with any remaining honey and leave to 'dry' slightly. Serve hot or cold, sliced thinly on a serving plate.

Pork Spare Ribs

PREPARATION TIME: 25 minutes
COOKING TIME: 40-45 minutes

16-20 spare ribs
5ml (1 tsp) salt
Oil
5ml (1 tsp) ginger paste
5ml (1 tsp) garlic paste

Pork Meat Balls in Sauce (left), Pork Spare Ribs (above) and Barbecued Pork (right).

5ml (1 tsp) onion paste
Pinch monosodium glutamate (optional)
5ml (1 tsp) light soya sauce
5ml (1 tsp) cornflour
1 egg
2.5ml (½ tsp) Shao Hsing wine
2.5ml (½ tsp) chilli oil

Sauce
45ml (3 tblsp) sugar
45ml (3 tblsp) black vinegar
15ml (1 tblsp) tomato ketchup (optional)
5ml (1 tsp) cornflour
5ml (1 tsp) water
15ml (1 tblsp) dark soya sauce
2.5ml (½ tsp) salt
2.5ml (½ tsp) freshly ground black pepper

Trim excess fat from spare ribs and rub with salt. Add 60ml (4 tblsp) oil to the wok and fry the ginger, garlic and onion for 1-2 minutes. Add the spare ribs and stir fry for 6 minutes. Remove to a dish and add the monosodium glutamate, light soya sauce, cornflour, egg, wine and chilli oil. Marinate for 10 minutes. Prepare the sauce by mixing all the ingredients together in the wok and bringing them gently to the boil. Simmer for 2-3 minutes and add the spare ribs along with their marinade. Stir fry until the liquid is reduced to half its original quantity. Put all the ingredients onto a baking tray and spread out evenly. Bake at 190°C, 375°F, Gas Mark 5, for 25 minutes. Baste occasionally with the liquid from the tray and oil. The spare ribs should have browned well and be well coated with seasoning. Serve hot or cold.

Pork Meat Balls in Sauce
(Sha Kwo Shih-tzu-Tou)

PREPARATION TIME: 25 minutes
COOKING TIME: 45 minutes

Seasoning
Pinch monosodium glutamate (optional)
15ml (1 tblsp) Shao Hsing wine
2cm (1") fresh root ginger, peeled and ground
2 spring onions, white part only, minced
2.5ml (½ tsp) salt
10ml (2 tsp) cornflour
450g (1lb) lean pork, minced
25g (1oz) bamboo shoots, chopped
50g (2oz) dried Chinese mushrooms, soaked, drained and sliced
1 egg, beaten
Cornflour to roll the meat balls in
175g (6oz) Chinese white cabbage, cut into 7.5cm (3") pieces or 225g (8oz) ordinary green leafy cabbage, cut into 7.5cm (3") pieces
15ml (1 tblsp) cooked oil
Oil for deep frying
15ml (1 tblsp) cornflour
45ml (3 tblsp) water
1 small onion, peeled and finely chopped
2.5cm (1") fresh root ginger, peeled and finely chopped
300ml (½ pint) chicken stock

Sauce
Salt to taste
2.5ml (½ tsp) monosodium glutamate (optional)
15ml (1 tblsp) light soya sauce
5ml (1 tsp) dark soya sauce
15ml (1 tblsp) cooked oil

Mix seasoning ingredients together. Add the pork, bamboo shoots, mushrooms and egg and mix well. Shape into 15-16 even-sized balls and roll them in cornflour. Keep aside on a dish. Blanch cabbage for 1 minute in boiling water and the cooked oil. Drain the cabbage and discard the water. Heat the wok and add the oil for deep frying. When quite hot deep-fry the meat balls, a few at a time, for 4-5 minutes. Remove and drain. Keep warm in a large casserole dish.

Keep oil for future use. Mix the 15ml (1 tblsp) cornflour with the 45ml (3 tblsp) water and keep aside. Reheat the wok and add 5ml (1 tsp) deep frying oil. Stir fry the onion and ginger for 2 minutes. Add the chicken stock and stir in the blended sauce ingredients. Bring to the boil and add the meat balls. Simmer gently for 30 minutes. Add the cabbage, sesame oil and the blended cornflour mixture. Stir over the heat until the sauce thickens.

Sesame Beef with Dates

PREPARATION TIME: 20 minutes, plus 30 minutes to marinate

COOKING TIME: 12-15 minutes

Seasoning A

2.5ml (½ tsp) bicarbonate of soda
15ml (1 tblsp) light soya sauce
15ml (1 tblsp) oil
7.5ml (1½ tsp) cornflour
450g (1lb) beef fillet, thinly sliced into 5cm (2") pieces
20 dried dates (red or dark), soaked and stoned

Seasoning B

5ml (1 tsp) monosodium glutamate (optional)
7.5ml (1½ tsp) sugar
10ml (2 tsp) bean paste
200ml (⅓ pint) beef stock, or made with stock cube
Salt to taste
60ml (4 tblsp) cooked oil or plain oil
2.5cm (1") fresh root ginger, peeled and thinly sliced
2 spring onions, sliced

Sauce

15ml (1 tblsp) cornflour
30ml (2 tblsp) water or stock
30ml (2 tblsp) sesame seeds

Mix the ingredients for seasoning A. Mix with the beef and marinate for 30 minutes. Drain meat and discard marinade. Drain soaked dates; slice most of them into 4 long pieces, leaving a few whole. Mix the dates with seasoning B. Heat oil in a wok and stir fry beef for 4-5 minutes. Add ginger, spring onions, dates and the seasoning B and gently bring to the boil. Add the blended sauce ingredients. Cover and simmer for 3-4 minutes over a gentle heat until the sauce thickens and becomes clear. Remove from the heat, place on a serving dish and keep warm. Heat a wok or frying pan and add the sesame seeds. Dry roast for 2 minutes until they begin to crackle and turn golden brown. Sprinkle over the beef and serve immediately.

Shredded Pork with Preserved Vegetables

PREPARATION TIME: 30 minutes

COOKING TIME: 6-8 minutes

Pinch monosodium glutamate (optional)
10ml (2 tsp) cornflour
Salt and freshly ground black pepper to taste
225g (½ lb) lean pork, shredded
Oil
2.5cm (1") fresh root ginger, peeled and shredded
50g (2oz) shelled green peas
2.5ml (½ tsp) sugar
10ml (2 tsp) Shao Hsing wine or dry sherry
225g (8oz) Shanghai preserved vegetables (mixed), in brine
5ml (1 tsp) sesame oil

Mix the monosodium glutamate, cornflour and a pinch of salt. Add the pork and let it stand for 15 minutes. Heat the oil in a wok and deep fry the pork for 3 minutes. Remove the pork and drain. Reserve oil for future use. Reheat wok and add 10ml (2 tsp) deep fried oil. Stir fry the ginger and green peas for 1 minute. Add the pork and sprinkle with the sugar, wine and salt and pepper to taste. Stir fry for another minute and add the well-drained, preserved vegetables. Allow to heat through and then stir gently. Sprinkle on the sesame oil and serve. Serve as a side dish or on a bed of plain fried noodles.

Beef Steak with Ginger

PREPARATION TIME: 20-25 minutes

COOKING TIME: 10-12 minutes

Seasoning

2.5ml (½ tsp) bicarbonate of soda
45ml (3 tblsp) light soya sauce
30ml (2 tblsp) rice wine or dry sherry
2.5ml (½ tsp) salt
2.5ml (½ tsp) ground black pepper
1.25cm (½ tsp) fresh root ginger, peeled and minced
225g (½lb) beef fillet, sliced into 2.5cm (1") pieces

Sauce

5ml (1 tsp) sugar
1.25ml (¼ tsp) monosodium glutamate (optional)
15ml (1 tblsp) dark soya sauce
45ml (3 tblsp) stock
Few drops sesame oil
5ml (1 tsp) Shao Hsing wine
60ml (4 tblsp) oil
2.5cm (1") fresh root ginger, peeled and thinly sliced
4 spring onions, chopped
50g (2oz) bamboo shoots, thinly sliced
2 green chillis, sliced

Mix the seasoning ingredients with the minced ginger. Add the beef and marinate for 20 minutes. Drain the beef and discard the marinade. Mix the sauce ingredients together. Heat 45ml (3 tblsp) oil in the wok and fry the sliced ginger and onions for 2 minutes. Add the bamboo shoots and chillis and stir fry for 1-2 minutes. Remove to a plate. Add the remaining oil to the wok and fry the beef for 2-3 minutes. Add fried vegetables and stir fry for 2 minutes. Add well-stirred sauce ingredients and simmer gently until the mixture thickens. Simmer for another 1-2 minutes. Remove from heat and serve.

Beef with Green Beans

PREPARATION TIME: 30 minutes

COOKING TIME: 12 minutes

Seasoning

2.5ml (½ tsp) bicarbonate of soda
5ml (1 tsp) cornflour
15ml (1 tblsp) light soya sauce
30ml (2 tblsp) water
5ml (1 tsp) cooked oil
450g (1lb) lean beef, thinly sliced into 2.5cm (1") pieces

Sauce

1.25ml (¼ tsp) salt
5ml (1 tsp) monosodium glutamate (optional)
5ml (1 tsp) light soya sauce
5ml (1 tsp) dark soya sauce
5ml (1 tsp) Shao Hsing wine (optional)
120ml (4 fl oz) stock
10ml (2 tsp) cornflour
45ml (3 tblsp) oil
2 cloves of garlic, peeled and sliced
1 onion, peeled and cut into wedges
2.5cm (1") fresh ginger root, peeled and sliced thinly
175g (6oz) Chinese long beans, cut into 7.5cm (3") pieces, or whole tender green beans
Salt and freshly ground black pepper to taste

Mix seasoning ingredients tog Add the beef and marinate fo minutes. Drain the meat and discard the marinade. Mix the sauce ingredients together. He 30ml (2 tblsp) oil in the wok u it smokes. Reduce the heat ad garlic and the beef, and stir fry 3-4 minutes. Remove the mea keep on one side. Add the remaining oil to the wok and a the onion, ginger and long bea and stir fry for 2-3 minutes. A fried beef. Cover and fry for a further 1 minute. Stir in the sa ingredients and bring to the b Simmer gently for 2-3 minute Season with salt and pepper. Remove from heat and serve.

Sweet and Sour Pork

PREPARATION TIME: 20 mi plus 20 minutes to marinate

COOKING TIME: 15-20 min

Batter

45ml (3 tblsp) flour
15ml (1 tblsp) cornflour
7.5ml (1½ tsp) bicarbonate of
30ml (2 tblsp) oil

350g (12oz) lean pork, cut into 2.5cm (1") cubes

Seasoning

5ml (1 tsp) sugar
5ml (1 tsp) salt
30ml (2 tblsp) light soya sauce
5ml (1 tsp) dark soya sauce
15ml (1 tblsp) cooked oil
15ml (1 tblsp) water

Cornflour
Oil for deep frying
2 cloves garlic, cut into thin stri
1 large onion, peeled and cut in 1cm (½") pieces
1 carrot, sliced into 3x25x50m (⅛x1x2") thin pieces
Pinch salt

Sweet and Sour Sauce

45ml (3 tblsp) sugar
15ml (1 tblsp) tomato purée
250ml (8 fl oz) chicken stock or
60ml (4 tblsp) red or white vine
5ml (1 tsp) light soya sauce
Few slices fresh root ginger, peel
15ml (1 tblsp) cornflour or arro
Few drops of red food colouring
10ml (2 tsp) cooked oil

Mix the batter ingredients to adding sufficient water to ma thick coating batter. Wash an drain the pork. Mix with the seasoning ingredients and ma

Sweet and Sour Pork (top right), Diced Pork with Walnuts (centre) and Shredded Pork with Preserved Vegetables (bottom left).

5-20 minutes. Drain the pork discard the marinade. Roll the cubes in cornflour. Heat the r deep frying. Dip the pork s in batter and fry in the hot atil golden brown. Fry a few at e until all the pork has been Drain well and keep warm in oven. Heat wok and add (2 tsp) deep fried oil. Stir fry the garlic, onions and carrots for 3-4 minutes. Season with salt and fry for a further minute. Mix the sweet and sour sauce ingredients together and add to the wok. Stir the mixture until it thickens. Pour over the fried pork cubes and serve immediately. Note: sliced green peppers can also be added along with the carrots and onions.

Diced Pork with Walnuts

PREPARATION TIME: 30 minutes

COOKING TIME: 16-18 minutes

100g (4oz) shelled walnuts
Oil for deep frying

Seasoning
7.5ml (1½ tsp) light soya sauce
Few drops sesame oil
Salt and freshly ground black pepper to taste
15ml (1 tblsp) oil
15ml (1 tblsp) water
15ml (1 tblsp) cornflour
Pinch monosodium glutamate (optional)

225g (½ lb) pork fillet, cut into cubes
1 carrot, thinly sliced
1 onion, peeled and cut into pieces
3 spring onions, chopped
2.5cm (1") fresh root ginger, peeled and thinly sliced

Sauce
90ml (6 tblsp) stock
5ml (1 tsp) cornflour

Cook the walnuts in boiling water for 3-4 minutes. Drain the nuts thoroughly. Deep fry the walnuts until lightly browned. Remove and drain. Use oil for cooking. Mix the seasoning ingredients together and add the pork. Leave to marinate for 15 minutes. Discard marinade. Heat 30ml (2 tblsp) oil in the wok and stir-fry the carrots for 2 minutes. Add the onions and root ginger and stir fry for 1 minute. Add 10ml (2 tsp) of the sauce stock and remove to a plate. Add the drained pork cubes and 15ml (1 tblsp) oil to the wok and stir fry for 4-5 minutes. Mix the remaining stock and the cornflour together for the sauce. Return the walnuts and carrots to the wok, together with the blended sauce ingredients. Mix well and simmer until the sauce thickens. Remove and serve immediately. Serve with rice noodles or fried rice.

Poultry Dishes

Roast Crispy Duck

PREPARATION TIME: 15-20 minutes plus 6-8 hours to dry

COOKING TIME: 1 hour 30 minutes

2kg (4½lb) duck or goose, prepared for cooking
250ml (8 fl oz) water
6 large scallions or 12 spring onions, cut into 5cm (2 inch) lengths
60ml (4 tblsp) maltose or golden syrup
2.5ml (½ tsp) red food colouring
30ml (2 tblsp) tomato purée

Wash the duck and pat it dry on a clean cloth. Ease the fingers between the skin and flesh of the duck, starting at the neck end and working the length of the bird. Put a stick or large skewer through the neck and the cavity of the duck to wedge it securely. This will make the duck easier to handle. Hold the duck over the sink and pour boiling water all over it. Pat the duck dry. Melt half the maltose and dissolve in the water. Stand the duck on a rack over a deep tray. Slowly pour the maltose liquid over the duck. Pour the maltose liquid over the duck 3 or 4 times. Leave the duck in a cool place for 6-8 hours, or overnight, until the skin is dry. Remove the stick. Stand the duck on a rack in a roasting tin. Preheat the oven to 200°C, 400°F, Gas Mark 6 and cook for 30 minutes. Turn over and cook the underside for a further 30 minutes. Melt the remaining maltose with the tomato purée and add the food colouring. Spread over the duck and cook for a further 30 minutes. (The duck should have a crisp, red skin.) Remove the duck skin in squares. Slice the duck flesh and serve with the skin on the top. Serve the following dip as an accompaniment.

Duck Dip

100g (4oz) sugar
60ml (4 tblsp) sweet bean paste
30ml (2 tblsp) sesame oil
120ml (4 fl oz) water

Heat the wok and add the mixed ingredients. Cook for 3-4 minutes until the sugar has dissolved and the dip is smooth. Serve in individual cups.

Sliced Duck with Bamboo Shoots

PREPARATION TIME: 30 minutes

COOKING TIME: 10 minutes

1kg (2¼lb) small duck
5ml (1 tsp) monosodium glutamate (optional)
12.5ml (2½ tsp) cornflour
30ml (2 tblsp) water
100g (4oz) broccoli, chopped
45ml (3 tblsp) oil
2-3 spring onions, chopped
2.5cm (1 inch) fresh root ginger, peeled and thinly sliced
1 clove garlic, peeled and finely chopped
100g (4oz) bamboo shoots, sliced
2.5ml (½ tsp) sugar
Salt and freshly ground black pepper to taste
60ml (4 tblsp) chicken stock
10ml (2 tsp) rice wine or sweet sherry
Few drops sesame oil

Cut the duck flesh into bite-size pieces, removing all the bones. Mix the MSG, 7.5ml (1½ tsp) cornflour and 15ml (1 tblsp) water together. Stir into the duck. Marinate for 20 minutes. Cook the broccoli in boiling water for 1 minute. Drain thoroughly. Heat the wok and add the oil. Stir fry the onions, ginger, garlic and bamboo shoots for 1-2 minutes. Add the duck pieces and stir fry for 2-3 minutes. Add the sugar, salt and pepper to taste, stock, rice wine and sesame oil. Stir fry for 3 minutes. Add the remaining cornflour and water blended together. Stir over the heat until the sauce thickens. Serve immediately, as a side dish.

Duck with Ginger and Pineapple

PREPARATION TIME: 20 minutes

COOKING TIME: 2 hours to 2 hours 45 minutes

1.25cm (½ inch) fresh root ging peeled and crushed
2kg (4½lb) duck
Salt and freshly ground black p to taste
45ml (3 tblsp) oil
10cm (4 inches) fresh root ginge peeled and thinly sliced
50g (2oz) bean sprouts
3 spring onions, chopped
2 carrots, peeled, sliced and bla in boiling water for 2 minute
10ml (2 tsp) brown sugar
15ml (1 tblsp) wine vinegar
5ml (1 tsp) white vinegar
225g (8oz) can pineapple chun syrup
15ml (1 tblsp) cornflour mixed 30ml (2 tblsp) water

Mix together the crushed ging half of the soya sauce and salt pepper to taste. Wash the duc pat it dry. Rub the outside of duck with salt and put on a w rack in a roasting tin. Roast at 180°C, 350°F, Gas Mark 4, fo minutes. Brush the ginger and sauce mixture over the duck. frequently with the sauces fro pan and roast for 2 hours, tur the bird occasionally to brow sides. Remove and slice the d small pieces. Heat the oil in a and stir fry the sliced ginger, b sprouts, onions and carrots fo minutes. Add the duck slices cook for 1 minute. Then add brown sugar, vinegar and pine chunks in their syrup. Bring to boil and cook for 2-3 minutes the blended cornflour and co until the sauce thickens. Serve main dish along with noodles rice.

This page: Stewed Chicken Pineapple (top right), Fried Shredded Chicken on Cabb (centre left) and Chicken an Cashew Nuts (bottom right

Facing page: Sliced Duck w Bamboo Shoots (top), Duck with Ginger and Pineapple (bottom left) and Roast Cri Duck (bottom right).

Chicken Green Chilli

PREPARATION TIME: 10 minutes, plus 10 minutes to marinate

COOKING TIME: 10 minutes

Sauce

5ml (1 tsp) light soya sauce
5ml (1 tsp) dark soya sauce
Salt to taste
10ml (2 tsp) cornflour
5ml (1 tsp) sesame oil
5ml (1 tsp) malt vinegar
250ml (8 fl oz) chicken stock

Seasoning

Salt to taste
Freshly ground black pepper to taste
Pinch monosodium glutamate (optional)
30ml (2 tblsp) dark soya sauce
15ml (1 tblsp) light soya sauce
5ml (1 tsp) cornflour
10ml (2 tsp) rice wine or dry sherry

450g (1lb) boned chicken, cut into bite-size pieces
45ml (3 tblsp) oil
3 spring onions, chopped
2.5cm (1") fresh root ginger, peeled and sliced
2 cloves of garlic, peeled and sliced
1 green pepper, seeded and chopped
2-3 green chillis, sliced lengthways

Mix the sauce ingredients together. Mix the seasoning ingredients together and add the chicken. Marinate for 10 minutes. Drain the chicken and discard the liquid. Heat 15ml (1 tblsp) oil and stir fry the onions, ginger and garlic for 2 minutes. Remove to a dish. Add the remaining oil and stir fry the chicken for 3 minutes. Add the blended green peppers and chillis and stir fry for 2 minutes. Add the onion mixture and the well-blended sauce ingredients and cook for 3-4 minutes until the sauce thickens. Serve immediately.

Chicken and Mushrooms

PREPARATION TIME: 15 minutes, plus 10 minutes to marinate

COOKING TIME: 10-12 minutes

Seasoning

2.5ml (1/2 tsp) salt
30ml (2 tblsp) light soya sauce
10ml (2 tsp) cornflour
5ml (1 tsp) rice wine or dry sherry
Pinch monosodium glutamate (optional)

225g (1/2lb) chicken breast, cut into bite-size pieces

Sauce

Salt to taste
Freshly ground black pepper to taste
15ml (1 tblsp) light soya sauce
250ml (8 fl oz) chicken stock
10ml (2 tsp) cornflour or arrowroot
5ml (1 tsp) oyster sauce
30ml (2 tblsp) oil

1 onion, peeled and chopped
1 clove of garlic, sliced
1cm (1/2") fresh root ginger, peeled and thinly sliced
3 dried black mushrooms, soaked and sliced
50g (2oz) open mushrooms, sliced
50g (2oz) button mushrooms, slice[d]

Mix the seasoning ingredients together. Marinate the chicken in the seasoning mixture for 10 minutes. Mix the sauce ingredients together. Heat the oil in a wok and fry the onion, garlic and ginger for 2-3 minutes. Remove and keep on one side. Fry the drained chicken in the remaining oil for 4 minutes. Add the mushrooms and stir fry for 1 minute. Add a little extra oil if necessary. Return the fried onion mixture to the wok and stir fry until well mixed. Pour the blended sauce ingredients into the wok and cook gently until the sauce thickens. Serve piping hot.

Chicken Fry with Sauce (below right), Chicken Green Chilli (below centre) and Chicken and Mushrooms (far right).

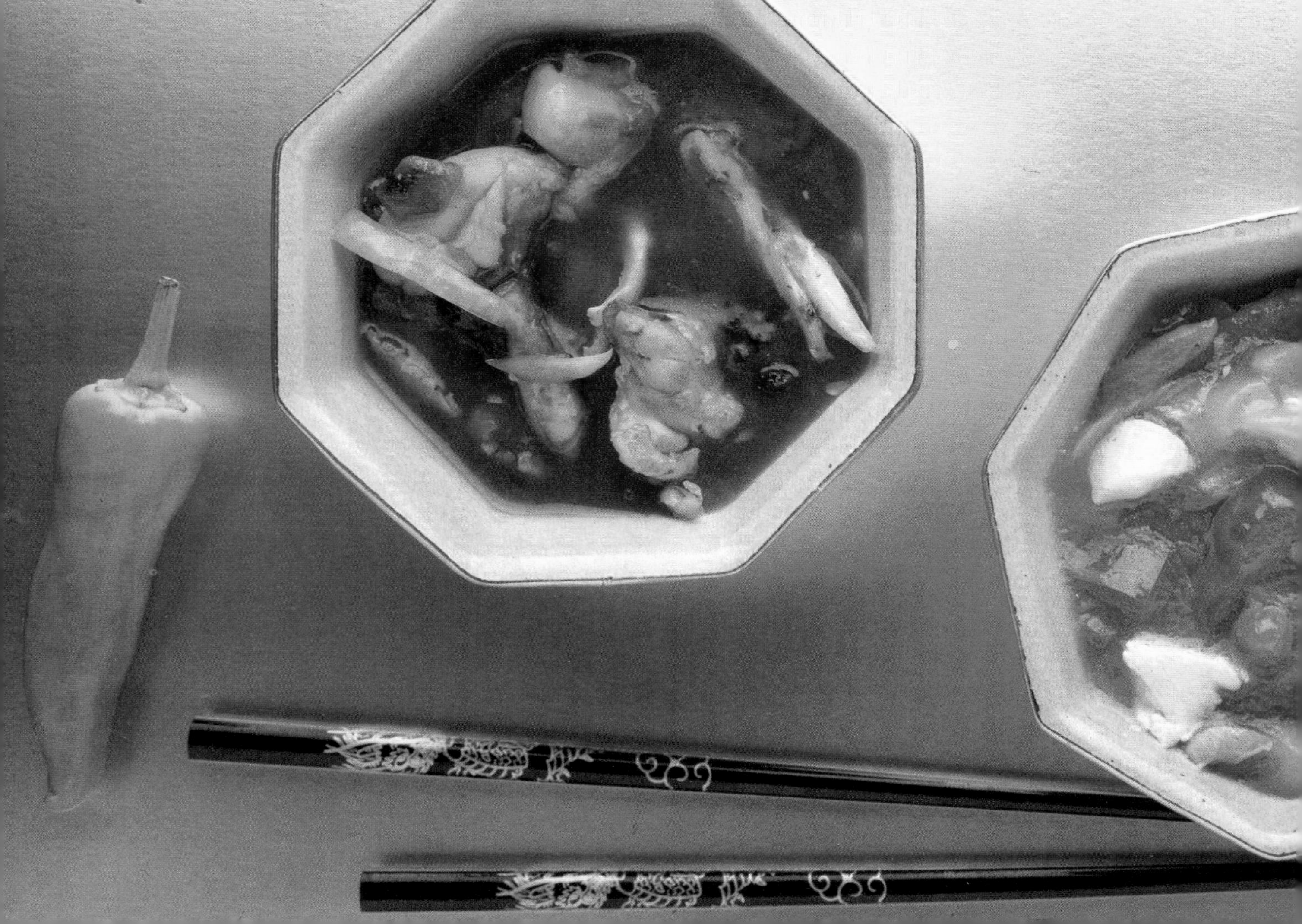

hicken Fry with Sauce

EPARATION TIME: 20 minutes
OKING TIME: about 24 minutes

nl (1 tblsp) cooked oil
l (1 tsp) sesame oil
g (1oz) sesame seeds

uce
oves of garlic, minced
ring onions, finely chopped or minced
l (1 tsp) Chinese black vinegar or rown malt vinegar
nl (3 tblsp) dark soya sauce
l (1 tsp) light soya sauce
ml (½ tsp) monosodium glutamate (optional)
2.5ml (½ tsp) salt
7.5ml (1½ tsp) sugar
8 chicken thighs, or 450g (1lb) chicken, cut into small joints

Heat the wok and add the oils. Stir fry the sesame seeds till they change colour to golden brown. Remove onto a dish. Mix sauce ingredients together and add the sesame seeds. Wipe the wok and add the chicken. Add sufficient water to cover, and cook for 20 minutes until the chicken is tender. De-bone the chicken and quickly cut into bite-size pieces. Arrange the chicken on a plate and spoon the sauce over the top. Serve immediately.

Stewed Chicken and Pineapple

PREPARATION TIME: 30 minutes
COOKING TIME: 15 minutes

Seasoning
30ml (2 tblsp) light soya sauce
15ml (1 tblsp) oil
15ml (1 tblsp) cornflour
5ml (1 tsp) salt
2.5ml (½ tsp) sesame oil
30ml (2 tblsp) water
750g (1½lb) boned chicken breast, cut into cubes

Sauce
7.5ml (1½ tsp) cornflour
250ml (8 fl oz) water or chicken stock
10ml (2 tsp) dark soya sauce
Salt to taste
30ml (2 tblsp) oil
1 onion, peeled and cut into chunks
2 spring onions, finely chopped
2.5cm (1") fresh root ginger, peeled and thinly sliced
4-5 pineapple rings, cut into chunks

Mix the seasoning ingredients together. Add the cubed chicken and marinate for 10-12 minutes. Mix the sauce ingredients together in a bowl. Heat the oil in a wok and fry the onions for 2 minutes until just tender. Add the drained chicken and fry for 3-4 minutes. Add the root ginger and fry for 1 minute. Add any remaining marinade and the sauce ingredients

and bring to the boil. Cook, stirring, until the sauce thickens then add the pineapple chunks. Heat through. Remove from the heat and serve with fried rice.

Chicken Chop Suey

PREPARATION TIME: 30 minutes
COOKING TIME: 15 minutes

30ml (2 tblsp) light soya sauce
5ml (1 tsp) brown sugar
Salt to taste
450g (1lb) boned chicken, cut into 2.5cm (1") pieces
30ml (2 tblsp) cooking oil
1 onion, cut into chunks
225g (8oz) bean sprouts
10ml (2 tsp) sesame oil
1.25g (¼ tsp) monosodium glutamate (optional)
15ml (1 tblsp) cornflour
250ml (8 fl oz) chicken stock

Mix the soya sauce with the sugar and salt and add the chicken pieces. Allow to marinate for 5 minutes. Drain the chicken and reserve the marinade. Heat the wok and add the oil. Fry the chicken for 2-3 minutes. Remove the chicken. Fry the onions for 2-3 minutes and add the beansprouts. Stir fry for 4-5 minutes. Return the chicken to the pan and add the sesame oil. Dissolve the monosodium glutamate and the cornflour in the stock and pour over the chicken mixture. Cook for 2-3 minutes, stirring, until the sauce thickens. Serve as a side dish.

Deep Fried Crispy Chicken

PREPARATION TIME: 3 hours
COOKING TIME: 13-14 minutes

1.5kg (3-3½lb) chicken, prepared for cooking

Seasoning
5ml (1 tsp) salt
2.5ml (½ tsp) five spice powder
40g (1½oz) maltose
30ml (2 tblsp) malt vinegar
150ml (¼ pint) white vinegar
Oil for deep frying

Wash the chicken and hang it up by a hook to drain and dry. The skin will dry quickly. Pour boiling water over the chicken 4-5 times, to partially cook the skin. This will make the skin crisp during frying. Rub salt and five spice powder well inside the chicken cavity. Dissolve the maltose and vinegars in a pan over a gentle heat. Pour over the chicken. Repeat several times, catching the maltose solution in a drip tray. Leave the chicken to hang and dry for 1½-2 hours, until the skin is smooth and shiny. Heat the oil for deep frying. Deep fry the chicken for 10 minutes. Ladle hot oil carefully over the chicken continually, until the chicken is deep brown in colour. (The skin puffs out slightly.) Cook for a further 3-4 minutes and remove from the oil. Drain on absorbent paper. Cut into small pieces and serve with a dip.

Chicken and Cashew Nuts

PREPARATION TIME: 15 minutes
COOKING TIME: 15 minutes

350g (12oz) chicken breast, sliced into 2.5cm (1") pieces
15ml (1 tblsp) cornflour

Seasoning
5ml (1 tsp) salt
5ml (1 tsp) sesame oil
15ml (1 tblsp) light soya sauce
2.5ml (½ tsp) sugar
Oil for deep frying
100g (4oz) cashew nuts
2 spring onions, chopped
1 small onion, peeled and cubed
2.5cm (1") fresh root ginger, peeled and sliced
2 cloves of garlic, sliced
75g (3oz) snow peas (mange tout)
50g (2oz) bamboo shoots, thinly sliced

Sauce
10ml (2 tsp) cornflour
15ml (1 tblsp) Hoi Sin sauce
250ml (just over ⅓ pint) chicken stock
Pinch monosodium glutamate (optional)

Roll the chicken pieces in cornflour. Discard the remaining cornflour. Mix the seasoning ingredients together and pour over chicken. Leave to stand for 10 minutes. Heat oil for deep frying and fry cashew nuts until golden brown. Remove the nuts and drain on kitchen paper. Heat 30ml (2 tblsp) oil in a wok and stir fry the onions, ginger and garlic for 2-3 minutes. Add snow peas and bamboo shoots and stir fry for 3 minutes. Remove the fried ingredients. Add 15ml (1 tblsp) oil to the wok and fry the chicken for 3-4 minutes. Remove the chicken. Clean the wok and add a further 10ml (2 tblsp) oil and return chicken, cashew nuts and fried onions etc. to the wok. Prepare the sauce by mixing the cornflour, Hoi Sin sauce, chicken stock and monosodium glutamate together. Pour over the chicken. Mix well and cook until the sauce thickens and becomes transparent. Serve hot with a chow mein dish. Alternatively, a few chunks of pineapple will add extra zest to the dish.

Fried Shredded Chicken on Cabbage

PREPARATION TIME: 20 minutes
COOKING TIME: 12 minutes

450g (1lb) Chinese white cabbage, cut into 2.5cm (1") pieces
Pinch bicarbonate of soda

Seasoning
15ml (1 tblsp) light soya sauce
15ml (1 tblsp) cornflour
1.25ml (¼ tsp) sesame oil
1.25ml (¼ tsp) freshly ground black pepper
2.5ml (½ tsp) sugar
2.5ml (½ tsp) salt
15ml (1 tblsp) water
15ml (1 tblsp) oil
Pinch monosodium glutamate (optional)
30ml (2 tblsp) oil
1 onion, peeled and roughly chopped
2.5cm (1") fresh root ginger, peeled and thinly sliced
450g (1lb) boned chicken breasts, shredded
4-6 mushrooms, sliced

Sauce
45ml (3 tblsp) chicken stock
1.25ml (¼ tsp) sesame oil
5ml (1 tsp) light soya sauce
5ml (1 tsp) cornflour
5ml (1 tsp) monosodium glutamate (optional)

Wash cabbage and blanch in boiling water with a pinch of bicarbonate of soda for 2 minutes. Drain well. Mix the seasoning ingredients together. Heat the wok and add the oil. Fry the onions, ginger and chicken for 2-3 minutes. Add the mushrooms and fry for further 2 minutes. Add the stock and cook for 4-5 minutes. Mix the sauce ingredients together and pour over the chicken. Cook fo[illegible] minutes. Serve immediately.

Steamed Chicken

PREPARATION TIME: 20-30 minutes
COOKING TIME: 15-20 minut[illegible]

750g (1½lb) boned chicken

Seasoning
15ml (1 tblsp) light soya sauce
5ml (1 tsp) brown sugar
5ml (1 tsp) salt
15ml (1 tblsp) cornflour
30ml (2 tblsp) oil or cooked oil
2.5ml (½ tsp) monosodium glutamate (optional)
100g (4oz) dried mushrooms, soa[illegible] in boiling water for 5 minutes [illegible] sliced, or ordinary mushrooms
1cm (½") fresh root ginger, peele[illegible] and sliced
4 spring onions, finely chopped
30ml (2 tblsp) stock or water, if needed

Cut the chicken into 2.5cm (1[illegible] pieces. Mix the seasoning ingredients together and mix w[illegible] the chicken. Leave to marinate 15 minutes. Place a plate in a steamer and put the chicken, mushrooms, ginger, half the oni[illegible] and the stock on top. Steam ov[illegible] boiling water for 15-20 minute[illegible] Serve with the remaining onio[illegible] sprinkled over the chicken. Th[illegible] steaming can also be done on a greased lotus leaf or a banana le[illegible] The flavour is quite stunning.

Tangerine Peel Chicke[illegible]

PREPARATION TIME: 30 minu[illegible]
COOKING TIME: 12-15 minut[illegible]

450g (1lb) boned chicken breast, into 2.5cm (1") pieces

Facing page: Chicken Chop Suey (top left), Steamed Chicken (centre right) and D[illegible] Fried Crispy Chicken (botto[illegible] left).

Seasoning
2.5ml (½ tsp) salt
7.5ml (1½ tsp) sugar
2.5ml (½ tsp) monosodium glutamate (optional)
5ml (1 tsp) dark soya sauce
10ml (2 tsp) light soya sauce
5ml (1 tsp) rice wine or dry sherry
10ml (2 tsp) malt vinegar
5ml (1 tsp) sesame oil
10ml (2 tsp) cornflour

Oil for deep frying
1-2 red or green chillis, chopped
1.25cm (½") fresh root ginger, peeled and finely chopped
5cm (2") dried tangerine peel, coarsely ground or crumbled
2 spring onions, finely chopped

Sauce
2.5ml (½ tsp) cornflour
15-30ml (1-2 tblsp) water or stock

Mix the chicken pieces with the seasoning ingredients and stir well. Leave to marinate for 10-15 minutes. Remove the chicken pieces and reserve the marinade. Heat wok and add the oil for deep frying. Once it starts to smoke add the chicken pieces and fry for 4-5 minutes until golden. Drain chicken on kitchen paper. Tip off the oil, leaving 15ml (1 tblsp) oil in the wok, and stir fry the chillis, ginger, tangerine peel and onions for 2-3 minutes. When they begin to colour add the chicken and stir fry for 1 minute. Mix the reserved marinade with the sauce ingredients and pour over the chicken. Stir and cook for 2-3 minutes until the sauce thickens and the chicken is tender. Serve immediately.

Roast Spiced Duck

PREPARATION TIME: 3-4 hours to dry, and 1 hour to glaze
COOKING TIME: 1 hour

2kg (4½lb) duck or small goose
5ml (1 tsp) five spice powder
7.5ml (1½ tsp) salt
60ml (4 tblsp) maltose or golden syrup
5ml (1 tsp) white vinegar
10ml (2 tsp) malt or red vinegar
Oil

Wash and dry the duck. Rub in the five spice powder and salt. Close the cavities of the duck by securing both ends with small skewers. Mix the maltose and vinegar together with a little water and bring to the boil. Spoon this liquid over the duck several times, collecting the liquid in a tray. Hang the duck by its neck for 3-4 hours to dry. Preheat the oven to 230°C, 450°F, Gas Mark 8. Place the duck in a roasting tin. Rub oil into the skin. Roast in the oven for 1 hour, basting with any remaining maltose and vinegar liquid. If the duck is not quite tender, cook for a little longer. Slice the duck onto a warmed serving dish and serve immediately.

Roast Peking Duck

PREPARATION TIME: 15 minutes plus 2-3 hours to dry out the skin
COOKING TIME: 1 hour 20 minutes

2kg (4½lb) duck or small goose
1 litre (1¾ pints) boiling water
30ml (2 tblsp) maltose or golden syrup
250ml (8 fl oz) water
2-3 seedless oranges, peeled and cut into rings
30ml (2 tblsp) oil
Salt and freshly ground black pepper

Sauce
10ml (2 tsp) cornflour
60ml (4 tblsp) water or stock
Pinch monosodium glutamate (optional)
10ml (2 tsp) light soya sauce
5ml (1 tsp) rice wine or dry sherry

To Garnish
4 spring onions, cut into 5cm (2 inch) lengths

Wash and dry the duck. Put a stick or skewer through the neck and the cavity of the duck so that it is easier to handle. Hold the bird over the sink and pour the boiling water over it. Hang the duck up to dry. Melt the maltose and water together and spoon over the duck several times, catching the liquid on a drip tray each time. Leave the duck to dry for 2-3 hours in a cool place. Save any liquid that drops off. Preheat the oven to 200°C, 400°F, Gas Mark 6. Place the duck, breast side down, in a roasting tin and roast for 30 minutes. Lift out the duck. Put the orange rings into the tin and sit the duck on top, breast side uppermost. Baste with the oil and season with salt and pepper. Roast for a further 45-50 minutes until tender. Cut off the duck joints and slice the breast meat. Arrange with the orange slices on a serving dish and keep warm.

To Make the Sauce
Mix the sauce ingredients together and add any reserved maltose liquid. Bring to the boil gently, stirring, until the sauce thickens. Pour over the cooked duck and sprinkle with the onions. This is served either as a main dish or as a side dish.

Steamed Duck in Wine Sauce

PREPARATION TIME: 20 minutes
COOKING TIME: 3 hours 30 minutes

2kg (4½lb) duck
150ml (¼ pint) Kao Liang wine or mild red wine
2.5ml (½ tsp) monosodium glutamate (optional)

Roast Spiced Duck (top), Roast Peking Duck (above) and Steamed Duck in Wine Sauce (right).

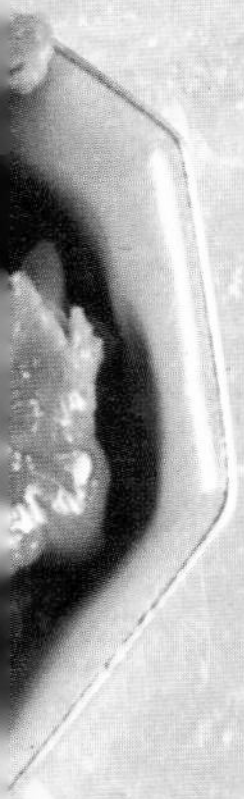

2.5cm (1 inch) fresh root ginger, peeled and thinly sliced
3 spring onions, chopped
5ml (1 tsp) salt
5ml (1 tsp) sugar
5ml (1 tsp) cornflour

Place the duck in a large pot. Add water to cover and boil for 5-7 minutes. Remove the duck and drain well. Mix all the remaining ingredients together apart from the cornflour. Place the duck in a deep dish and stand over a steamer. Pour the wine mixture over the duck. Cover and steam for 2-3 hours until the duck is quite tender. Remove the duck and strain the cooking liquid. Place the duck on a serving dish, either whole or cut into slices. Blend the cooking liquid with the cornflour. Bring to the boil and stir until thickened. Pour over the duck. Serve immediately.

Chicken Chow Mein

PREPARATION TIME: 30 minutes
COOKING TIME: 20 minutes

450g (1lb) egg noodles or spaghetti, broken into small pieces
1 onion, peeled and thinly sliced
50g (2oz) mushrooms, sliced
3 spring onions, chopped
2 cloves of garlic, peeled and chopped
Salt to taste
Pinch monosodium glutamate
60ml (4 tblsp) oil
175g (6oz) chicken meat, finely shredded
30ml (2 tblsp) light soya sauce
5ml (1 tsp) sugar
15ml (1 tblsp) rice wine or dry sherry
90ml (6 tblsp) chicken stock

Cook the noodles in boiling, salted water for 4-5 minutes until tender. Drain and rinse under cold water. Drain once again and add 30ml (2 tblsp) oil; mix well to prevent the noodles from sticking together. Heat 30ml (2 tblsp) oil in a wok and fry the onions and garlic for 2 minutes. Add chicken and stir fry for 3-4 minutes. Add mushrooms. Sprinkle over the wine, sugar, soya sauce, monosodium glutamate and salt to taste. Cook until the mixture is fairly dry. Add noodles and stir well to mix. Sprinkle over the stock and cook once again until dry. Serve with chilli sauce and dark soya sauce. 50g (2oz) sliced green beans, 50g (2oz) peas or 50g (2oz) shredded carrot may also be added, along with the chicken pieces.

Peking Duck with Pancakes

PREPARATION TIME: for duck 2-3 hours; for pancakes 6 minutes
COOKING TIME: for duck 1 hour 20 minutes; for pancakes 15 minutes

2kg (4½lb) Peking duck, roasted
16-20 spring onions, sliced into 7.5cm (3 inch) pieces

Pancakes (Po Ping)
450g (1lb) flour
Pinch salt
15ml (1 tblsp) corn oil
5ml (1 tsp) sesame oil
Tepid water for kneading
Flour for rolling

To Make Pancakes
Sift the flour and salt into a mixing bowl. Make a well in the centre and add the corn oil and water, a little at a time, and work in the flour. Make a pliable dough. Remove from the bowl and knead well for 2-3 minutes. Cover with a damp,

clean cloth and allow to rest for 10 minutes. Knead again for 1 minute and divide the dough into 16-20 even-sized balls. Roll each ball in flour and roll out into a 10-15cm (4-6 inch) circle. Place a frying pan on the heat and when moderately hot place the rolled circle of dough on it; cook for ½-1 minute. Little bubbles will appear; flip over and allow to cook for 1-1½ minutes. Pick the pancake up and check whether little brown specks have appeared on the undersides; if not, then cook for a few seconds more. Use a clean tea towel to press the pancakes gently, this will circulate the steam and cook the pancakes. Prepare the rest of the pancakes in the same way and keep them stacked, wrapped in foil to keep them warm.

To Make Dip
60ml (4 tblsp) sugar
60ml (4 tblsp) bean paste (sweet)
15ml (1 tblsp) sesame oil
15ml (1 tblsp) corn oil or peanut oil
120ml (4 fl oz) water

Other Dips, Ready Prepared
60ml (4 tblsp) Hoi Sin sauce
60ml (4 tblsp) Chinese barbecue sauce

Mix sugar, bean paste and water together. Warm the wok, add the oil and then the sugar mixture. Bring to boil and, when the sugar has melted, remove and put in a bowl. Place the duck on a cutting board and cut thin slices from the breast area and thighs. Place a pancake on an individual plate, cover with a slice of duck and a few strips of onion, spread on a dip of your choice, roll up like a pancake and eat. To make very crisp duck, cut duck into large joints and deep fry them till crispy.

Sweet and Sour Chicken

PREPARATION TIME: 30 minutes
COOKING TIME: 20 minutes

2.5ml (½ tsp) salt
10ml (2 tsp) cornflour or arrowroot
1 chicken breast, cut into 1cm (½") cubes
1 onion, peeled and roughly chopped into 1cm (½") chunks
25g (1oz) bamboo shoots, sliced
1 green pepper, seeded and thinly sliced
2.5cm (1") fresh root ginger, peeled and thinly sliced
2 carrots, scraped and thinly sliced into 2.5cm (1") long pieces
1 garlic clove, peeled and chopped
30ml (2 tblsp) oil

Batter
100g (4oz) plain flour
25g (1oz) cornflour
1 small egg
Oil for deep frying

Sauce
15ml (1 tblsp) soft brown sugar
15ml (1 tblsp) red wine vinegar or white vinegar
15ml (1 tblsp) soya sauce
15ml (1 tblsp) tomato purée
450ml (¾ pint) chicken stock
Pinch monosodium glutamate (optional)
10ml (2 tsp) cornflour or arrowroot

Mix salt and cornflour and roll chicken pieces in it. Make the batter by mixing the sieved flour and cornflour with the egg and sufficient water to make a thick batter. Beat well. Heat oil for deep frying. Dip the chicken pieces into the batter and deep-fry until golden brown and crisp. Drain on absorbent paper and keep warm.

Heat the 30ml (2 tblsp) oil in a wok and stir fry the onions, gin and garlic for 2-3 minutes. Add carrots and fry for 2 minutes. A the green peppers and fry for 2 minutes. Add bamboo shoots, season with salt and stir well. M all the sauce ingredients togeth Pour over the cooked vegetable Cook for 2-3 minutes, until the sauce thickens. The sauce shou become transparent. Arrange fr chicken pieces on a serving dish and pour the sweet and sour sa over them. Serve as a side dish.

This page: Peking Duck with Pancakes.

Facing page: Tangerine Peel Chicken (top), Sweet and So Chicken (centre left) and Chicken Chow Mein (botto

Fish and Seafood

Prawns with Broccoli

PREPARATION TIME: 10 minutes

COOKING TIME: 8-10 minutes

450g (1lb) peeled prawns
Oil for deep frying

Sauce
120ml (4 fl oz) chicken stock
10ml (2 tsp) cornflour
Freshly ground black pepper and salt to taste
Pinch monosodium glutamate (optional)
5ml (1 tsp) sugar

Seasoning
30ml (2 tblsp) cooked oil, or oil from deep frying the prawns
Pinch salt
2.5ml (½ tsp) sugar
Pinch monosodium glutamate (optional)
10ml (2 tsp) cornflour

250g (8oz) Chinese broccoli, or English broccoli, cut into 8cm (3") pieces
1 carrot, peeled and sliced
2 cloves garlic, peeled and chopped
1cm (½") fresh root ginger, peeled and chopped

Deep fry the prawns in hot oil for 1-2 minutes. Drain the prawns and keep on one side. Keep the oil. Mix the sauce ingredients together. Mix the seasoning ingredients together in a separate bowl. Cook the broccoli in boiling water for 1 minute. Drain and add cold water to cover. Drain once again and mix the broccoli with the seasoning ingredients. Heat the wok and add 30ml (2 tblsp) cooked oil. Add the carrot, garlic and ginger and stir fry for 1 minute. Add the broccoli and stir fry for 1 minute more. Add the prawns and stir fry for ½ minute then add the blended sauce ingredients. Cook gently until the sauce thickens. Serve immediately.

Shrimps with Beancurd

PREPARATION TIME: 10 minutes

COOKING TIME: 8 minutes

450g (1lb) peeled shrimps

Seasoning
5ml (1 tsp) light soya sauce
Pinch salt
5ml (1 tsp) sugar
5ml (1 tsp) cornflour

2.5cm (1") fresh root ginger, peeled and finely chopped
30ml (2 tblsp) oil
1 clove of garlic, peeled and chopped
1 red chilli, chopped
2-3 beancurd cakes, cubed
60ml (4 tblsp) chicken stock
5ml (1 tsp) cornflour
30ml (2 tblsp) water

Mix the shrimps with the seasoning ingredients and half of the ginger. Heat the oil and stir fry the ginger and shrimps for 2 minutes. Add the garlic and fry for 1 minute. Add the chilli, cubed beancurd and stock. Simmer for 2-3 minutes. Mix the cornflour with the water and remaining crushed ginger and pour over the shrimp mixture. Simmer gently until the sauce thickens. Serve immediately.

Prawns in Hot Sauce

PREPARATION TIME: 10 minutes

COOKING TIME: 6 minutes

350g (12oz) cooked unshelled prawns

Seasoning
5ml (1 tsp) malt vinegar
5ml (1 tsp) Shao Hsing wine
Pinch salt

Sauce
5ml (1 tsp) cornflour mixed with 15ml (1 tblsp) water
10ml (2 tsp) tomato purée
Salt and freshly ground black pepper to taste
10ml (2 tsp) sugar
2.5ml (½ tsp) monosodium glutamate (optional)
5ml (1 tsp) hot chilli sauce
180ml (6 fl oz) chicken stock
30ml (2 tblsp) cooked oil

Wash prawns and drain well. Mi the seasoning ingredients togeth Mix the sauce ingredients togeth in a separate bowl. Heat the oil in wok and deep fry the prawns for minute. Remove the prawns and drain. Keep the oil. Reheat the w and add 10ml (2 tsp) oil and stir the onion, celery and garlic for 1 minute. Add prawns and the blended sauce ingredients. Bring the boil and simmer gently for 3- minutes. Stir in the seasoning mixture.

Fish in Wine Sauce

PREPARATION TIME: 20 minut

COOKING TIME: 15 minutes

Marinade
1.25ml (¼ tsp) salt
1 egg white
10ml (2 tsp) cornflour
5ml (1 tsp) wine vinegar

275-350g (10-12oz) mullet or carp fillet, cut into 5cm (2 inch) slices
Oil for deep frying
250ml (8 fl oz) chicken stock

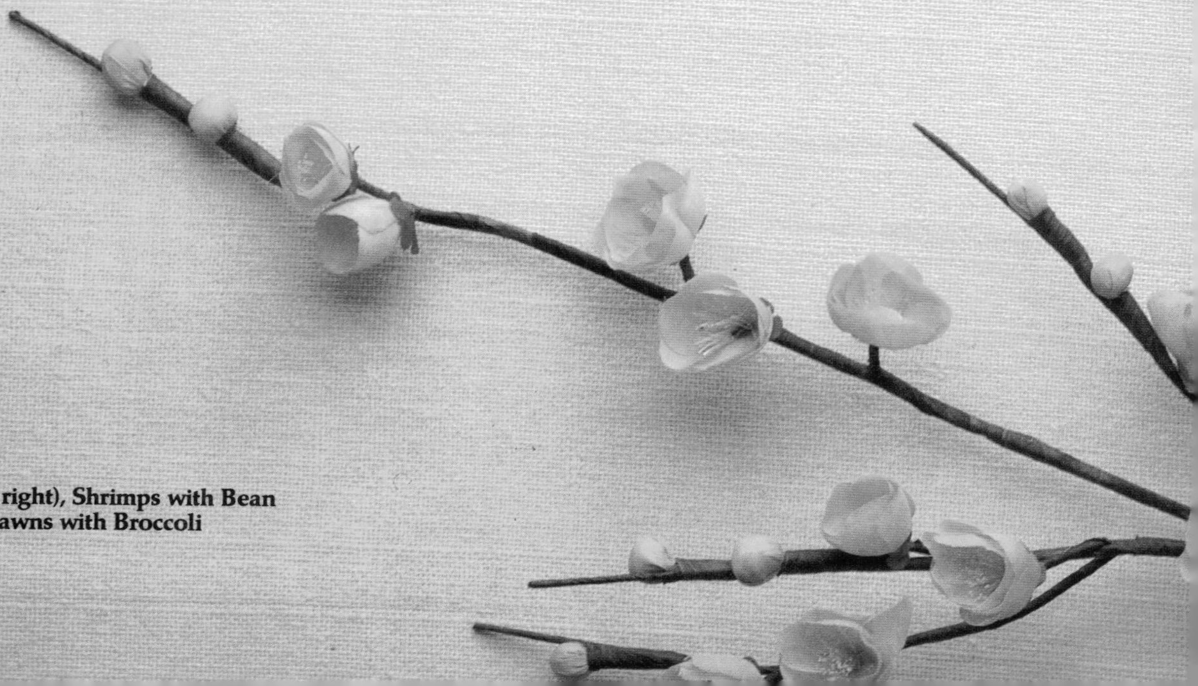

Prawns in Hot Sauce (top right), Shrimps with Bean Curd (centre right) and Prawns with Broccoli (bottom right).

Seasoning
Pinch monosodium glutamate (optional)
Pinch salt
Pinch freshly ground black pepper
5ml (1 tsp) sugar
10ml (2 tsp) cornflour
15ml (1 tblsp) water
1 cloud ear fungus, soaked and boiled for 2 minutes, and then chopped
2 dried Chinese mushrooms, soaked and sliced

Mix the marinade ingredients together. Marinate the fish in the marinade for 10 minutes. Heat a generous quantity of oil in the wok and deep fry the fish pieces, a few at a time, until the flesh is white. Remove and drain the fish. Keep the oil for future use. Clean the wok. Add the chicken stock to the wok and bring to the boil. Simmer gently and stir in the seasoning ingredients. Simmer for a few seconds and then add the cornflour blended with the water. Add the fish and simmer until the sauce thickens. Add the fungus and mushrooms. Simmer for 1 minute. Serve immediately.

Fish with Chicken and Vegetables

PREPARATION TIME: 25 minutes
COOKING TIME: 15 minutes

450g (1lb) pomfret, plaice or lemon sole fillets, cut into 5cm (2 inch) pieces
225g (8oz) boned chicken, cut into 5cm (2 inch) slices
6 dried Chinese mushrooms, soaked and sliced
50g (2oz) button mushrooms, sliced
50g (2oz) bamboo shoots, sliced
50g (2oz) mustard green, kale, or broccoli or 4 asparagus tips
100g (4oz) mixed vegetables (peas, carrots, bean sprouts, etc)
1 small onion, peeled and sliced
5ml (1 tsp) salt
Cooked oil

Marinade
1.25ml (¼ tsp) salt
5ml (1 tsp) white pepper
2.5ml (½ tsp) monosodium glutamate (optional)
10ml (2 tsp) cornflour
15ml (1 tblsp) cooked oil
1.25ml (¼ tsp) sesame oil

Sauce
250ml (8 fl oz) chicken stock
Salt to taste
Freshly ground black pepper to taste
2.5ml (½ tsp) monosodium glutamate (optional)
10ml (2 tsp) cooked oil
5ml (1 tsp) lemon juice

Wash the fish and drain. Mix the marinade ingredients together and marinate fish for 10-15 minutes. Blanch the mustard green, kale or broccoli in boiling, salted water for 1 minute. Drain and keep on one side. Heat the wok with 15ml (1 tblsp) cooked oil and stir fry the mixed vegetables and the onions for 2 minutes. Add the mustard green and stir fry for 1 minute. Drain and remove onto a plate. Brush a deep plate with cooked oil and arrange the drained fish, mushrooms, chicken and bamboo shoots in alternate rows. Place the dish over a steamer. Cover and steam over boiling water for 7 minutes until cooked. Remove the steamer from heat and keep on one side. Heat the wok and add the sauce ingredients and fish marinade. Bring to the boil and simmer for 1 minute, until thickened. Put the steamed fish, mushrooms etc. onto a serving plate and pour the hot sauce over the top. Serve immediately.

Fish with Vegetables and Bean Curd

PREPARATION TIME: 20 minutes
COOKING TIME: 15 minutes

4 squares bean curd, cut into 2.5cm (1 inch) squares

Sauce B
15ml (1 tblsp) Shao Hsing wine
15ml (1 tblsp) dark soya sauce
15ml (1 tblsp) light soya sauce
10ml (2 tsp) sugar
Pinch salt
Pinch white pepper
900ml (1½ pints) chicken stock
225g (8oz) cod fillet, cut into 5cm (2 inch) slices

Seasoning for Fish A
2.5ml (½ tsp) salt
2.5ml (½ tsp) Shao Hsing wine
22.5ml (1½ tblsp) cornflour
45ml (3 tblsp) oil

Seasoning for Cabbage C
2.5ml (½ tsp) sugar
Pinch salt
5ml (1 tsp) cornflour
2.5cm (1 inch) fresh root ginger, peeled and shredded
2 spring onions, chopped
22.5ml (1½ tblsp) cornflour mixed with 30ml (2 tblsp) water
25g (1oz) bean sprouts
Few slices of pepper, diced
1 small carrot, chopped
25g (1oz) shelled or frozen peas

Soak the bean curd in cold water for 2 minutes. Drain well. Mix the sauce B ingredients and keep on one side. Wash the fish and drain well. Mix seasoning A ingredients and marinate fish for 10-12 minutes. Heat the wok and add half the oil. When very hot, add the cabbage and seasoning C ingredients and stir fry for about 2 minutes. Drain the cabbage well. Discard any liquid. Heat wok and add the remaining oil. Add the ginger and onions and stir fry for 1 minute. Add sauce B ingredients and bring to the boil. Add fish and boil for 1 minute. Add the beancurd and simmer over a low heat for 5-6 minutes. (The bean curd should become spongy to the touch.) Add the blended cornflour and water. Stir and simmer until the sauce thickens. Add the cabbage and simmer for a further 2 minutes. Serve immediately.

Boiled Prawns

PREPARATION TIME: 5 minut
plus 10 minutes for the sauce
COOKING TIME: 10-15 minute

Sauce
30ml (2 tblsp) dark soya sauce
45ml (3 tblsp) light soya sauce
1cm (½") fresh root ginger, peeled and shredded
2 spring onions, finely chopped
1 red chilli, seeded and shredded
60ml (4 tblsp) cooked oil
10ml (2 tsp) tomato purée

1kg (2 lb) medium or large uncooked prawns in their shells
Salt

Mix the sauce ingredients togetl Wash the prawns and drain. Pla the prawns into a wire basket ar lower into a large pan of boiling, salted water. Boil for 10-12 minutes. Drain. Serve the drain hot prawns with small bowls of sauce for dipping.

Cantonese Prawns

PREPARATION TIME: 10 minut
COOKING TIME: 15 minutes

45ml (3 tblsp) oil
2 cloves garlic, finely crushed
450g (1lb) peeled prawns
5cm (2") root ginger, peeled and finely chopped
100g (4oz) uncooked pork or baco finely chopped

Sauce
15ml (1 tblsp) rice wine or dry she
15ml (1 tblsp) light soya sauce
5ml (1 tsp) sugar
250ml (8 fl oz) stock or water
15ml (1 tblsp) cornflour mixed wit 30ml (2 tblsp) stock or water

2-3 spring onions, chopped
2 eggs, lightly beaten

Heat 15ml (1 tblsp) oil in a wok. Add the garlic and fry for 1 minu Add the prawns and stir fry for 4 minutes. Remove to a dish. Keep warm. Add the remaining oil to t wok and fry the ginger and pork 3-4 minutes until it loses its colour. Add the mixed sauce ingredients to the wok and cook for 1 minute. Add the onions an cook for 1 minute. Add the beat eggs and cook for 1-2 minutes, without stirring, until it sets. Spo the egg mixture over the prawns.

Alternatively, add the prawns along with the beaten eggs. Allow the eggs to set and then mix gently. Serve at once.

Prawns and Ginger

PREPARATION TIME: 10 minutes
COOKING TIME: 10 minutes

30ml (2 tblsp) oil
675g (1½ lb) peeled prawns
2.5cm (1") fresh root ginger, peeled and finely chopped
2 cloves garlic, peeled and finely chopped
2-3 spring onions, chopped lengthways into 2.5cm (1") pieces
1 leek, white part only, cut into strips.
100g (4oz) shelled peas
175g (6oz) bean sprouts

Seasoning
30ml (2 tblsp) dark soya sauce
5ml (1 tsp) sugar
Pinch monosodium glutamate (optional)
Pinch of salt

Heat the oil in a wok and stir fry the prawns for 2-3 minutes. Remove the prawns to a dish. Reheat the oil and add the ginger and garlic and fry for 1 minute. Add the onions and stir fry for 1 minute. Add the leek, peas and bean sprouts. Stir fry for 2-3 minutes. Sprinkle over the seasoning ingredients and return the prawns to the wok. Cover and cook for 2 minutes. Serve immediately.

Shrimp and Cauliflower

PREPARATION TIME: 15 minutes
COOKING TIME: 14-15 minutes

45ml (3 tblsp) oil
1 clove of garlic, peeled and finely chopped
450g (1lb) shrimps, peeled
275g (10oz) cauliflower florets, cut into smaller pieces
250ml (8 fl oz) water or stock
Salt to taste
175g (6oz) shelled peas

Facing page: Fish with Vegetables and Bean Curd (top), Fish in Wine Sauce (centre right), Fish with Chicken and Vegetables (bottom). This page: Prawns and Ginger (top), Boiled Prawns (centre) and Cantonese Prawns (bottom right).

Sauce
10ml (2 tsp) cornflour
30ml (2 tblsp) stock or water
Freshly ground black pepper to taste

Heat the oil in a wok and fry the garlic for 2 minutes. Add the shrimps and cook for 3 minutes. Remove the shrimps. Add cauliflower and fry for 2-3 minutes, stirring constantly. Add stock, cover and simmer for five minutes. Add salt to taste and the peas and cook for a further 2-3 minutes. Return the shrimps to the wok and stir well. Add the blended sauce ingredients and gently simmer until it thickens. Serve immediately.

Snow Peas with Shrimps

PREPARATION TIME: 10 minutes
COOKING TIME: 6-8 minutes

5ml (1 tsp) cornflour
5ml (1 tsp) sugar
5ml (1 tsp) dark soya sauce
15ml (1 tblsp) water
45ml (3 tblsp) oil
450g (1lb) peeled shrimps
180ml (6 fl oz) chicken stock
2.5ml (½ tsp) salt
100g (4oz) snow peas (mange tout)
75g (3oz) water chestnuts, sliced
1 small onion, peeled and cut into small pieces
1 stem celery, cut into 5mm (¼") pieces
Pinch monosodium glutamate (optional)

Mix together the cornflour, sugar, soya sauce and water. Heat the oil in a wok. Add the shrimps and stir fry for 2 minutes. Add the stock, salt, snow peas, water chestnuts, onions and celery. Cover and cook for 2 minutes. Stir in the monosodium glutamate. Stir in the cornflour mixture and simmer gently until the sauce thickens. Serve as a side dish.

Prawns with Cashew Nuts

PREPARATION TIME: 10 minutes
COOKING TIME: 7-8 minutes

45ml (3 tblsp) oil
50-75g (2-3oz) cashew nuts
10ml (2 tsp) cornflour
250ml (8 fl oz) chicken stock or water
1 onion, peeled and cut into small pieces
25g (1oz) sliced green beans
50g (2oz) Chinese cabbage or white cabbage, shredded
50g (2oz) bamboo shoots, sliced
450g (1lb) peeled prawns
Salt and freshly ground black pepper to taste
4 rings pineapple, cut into chunks
Pinch monosodium glutamate (optional)

Heat 15ml (1 tblsp) oil in a wok and stir fry the cashew nuts until light brown. Remove the nuts and keep on one side. Mix the cornflour with 30ml (2 tblsp) water or stock and keep on one side. Reheat the wok with the remaining oil and fry the onion for 1 minute. Add the beans, cabbage and bamboo shoots and stir fry for 2-3 minutes. Add the cashew nuts and prawns and then add the remaining stock, salt and pepper, and the pineapple. Simmer for 1 minute and then add the MSG and cornflour mixture and cook unt the sauce thickens. Serve immediately.

Shrimp and Cauliflower (top right), Prawns with Cashew Nuts (centre left) and Snow Peas with Shrimps (bottom).

?egetables

?ised Cauliflower ?h Chilli

?ARATION TIME: 5 minutes
?KING TIME: 10 minutes

(4 tblsp) oil
?n (1 inch) fresh root ginger, ?eled and thinly sliced
?ll cauliflower, cut into 2.5cm (1 ?h) florets
?reen or red chillis, sliced into ?arters and seeded
?ing onions
?o taste
?1 tsp) sugar
?l (½ pint) chicken stock
?1 tsp) cornflour or arrowroot
(1 tblsp) water

? the wok and add the oil. Stir ?e ginger for 1 minute. Reduce ?eat and add the cauliflower ?hillis. Stir fry for 3-4 minutes. ? the spring onions, season with ?nd sprinkle with sugar. Mix ? minute and then add the ?. Cover and cook for 2 ?tes. Add the blended ?flour and water and stir over ?eat until the sauce has ?ened.

?d Bean Curd with ?shrooms

?ARATION TIME: 15 minutes
?KING TIME: 12-15 minutes

? (8oz) mushrooms (button or ?en) sliced

?soning
? (1 tblsp) rice wine or dry sherry
? (2 tsp) sugar
?ed Chinese mushrooms, soaked ?d sliced
?h bicarbonate of soda
? (8oz) mustard green or spinach, ?t into 7.5cm (3 inch) pieces
?ares bean curd (tau fu), cubed

?n (1 inch) fresh root ginger, ?eled and shredded
?ing onions, chopped
?(2oz) cooked ham, shredded

?ce
? (1 tblsp) oyster sauce
?(1 tsp) dark soya sauce

Fried Vegetables with Ginger (top right), Mustard Green with Crab Sauce (centre left) and Fried Bean Curd with Mushrooms (bottom).

15ml (1 tblsp) cornflour
60ml (4 tblsp) stock or water
Freshly ground black pepper

Blanch the fresh mushrooms in water for 1 minute. Drain the mushrooms and discard the water. Mix the seasoning ingredients together and marinate the mushrooms for 5-6 minutes. Discard marinade. Bring 1.2 litres (2 pints) of water to the boil and add the bicarbonate of soda and salt. Blanch the greens for 2 minutes. Drain the greens. Discard water. Sprinkle 2.5ml (½ tsp) salt over the bean curd. Deep fry in hot oil until golden brown. Drain and remove. Heat 30ml (2 tblsp) oil in the wok and stir fry the ginger, onions and ham for 2-3 minutes. Return the mushrooms to the wok and mix with the ginger and onions. Add the blended sauce ingredients and bring to boil. Add the bean curd and simmer until the sauce thickens. Arrange the greens on a dish and pour the sauce over them. Sprinkle with freshly ground black pepper.

Fried Vegetables with Ginger

PREPARATION TIME: 10 minutes
COOKING TIME: 13-15 minutes

1kg (2¼ lb) mixed Chinese green vegetables (cabbage, spinach, kale, broccoli, Chinese leaf etc.)
50g (2oz) snow peas (mange tout)
5ml (1 tsp) bicarbonate of soda
10ml (2 tsp) sugar
5ml (1 tsp) salt
15ml (1 tblsp) cooked oil
45ml (3 tblsp) oil
2.5cm (1 inch) fresh root ginger, peeled and shredded
1 green pepper, seeded and diced
1 green or red chilli, sliced into strips

Sauce
10ml (2 tsp) dark soya sauce
5ml (1 tsp) sugar
250ml (8 fl oz) chicken stock
10ml (2 tsp) cornflour
5ml (1 tsp) five spice powder

To Serve
2.5ml (½ tsp) sesame oil
Freshly ground black pepper to taste

Cut greens into 7.5cm (3 inch) pieces. Bring a large pan of water to the boil and add the seasoning ingredients. Add the snow peas and greens and cook for 4-5 minutes. Drain green vegetables and discard water. Add 15ml (1 tblsp) oil to the vegetables and keep covered. Heat the remaining oil in the wok and stir fry the ginger for 1 minute. Add the green pepper and chillis and stir fry for 1-2 minutes. Add the blended sauce ingredients and stir well. Simmer gently for 3-4 minutes. Add the green vegetables and cook for 1 minute. Serve immediately, sprinkled with sesame oil and pepper.

Bamboo Shoots with Green Vegetables

PREPARATION TIME: 10 minutes
COOKING TIME: 10-12 minutes

Oil for cooking
225g (8oz) spinach, or chopped broccoli

Seasoning
120ml (4 fl oz) chicken stock or water
1.25ml (¼ tsp) monosodium glutamate (optional)
1.25ml (¼ tsp) salt
1.25ml (¼ tsp) sugar
100g (4oz) bamboo shoots, sliced

Sauce
5ml (1 tsp) light soya sauce
Pinch monosodium glutamate
5ml (1 tsp) cornflour
10ml (2 tsp) water
15ml (1 tblsp) cooked oil

Heat 30ml (2 tblsp) oil in the wok. Fry the spinach for 2 minutes and add the mixed seasoning ingredients. Simmer for 1 minute and remove from the wok onto a

dish. Heat the wok and add 15ml (1 tblsp) oil. Add the bamboo shoots and fry for 1-2 minutes. Return the spinach mixture to the wok. Cook for 3 minutes. Mix together the ingredients for thickening the sauce. Add to the wok and cook for 1-2 minutes. Serve with roast Peking duck, or as a side dish.

Braised Aubergine and Chicken with Chilli

PREPARATION TIME: 10 minutes

COOKING TIME: about 15 minutes

90ml (3 fl oz) oil
2 cloves of garlic, peeled and sliced
450g (1lb) aubergine, cut into 5x6cm (2x2½ inch) pieces
15ml (1 tblsp) soya bean paste (or canned red kidney beans, made into paste)
2.5ml (½ tsp) ground dry chilli or chilli powder
Salt
450ml (¾ pint) chicken stock
2.5cm (1 inch) fresh root ginger, peeled and sliced
2-3 spring onions, chopped
225-275g (8-10oz) chicken, shredded (cooked or uncooked)

Seasoning
30ml (2 tblsp) light soya sauce
2.5ml (½ tsp) sugar
15ml (1 tblsp) cornflour or arrow
30ml (2 tblsp) stock or water, if needed

Heat 60ml (4 tblsp) oil in the w and stir fry the garlic for 2 minu Add the aubergine, which will s up all the oil. Stir fry for 3-4 minutes, stirring constantly to avoid burning. Add the bean pa chilli powder and salt to taste, a mix well. Add the chicken stock Cover and cook for 4-6 minute simmering gently. Remove the aubergine and arrange on a dish Save the sauce. Clean the wok heat the remaining oil. Stir fry t ginger for 1 minute. Add the onions and chicken and stir fry 2 minutes. Add the blended seasoning ingredients and the reserved aubergine sauce and simmer gently until it thickens. Pour over the aubergine and se immediately.

Szechuan Aubergine

PREPARATION TIME: 15 minu

COOKING TIME: 18-20 minut

Oil
1 large European aubergine or 450g (1lb) oriental aubergines, c into 5cm (2 inch) long and 1cm (½ inch) thick strips
3 cloves garlic, peeled and finely sliced
2.5cm (1 inch) fresh root ginger, peeled and shredded
1 onion, peeled and finely choppe
2 spring onions, chopped
100g (4oz) cooked and shredded chicken
1 red or green chilli, cut into strips

Seasoning
120ml (4 fl oz) chicken stock
5ml (1 tsp) sugar
5ml (1 tsp) red vinegar or wine vinegar
2.5ml (½ tsp) salt
2.5ml (½ tsp) freshly ground blac pepper.

Sauce
5ml (1 tsp) cornflour
15ml (1 tblsp) water
5ml (1 tsp) sesame oil

ı the wok and add 45ml (3
ı) oil. Add the aubergine and
ry for 4-5 minutes. The
ergines absorb a lot of oil; keep
ing or else they will burn.
ove from wok and keep on
side. Heat the wok and add
l (2 tblsp) oil. Add the garlic
ginger and fry for 1 minute.
the onions and fry for 2
ites. Add the chicken and
. Cook for 1 minute. Return
aubergines to the wok. Add the
ded seasoning ingredients and
ner for 6-7 minutes. Stir in the
ded sauce ingredients and
ner until the sauce thickens.
e with extra sesame oil if
red. This dish goes well with
g Chow fried rice or rice
eme.

ttuce and Bean routs with Soya uce

PARATION TIME: 15 minutes

OKING TIME: 5 minutes

100g (4oz) bean sprouts (moong or soya)
225g (8oz) sweet lettuce
15ml (1 tblsp) oil
2.5cm (1 inch) fresh root ginger, peeled and shredded
1 green or red chilli, seeded and split in half
Salt and freshly ground black pepper

Sauce
30ml (2 tblsp) light soya sauce
5ml (1 tsp) dark soya sauce
10ml (2 tsp) medium white wine or rice wine
2.5ml (½ tsp) sugar
Salt and freshly ground black pepper to taste
2.5ml (½ tsp) sesame oil

Trim the bean sprouts by pinching off the grey and brown ends, as they impart a bitter taste to the dish. Pick off bean seed skin if using soya beans. Cut soya bean sprouts in 2-3 pieces. Rinse in cold water and drain. Wash and drain lettuce before shredding into 5cm (2 inch) pieces. Heat the oil in the wok and stir fry the ginger and chilli for 1 minute. Add the lettuce and toss for 1 minute. Drain and remove on to a plate. Place the bean sprouts in a colander and pour boiling water over them. Drain thoroughly and add to the lettuce. Sprinkle with salt and pepper and keep covered. Mix the sauce ingredients together in the wok. Stir over the heat until blended. Pour this sauce over the vegetables and serve immediately.

Sweet and Sour Cabbage

PREPARATION TIME: 10 minutes

COOKING TIME: 10 minutes

450g (1lb) white cabbage, shredded
2.5ml (½ tsp) bicarbonate of soda
5ml (1 tsp) salt
10ml (2 tsp) sugar
15ml (1 tblsp) oil

Sauce
30ml (2 tblsp) sugar
30ml (2 tblsp) wine vinegar
250ml (8 fl oz) chicken stock or water
Pinch salt
15ml (1 tblsp) cornflour or arrowroot
Few drops red food colouring
5ml (1 tsp) tomato purée

Boil the cabbage in a large pan of water with the bicarbonate of soda, salt and sugar for 2-3 minutes. Drain the cabbage and discard the boiling water. Keep the cabbage in cold water for 5 minutes. Drain and keep on one side. Heat the wok and add the oil. Fry the cabbage until it is heated through. Remove on to a serving dish. Add the well-stirred sauce ingredients to the wok and gently bring to the boil, stirring. Stir over the heat until the sauce thickens. Pour over the cabbage and serve immediately.

Facing page: Bamboo Shoots with Green Vegetables (top right), Sweet and Sour Cabbage (centre left), Szechuan Aubergine (bottom).

This page: Lettuce and Bean Sprouts with Soya Sauce (left), Braised Aubergine and Chicken with Chilli (centre) and Braised Cauliflower with Chilli (right).

Egg Dishes and Curry

Lamb Curry

PREPARATION TIME: 15 minutes

COOKING TIME: 50 minutes

30ml (2 tblsp) oil
1 onion, peeled and chopped
2.5cm (1 inch) fresh root ginger, peeled and chopped
2 cloves of garlic, chopped
450g (1lb) lean, boned lamb, cut into cubes
1-2 carrots, scraped and sliced
5ml (1 tsp) five spice mixture
Salt to taste
2 chillis, chopped
15ml (1 tblsp) tomato purée
10ml (2 tblsp) cornflour
1 green pepper, seeded and chopped

Heat the oil and fry the onion for 2 minutes. Add the ginger and garlic and fry for 1 minute. Add the lamb and carrots and stir fry for 3-4 minutes. Sprinkle over the five spice powder and add the salt, chillis and tomato purée. Stir in 300ml (1/2 pint) water. Cover and simmer for 30-35 minutes. Mix 30ml (2 tblsp) water with the cornflour and add to the curry. Add the green pepper and simmer for 5 minutes. Serve with rice.

Prawn Curry

PREPARATION TIME: 10 minutes

COOKING TIME: 8 minutes

30ml (2 tblsp) oil
1 onion, peeled and chopped
1 carrot, cut into strips
75g (3oz) snow peas (mange tout)
2.5cm (1 inch) fresh root ginger, peeled and chopped
2 cloves garlic, chopped
450g (1lb) prawns, peeled
7.5ml (1½ tsp) curry powder
Salt to taste
2 green chillis, sliced
10ml (2 tblsp) cornflour

Heat the oil and fry the onions for 2 minutes. Add the carrot and snow peas and fry for 2 minutes. Add the ginger, garlic and prawns and stir fry for 1-2 minutes. Sprinkle over the curry powder and add the salt, green chillis and 300ml (1/2 pint) water. Mix the cornflour with 15ml (1 tblsp) water and add to the curry. Cook gently until the curry thickens. Serve with rice.

Chicken Curry

PREPARATION TIME: 15 minutes

COOKING TIME: 40 minutes

30ml (2 tblsp) oil
1 onion, peeled and chopped
2 cloves of garlic, peeled and chopped
2.5cm (1 inch) fresh root ginger, peeled and finely chopped
1.5kg (3lb) chicken, boned and cut into small pieces
10ml (2 tsp) curry powder
5ml (1 tsp) chilli powder
2.5ml (½ tsp) salt
100g (4oz) mixed frozen vegetables
1 green pepper, seeded and chopped
10ml (2 tsp) cornflour

Heat the oil and fry the onions for 2 minutes. Add the garlic, ginger and chicken and fry gently for 5 minutes. Add the curry powder, chilli powder, salt and 450ml (3/4 pint) of water. Cover and cook gently until the chicken is tender. Add the mixed vegetables and green pepper and cook for 3-4 minutes. Add the cornflour, dissolved in 30ml (2 tblsp) water, and simmer until the sauce thickens. Serve with plain boiled rice.

Shrimp Fu Yung

PREPARATION TIME: 10 minutes

COOKING TIME: 4 minutes for filling; 3-4 minutes for each pancake

Oil
1-2 cloves of garlic, chopped
100g (4oz) shrimps, peeled
100g (4oz) green beans, sliced
1 carrot, shredded
6 eggs
Salt and freshly ground black pepper to taste
250ml (8 fl oz) chicken stock
1.25ml (¼ tsp) salt
10ml (2 tsp) soya sauce
5ml (1 tsp) sugar
5ml (1 tsp) vinegar
5ml (1 tsp) cornflour

Heat 30ml (2 tblsp) oil in a wok. Add the garlic and stir fry for 1 minute. Add the shrimps and stir fry for 1 minute. Add the beans and carrots and stir fry for 2 minutes. Remove and keep on one side. Beat the eggs with salt and pepper to taste, and add the cooled shrimp mixture. Clean the wok and heat 5ml (1 tsp) oil. Pour in 60ml (4 tblsp) of the egg mixture and cook like a pancake. When the egg is set, turn the pancake over and cook on the other side until lightly golden. Place on a warm platter and keep warm.

To Make the Sauce
Beat the stock with the other sauce ingredients and stir over a gentle heat until the sauce thickens. Serve the pancakes with this sauce.
Makes 6-8 servings.

Egg Fu Yung

PREPARATION TIME: 5 minutes

COOKING TIME: 8-10 minutes

6 eggs
22.5ml (1½ tblsp) soya sauce
3-4 spring onions, chopped
Salt and freshly ground black pepper to taste
45ml (3 tblsp) oil
100g (4oz) bean sprouts

Beat the eggs and soya sauce together and add the spring onions and salt and pepper to taste. Heat the oil in a frying pan or wok and stir fry the bean sprouts for 2-3 minutes. Pour in the beaten egg mixture. Leave over a moderate heat to set and then put under the grill to set and brown the top. Cut into wedges and serve immediately. Alternatively, stir the mixture while it is cooking so that it turns out like scrambled egg.

Prawns in Egg Custard

PREPARATION TIME: 5 minutes

COOKING TIME: 20 minutes

8 eggs
Salt and freshly ground black pepper to taste
Pinch monosodium glutamate (optional)
5ml (1 tsp) Shao Hsing wine
300ml (½ pint) chicken stock
300ml (½ pint) water
450g (1lb) prawns, peeled
10ml (2 tsp) cooked oil

Beat the eggs in a bowl, add the seasoning, MSG and wine. Bring the stock and water to the boil and add to the eggs. Add prawns an set the bowl over a steamer. Co and steam over simmering water for about 15-20 minutes, until t custard has set. Serve with the cooked oil spooned over the top

Stir Fried Eggs with Shredded Meats and Vegetables

PREPARATION TIME: 15-20 minutes

COOKING TIME: 15 minutes

50g (2oz) cooked chicken, shredde
75g (3oz) cooked pork or beef, shredded
Salt to taste
1.25ml (1/4 tsp) soya sauce
60ml (4 tblsp) oil
4 eggs, beaten
2 spring onions, chopped
50g (2oz) dried mushrooms, soake and sliced
50g (2oz) button mushrooms, slice
2 cloud ear fungus, boiled in wate for 3 minutes and thinly sliced
175g (6oz) Chinese white cabbag broccoli or green leafy cabbage, shredded.
1-2 green or red chillis, chopped
2 sprigs Chinese parsley, chopped
Pinch monosodium glutamate (optional)

Put the chicken and pork into a bowl with 1.25ml (¼ tsp) salt a the soya sauce. Leave for 10 minutes. Heat the wok and add 30ml (2 tblsp) oil. Add the beat eggs and stir fry for 2-3 minutes until they resemble scrambled e Keep on one side. Reheat the w and add the remaining oil. Fry th onions and meats for 2 minutes. Remove from the wok and keep one side. Stir fry the cabbage an chillis in the wok for 1-2 minute Cover and gently cook in its ow juice until tender – approx 3-4 minutes. Return the meats, mushrooms and egg to the cabb and add the parsley and MSG. S fry for 1-2 minutes. Serve with extra soya sauce and Shao Hsing wine sprinkled over it, if desired

nb Curry (right), Prawn rry (below) and Chicken rry (bottom).

Marbled Eggs

PREPARATION TIME: 10 minutes

COOKING TIME: 1 hour 10 minutes to 1 hour 15 minutes

These are eaten cold, dipped in a sauce, as a starter or a snack. Allow 1 egg per person.

6-8 eggs
45ml (3 tblsp) tea leaves
2.5cm (1 inch) cinnamon stick
2-3 star anise
30ml (2 tblsp) dark soya sauce
30ml (2 tblsp) light soya sauce

Boil the eggs for 8-10 minutes until hard boiled. Drain and cool quickly by placing in iced water. Tap each egg shell with the back of a spoon until cracks appear all over. Bring enough water to the boil to cover the eggs. Add tea leaves, cinnamon, star anise, soya sauces and stir. Add the eggs and simmer gently for at least 1 hour. Allow to cool and then shell before serving.

Noodles with Pork Fu Yung

PREPARATION TIME: 20 minutes
COOKING TIME: about 20 minutes

2.5ml (½ tsp) bicarbonate of soda
15ml (1 tblsp) water
225g (8oz) pork, thinly sliced
225g (8oz) cake noodles
10ml (2 tsp) cornflour
Few drops sesame oil
Salt and freshly ground black pepper to taste
2.5ml (½ tsp) sugar
Oil
2 cloves of garlic, finely chopped
2.5cm (1 inch) fresh root ginger, peeled and sliced
2-3 spring onions, chopped
6 eggs, well beaten

Mix the bicarbonate of soda and the water together. Mix in the pork and marinate for 10-12 minutes. Drain. Cook the noodles in boiling, salted water for 3-4 minutes. Drain, rinse in cold water and drain once again. Toss in 15ml (1 tblsp) oil. Heat 30ml (2 tblsp) oil in the wok and brown the garlic. Add 5ml (1 tsp) salt and the noodles and stir fry for 3-4 minutes, until they turn light brown. Remove and keep on one side. Heat sufficient oil for deep frying in the wok and deep fry the pork for 3-4 minutes, drain and remove. Tip off the oil. Heat 15ml (1 tblsp) oil in the wok. Add the ginger and onions and stir fry for 1 2 minutes. Add the pork and then pour in the beaten eggs, mixing well. Add the cornflour, sesame oil and sugar and cook until the mixture thickens. Pour over the noodles and serve immediately.

Egg Pancakes with Filling

PREPARATION TIME: 10 minu
COOKING TIME: 6-7 minutes f each pancake

6 eggs
Salt and freshly ground black pep to taste
100g (4oz) lean pork, finely chop or ground
50g (2oz) button mushrooms, chopped
5ml (1 tsp) rice wine or dry sherry
5ml (1 tsp) light soya sauce
2.5ml (½ tsp) sugar
2.5ml (½ tsp) fresh root ginger, mi
Oil

Beat the eggs and season with s and pepper. Mix the pork with t mushrooms, wine, soya sauce, sugar and ginger. Add salt and pepper to taste and mix well. H the wok and add 5ml (1 tsp) oil Spoon in 30ml (2 tblsp) of the beaten egg and spread into a 7½ (3 inch) circle. Place 10ml (2 tsp filling into the centre of the egg. When the underside of the egg but the top is still moist, fold th egg circle over to make a crescen shape; press gently to seal the edges. Cook for 4 minutes on a heat to cook the filling. Make th remaining pancakes in the same way. Serve with a chilli sauce or dip, or with stir fried vegetables a main dish.

This page: Marbled Eggs (top Noodles with Pork Fu Yung (centre right) and Stir Fried E with Shredded Meats and Vegetables (bottom left).

Facing page: Prawns in Egg Custard (top left), Egg Pancak with Filling (top right), Shrim Fu Yung (centre left) and Egg Yung (bottom right).

Rice and Noodles

Rice with Minced Beef

PREPARATION TIME: 10 minutes
COOKING TIME: 25 minutes

30ml (2 tblsp) cooking oil
225g (8oz) minced beef
3 spring onions, chopped
1.25cm (½ inch) fresh root ginger, peeled and sliced
2 cloves garlic, peeled and sliced
15ml (1 tblsp) soya sauce
1 green pepper, seeded and chopped
450g (1lb) rice, thoroughly washed
2.5ml (½ tsp) salt
5ml (1 tsp) freshly ground black pepper, or to taste

Heat the oil and fry the mince, onions, ginger and garlic for 5 minutes. Add the soya sauce and green pepper and fry for 5-6 minutes. Cook the rice with 2.5cm (1 inch) water above the rice level with the salt for 5-6 minutes or until the rice is semi-cooked and the water is almost absorbed. Spread the mince evenly over the rice. Cover and cook for 6-8 minutes over a very gentle heat. Remove and serve well mixed. Season with salt and pepper to taste.

Assorted Meat Congee

PREPARATION TIME: 20 minutes
COOKING TIME: 1 hour 45 minutes

450g (1lb) rice
Scant 2½ litres (4 pints) chicken stock
100g (4oz) tripe, well washed and chopped (optional)
100g (4oz) pig's or lamb's liver, sliced
100g (4oz) cooked beef, ham, lamb, chicken or pork, chopped
100g (4oz) white fish fillets, thinly sliced
5ml (1 tsp) sesame oil
3 spring onions, chopped
7.5ml (1½ tsp) salt, or to taste
7.5ml (1½ tsp) freshly ground black pepper
1.25cm (½ inch) fresh root ginger, peeled and sliced

Wash the rice well and put it into a large saucepan. Add the chicken stock and the tripe (if used). Cook gently for 1-1½ hours or until the tripe is well cooked and the rice has become a soft pulp. In a separate saucepan, boil the sliced liver for 5 minutes in water. Drain and add to the rice. Add the cooked meat, fish, sesame oil, half the onions, salt and pepper and the slices of ginger. Cook for further 10-15 minutes covered. Pour into large bowls and serve topped with the remaining chopped onions.

Rice Supreme

PREPARATION TIME: 10 minutes
COOKING TIME: 15 minutes

45ml (3 tblsp) cooking oil
15ml (1 tblsp) light soya sauce
2 eggs, beaten
1 small onion, peeled and finely sliced
50g (2oz) shrimps, peeled
50g (2oz) prawns, peeled
50g (2oz) white fish, cubed
2 spring onions, finely chopped
50g (2oz) green pepper, seeded and cut into strips
450g (1lb) rice, cooked and cooled
Salt to taste
5ml (1 tsp) freshly ground black pepper
45ml (3 tblsp) tomato ketchup
50g (2oz) frozen peas

Heat 15ml (1 tblsp) oil in the wok and pour in the beaten eggs. Cook to make a thin omelette. Cut into thin strips. Heat 15ml (1 tblsp) oil in the wok and stir fry the onion for 2 minutes. Add the shrimps, prawns and fish and stir fry for 3-4 minutes. Remove the fish mixture to a plate. Heat the remaining oil in the wok. Add half the spring onions and the green pepper and stir fry for 2 minutes. Add the rice and season with salt and pepper. Add the tomato ketchup, peas, fried fish, prawns and shrimps. Add the soya sauce and stir fry for 3 minutes. Serve with the egg strips arranged on top of the rice.

Vegetable Rice

PREPARATION TIME: 10 minu
COOKING TIME: 5-8 minutes

450g (1lb) rice, cooked
175g (6oz) Chinese cabbage or Chinese leaves, shredded
100g (4oz) sliced green beans
100g (4oz) frozen peas
3 spring onions, chopped
15ml (1 tblsp) light soya sauce
Salt to taste

Rinse the cooked rice in cold w and drain. Put the moist rice in pan. Arrange the Chinese cabb sliced beans, peas and onions o top. Cover and cook over a ger heat for 4-6 minutes. Sprinkle soya sauce and add salt to taste Stir the vegetables evenly into rice and raise the heat for a few seconds. Serve immediately.

Plain Fried Rice

PREPARATION TIME: 5 minut plus cooling time
COOKING TIME: 10-11 minut

450g (1lb) Patna or long grain ri
1.25ml (¼ tsp) monosodium glutamate
30ml (2 tblsp) oil
Salt

Wash the rice in 4-5 changes o cold water. Drain the rice and p into a large pan or wok. Add sufficient cold water to come 2.5cm (1 inch) above the level the rice. Bring to the boil. Stir and reduce the heat to simmer. Cover and cook gently for 5-7 minutes until the water has be

This page: Vegetable Rice (t Assorted Meat Congee (cen right) and Rice Supreme (bottom).

Facing page: Yang Chow Fri Rice (top), Plain Fried Rice (centre left) and Rice with Minced Beef (bottom).

totally absorbed and the rice is separate and fluffy, with the necessary amount of stickiness to be handled by chopsticks. (If necessary cook for a little longer.) Spread the rice out on a tray and cool. Sprinkle with the monosodium glutamate. Heat the oil in a wok or large frying pan and add the rice. Stir fry for 1-2 minutes. Add salt to taste and stir fry for a further 1-2 minutes.

Yang Chow Fried Rice

PREPARATION TIME: 10 minutes

COOKING TIME: 6-8 minutes

45ml (3 tblsp) cooking oil
1 egg, beaten
100g (4oz) cooked meat, chopped (pork, lamb, beef)
100g (4oz) cooked prawns or shrimps, shelled and chopped
50g (2oz) shelled green peas
2 spring onions, chopped
450g (1lb) dry, cooked rice
Salt to taste
5ml (1 tsp) monosodium glutamate (optional)

Heat 15ml (1 tblsp) oil in a wok. Fry the beaten egg until set, and break into small lumps. Remove the egg. Add the remaining oil and fry the meat, shrimps, peas and onions for 1-2 minutes. Add the cooked rice and sprinkle with salt and monosodium glutamate. Fry for 3 minutes. Mix in the cooked egg and serve immediately.

Sizzling Rice or Singing Rice

PREPARATION TIME: 50 minutes

COOKING TIME: 2 hours, plus time for deep frying sizzling rice

100g (4oz) short grained rice

When rice is cooked, the crust that forms on the bottom of the pot can be dried and then deep fried. When it is immersed in gravy or soup it makes a sizzling noise, hence the name. Once made or collected, the rice crusts can be kept for months.

To Make a Rice Crust
Wash rice in 4-5 changes of water until the water runs clear. Drain the rice and put it into a pan with 300ml (½ pint) of water; bring to the boil. Reduce heat to low and cook for 20 minutes, simmering gently. Turn off the heat and let the rice stand covered for 25-30 minutes. Take a non-stick frying pan and transfer the rice to it. Spread evenly to a thickness of 1cm (½ inch). Cook on a very gentle heat for 40-50 minutes. Turn over and cook gently for another hour. The rice should be very dry. Break into 5cm (2 inch) squares and store in a glass jar with a lid.

To Cook Sizzling Rice
Pour oil into a pan to a depth of 5cm (2 inches) and bring to a moderately high temperature (190°C or 375°F). Add the rice squares and fry until golden brown. Remove and drain on kitchen paper. Serve with soup or any stir fried dish.

Shrimp Egg Rice

PREPARATION TIME: 20 minutes

COOKING TIME: 17-18 minutes

450g (1lb) long or medium grained rice
2 eggs
2.5ml (½ tsp) salt
60ml (4 tblsp) oil
2 spring onions, chopped
1 large onion, peeled and chopped
2 cloves garlic, peeled and chopped
100g (4oz) peeled shrimps
50g (2oz) shelled peas
30ml (2 tblsp) dark soya sauce

To Cook the Rice
Wash rice in 4-5 changes of wa
Add cold water to 2.5cm (1 inc
above the rice level and bring t
the boil. Stir once and reduce t
heat to simmer. Cover the pan
gently cook the rice for 5-7
minutes until the rice is dry and
the liquid has been totally
absorbed. Remove from the he
add cold water to cover and dr
thoroughly. Spread the rice on
serving tray and separate the gr
with a fork.
Beat the eggs in a bowl and sea
with a pinch of salt. Heat the w
and add 15ml (1 tblsp) oil. Add
onions and stir fry for 2 minute
Add the beaten eggs. Allow to
slightly and then stir the mixtu
until it scrambles. Remove onto
plate. Heat the wok and add 15
(1 tblsp) oil. Fry the garlic for 1
minute then add the shrimps a
cook for 2 minutes. Add the pe
and stir fry for 1 minute. Remo

ɔ a plate. Heat the wok and add remaining oil, a little salt to e and the cooked rice. Stir fry eat the rice through. Stir in the ı sauce, shrimp mixture and the ked eggs, gently stirring the ture to blend. Serve nediately.

Shrimp Egg Rice (below), Sizzling Rice or Singing Rice (bottom left) and Plain Rice (bottom right).

Plain Rice

PREPARATION TIME: 5 minutes
COOKING TIME: 5-7 minutes

450g (1lb) rice
Pinch salt
10ml (2 tsp) oil

To make a bowl of plain rice, take any grade of long or medium grained rice. Wash the rice in 4-5 changes of water and then add enough cold water to come 2.5cm (1 inch) above the rice level. Add the salt and oil and bring to the boil. Stir once. Cover and simmer gently for 5-7 minutes until the water has been totally absorbed. Remove from the heat and serve. Plain boiled rice should be fluffy, yet have enough moisture around the rice so that the grains can be picked up easily by chopsticks.

Noodles in Soup

PREPARATION TIME: 10 minutes
COOKING TIME: 6-8 minutes

450g (1lb) small rounds of noodle cakes.
Salt
1.3 litres (2¼ pints) chicken or beef broth, or thick stock
100g (4oz) cooked shredded chicken
2 eggs, hard boiled and sliced
100g (4oz) Chinese napa cabbage, finely shredded (or iceberg lettuce)
2 spring onions, thinly sliced

Cook the noodles in boiling, salted water for 5 minutes. Drain thoroughly. Heat the broth or stock and add salt to taste. Serve the cooked noodles in bowls, and pour over the hot broth. Garnish with chicken, sliced eggs, cabbage and spring onions.

Stir Fried Shanghai Noodles

PREPARATION TIME: 10 minutes
COOKING TIME: 5-6 minutes

100g (4oz) white cabbage, shredded
2.5ml (½ tsp) sesame oil
45ml (3 tblsp) cooked oil
100g (4oz) cooked chicken or pork, shredded
450g (1lb) thick Shanghai noodles, cooked until just tender
30ml (2 tblsp) soya sauce
2.5ml (½ tsp) monosodium glutamate (optional)
Freshly ground black pepper to taste

Cook the cabbage in boiling water for 1 minute. Drain thoroughly. Heat the oils in a wok. Add the meat and stir fry for 2-3 minutes. Add the cooked noodles, soya sauce, monosodium glutamate and salt and pepper to taste. Add the cabbage, heat through and serve immediately.

Deep Fried Noodles
Boil noodles for 5 minutes. Drain thoroughly on absorbent paper. Deep fry in hot oil until crisp and golden.

Fried Rice Noodles

PREPARATION TIME: 25 minutes
COOKING TIME: 10 minutes

450g (1lb) rice noodles
45ml (3 tblsp) oil
100g (4oz) cooked chicken, shredded
50g (2oz) peeled shrimps
50g (2oz) bamboo shoots, sliced
2 sticks celery, chopped
50g (2oz) leek, chopped
2 spring onions, shredded
60ml (4 tblsp) stock
30ml (2 tblsp) soya sauce

Soak the rice noodles in warm water for 10-15 minutes. Drain thoroughly. Heat half the oil in wok. Add the chicken, shrimps, bamboo shoots, celery, leeks an spring onions and stir fry for 2- minutes. Add the stock and salt and pepper to taste. Simmer for minutes and then drain the chicken and vegetables. Heat th remaining oil, add the rice nood and stir over the heat for 1 min Add the soya sauce and stir int the chicken and vegetable mixt Cook together for 2-3 minutes. Serve immediately. Boiled praw may also be added along with t chicken.

Meat and Prawn Cho Mein

PREPARATION TIME: 20 minu
COOKING TIME: 12-15 minut

450g (1lb) dried Chinese noodles broken spaghetti
Salt to taste
60ml (4 tblsp) oil
2-3 spring onions, chopped
100g (4oz) cooked ham, shreddec
100g (4oz) peeled prawns
100g (4oz) shredded carrots
100g (4oz) green beans, sliced
5ml (1 tsp) sugar
15ml (1 tblsp) rice wine or dry sh
100g (4oz) cooked chicken, shred
100g (4oz) bean sprouts
37ml (2½ tblsp) soya sauce

Cook the noodles in boiling, sal water for 4-5 minutes. Rinse un cold water and drain thoroughl Toss in 15ml (1tblsp) oil. Heat t remaining oil in a wok. Add the onions, ham, prawns, carrots an green beans and stir fry for 2-3 minutes. Add the salt, sugar, wi chicken and bean sprouts. Cool for 2 minutes. Add the cooked noodles and soya sauce. Cook f 1-2 minutes. Serve immediately

This page: Deep Fried Nood (top), Stir Fried Shanghai Noodles (centre), Fried Rice Noodles (bottom). Facing pa Meat and Prawn Chow Mei (top), Noodles in Soup (cent Rice Noodles Singapore Sty (bottom).

P
S

Rice Noodles Singapore Style

PREPARATION TIME: 15 minutes, plus soaking time for noodles

COOKING TIME: about 15 minutes

225g (8oz) rice noodles
Oil
2 eggs, beaten
1.25cm (½ inch) fresh root ginger, peeled and shredded
100g (4oz) bean sprouts
100g (4oz) cooked ham, pork or chicken, shredded
50g (2oz) chives, finely chopped
2 cloves garlic, finely chopped
Salt to taste
15ml (1 tblsp) chicken stock
30ml (2 tblsp) soya sauce
3 spring onions, chopped

Soak the rice noodles in warm water for 10 minutes and then drain well. Heat 15ml (1 tblsp) oil in a frying pan or wok and fry the beaten eggs to make a thin pancake. Slide onto a plate and cut into thin strips. Heat the wok or frying pan and add 15ml (1 tblsp) oil. Fry the ginger and bean sprouts for 2 minutes. Slide onto a plate. Heat the wok or frying pan with a further 15ml (1 tblsp) oil and fry the pork or chicken and the chives for 1-2 minutes. Slide onto a plate. Heat 30ml (2 tblsp) oil in the wok or frying pan and brown the garlic. Add the rice noodles and stir fry for 2-3 minutes. Add salt to taste, chicken stock, bean sprouts and pork or chicken. Mix well, sprinkle with soya sauce and stir over the heat for 1 minute. Top with the strips of egg pancake and spring onions and serve immediately.

Noodles with Beef and Almonds

PREPARATION TIME: 15 minutes

COOKING TIME: 10 minutes

45ml (3 tblsp) oil
1 onion, chopped
4 cloves of garlic, chopped
2.5cm (1 inch) fresh root ginger, peeled and sliced
225g (8oz) beef, thinly sliced
50g (2oz) carrots, diced
50g (2oz) sliced green beans
50g (2oz) water chestnuts, sliced
50g (2oz) mushrooms, sliced
2 green chillis, sliced in half
Salt

5ml (1 tsp) sugar
5ml (1 tsp) monosodium glutamate (optional)
250ml (8 fl oz) chicken stock
100g (4oz) blanched almonds
450g (1lb) noodles, cooked until just tender

Heat 30ml (2 tblsp) oil in a wok. Fry the onion, garlic, ginger and beef for 3 minutes. Add the carrots and green beans and fry for 2 minutes. Add the water chestnuts, mushrooms and green chillis and fry for 1 minute. Add salt, sugar, MSG and stock. Simmer for 1 minute. Remove to a dish and keep warm. Clean the wok and add the remaining oil. Fry the almonds and noodles for 1-2 minutes. Mix with the cooked vegetables and season with soya sauce. Serve immediately.

Egg Noodles with Meat Sauce

PREPARATION TIME: 15 minutes

COOKING TIME: 20-22 minutes

45ml (3 tblsp) oil
3 cloves garlic, chopped
2.5cm (1 inch) fresh root ginger, peeled and shredded
1 onion, chopped
1 green pepper, seeded and sliced
450g (1lb) beef mince
2.5ml (½ tsp) salt
10ml (2 tsp) tomato purée
15ml (1 tblsp) soya sauce
2.5ml (½ tsp) freshly ground black pepper
120ml (4 fl oz) chicken stock
5ml (1 tsp) cornflour
450g (1lb) egg noodles
2 spring onions, chopped

Heat 30ml (2 tblsp) oil in a wok. Fry the garlic and ginger for 1-2 minutes. Add the onion and fry for 2-3 minutes. Add the green pepper and the beef mince and fry for 1 minute. Add half the salt, tomato purée, soya sauce and ground pepper. Fry for a further 3 minutes. Blend the stock and cornflour and add to the wok. Cook until thickened and the meat is tender. Meanwhile, cook noodles in boiling, salted water for 3-4 minutes, and drain. Rinse in cold water and drain once again. He the remaining oil in a pan. Add noodles and toss over the heat until heated through. Arrange plate and top with the meat sa Garnish with chopped spring onions.

Fried Noodles with Shredded Chicken

PREPARATION TIME: 15 min

COOKING TIME: about 10 minutes

Oil
225g (8oz) cooked chicken, shre
1 clove of garlic, chopped
2-3 spring onions, chopped
100g (4oz) whole green beans (c long Chinese beans, cut into 7 (3 inch) pieces)
450g (1lb) noodles, cooked until tender
15ml (1 tblsp) cornflour
250ml (8 fl oz) chicken stock
15ml (1 tblsp) soya sauce
15ml (1 tblsp) oyster sauce
5ml (1 tsp) wine
5ml (1 tsp) sugar
1.25ml (¼ tsp) salt

Heat 30ml (2 tblsp) oil in a wo and cook the chicken for 2 minutes. Remove the chicken. the garlic, spring onions and be and fry for 2 minutes. Remove vegetables. Heat 30ml (2 tblsp in the wok and toss the pre-bo noodles over the heat for 2 minutes. Arrange on a plate an keep warm. Return the fried chicken, onion and green bean the wok and stir fry for 1 minu Dissolve the cornflour in the chicken stock and add to the w Add the soya sauce, oyster sau wine, sugar and salt and peppe taste. Simmer until the sauce is thick. Pour over the bed of noo and serve immediately.

This page: Noodles with Be and Almonds (top), Egg Noodles with Meat Sauce (centre) and Fried Noodles Shredded Chicken (bottom).

Facing page: Chinese Bean Buns (top), Red Bean Filled Sums (centre right) and Can Apples (bottom).

Sweets

'hinese Bean Buns

:PARATION TIME: about 2 ırs, including proving time

OKING TIME: about 30 minutes

ıl (2 fl oz) milk
(2 oz) sugar
nl (½ tsp) salt
(1oz) lard
ıl (2 fl oz) warm water
ıl (2 tsp) dried yeast
g, beaten
g (10oz) plain flour

Bring the milk almost to the boil. Stir in the sugar, salt and lard. Cool slightly. Put the warm water and yeast into a bowl and stir to mix. Add the lukewarm milk mixture. Add the beaten egg and 225g (8oz) of the flour and beat until smooth. Add the remaining flour and mix to a dough. Turn dough out onto a well-floured board and knead until smooth and elastic. Place in a greased bowl. Brush the dough with oil and cover. Leave to rise in a warm place until doubled in size (about 1 hour).

Filling
100g (4oz) sweet bean paste
25g (1oz) sugar
25g (1oz) chopped walnuts
15ml (1 tblsp) lard

Heat the filling ingredients together in a wok for 5-6 minutes until smooth and shiny. Remove and cool. Divide the filling into 12-14 portions. Knead the risen dough again for 2 minutes and then divide the dough into 12-14 portions. Flatten into thick, circular shapes 10cm (4 inches) in diameter. Place a chopstick on each circle of dough to mark it in half, and then in half again. Cut along the marks to within ⅓ of the centre. Place one portion of filling in the centre of the dough circle and fold the cut ends in to meet in the centre, to form a rosette. Secure by pinching ends of dough together. Place a piece of greased foil over the pinched ends and place the buns on a greased baking tray. Brush with a little milk. Bake at 190°C, 375°F, Gas Mark 5 for 20-25 minutes.

Red Bean Filled Dim Sums

PREPARATION TIME: 45-50 minutes

COOKING TIME: 10-12 minutes

50g (2oz) sugar
300ml (½ pint) warm water
15ml (1 tblsp) dried yeast
450g (1lb) plain flour
30ml (2 tblsp) melted lard
1 egg white, beaten

Filling
275g (10oz) sweet bean paste, ready made
Red food colouring

Dissolve the sugar in the warm water and add the yeast. Stir until dissolved. Leave in a warm place until frothy. Sift the flour into a mixing bowl and add the melted lard and the yeast mixture. Mix together. Turn the mixture onto a floured surface and knead to a smooth and elastic dough. Roll into a long sausage and divide into 24 equal portions. Roll each portion into a 5cm (2 inch) flat circle. Brush edges of dough with beaten egg white. Place 15ml (1 tblsp) of filling into the centre of each circle and pull the dough around it to enclose the filling. Pleat the open edges in a circular fashion, so that a small opening is left in the middle of the pleating. Place a small piece of greased foil over the pleats on each dim sum. Leave for 10-12 minutes until the dough becomes springy to the touch. Put a dab of red food

Below: Stuffed Lychees (left), Sweet Almon Pudding (centre) and Agar-Agar Pudding (right

colouring on each dim sum. Arrange the dim sums in a bamboo steaming basket and steam over boiling water for 10-12 minutes. The dim sums are ready when they are dry and smooth. Alternatively they can be baked at 180°C, 350°F, Gas Mark 4, for about 20 minutes.

Agar-Agar Pudding

PREPARATION TIME: 5 minutes

COOKING TIME: 4-5 minutes

600ml (1 pint) milk
100g (4oz) sugar
25g (1oz) ground almonds
50g (2oz) agar-agar (also called Chinese grass)
25g (1oz) blanched and chopped almonds

Mix the milk, sugar and ground almonds together in a pan and stir over the heat for 4 minutes. Add the agar-agar and stir until dissolved. Stir in the chopped almonds. Pour into a shallow dish 2.5cm (1 inch) deep. Cool and keep in refrigerator until set. Serve chilled, cut into diamond or square shapes.

Almond Cookies

Makes 60 cookies

PREPARATION TIME: 20 minutes

COOKING TIME: 12-15 minutes

225g (8oz) lard
100g (4oz) caster sugar
50g (2oz) brown sugar
1 egg, beaten
Few drops almond essence
275g (10oz) plain flour
Pinch salt
7.5ml (1½ tsp) baking powder
75g (3oz) blanched almonds
1 egg yolk
30ml (2 tblsp) water

Cream the lard with the caster sugar and the brown sugar until light and fluffy. Add the egg and almond essence and beat until smooth. Sift the flour, salt and baking powder. Mix the dry ingredients into the creamed mixture. Shape into small balls on a lightly floured surface. Flatten slightly and press an almond into the centre of each one. Place onto a greased baking sheet. Mix the egg yolk with the water. Brush the cookies with the egg glaze. Bake at 180°C, 350°F, Gas Mark 4, for 12-15 minutes.

Sweet Almond Pudding

PREPARATION TIME: 4-5 minutes

COOKING TIME: 6 minutes

175g (6oz) blanched almonds
450ml (¾ pint) water
175g (6oz) sugar
45ml (3 tblsp) rice powder, or ground rice
150ml (¼ pint) milk

Blend the blanched almonds and water in the liquidiser. Put into a pan and bring to the boil. Add the sugar and stir over the heat until the sugar has dissolved. Add the rice slowly to the milk and stir gradually into the simmering sugar and almond mixture. Cook gently until the mixture thickens. Remove from the heat and pour into a serving dish. Serve hot or cold.

Sweet Dumplings

PREPARATION TIME: 10 minutes

COOKING TIME: 15-20 minutes

Oil
75g (3oz) sugar
100g (4oz) plain red bean paste
50g (2oz) desiccated coconut
4 egg whites
15ml (1 tblsp) plain flour
45ml (3 tblsp) cornflour
Icing sugar

Heat 15ml (1 tblsp) oil in a wok and add the sugar, bean paste and coconut. Stir fry for 4-5 minutes until the sugar melts and the paste is smooth and shiny. Fry for a few minutes more and then allow to cool on a dish. Whisk the egg whites until stiff and mix with the plain flour and cornflour to a smooth batter. Beat well. Clean the wok and heat sufficient oil for deep frying. Make 10-12 even-sized balls from the bean paste mixture. Dip each ball into the batter and then deep fry for 3-4 minutes until golden and crisp. Fry a few at a time and drain on kitchen paper. Dust with icing sugar before serving.

Stuffed Lychees

PREPARATION TIME: 20 minu

450g (1lb) canned lychees, stones removed
225g (8oz) canned pineapple ring
Few drops vanilla essence or almo essence

Drain the lychees into a bowl, reserving the juice. Drain the pineapple rings and reserve the liquid. Slice each pineapple ring into 2.5cm (½ inch) long strips. Press one or two strips of pinea into each lychee. Arrange the pineapple-filled lychees in a dee serving dish. Mix the pineapple and lychee liquid with a few drc of essence. Spoon over the stuf fruits. Serve well chilled. Alternatively, stuff the lychees maraschino cherries, mango, canned pears, oranges etc.

Facing page: Sweet Dumplin (top), Almond Cookies (cent left) and Date Cake (bottom right).

Chocolate Roulade (above), Devil's Food Cake (right) and Family Chocolate Cake (far right).

COOKING WITH CHOCOLATE

Introduction

Rich, dark and luxuriously smooth and enticing, chocolate remains one of the most popular ingredients for both everyday and exotic desserts, cakes and confectionery. These mouth-watering recipes have been specially selected for their variety as well as their relative ease of preparation: recipes which are bound to delight all those with a passion for chocolate cuisine.

Hints For Cooking With Chocolate
The amount of cocoa butter added to chocolate determines how the chocolate can be used.

Cooking Chocolate
This is not to be confused with cake covering. Cooking chocolate has some cocoa butter replaced with palm kernel oil or coconut oil. Flavourings are used to make the chocolate less expensive and easy to use; it can be used for any chocolate cooking or decoration.

Milk Chocolate
This is rarely used in cooking as it does not give a strong enough flavour, but it can be used for making Easter Eggs and in other recipes that require a delicate flavour.

Couverture
This is a chocolate containing a high proportion of cocoa butter, which gives it a smooth, glossy appearance. Couverture chocola requires repeated heating and cooling, or tempering; a professior method of working with chocolate.

White Chocolate
This variety has a relatively high sugar content. It is used in son recipes in this book but great care should be taken when using this it is difficult to melt and has a tendency to go grainy if overheate

Plain Chocolate
This chocolate has a rich, dark flavour and is used in most recip where chocolate is called for. Plain eating chocolate can always l used but there are also some varieties of plain chocolate availab which are specially recommended for cooking.

Bitter Chocolate
This is not easy to buy but it can be made as required. To make pla chocolate bitter add 5ml (1 tsp) instant coffee powder or granules (5ml (1 tsp) cocoa powder) for every 50g (2oz) of chocolate.

Chipped and Grated Chocolate
Chocolate can be chipped and grated either manually or in a fo

ocessor. When grating chocolate, refrigerate for 30 minutes, then ld the chocolate with kitchen paper to prevent it from melting.

ocoa Powder and Drinking Chocolate

ten used in baking but make sure the lumps are removed. It is best ed blended with hot (not boiling) water, so that it forms a smooth ste. Add the paste to the recipe as required.

elting Chocolate

is should be done carefully as it is particularly important. Break chocolate into pieces and put in a bowl over a pan of simmering ter, or into the top of a double boiler if you have one. When using electric cooker turn off the heat once the water has boiled. Make e the bowl fits well into the saucepan so that no steam or water es into the chocolate. Note: if the chocolate goes solid add a little getable oil and beat well.

icrowave Melting

is is a clean and easy way to work with chocolate. Break the ocolate into pieces and put into a suitable bowl. Cover with cling n and melt following the manufacturers instructions. The timing l depend on the quantity of chocolate and the size of the bowl.

ecorating with Chocolate

hocolate for Dipping

is chocolate has a high proportion of vegetable fat and is less pensive than couverture. Melt the chocolate, which you may find sier to use if you add 15ml (1 tblsp) of vegetable oil to every 175g oz) of chocolate.

Chocolate Leaves

These are made by using rose leaves, although any leaves with good strong veins can be used. *Make sure that the leaves you select are not poisonous.* Wash and dry the leaves thoroughly, melt the chocolate and, using a small paintbrush, brush the underside of the leaves with the chocolate. Alternatively you can dip the undersides of the leaves in the chocolate, then place them on non-stick silicone paper or greaseproof paper, chocolate side up. When the chocolate is hard peel off the leaves.

Chocolate Curls

Make sure the chocolate is neither too warm, as it will be too soft to hold a cult, nor too cold, since it will become brittle and may crumble. Using a small knife or even a vegetable peeler make curls by gently shaving the chocolate with the blade.

Craque

To produce these glamorous, long curls, melt the chocolate and spread it with a palette knife onto an ungreased, laminated or marble surface. The chocolate should be 0.5cm (¼ inch) thick. Leave it to set, then scrape it up in curls by holding a knife at an angle of 45° and pushing it away from you.

Shapes

To make shapes, melt and pour the chocolate onto an ungreased, laminated or marble surface then, when set, cut into shapes with a sharp knife.

Cakes and Gateaux

Chocolate Fudge Cake

PREPARATION TIME: 15 minutes
COOKING TIME: 45-50 minutes
OVEN TEMPERATURE: 160°C, 325°F, Gas Mark 3
MAKES: 1 cake, 23cm (9 inches) in diameter

200g (7oz) plain flour
5ml (1 tsp) bicarbonate of soda
5ml (1 tsp) baking powder
30ml (2 tblsp) cocoa powder
150g (5oz) brown sugar
30ml (2 tblsp) golden syrup
2 eggs
150ml (¼ pint) oil
300ml (½ pint) milk

Chocolate Icing
175g (6oz) plain chocolate, grated
30ml (2 tblsp) single cream

To Decorate
Chocolate shavings

Grease and line a 23cm (9 inch) cake tin. Sieve the dry ingredients together in a bowl and add the sugar. Make a well in the centre and add the syrup, eggs, oil and the milk. Beat them all together until smooth. Pour the cake mixture into the cake tin. Bake in the oven for 45 minutes. When cooked, leave the cake in the tin for a few minutes before turning it out onto a wire rack. To make the icing: heat the chocolate and cream in a small, heavy saucepan until melted. Cool the mixture slightly and pour over the cake; drag the surface with a fork when it is nearly dry, and decorate with the chocolate shavings.

Chocolate Spice Cake

PREPARATION TIME: 30 minutes
COOKING TIME: 40-50 minutes
OVEN TEMPERATURE: 180°C, 350°F, Gas Mark 4
MAKES: 1 cake, 20cm (8 inches) in diameter

5 eggs, separated
175g (6oz) caster sugar
75g (3oz) plain chocolate, melted
75g (3oz) plain flour
2.5ml (½ tsp) ground nutmeg
2.5ml (½ tsp) ground cinnamon
2.5ml (½ tsp) ground cloves

Cinnamon Topping
Ground cinnamon
Icing sugar

Butter and line a 20cm (8 inch) spring form cake tin with greaseproof paper (use a tin that has a central funnel). Brush the paper with melted butter and dust with flour. Put the egg yolks and sugar into a mixing bowl and beat them well until the mixture will fall from the whisk in a thick ribbon. Stir in the melted chocolate. Sieve together the flour, nutmeg, cinnamon and cloves, and fold into the cake mixture. Whisk the egg whites until stiff but not dry. Gently fold in the beaten egg whites, a little at a time. Pour the mixture into the tin. Bake in a pre-heated oven for 40-50 minutes, or until a skewer inserted into the middle comes out clean. Remove the cake from the oven and let it

This page: Chocolate Fudge Cake (top) and Chocolate Almond Cake (bottom).

Facing page: Chocolate Spice Cake (top) and Chocolate Potato Cake (bottom).

Chocolate Roulade (above) and
Chocolate Orange Cake (right).

ol in the tin on a wire rack, for 10 nutes. Turn the cake out to cool npletely. Dust the top of the e with a little ground cinnamon d/or icing sugar.

hocolate Roulade

EPARATION TIME: 35 minutes
OKING TIME: 15-20 minutes
EN TEMPERATURE: 180°C
0°F, Gas Mark 4
KES: 1 roulade, 23cm (9 inch) long

nl (1 tblsp) instant coffee
nl (1 tblsp) hot water
0g (4oz) plain chocolate, chopped
r grated
4 eggs, separated
100g (4oz) caster sugar

To Decorate
300ml (½ pint) double cream
Icing sugar

Grease and line a 33x23cm (13x9 inch) Swiss roll tin. Mix the coffee with the hot water and add the chocolate; stand in a bowl over a saucepan of hot water, and stir until the chocolate has melted. Allow the mixture to cool. Whisk together the egg yolks and sugar until thick, then fold into the chocolate mixture. Whisk the egg whites until stiff but not dry, and fold lightly into the mixture. Pour the mixture into the prepared tin. Bake in the oven for 15-20 minutes. Immediately after taking the cake out of the oven, cover the cake in its tin with a damp tea towel, and leave it to stand overnight. To decorate: carefully turn the cake out onto a sheet of greaseproof paper which has been sprinkled with caster sugar; remove the lining paper. Whip the cream until it holds its shape and spread over the cake (reserve a little for piping). Roll up the cake, like a Swiss roll, and dust it with icing sugar. Pipe the remaining cream down the centre or around the roulade.

Chocolate Orange Cake

PREPARATION TIME: 30 minutes
COOKING TIME: 40 minutes
OVEN TEMPERATURE: 180°C, 350°F, Gas Mark 4
MAKES: 1 cake, 20cm (8 inches) in diameter

225g (8oz) plain flour
75g (3oz) cocoa powder
225g (8oz) butter
275g (10oz) caster sugar
2 eggs, beaten
250ml (8 fl oz) buttermilk

Icing
225g (8oz) butter
Grated rind of 1 orange
225g (8oz) icing sugar, sieved
Juice of ½ an orange

To Decorate
Fresh orange segments or slices

Grease and line two 20cm (8 inch) sandwich tins. Sieve together the cocoa and the flour. Cream the butter and sugar together until light and fluffy; gradually add the beaten eggs. Stir the buttermilk into the mixture, and then fold in the cocoa and flour. Turn the mixture into the prepared tins. Bake for 40 minutes. Remove the cakes from the oven; turn out of the tins and allow to cool on a wire rack. When the cakes are cold, split each cake into two layers. To make the icing: cream the butter with the orange rind until soft; beat in the icing sugar, alternately with the orange juice. Sandwich the cakes together with some of the butter icing and spread the remaining icing on the top and the sides of the cake. "Rough" with a fork and decorate with the orange slices or segments.

Chocolate and Almond Cake

PREPARATION TIME: 45 minutes

COOKING TIME: 40-45 minutes

OVEN TEMPERATURE: 160°C, 325°F, Gas Mark 3

MAKES: 1 cake, 20cm (8 inches) in diameter

175g (6oz) butter or margarine
175g (6oz) caster sugar
100g (4oz) plain chocolate, melted
50g (2oz) ground almonds
4 eggs, separated
50g (2oz) self-raising flour
25g (1oz) cornflour

Icing
30ml (2 tblsp) cocoa powder
30ml (2 tblsp) hot water
75g (3oz) butter or margarine
225g (8oz) icing sugar

To Decorate
50g (2oz) chopped toasted almonds
16 whole almonds, half dipped in melted chocolate

Grease and line two 20cm (8 inch) sandwich tins. Cream the butter and sugar together until light and fluffy. Beat together the melted chocolate, ground almonds, and egg yolks, and add to the butter and sugar mixture. Fold the flour and cornflour into the mixture. Whisk the egg whites until stiff but not dry; fold into the cake mixture. Divide the mixture between the two tins. Bake in the oven for 40-45 minutes. Turn out and cool on a wire rack. To make the icing: blend the cocoa powder with the hot water. Beat together the butter and icing sugar until well mixed. Mix in the cocoa mixture. Use two-thirds of the icing to sandwich the cakes together, and cover the sides. Put the toasted nuts on a sheet of greaseproof paper and roll the sides of the sandwiched cakes over the nuts. Smooth the remaining icing over the top of the cake. Decorate with the whole almonds, half dipped in melted chocolate.

Austrian Sachertorte

PREPARATION TIME: 40 minu[tes] plus cooling time

COOKING TIME: 1 hour 15 minutes

OVEN TEMPERATURE: 180°C, 350°F, Gas Mark 4

MAKES: 1 cake, 20cm (8 inches) diameter

Torte
150g (5oz) plain dark chocolate, grated
15ml (1 tblsp) warm water
150g (5oz) butter
150g (5oz) icing sugar
5 eggs, separated
150g (5oz) self-raising flour
25g (1oz) cornflour
15ml (1 tblsp) rum, or strong black coffee
75ml (5 tblsp) sieved apricot jam

Icing
120ml (4 fl oz) double cream
10ml (2 tsp) brandy
100g (4oz) plain dark chocolate, grated
50g (2oz) milk chocolate, grated
Icing sugar to dust

Grease and flour a 20cm (8 inch) round cake tin. Melt the chocola[te] in a basin with the warm water. Cream the butter and icing suga[r] together until light and fluffy. Be[at] in the chocolate gradually. Beat i[n] the egg yolks one at a time. Siev[e] together the flour and the cornflour and fold it into the chocolate mixture. Whisk the eg[g] whites until stiff but not dry. Bea[t a] third of the egg whites into the mixture then fold in the remaind[er]. Spoon the mixture into the prepared cake tin. Bake for 50 minutes to 1 hour, until firm to t[he] touch. Turn out and cool on a w[ire] rack. Split the cake in half horizontally, sprinkle with rum o[r] coffee, and sandwich together w[ith] 30ml (2 tblsp) apricot jam. Place

This page: Humpty Dumpty (top) and Moon Cake (bottom).

Facing page: Loganberry Tort[e] (top) and Austrian Sachertort[e] (bottom).

Sachertorte

the cake on a wire rack. Brush all over with the remaining jam. To make the icing: place the cream in a saucepan with the brandy and bring just to the boil. Add the grated plain dark chocolate and stir until thick and smooth. Pour the chocolate mixture evenly over the cake and leave it to set. Melt the milk chocolate and place in a greaseproof piping bag fitted with a plain "writing" nozzle. Pipe "Sachertorte" across the top. Dust with icing sugar if liked.

Chocolate Raspberry Torte

PREPARATION TIME: 45 minutes
COOKING TIME: 35-40 minutes
OVEN TEMPERATURE: 160°C, 325°F, Gas Mark 3
MAKES: 1 cake, 30cm (12 inches) in diameter

1 recipe Family Chocolate Cake mixture (see recipe)
65ml (2½ fl oz) rum or Framboise
75g (3oz) raspberry jam
450g (1lb) fresh raspberries
Bittersweet Butter Cream (see recipe)
20 chocolate leaves (see recipe)

Chocolate Icing
10ml (2 tsp) oil
25g (1oz) butter
175g (6oz) plain dark chocolate, grated
15ml (1 tblsp) Framboise or rum

Grease and flour a 30cm (12 inch) deep pizza pan. Fill with the cake mixture. Bake until it springs up when pressed on top. Leave to cool in the tin for 5 minutes. Remove from the tin and let the cake cool on a wire rack for at least 2 hours. Slice the cake into two layers, horizontally, using a long knife. Sprinkle the cut surfaces with either the Framboise or rum. Spread one layer of the cake with raspberry jam and then with bittersweet butter cream; sandwich the cake back together again. Turn the cake upside down and chill. To make the icing, put the oil and butter into a saucepan and stir constantly over a medium heat. Let the mixture simmer for a minute. Remove from the heat and add the chocolate and the Framboise or rum. Whisk until the chocolate has melted and the icing is smooth. Let the icing cool and spread the icing over the top and sides of the cake. Put the raspberries on the top of the cake, in the middle, and put the chocolate leaves round the circle of raspberries. Refrigerate the cake for 1 hour. Note: this cake is best consumed on the day it is made.

Loganberry Torte

PREPARATION TIME: 25 minutes
COOKING TIME: 45 minutes
OVEN TEMPERATURE: 180°C, 350°F, Gas Mark 4
MAKES: 1 cake, 20cm (8 inches) in diameter

4 eggs, separated
100g (4oz) caster sugar
25g (1oz) cocoa powder
50g (2oz) fresh white breadcrumbs
100g (4oz) ground almonds

Filling
60ml (4 tblsp) loganberry jam
150ml (¼ pint) double cream, whipped

To Decorate
Fresh loganberries (or raspberries)
Cocoa powder to dust

Grease and line a 20cm (8 inch) round cake tin. Beat the egg yolks and sugar until thick and fluffy. Sieve the cocoa powder into the breadcrumbs. Fold into the egg yolks. Whisk the egg whites in a large, dry bowl until they are fluffy and stiff. Fold half the egg whites into the cake mixture taking care not to deflate the meringue; fold in the almonds followed by the remaining egg whites. Put the mixture into the prepared cake tin. Bake in the oven for 45 minutes. Cool in the tin for a few minutes, and then turn onto a wire rack to cool. Split the cake in half horizontally. Spread one layer of the cake with the jam, and then with half the whipped cream. Pipe the remaining cream on the top of the cake and garnish with loganberries, or raspberries. Dust the cake with cocoa powder.

Devil's Food Cake

PREPARATION TIME: 35 minutes
COOKING TIME: 1 hour 45 minutes-2 hours
OVEN TEMPERATURE: 150°C, 300°F, Gas Mark 2
MAKES: 1 cake, 20cm (8 inches) in diameter

175g (6oz) butter or margarine
175g (6oz) soft brown sugar
2 eggs, beaten
175g (6oz) golden syrup
50g (2oz) ground almonds
175g (6oz) plain flour
50g (2oz) cocoa powder
150ml (¼ pint) milk
1.25ml (¼ tsp) bicarbonate of soda

American Frosting
1 egg white
175g (6oz) icing sugar
15ml (1 tblsp) golden syrup
45ml (3 tblsp) water
Pinch of salt
5ml (1 tsp) lemon juice

To Decorate
Chocolate curls

Grease and line a 20cm (8 inch) cake tin with greaseproof paper. Cream the butter and sugar together until light and fluffy. Add the eggs gradually, beating well after each addition. Sieve together all the dry ingredients. Add the golden syrup and the milk to the creamed mixture. Fold in the dry ingredients and beat well with a wooden spoon. Pour the mixture into the prepared cake tin. Bake until a skewer inserted in the centre comes out clean. Turn out and cool on a wire rack. To make the frosting: place all the frosting ingredients into a basin over a saucepan of hot water; whisk until the icing stands in peaks. Remove from the heat and continue whisking until the mixture has cooled. Spread over the cake using a palette knife. (The frosting must be used as soon as it is made.) Decorate with the chocolate curls.

Truffle Torte (top) and Chocolate Raspberry Torte (right).

Humpty Dumpty

PREPARATION TIME: 50 minutes
COOKING TIME: 40-50 minutes
OVEN TEMPERATURE: 160°C, 325°F, Gas Mark 3
MAKES: 1 cake

225g (8oz) butter or margarine
225g (8oz) caster sugar
4 eggs, lightly beaten
175g (6oz) self-raising flour
5ml (1 tsp) baking powder
30ml (2 tblsp) cocoa powder
350g (12oz) Butter Icing (see recipe)
Smarties
Liquorice strips
225g (8oz) marzipan

Grease a 600ml (1 pint) pudding basin, and grease and line an 18cm (7 inch) square shallow tin. Cream the butter and sugar together until light and fluffy. Beat in the eggs and then sieve the flour and baking powder into the mixture. Mix the cocoa powder with a little water to make a paste. Mix this into the cake mixture. Put two-thirds of the cake mixture into the pudding basin and the rest into the tin. Bake the pudding cake for 40-50 minutes, and the square cake for 30 minutes. Cool on a wire rack. To ice the cake: cut the square cake in half and then cut each half into 4 rectangles. Using the rectangles of cake as bricks, make a wall 2 bricks high and 4 across, sandwiching them together with butter icing. Spread some of the remaining icing on the top of the wall. Cover the pudding basin cake completely with butter icing and put Humpty's eyes and nose on, using smarties.

Use the liquorice to make a mouth. Roll out the marzipan and shape legs and arms. Fix in position with cocktail sticks. You can even make a little hat, by making a marzipan cup and pulling out a brim.

Chocolate Potato Cake

PREPARATION TIME: 55 minutes, plus cooling time

COOKING TIME: 30 minutes

OVEN TEMPERATURE: 190°C, 375°F, Gas Mark 5

MAKES: 1 two layer cake, 18cm (7 inches) in diameter

100g (4oz) hot mashed potato
30ml (2 tblsp) double cream
200g (7oz) sugar
50g (2oz) plain chocolate, melted
65g (2½oz) unsalted butter, softened
15-20ml (3-4 tsp) bicarbonate of soda
30ml (2 tblsp) water
3 eggs, separated
100g (4oz) plain flour
5ml (1 tsp) baking powder
2.5ml (½ tsp) rum
50ml (2 fl oz) milk
1.25 (¼ tsp) salt

Cocoa and Rum Icing

40g (1½oz) unsalted butter
225g (8oz) icing sugar
30ml (2 tblsp) cocoa powder
1.25ml (¼ tsp) salt
10ml (2 tsp) rum
22ml (1½ tblsp) strong black coffee

Butter and line two 18cm (7 inch) round sandwich tins with greaseproof paper. Brush the paper with a little melted butter and dust with flour. Mix the mashed potato and cream together in a bowl over a saucepan of hot water. Beat the softened butter and sugar together until soft and creamy. Add the potato and cream mixture to the butter and sugar and stir in the melted chocolate. Dissolve the bicarbonate of soda in the water and add to the mixture. Beat the egg yolks into the mixture one at a time. Sieve together the flour, baking powder and salt. Fold the flour into the mixture, adding the milk and rum alternately. Whisk the egg whites until stiff but not dry. Gently fold in a third of the egg whites, and then fold in the remainder. Divide the mixture between the tins. Bake in a preheated oven for 30 minutes, or until a skewer inserted into the centre comes out clean. Leave the cakes in the tins for 5 minutes before turning them out onto a wire rack to cool. For the icing: beat the butter until soft and creamy. Sieve together the icing sugar, cocoa powder and salt; beat into the butter. Stir in the rum and coffee. Spread a layer of icing on top of one cake and sandwich the cakes together; ice the top and sides of the cake with the remaining icing.

This page: Chocolate Mushroom Cake (top) and Chocolate Valentine Baske[t] (bottom).

Facing page: Black Forest Gateau (top) and Devil's Fo[od] Cake (bottom).

Black Forest Gateau

PREPARATION TIME: 35 minutes

COOKING TIME: 55 minutes

OVEN TEMPERATURE: 160°C, 325°F, Gas Mark 3

MAKES: 1 cake, 18cm (7 inches) in diameter

100g (4oz) plain chocolate, grated
100g (4oz) self-raising flour
25g (1oz) cornflour
Generous pinch salt
150g (5oz) butter, softened
100g (4oz) caster sugar
4 eggs, separated
300ml (½ pint) double cream, whipped
45ml (3 tblsp) black cherry jam

To Decorate

100g (4oz) plain chocolate, grated

Grease and line an 18cm (7 inch) round cake tin. Melt the chocolate in a basin over hot water. Sieve the flours and salt together. Cream the butter and sugar together until light and fluffy. Add the melted chocolate and egg yolks and beat well. Beat the egg whites until they are stiff and form peaks. Fold the egg whites lightly but thoroug[hly] into the cake mixture. Spoon [the] mixture into the prepared cak[e]. Bake in the oven for 55 minut[es]. Cool the cake in the tin and t[hen] turn it out onto a wire rack. S[...]

the cake into two, horizontally. Spread one half with the jam and then with a third of the cream; sandwich together with the remaining cake layer. Spread one half of the remaining cream over the top of the cake. Fit a large star nozzle to a piping bag and fill with the remaining cream. Pipe 8 rosettes on the top of the cake. Sprinkle the grated chocolate on the top of the cake. (You can top each rosette of cream with a black cherry, if liked.)

Chocolate Lemon Cake

PREPARATION TIME: 30 minutes
COOKING TIME: 40-45 minutes
OVEN TEMPERATURE: 180°C, 350°F, Gas Mark 4
MAKES: 1 1kg (2lb) cake

175g (6oz) butter or margarine
175g (6oz) soft brown sugar
3 eggs
Grated rind of 1 lemon
225g (8oz) self-raising flour
100g (4oz) plain chocolate, melted

Icing
175g (6oz) butter
450g (1lb) icing sugar, sieved
30ml (2 tblsp) lemon juice

To Decorate
Crystallised orange and lemon slices

Grease and line a 1kg (2lb) rectangular tin or loaf tin. Cream the butter and sugar together until light and fluffy. Beat in the eggs, one at a time, adding a little sieved flour with each egg. Beat in the lemon rind and remaining flour, and then the chocolate. Pour into the prepared tin. Bake in the oven for 40-45 minutes. Turn onto a wire rack to cool. To make the icing: put all the ingredients into a mixing bowl and beat together with a wooden spoon until well mixed. Cut the cake in half and use half the butter cream to sandwich the cake together. Spread the remaining icing on the top of the cake and decorate with crystallised orange and lemon slices.

Chocolate Valentine Basket

PREPARATION TIME: 25 minutes
COOKING TIME: 40-45 minutes
OVEN TEMPERATURE: 160°C, 325°F, Gas Mark 3
MAKES: 1 heart-shaped cake

1 recipe Family Chocolate Cake mixture (see recipe)

Icing
150g (5oz) butter
350g (12oz) icing sugar
15ml (1 tblsp) milk
30ml (2 tblsp) hot water
15ml (1 tblsp) cocoa powder
Sweets for filling

Bake the Family Chocolate Cake mixture in two 20cm (8 inch) heart-shaped sandwich tins, for 40-45 minutes. Leave to cool on a wire rack. Cream the butter and the icing sugar together with the milk. Mix the hot water and cocoa powder into a paste. Add this to the butter mixture and cream well. Fit two piping bags with nozzles; one a ribbon nozzle, and the other a plain writing nozzle. Fill the bags with the butter cream. Hold the ribbon nozzle sideways and pipe three evenly-spaced lines, one above the other, on one of the cakes. The three lines should all be the same length. Pipe a vertical line, using the writing tube, along the edge of the basket weaving. Continue this process until the cake is covered. Cover the outermost edge and the sides of the remaining cake in the same way. This will now be the base, and the completely covered cake the lid. Arrange the lid at an angle on top of the lower cake and fill the inside with sweets.

Moon Cake

PREPARATION TIME: 20 minutes
COOKING TIME: 35 minutes
OVEN TEMPERATURE: 180°C, 350°F, Gas Mark 4
MAKES: 1 cake, 23cm (9 inches) in diameter

This cake is fun to make and to eat. The mixture bubbles during baking and leaves a cake with a rocky, moon-like surface.

200g (7oz) self-raising flour
100g (4oz) granulated sugar
100g (4oz) brown sugar
5ml (1 tsp) salt
60ml (4 tblsp) cocoa powder
75ml (5 tblsp) melted butter
5ml (1 tsp) vanilla essence
5ml (1 tsp) baking powder
15ml (1 tblsp) white wine vinegar
150ml (1/4 pint) milk
100g (4oz) marshmallows
Icing sugar

Put the flour, sugar, salt and cocoa directly into a 23cm (9 inch) cake tin and stir well until you have a light brown moon sand texture. Make a big crater in the middle of the sand so you can see the base of the tin, then a medium sized crater somewhere else in the sand, and a smaller crater on the other side (make sure that they are well apart). Spoon the baking powder into the medium sized crater. Spoon the melted butter into the large crater and the vanilla into the smallest crater. Now pour the vinegar into the medium sized crater and it will bubble and foam, and become "volcanic". When this stops, pour the milk over the moon sand and stir well. The sand will now look like mud. Scatter the marshmallows over the surface. Bake for 35 minutes. (Test with a cocktail stick or skewer to see that the cake is done.) Dust with icing sugar and serve from the tin.

Chocolate Mushroom Cake

PREPARATION TIME: 1 hour
COOKING TIME: 3 hours
OVEN TEMPERATURE: 110°C, 225°F, Gas Mark 1/4
MAKES: 1 cake, 23cm (9 inches) in diameter

1 recipe Family Chocolate Cake mixture (see recipe)
Icing recipe for Family Chocolate Cake
50g (2oz) white chocolate, melted
3 chocolate flakes
Icing sugar

Meringue Mushrooms
2 egg whites
100g (4oz) caster sugar
Oil for greasing
Cocoa powder
75g (3oz) plain chocolate, melted

Make the Family Chocolate Cake as instructed. Bake as directed and coat with icing. Fill a piping bag fitted with a small writing nozzle with the melted white chocolate. Pipe a spiral of melted white chocolate on top of the cake, working from the middle outwards. Cut the chocolate flakes in half, dust them with icing sugar, and stick them around the sides of the cake to represent bark. To make the meringues: beat the egg whites in a bowl until they are stiff but not dry. Add the sugar slowly, beating well after each addition. Lightly oil a baking tray and cover with greaseproof paper. Fit a piping bag with a 1-2cm (1/2-3/4 inch) plain nozzle. Fill the bag with the meringue mixture. Pipe 12 mushroom stems on half the baking sheet. Lift the bag vertically until the stems are 4-5cm (1½-2 inches) high. Cut the meringue away from the nozzle. Then pipe even rounds of meringue 4-5cm (1½-2 inches) in diameter and 2c (3-4 inches) thick. (These make the mushroom tops; make sure that they are flat.) Sieve the coco powder over the meringues and then bake in a pre-heated oven until they are dried out (about 3 hours). Leave to cool. When the meringues are cool, spread melte chocolate on the underside of ea mushroom top and fix the stem onto the chocolate. Leave to coo until the chocolate has set. Remove the mushrooms and stic a few of them on the cake, using little more melted chocolate. Lay the others around the cake, to b eaten separately.

Chocolate Brandy Sna Gateau

PREPARATION TIME: 40 minut
COOKING TIME: 25-30 minutes
OVEN TEMPERATURE: 180°C, 350°F, Gas Mark 4
MAKES: 1 gateau, 20 cm (8 inche in diameter

3 eggs
75g (3oz) caster sugar
15g (½oz) cocoa powder
2.5ml (½ tsp) baking powder
65g (2½oz) plain flour

Filling and Decoration
300ml (½ pint) double cream
100g (3.5oz) packet brandy snaps
25g (1oz) plain chocolate, melted

Grease and line two 20cm (8 inc sandwich tins. Place the eggs and sugar in a basin and whisk over a saucepan of hot water until thick and pale. Remove from the heat and whisk until cool. Sieve together the cocoa powder, bakir powder and flour, and gently fold into the mixture. Divide the mixture between the two prepare tins. Bake for 25-30 minutes. Tur out carefully onto a wire rack and cool. Whip the cream until thick and use a little to sandwich the cakes together. Spread a little cream around the sides and secu the brandy snaps round the edge the cake. Spread the remaining cream on the top of the cake. Put the melted chocolate into a greaseproof piping bag with a small hole, and drizzle over the cream; swirl it with a skewer.

Chocolate Brandy Snap Gateau (right) and Chocolate Lemon Cake (below).

Truffle Torte

PREPARATION TIME: 1 hour

COOKING TIME: 1 hour 15 minutes

OVEN TEMPERATURE: 180°C, 350°F, Gas Mark 4

MAKES: 1 cake, 18cm (7 inches) in diameter

100g (4oz) unsalted butter, softened
100g (4oz) caster sugar
3 eggs, separated
100g (4oz) plain chocolate, melted
25g (1oz) plain flour
150g (5oz) finely ground hazelnuts

Chocolate Icing
150ml (¼ pint) double cream
150g (5oz) plain chocolate, broken into pieces

Butter and line an 18cm (7 inch) springform cake tin with greaseproof paper. Brush the paper with a little melted butter and dust with flour. Beat the butter until soft and creamy. Add the sugar and continue to beat until light and fluffy. Add the egg yolks, one at a time, and beat well. Stir in the melted chocolate. Sieve together the flour and the ground hazelnuts and fold them into the cake mixture. Beat the egg whites until stiff but not dry. Gently fold in the beaten egg whites. Pour the mixture into the prepared tin. Bake in the pre-heated oven for about 1 hour. (When cooked the cake should be springy to the touch.) Remove from the oven and leave the cake in its tin for 5 minutes. Turn onto a wire rack and cool completely. To make the chocolate icing: put the cream into a saucepan and bring to the boil. Add the chocolate, stirring until the chocolate has melted, and the mixture is thick and smooth. Pour the icing evenly over the cake before it has a chance to set. Decorate with piped chocolate wirls (see Cookies and Confections recipe).

Family Chocolate Cake

PREPARATION TIME: 25 minutes

COOKING TIME: 45-50 minutes

OVEN TEMPERATURE: 160°C, 325°F Gas Mark 3

MAKES: 1 cake, 23cm (9 inches) in diameter

200g (7oz) plain flour
5ml (1 tsp) bicarbonate of soda

5ml (1 tsp) baking powder
30ml (2 tblsp) cocoa powder
150g (5oz) soft brown sugar
30ml (2 tblsp) golden syrup
2 eggs
150ml (¼ pint) oil
150ml (¼ pint) milk

Icing
175g (6oz) plain chocolate, chopped or grated
30ml (2 tblsp) single cream

To Decorate
Walnut halves

Grease and line a 23cm (9 inch) cake tin. Sieve all the dry ingredients together in a large bowl. Put the sugar, syrup, eggs, oil and milk into a well in the centre of the dry ingredients. Beat thoroughly until the mixture is smooth. Pour the mixture into the prepared cake tin. Bake for 45-50 minutes until a skewer inserted in the centre of the cake comes out clean. Leave the baked cake in its tin for a few minutes and turn onto a wire rack to cool. To make the icing: place the chocolate and cream into a small, heavy-based pan and heat gently until melted. Cool slightly and pour evenly over the cake. Decorate with walnuts.

Chocolate Cup Cakes

PREPARATION TIME: 20 minutes

COOKING TIME: 15 minutes

OVEN TEMPERATURE: 180°C, 350°F, Gas Mark 4

MAKES: 18

100g (4oz) soft margarine
100g (4oz) caster sugar
2 eggs
75g (3oz) self-raising flour
25g (1oz) cocoa powder

Fudge Icing
15ml (1 tblsp) golden syrup
450g (1lb) granulated sugar
50g (2oz) unsalted butter
50g (2oz) cocoa powder

Line 2 bun trays with 18 paper cake cases. Put all the cake ingredients into a bowl and beat together with a wooden spoon, until smooth and glossy. Put one small spoonful of the mixture into each of the cake cases. Bake in the centre of the oven for 15 minutes or until they are firm to touch. To make the icing: put the syrup into a saucepan with 250ml (8 fl oz) cold water, the sugar, butter and cocoa powder; stir over a low heat until the sugar dissolves. Boil the mixture until a little will form a soft ball when dropped into cold water. (Do nc stir the mixture, just cut it with a wooden spoon occasionally.) Remove the mixture from the h and allow it to cool for 10 minut Beat it with a wooden spoon un the mixture begins to thicken to coating consistency. Pour the mixture over the cup cakes and allow it to set. (If the icing sets before it has covered all the cake melt it gently.)

Spider's Web

PREPARATION TIME: 50 minut

COOKING TIME: 35 minutes

OVEN TEMPERATURE: 190°C, 375°F, Gas Mark 5

MAKES: 1 cake, 19cm (7½ inche in diameter

150g (5oz) self-raising flour
50g (2oz) cocoa powder
2.5ml (½ tsp) bicarbonate of soda
100g (4oz) soft margarine
225g (8oz) dark soft brown sugar
2 eggs
10ml (2 tsp) peppermint essence
25g (1oz) ground almonds
150ml (¼ pint) soured cream

To Decorate
100g (4oz) dark plain chocolate, grated
175g (6oz) icing sugar
1 plain chocolate drop
Green food colouring
Peppermint essence
225g (8oz) Butter Icing (see recipe
1 liquorice shoe-lace
1 chocolate-covered marshmallow
1 packet white chocolate buttons

Grease and line two 19cm (7½ inch) cake tins. Sieve the flour, cocoa powder and bicarbonate o soda into a bowl and then add al the other ingredients. Mix well

This page: Chocolate Cup Cakes (top) and Family Chocolate Cake – shown with candy covered chocolate swee – (bottom).

Facing page: Nouvelle – Truff Cake (top) and Sherry Cream Pie (bottom).

until they are blended. Divide the mixture between the two tins. Slightly hollow out the centres so that the tops will be flat when baked. Bake in the oven for 35 minutes, until a knife inserted through the centre comes out clean. Cool the cakes slightly in their tins and then turn onto a wire rack. Melt half the chocolate in a bowl over a pan of simmering water. Mix the sieved icing sugar with a few drops of water to give a coating consistency. Put the melted chocolate into a piping bag fitted with a small, plain nozzle. Cover the top of one of the cakes with the white icing. Immediately pipe a spiral of chocolate onto the white iced cake, working outwards from the centre. To make the web, mark out 12 lines by drawing a skewer across the icing, from the centre outwards. Put the plain chocolate drop in the centre and leave to set. Add a little green colouring and peppermint essence to the butter icing. Spread some of the green peppermint butter icing over the un-iced cake and place the iced cake on top. Spread some of the remaining green icing around the sides of the cake. Sprinkle the remaining grated chocolate around the sides of the cake. To make the spider: cut the liquorice into 8 equal lengths. Stick each length into the side of the chocolate marshmallow and trim the two front legs, making them a little shorter than the others. Using a little icing, stick two white buttons on the front of the marshmallow for eyes. Put small liquorice trimmings onto the white chocolate drops, fixing them in place with a little more icing. Place the spider on the cake.

Birthday Salute
Tanks

PREPARATION TIME: 45 minutes
COOKING TIME: 25 minutes
OVEN TEMPERATURE: 190°C, 375°F Gas Mark 5

1 recipe Family Chocolate Cake mixture (see recipe)
350g (12oz) Chocolate Butter Icing (see recipe)
1 packet chocolate buttons
6 chocolate flakes

Grease and line an 18cm (7 inch) square cake tin. Fill the tin with the family chocolate cake mixture and spread evenly in the tin. Bake as instructed, then leave to cool on a wire rack. Cut the cake in half. Cut off a piece from each half, measuring 9x5cm (3½x2 inches).

Spider's Web (above) and Birthday Salute (right).

Cover the larger cake pieces with butter icing. Put the smaller pieces of cake on top of the larger pieces of cake, slightly towards the back. Stick 5 chocolate buttons along both of the longer sides of each lower cake. Then put one button on top for the hatch lid. Reserve two chocolate flakes, then cut the rest into short lengths. Lay the short lengths as tracks around the outer edges of the cakes. Push the whole flakes into the front of the smaller cakes to make the gun barrels.

Cannon

PREPARATION TIME: 10 minutes
COOKING TIME: 12 minutes
OVEN TEMPERATURE: 200°C, 400°F, Gas Mark 6

3 eggs
75g (3oz) caster sugar
Vanilla essence
75g (3oz) plain flour
25g (1oz) cocoa powder
22ml (1½ tblsp) warm water
1 recipe Chocolate Butter Icing

To Decorate
Icing sugar
4 large chocolate flakes
Chocolate balls

Grease and line a 23cm (9 inch) Swiss roll tin. Whisk the eggs, sugar, and a few drops of vanilla essence in a bowl over a pan of hot water until pale and thick. (Use an electric whisk if possible.) Sieve together the flour and cocoa powder, and then fold into the egg mixture with the water. Turn the mixture into the prepared tin and spread evenly. Bake for 12 minutes until the cake has risen. Sprinkle some caster sugar onto a sheet of greaseproof paper and turn the cake out onto the paper. Peel off the lining paper which may be stuck to the cake, and trim off any crisp edges that may be around the cake. Lay a piece of greaseproof paper over the top of the cake and roll up the cake with the greaseproof paper inside. Leave to cool on a wire rack. Unroll the cake and remove the paper. Spread with some of the butter icing and re-roll.

Dust the cake with icing sugar. To decorate: fit a star nozzle onto a piping bag and fill with some of the butter cream. Cut the Swiss roll into 12 pieces, then cut 4 of the slices in half. Place two halves side by side, standing them on their flat edges. With a dab of butter cream, attach two whole slices on each of the sides. Pipe stripes of butter icing down the middle of each cannon and lay the flake on it, angled up at one end. Next to the cannon place a pile of chocolate balls, to represent cannon balls.

Chocolate Nut Gateau

PREPARATION TIME: 30 minutes, plus chilling

MAKES: 1 gateau, 18cm (7 inches) in diameter

25g (1oz) butter
15ml (1 tblsp) golden syrup
40g (1½oz) Rice Krispies

Filling
40g (1½oz) cornflour
15ml (1 tblsp) cocoa powder
450ml (¾ pint) milk
150ml (¼ pint) chocolate flavoured yogurt
15ml (1 tblsp) hazelnuts, skinned and roughly chopped

Topping
150ml (¼ pint) hazelnut-flavoured yogurt
75ml (5 tblsp) double cream, whipped

To Decorate
Grated chocolate
8 whole hazelnuts

Melt the butter and syrup in a saucepan. Add the Rice Krispies and mix well until they are coated with the butter syrup. Press the mixture into the base of an 18cm (7 inch) fluted flan ring, placed on a serving plate. Leave to cool. For the filling: mix the cornflour and cocoa powder with a little of the milk. Heat the remaining milk until boiling and pour onto the cornflour mixture, stirring constantly. Return the mixture to the pan and return to the heat; simmer for a few minutes, until thickened. Remove the saucepan from the heat and stir in the chocolate yogurt and chopped hazelnuts. Pour the mixture over the crisp base. For the topping: mix the nut yogurt with the whipped cream and spread it over the chocolate mixture. Put the flan in the refrigerator and chill until set. Carefully remove the flan ring and decorate with grated chocolate and whole hazelnuts. Serve with chocolate sauce if desired.

Chocolate Pistachio Loaf

PREPARATION TIME: 20 minutes

COOKING TIME: 1 hours 15 minutes-1 hour 30 minutes

OVEN TEMPERATURE: 180°C, 350°F, Gas Mark 4

MAKES: One 450g (1lb) loaf

100g (4oz) self-raising flour
100g (4oz) butter or margarine, softened
50g (2oz) caster sugar
50g (2oz) plain chocolate, chopped
50g (2oz) pistachio nuts, chopped
25g (1oz) ground almonds
2 eggs
30ml (2 tblsp) milk

Icing
175g (6oz) plain chocolate, chopped or grated
A knob of butter

To Decorate
A few pistachio nuts, chopped

Grease and line a 450g (1lb) loaf tin. Put all the cake ingredients into a mixing bowl and beat until they are well mixed. Pour the mixture into the prepared tin. Bake in a preheated oven for 1 hour 15 minutes, or until cooked. Turn the cake out of the tin and leave to cool on a wire rack. For the icing: melt the chocolate in a basin over a pan of hot water; beat the knob of butter (the size of a walnut) into the chocolate and pour evenly over the cake. Sprinkle with chopped pistachio nuts.

Chocolate Knitting

PREPARATION TIME: 45 minutes

COOKING TIME: 40-45 minutes

OVEN TEMPERATURE: 160°C, 325°F, Gas Mark 3

MAKES: 1 cake, 23cm (9 inches) square

1 recipe Family Chocolate Cake mixture (see recipe)
Butter Icing (see recipe)
10ml (2 tsp) cocoa powder
1 packet of sugar strand cake decorations
2 large wooden knitting needles
10 chocolate flakes
25cm (10 inch) square cake board

Bake the family chocolate cake mixture in a 23cm (9 inch) square cake tin, as directed. Cut the cake in half and sandwich the two halves together using some of t butter icing. Put on the cake bo Mix the cocoa powder with 10m (2 tsp) boiling water and add th to the remaining butter icing. M until smooth. Then add an ext 15ml (1 tblsp) icing sugar to the icing so it will pipe better. Spre some of this icing over the top the cake. With a warmed knife 4 flakes in half and arrange the along the edge of the cake. Cut flakes into quarters and place t with two pieces alternately, vertically and horizontally. The cut two flakes into eight and re this process. Put the knitting needles into the cake; one goes top, and the other goes throug the centre filling, so that the handles cross. Use the remainin icing to fill a piping bag fitted w star nozzle. Pipe sticks of icing the top needle. Sprinkle the su strands over the top of the cak a flaked pattern.

Dart Board

PREPARATION TIME: 45 minu

COOKING TIME: 35 minutes

OVEN TEMPERATURE: 160°C 325°F, Gas Mark 3

MAKES: 1 cake, 25cm (10 inche in diameter

225g (8oz) butter
175g (6oz) soft light brown sugar
4 eggs
175g (6oz) golden syrup
25g (1oz) cocoa powder
225g (8oz) self-raising flour
5ml (1 tsp) mixed ground spice
2.5ml (½ tsp) ground ginger

To Decorate
30cm (12 inch) cake board
45ml (3 tblsp) apricot jam
350g (12oz) Butter Icing (see reci
Generous pinch ground ginger
Grated chocolate
1 liquorice wheel
Small darts

Grease and line two 25cm (10 inch) round cake tins. Cream t butter and sugar together; beat the eggs slowly, followed by the golden syrup. Mix the cocoa powder with a few drops of wa and make into a paste. Fold the flour into the cake mixture and then divide the mixture into tw Add the cocoa paste to one portion; sieve the mixed spice ground ginger into the other portion, and add a little milk if

ecessary. Spread the two mixtures into their separate tins and hollow out the centres so the cakes will have a flat top when cooked. Bake in a pre-heated oven for 35 minutes. Leave to cool upside down on a wire rack, removing the paper. Put an 18cm (7 inch) round plate on each cake and, using it as a guide, cut out a circle from the middle of each cake. Remove the circles and cut them into 20 even wedges. Put the ginger outer circle on the cake board and put the wedge slices – alternating between chocolate and ginger – in a circular pattern in the centre. Spread the top of the cake with jam and lay the chocolate ring on top of the ginger ring. Then repeat the process with the remaining wedges, reversing the colours to get a chequered effect. Beat the butter icing with the ginger and spread some of it around the sides of the cake. Cover the sides of the cake with grated chocolate. Fill a piping bag fitted with a plain writing nozzle with butter icing. Pipe the numbers on the cake in the correct order. Fit a star nozzle to the piping bag, refill with the remaining butter icing, and pipe shells for the scoring circles. Pipe a line around the top and bottom of the outer edges and stick the liquorice wheel in the centre for the bullseye. Put on the darts for decoration.

Facing page: Chocolate Knitting (top) and Dart Board (bottom).

This page: Chocolate Pistachio Loaf (top) and Chocolate Nut Gateau (bottom).

Desserts and Pastries

Chocolate Pear Flan

PREPARATION TIME: 25 minutes, plus chilling

SERVES: 4-6 people

75g (3oz) butter
225g (8oz) plain chocolate digestive biscuits, crushed
425g (14½oz) can of pear halves
10ml (2 tsp) arrowroot

To Decorate
Grated chocolate

Melt the butter in a saucepan and mix with the crushed biscuits. Press the crumb mixture into the base and up the sides of an 18cm (7 inch) loose-bottomed fluted flan tin. Place in the refrigerator to set. Carefully remove the crumb case from the flan tin; leave it on the base, as this will make serving easier. Drain the juice from the pears and reserve it. Arrange the pear halves in the flan case. Mix the arrowroot with half of the pear juice in a small saucepan and bring to the boil. Stir gently until the mixture thickens and clears. Cool slightly and then spoon over the pears. Chill briefly. Sprinkle with grated chocolate and serve with cream.

Chocolate Orange Pudding

PREPARATION TIME: 25 minutes

COOKING TIME: about 1¾ hours

SERVES: 4-6 people

1 recipe Steamed Chocolate Pudding mixture (see recipe)
2 oranges

Make the chocolate pudding mixture as directed. Finely grate the rind of 1 orange and add this to the mixture. Thinly slice the second orange and press the orange circles around the inside of a greased 1 litre (2 pint) pudding basin; put one orange slice in the base. Fill with the pudding mixture. Cover and steam the pudding for about 1¾ hours. Serve with orange sauce or chocolate sauce.

Chocolate Mousse

PREPARATION TIME: 20 minutes, plus chilling time

SERVES: 4-6 people

100g (4oz) plain chocolate, grated
30ml (2 tblsp) water
15ml (1 tblsp) instant coffee
4 egg whites
100g (4oz) caster sugar

To Decorate
A little reserved chocolate

Put most of the chocolate, and the water and coffee into a bowl; stand it over a pan of hot water. Stir the mixture occasionally until the

This page: Chocolate Brandy Cheesecake (top left), Chocol[ate] Orange Pudding (top right) a[nd] Chocolate Pear Flan (bottom)

Facing page: Chocolate Eclair (top) and Chocolate Strudel (bottom).

chocolate has melted and the mixture is smooth. Whisk the egg whites until stiff but not dry, gradually whisking in half the sugar. Mix the remaining sugar into the chocolate mixture and fold in the meringue. Divide the mixture among 4-6 glasses and sprinkle with remaining grated chocolate. Chill briefly.

Strawberry Box

PREPARATION TIME: 50 minutes, plus chilling

SERVES: 6 people

Chocolate Case
225g (8oz) plain chocolate, chopped or grated
15g (½oz) vegetable oil

Filling
175g (6oz) plain chocolate, chopped or grated
15ml (1 tblsp) kirsch
2 egg yolks
150ml (¼ pint) double cream
150ml (¼ pint) single cream

Topping
225g (8oz) strawberries, hulled and halved
45ml (3 tblsp) strawberry jam, sieved
15ml (1 tblsp) kirsch
25g (1oz) plain chocolate, chopped or grated
150ml (¼ pint) double cream

Line either a 15cm (6 inch) square cake tin or an 18cm (7 inch) round cake tin, with a double thickness of foil. (Make sure that the foil comes above the top of the tin to make removal of the set chocolate case easy.) For the chocolate case: melt the chocolate with the vegetable oil; pour two-thirds into the prepared tin and turn and tilt the tin so that the sides and base are coated evenly. Allow the chocolate to set slightly and then repeat the process with the remaining melted chocolate. Leave it in a cool place until the chocolate has set completely. Remove the chocolate case from the tin by pulling the foil lining gently; peel the foil away carefully from the chocolate case. To make the filling: melt the chocolate. Remove from the heat and beat the kirsch and the egg yolks into the chocolate. Whip the double and single creams together until thick and then fold into the chocolate. Pour the chocolate cream into the prepared chocolate case. Chill until set. Arrange the stawberries on the top of the filled case. Bring the jam and the kirsch to the boil together and remove from the heat; allow to cool slightly. Spoon the topping glaze over the strawberries, but do not allow the hot jam to run to the edge of the chocolate case or it will melt. The glaze will set in about 5 minutes. Melt the chocolate and allow it to cool. Whip the double cream until thick and beat in the chocolate. Pipe the chocolate mixture decoratively around the case.

Chocolate Eclairs

PREPARATION TIME: 20 minutes

COOKING TIME: 20-25 minutes

OVEN TEMPERATURE: 220°C, 425°F, Gas Mark 7

MAKES: 10-12

50g (2oz) butter or margarine
150ml (¼ pint) water
65g (2½oz) plain flour, sieved
2 eggs, beaten
175ml (6 fl oz) double cream, whipped

Icing
100g (4oz) plain chocolate, chopped or grated
15g (½oz) butter

Melt the butter (or margarine) in a saucepan over a gentle heat. Add the water and bring it just to the boil. Remove the pan from the heat and add the flour. Beat the mixture well until it leaves the sides of the pan clean. Cool the mixture slightly, and beat in the eggs gradually, beating between each addition. Spoon the mixture into a piping bag fitted with a 1cm (½ inch) plain nozzle. Pipe 7.5cm (3 inch) lengths onto a lightly dampened baking sheet. Bake in a preheated oven for 20-25 minutes until crisp and golden brown. Make a slit in the side of each eclair to allow the steam to escape and cool on a wire rack. Fit a piping bag with a 1cm (½ inch) plain nozzle and spoon the whipped cream into the bag. Pipe the cream into each of the eclairs. Melt the chocolate and butter on a plate over a pan of hot water, stirring until smooth. Dip each eclair into the chocolate to give an even top coating and place on a wire rack to set.

Chocolate Strudel

PREPARATION TIME: 1 hour 30 minutes

COOKING TIME: 40 minutes

OVEN TEMPERATURE: 190°C, 375°F, Gas Mark 5

MAKES: a 36cm (14 inch) strudel

100g (4oz) plain flour
½ a beaten egg
2.5ml (½ tsp) salt
65ml (2½ fl oz) water
A few drops of vinegar
75g (3oz) butter, melted and cooled

Filling
40g (1½oz) butter
50g (2oz) vanilla sugar
2 eggs, separated
40g (1½oz) raisins
65ml (2½ fl oz) double cream
A pinch of ground cinnamon
22ml (1½ tblsp) caster sugar
50g (2oz) plain chocolate, grated
65g (2½oz) chopped walnuts
Icing sugar

Sieve the flour into a large mixing bowl and make a well in the centre. Beat together the egg, salt, water, vinegar and 15ml (1 tblsp) of the melted butter. Pour this mixture into the well. Mix all the ingredients together to a dough. Knead the dough on a well-floured board until smooth and elastic (this will take about 15 minutes). Put the dough into a floured bowl and cover with a cloth. Leave for 15 minutes. While the dough is resting make the filling. Beat together the butter and vanilla sugar until light and fluffy. Add the egg yolks one at a time, beating after each addition. Add the walnuts, cream, cinnamon, chocolate and raisins and mix well. Whisk the egg whites until stiff but not dry, and then gradually whisk in the caster sugar. Fold this mixture gently into the chocolate mixture. Cover the work surface with a large, clean cloth and dust the cloth with flour. Put the doug into the middle of the cloth and brush the top with melted butter. Working around the dough, roll i out to a thickness of 3mm (⅛ inch). Brush it with more butter and, using four hands (you'll nee to enlist help!), stretch the dough outwards as thinly as possible. Tr to work around the dough so it does not tear. Cut the dough int rectangle measuring 36x18cm (14x18 inches). Butter a large baking sheet. Spoon the filling or the strudel pastry, leaving a marg of 5cm (2 inches) around three c the edges. Fold the margins over the filling and brush the remainir pastry with the melted butter. Gently lift the cloth so that the dough rolls itself up. Roll the dough onto the prepared baking sheet. Bake for 40 minutes, basti with melted butter once or twice until golden and crisp. Remove t strudel from the oven and dust with icing sugar. Serve warm or cold. (Do not be put off by the thought of handling strudel pastr Although a professionally thin pastry is needed for good results, is not as difficult to achieve as its reputation would suggest.)

Strawberry Box (top right) and Chocolate Mousse (right).

Chiffon Pie

PREPARATION TIME: 40 minutes, plus chilling
COOKING TIME: 1 hour
OVEN TEMPERATURE: 190°C, 375°F, Gas Mark 5
MAKES: 1 pie, 23cm (9 inches) in diameter

Shortcrust Pastry
225g (8oz) plain flour
30ml (2 tblsp) caster sugar
5ml (1 tsp) salt
50g (2oz) ground almonds
150g (5oz) unsalted butter, cut into pieces
1 egg yolk

Filling
250ml (8 fl oz) milk
120g (4½oz) caster sugar
200g (7oz) plain chocolate, broken into pieces
2 eggs, separated
15ml (1 tblsp) powdered gelatine
45ml (3 tblsp) strong black coffee
350ml (12 fl oz) double cream, whipped

Topping
250ml (8 fl oz) double or whipping cream, whipped
Grated chocolate

To make the pastry: sieve the flour, sugar and salt and add the almonds. Make a well in the centre of the dry ingredients and add the butter and egg yolk. Working quickly, use the fingertips to mix all the ingredients together. Shape the dough into a ball and wrap in foil or cling film. Leave to chill for 1 hour. Roll out the pastry on a floured work surface to a thickness of 3-5mm (⅛-¼ inch) and use to line a 23cm (9 inch) fluted deep pie tin. Cover the pastry with a sheet of greaseproof paper and weight it down with rice or beans. Bake blind in a pre-heated oven for 15 minutes, or until the edges begin to colour. Remove the paper and beans and bake for a further 15 minutes. Leave to cool on a wire rack before removing from the tin. To make the filling: mix the milk, 75g (3oz) of the sugar and the chocolate pieces in a saucepan; cook over a moderate heat. Stir constantly until the chocolate melts. The chocolate mixture should be thick and smooth when removed from the heat. Leave to cool. Whisk the egg yolks into the chocolate mixture. Dissolve the gelatine in the coffee, over a low heat, and stir into the warm chocolate mixture. Chill until it begins to set. Whisk the egg whites until stiff but not dry. Whisk the remaining sugar into the beaten egg whites until stiff and glossy. Gently fold the egg whites into the chocolate mixture, followed by the whipped cream. Pour the mixture into the pie shell. Decorate with whipped cream and grated chocolate.

Chocolate Terrine with Cherry Sauce

PREPARATION TIME: 40 minutes, plus freezing
COOKING TIME: about 8 minutes
MAKES: 1 1¼kg (3lb) terrine

225g (8oz) plain chocolate, chopped or grated
225g (8oz) unsalted butter
100g (4oz) caster sugar
50g (2oz) icing sugar
50g (2oz) cocoa powder
100g (4oz) granulated sugar
150g (¼ pint) water
4 egg yolks, beaten
300ml (½ pint) double cream
100g (4oz) pitted black cherries

Sauce
30ml (2 tblsp) cornflour
300ml (½ pint) water
450g (1lb) pitted black cherries
100g (4oz) granulated sugar
60ml (4 tblsp) kirsch

Grease a 1¼kg (3lb) loaf tin, and line with greased greaseproof paper. Melt the chocolate in a bowl over a pan of hot water; remove from the heat and cool. Cream the butter and caster sugar until light and fluffy. Sieve the icing sugar and cocoa together and beat into the butter mixture; beat in the cooled melted chocolate. Put the granulated sugar and water into a small, heavy-based pan and stir over a gentle heat until the sugar has dissolved. Boil quickly to 110°C (225°F) on a sugar thermometer. Beat the egg yolks in a basin and add the sugar syrup; whisk into a mousse-like consistency. Beat into the butter and chocolate mixture. Whip the cream and lightly fold it into the mixture. Fold in the pitted cherries and turn the mixture into the prepared tin. Freeze for 6 hours or until firm.

Cherry Sauce
Blend the cornflour with 45ml (3 tblsp) water in a small bowl. Pu the cherries into a pan with the remaining water and sugar and bring to the boil. Remove the p from the heat and stir in the cornflour mixture. Bring back t the boil, stirring continuously. Remove from the heat and add kirsch. Serve the Chocolate Te in slices, accompanied by the h cherry sauce.

Banana and Chocola Trifle

PREPARATION TIME: 30 minu
SERVES: 6 people

1 packet pineapple jelly
3 bananas
1 chocolate Swiss roll
15ml (1 tblsp) cornflour
30ml (2 tblsp) caster sugar
600ml (1 pint) milk
30ml (2 tblsp) cocoa powder
150ml (¼ pint) double cream

To Decorate
4 glace cherries

Make up the jelly, following the instructions on the packet. As t jelly is about to set, slice two bananas and stir them into the j Pour into a pretty glass dish. W the jelly has cooled (but not set cut the Swiss roll into eight piec and arrange the slices around th sides of the dish, standing up in jelly. Mix the cornflour and the sugar with a little of the milk; ac the cocoa powder and mix well. Add the remaining milk. Put the chocolate mixture into a small saucepan and boil for a few minutes, stirring until it thicken Leave to cool. Lightly whip the cream and fold into the cold custard. Pour the mixture into th dish on top of the jelly. Before serving, decorate the top of the trifle with slices of the remaining banana and the glace cherries.

This page: Chocolate Terrine with Cherry Sauce (top) and Tarte au Chocolat (bottom).

Facing page: Banana and Chocolate Trifle (top) and Chiffon Pie (bottom).

Chocolate Rum Fool

PREPARATION TIME: 20 minutes, plus chilling

SERVES: 4-6 people

75g (3oz) raisins
60ml (4 tblsp) dark rum
225g (8oz) cold cooked potato
50g (2oz) caster sugar
200g (7oz) plain chocolate cake covering
225g (8oz) butter
150ml (¼ pint) double cream

Soak the raisins in the rum for one hour. Sieve the potato and beat in the rum-soaked raisins and the sugar. Melt the chocolate and the butter together. Remove from the heat and beat into the potato mixture. Whip the cream until thick, and gently fold two-thirds of it into the mixture. Turn the mixture into a serving dish and chill in the refrigerator for at least one hour. Decorate with the remaining cream when ready to serve.

Chocolate and Cherry Mousse

PREPARATION TIME: 35-40 minutes, plus chilling

SERVES: 6 people

Cherry Mousse
350g (12oz) pitted cherries, fresh or canned
7.5ml (1½ tsp) gelatine powder
30ml (2 tblsp) cold water
50g (2oz) caster sugar
2 eggs, separated
150ml (¼ pint) double or whipping cream

Chocolate Mousse
175g (6oz) plain chocolate, chopped or grated
10ml (2 tsp) instant coffee
15ml (1 tblsp) water
4 eggs, separated
150ml (¼ pint) double or whipping cream

To Decorate
150ml (¼ pint) whipped cream
A few whole cherries

Rub the cherries through a sieve, or puree them in a blender or food processor. Sprinkle the gelatine over the cold water and leave in a basin to soften for a few minutes; dissolve the gelatine over a pan of simmering water. Remove from the heat and cool. Whisk the sugar and egg yolks together until thick and creamy and then whisk in the gelatine; stir in the cherry puree and mix well. Whisk the egg whites in a dry bowl until stiff but not dry. Whip the cream lightly until it holds its shape and then fold the cream gently into the cherry mixture. Fold the egg whites into the cherry mixture lightly but thoroughly. Pour into 6 individual serving dishes and chill for 30 minutes. For the chocolate mousse: melt the chocolate with the coffee and the water. Remove from the heat and beat in the egg yolks. Whip the cream lightly until it holds its shape, then whisk the egg whites in a separate bowl until stiff but not dry. Fold the cream into the chocolate mixture and then the egg whites. Pour the chocolate mousse over the chilled cherry mousse and chill for at least an hour. Decorate with whipped cream and cherries before serving.

Chocolate Quiche

PREPARATION TIME: 30 minutes, plus chilling time

COOKING TIME: about 1 hour

OVEN TEMPERATURE: 190°C, 375°F, Gas Mark 5 and then 180°C, 350°F, Gas Mark 4

SERVES: 10 people

100g (4oz) self-raising flour
Pinch of salt
100g (4oz) ground almonds
150g (5oz) butter
1 egg yolk
Cold water

Filling
500g (1lb 2oz) cooking chocolate, grated
750ml (1¼ pints) double cream
7 egg yolks

Mix the flour, salt and almonds in a bowl. Add the butter in small pieces and rub into the texture of crumbs. Beat the egg yolk with 30ml (2 tblsp) of water. Add to the crumble mixture and mix to a firm dough, adding a little extra water if required. Shape the dough into a ball; wrap and chill in the refrigerator. Flour a pastry slab or work surface and roll out the dough; use to line a large loose-bottomed flan tin, 30cm (12 inches) in diameter. Line the pastry with greaseproof paper and beans and bake "blind" at the higher temperature for 10 minutes. Remove the paper and beans and bake for a further 3 minutes. Leave to cool. Melt the chocolate and cool slightly. Beat the cream and the egg yolks until they are well blended, and add the melted chocolate. Pour into the pastry case. Bake for 45 minutes, at the lower temperature, until the top is firm to the touch. Allow the quiche to cool a little, and then serve in small portions with whipped cream and/or fruit.

Nouvelle – Truffle Cakes

PREPARATION TIME: 40 minutes

COOKING TIME: 18-20 minutes

OVEN TEMPERATURE: 190°C, 375°F, Gas Mark 5

MAKES: 6

This is a very rich, sophisticated dessert, ideal for special occasions.
5 eggs, separated
40g (1½oz) granulated sugar
40g (1½oz) self-raising flour
25g (1oz) cocoa powder
5ml (1 tsp) baking powder
Pinch salt
30ml (2 tblsp) melted unsalted butter
75g (3oz) dark plain chocolate, melted
Cocoa powder
Rum, Grand Marnier or Amaretto liqueur
150ml (¼ pint) double cream, well chilled
Icing or vanilla sugar
1 recipe Nouvelle Chocolate Sauce (see recipe)
100g (4oz) split almonds, lightly toasted, and broken into pieces

To make the cake mixture: butter and flour six 10cm (4 inch) individual souffle dishes. Line the base of each dish with buttered greaseproof paper. Put the egg yolks and half the sugar into a bowl and beat well, preferably with an electric beater, until the eggs are thick and pale. Sieve the flour, cocoa, baking powder and salt together. Whisk the egg whites until stiff but not dry, gradually adding the remaining sugar. Fold the flour and melted butter alternately into the egg yolk mixture. Fold in the whisked egg whites lightly but thoroughly. Divide the mixture among the prepared dishes. Stand them on a baking sheet and bake for 18-20 minutes, or until a skewer inserted in the centre comes out clean. Take the cakes out of the oven and let them cool in their dishes. Remove them from their dishes, right way up, and cool on a wire rack. Trim the cakes a little so that they are rounded. Brush the tops and sides of the cakes with the melted chocolate and let it harden slightly before rolling them in the cocoa powder. Dig a little hole in the top of each cake. Sprinkle the inside of each cake with some of the liqueur you have chosen. About 30 minutes before serving, whip th[e] cream until thick and flavour it with icing or vanilla sugar and m[...] of the chosen liqueur. Fit a pipin[g] bag with a small rosette nozzle a[nd] fill with the cream. Fill the little hole in each cake with the crea[m] and place the truffle cake hole si[de] down on a small plate. Pipe a sm[...] rosette of cream to decorate eac[h] cake. Mix the Nouvelle Sauce w[ith] the almonds: spoon it around th[e] bottom of each cake, and a little over the top.

Chocolate and Cherry Mouss[e] (right) and Chocolate Quiche (below).

Tarte au Chocolat

PREPARATION TIME: 25 minutes, plus chilling

COOKING TIME: 45 minutes

OVEN TEMPERATURE: 190°C, 375°F, Gas Mark 5

MAKES: 1 tart, 25cm (10 inches) in diameter

225g (8oz) plain flour
5ml (1 tsp) salt
50g (2oz) ground almonds
30ml (2 tblsp) caster sugar
150g (5oz) unsalted butter
1 egg yolk

Filling
200ml (⅓ pint) double cream
22ml (1½ tblsp) brandy
200g (7oz) plain chocolate, chopped or grated
2 egg whites, beaten
50g (2oz) caster sugar

Topping
300ml (½ pint) double cream
22ml (1½ tblsp) caster sugar
Praline (see recipe) or grated chocolate

Grease and line a 25cm (10 inch) flan tin with greaseproof paper. Sieve together the flour and salt and add the almonds and sugar; make a well in the centre. Add the butter and egg yolk. Mix all the ingredients together, using the fingertips, to form a dough. Shape the dough into a ball and wrap in foil or cling film. Chill for 1 hour. Roll the dough out on a floured work surface to about 3-5cm (⅛-¼ inch) thick. Use the dough to line the prepared flan tin. Cover with greaseproof paper and weight it down with rice or beans. Bake "blind" for 10-15 minutes until it begins to turn pale golden. Remove the paper and beans and bake for a further 15 minutes. Leave the flan case to cool in its tin. To make the filling: put the cream and brandy into a saucepan and bring just to the boil. Add the chocolate and stir until the mixture is thick and smooth. Leave to cool for at least 1 hour. Whisk until fluffy. Whisk the egg whites until stiff but not dry, adding the sugar slowly. Fold the meringue into the chocolate mixture. Remove the pastry case from its tin and fill it with the chocolate mixture. For the topping: whisk the cream with the sugar until it is light and fluffy, and then spread it over the chocolate filling. Decorate with crushed praline or chocolate.

Chocolate Honeycomb

PREPARATION TIME: 20 minutes, plus chilling

SERVES: 4-6 people

15g (½oz) gelatine
3 eggs, separated
50g (2oz) caster sugar
450ml (¾ pint) milk
75g (3oz) plain dark chocolate, grated
Vanilla essence

Put the gelatine, sugar and egg yolks into a basin and beat until creamy. Heat the milk in a small saucepan; add the grated chocolate to it and stir until dissolved. Pour the chocolate milk over the beaten egg yolk and gelatine mixture; put the bowl over a pan of gently simmering water and stir continuously until the mixture is thick. Leave the mixture to cool. Add a few drops of vanilla essence to the thickened chocolate mixture. Whisk the egg whites until stiff but not dry and fold in. Turn the mixture into a dampened mould and chill until set. Unmould carefully before serving.

Marbled Rum Cream Pie

PREPARATION TIME: 35 minutes, plus chilling

COOKING TIME: 10 minutes

SERVES: 6-8 people

225g (8oz) caster sugar
A pinch of salt
60ml (4 tblsp) water
15ml (1 tblsp) gelatine
2 eggs, separated
175ml (6 fl oz) milk
60ml (4 tblsp) dark rum
350g (12oz) plain chocolate, finely chopped
250ml (8 fl oz) double or whipping cream
5ml (1 tsp) vanilla essence
1 baked sweet shortcrust pastry flan case, 23cm (9 inches) in diameter

Mix 50g (2oz) of the sugar with the salt, water and gelatine in a small, heatproof bowl; stand over a pan of simmering water and stir until the gelatine has dissolved. Remove the bowl from the heat and beat in the egg yolks, milk and rum. Return to the heat, and continue to beat until the mixture has thickened slightly. Remove from the heat and stir in the chocolate until it has melted. Chill until thickened but not set. Beat the egg whites until stiff but not dry and gradually beat in 100g (4oz) of the remaining sugar. Fold the meringue mixture into the chilled chocolate mixture. Whip the cream with the remaining sugar and vanilla essence until thick. Pile alternate spoons of cream and chocolate mixture into the cold cooked pastry flan case. Cut through the layers with a knife, to give a marbled effect. Chill well until firm.

Sherry Cream Pie

PREPARATION TIME: 30 minutes, plus chilling time

COOKING TIME: 35 minutes

OVEN TEMPERATURE: 190°C, 375°F, Gas Mark 5

MAKES: 1 flan, 20cm (8 inches) in diameter

150g (5oz) plain flour
50g (2oz) caster sugar
75g (3oz) butter
1 egg yolk

Filling
225g (8oz) plain dark chocolate, chopped or grated
45ml (3 tblsp) medium sherry
5ml (1 tsp) gelatine
4 eggs, separated

To Decorate
50g (2oz) plain dark chocolate, melted
150ml (¼ pint) double cream
15ml (1 tblsp) sherry

Put the flour and the sugar into a bowl; add the butter, cut into small pieces, and egg yolk. Knead to a smooth dough. Wrap the dough and chill for 30 minutes. Lightly flour the work surface and roll out the dough; use to line a 20cm (8 inch) loose-bottomed flan tin. Prick the base of the flan with a fork. Line with greaseproof paper and baking beans. Bake for 15 minutes; remove the paper and beans and bake for a further 15 minutes. Remove the pastry case from the tin and cool on a serving plate or platter. Put the chocolate into a small, heavy-based saucepan with the sherry and 30ml (2 tblsp) cold water. Sprinkle the gelatine over the top and stir over a low heat until the gelatine has dissolved. Beat the egg yolks into the sauce,

e at a time, and cool the mixture. nisk the egg whites until stiff but : dry and then fold it into the ce. Pour the mixture into the pared flan case and chill until . Melt the chocolate. Lightly ip the double cream. Divide the am in half; stir the sherry into e half, and the chocolate into the er. Fit two piping bags with star zzles and fill each bag with a erent cream. Decorate the top of pie with alternate stars of the erent creams.

Steamed Chocolate Pud

PREPARATION TIME: 25 minutes

COOKING TIME: 1¾-2 hours

SERVES: 6 people

225g (8oz) caster sugar
225g (8oz) butter
4 eggs, beaten
175g (6oz) self-raising flour
50g (2oz) cocoa powder
30ml (2 tblsp) rum

Butter a 1 litre (2 pint) pudding basin. Beat the sugar and butter together until light and fluffy. Add the eggs gradually, beating well after each addition. Fold in the sieved flour and cocoa and the rum and mix well. Turn the mixture into the greased pudding basin. Cover the top with a double thickness of greaseproof paper or foil, making a pleat in the top to give room for the pudding to rise. Tie round with string. Steam for 1¾-2 hours until well risen and spongy to the touch. Unmould the pudding and serve hot with a sauce of your choice.

Facing page: Marbled Rum Cream Pie (top) and Chocolate Honeycomb (bottom).

This page: Steamed Chocolate Pud (top) and Chocolate Rum Fool (bottom).

Fruits and Fantasies

Chocolate Dipped Pineapple with Melba Sauce

PREPARATION TIME: 40 minutes, plus chilling

SERVES: 6-8 people

1 good sized fresh pineapple
Rum
100g (4oz) granulated sugar
450g (1lb) raspberries
175g (6oz) bitter chocolate, chopped or grated

Peel and slice the pineapple into rings, 1cm (½ inch) thick. Sprinkle the slices first with the rum, and then with a little sugar. Cover and chill for at least one hour. Puree the raspberries and sieve them to remove the seeds. Sweeten with a little sugar to taste and add a little rum. Chill until needed. Melt the chocolate in a bowl over a saucepan of hot water. Remove the pineapple from the refrigerator and pat dry with absorbent paper. Cover a baking sheet with waxed paper and partially dip each ring of pineapple into the melted chocolate. Leave on the waxed paper to harden (you can put them in the refrigerator). Put each pineapple ring onto an individual plate and pour a pool of melba sauce over just before serving.

Chocolate Souffle with Sour Cherries

PREPARATION TIME: 40 minutes

COOKING TIME: 10-12 minutes

OVEN TEMPERATURE: 200°C, 400°F, Gas Mark 6

SERVES: 6 people

100g (4oz) caster sugar
3 eggs, separated
Vanilla essence
Grated rind of half a lemon
5 egg whites
5ml (1 tsp) instant mashed potato powder
Melted butter for greasing
Sugar to dust
5ml (1 tsp) arrowroot
375g (13oz) can sour cherries

Beat 25g (1oz) of the sugar with the egg yolks, vanilla essence and lemon rind. Whisk the egg whites with the remaining sugar until stiff but not dry; whisk in the potato powder. Fold the snowy egg whites into the egg yolk mixture. Brush the surface of a metal serving dish with melted butter and sprinkle with a little sugar. Put ¾ of the souffle mixture into the dish with a spatula and smooth it out into a boat shape, hollowing out the middle. Fit a piping bag with a star nozzle and fill with the remaining souffle mixture. Pipe a border around the top and bottom of the boat. Bake in the oven for 10-12 minutes. Drain the canned cherries and keep the juice. Mix the juice

This page: Locksmiths Lads (top) and Banana Fritters with Chocolate Rum Sauce (bottom).

Facing page: Chocolate Souffle with Sour Cherries (top) and Chocolate Dipped Pineapple with Melba Sauce (bottom).

with the arrowroot and stir over a low heat until it thickens. Add most of the cherries. Fill the top of the souffle with the reserved cherries. Serve the cherry sauce separately. Note: the metal of the dish will conduct the heat evenly through the souffle.

Chocolate Waffles and Fruit Kebabs

PREPARATION TIME: 15 minutes

COOKING TIME: 15 minutes

SERVES: 4 people

50g (2oz) plain chocolate, chopped or grated
50ml (2 fl oz) water
75g (3oz) unsalted butter
2 eggs
75-90g (3-3½oz) sugar
175g (6oz) plain flour
10ml (2 tsp) baking powder
120ml (4 fl oz) milk
75g (3oz) chopped walnuts
Whipped cream or ice cream to serve

Stir the chocolate and water together in a small, heavy-based saucepan until the chocolate melts. Remove the pan from the heat when the chocolate forms a paste. Beat the butter into the melted chocolate, and then add the eggs and the sugar. Sieve the flour and baking powder onto a sheet of greaseproof paper. Add the sieved flour and milk alternately to the chocolate mixture. Stir in the walnuts. Pour the batter into a hot, oiled waffle iron. Bring the cover down and cook for 2-3 minutes on either side. Serve with whipped cream, ice cream, and cocktail sticks threaded with pieces of fresh fruit.

Banana Fritters with Chocolate Rum Sauce

PREPARATION TIME: 20 minutes, plus standing time

COOKING TIME: 14-15 minutes

SERVES: 6 people

Almost any kind of fruit can be battered, and the accompanying sauces that can be used range from fruit purees to liqueured sauces, like the rum sauce in this recipe.

150g (5oz) flour
150ml (¼ pint) white wine
2 eggs, separated
15g (½oz) drinking chocolate
15g (½oz) caster sugar
6 bananas
Oil for deep frying
Icing sugar for dusting

Sauce
100g (4oz) butter
100g (4oz) caster sugar
A pinch of salt
30ml (2 tblsp) dark rum
50g (2oz) cocoa powder
150ml (¼ pint) double cream
5ml (1 tsp) vanilla essence

Sieve the flour into a bowl and whisk in the wine, egg yolks and drinking chocolate. Beat until smooth and let the batter stand for 15 minutes. Whisk the egg whites and sugar until fluffy. Fold the fluffy egg whites into the batter. Slice the bananas into bite-sized pieces. Put each piece onto a fork and dip into the batter. Lower immediately into the hot oil, frying until the batter is golden brown. Lift out of the oil with a slotted spoon and leave to drain on a piece of absorbent paper. Dust with icing sugar and serve with the sauce. To make the sauce: melt the butter in a small saucepan. Stir in the sugar, salt, rum and cocoa powder. Mix well over a low heat. Add the cream and bring to the boil. Simmer very gently for 5 minutes. Remove from the heat and add the vanilla essence. Note: you can use fresh butter to fry the fritters and this will give a very rich flavour, unlike lard or vegetable oil, which are usually well refined, and will not alter the natural flavour of the ingredients. The crisper the better, but be careful not to burn the fritters. You may have a tempura set which can be used when entertaining informally, or a thermostatically controlled deep fat fryer which will give you perfect results.

Locksmiths Lads

Beignets De Prunes Au Chocolat

PREPARATION TIME: 35 minutes

COOKING TIME: about 4 minutes

SERVES: 4 people

150g (5oz) plain flour
2 eggs, separated
150ml (¼ pint) white wine
A pinch of salt
30ml (2 tblsp) cooking oil
25g (1oz) caster sugar
16 large tenderised prunes
16 blanched almonds
Oil for deep frying
50g (2oz) grated chocolate
Icing sugar to dust

Zabaione Sauce
3 egg yolks
1 whole egg
120g (4½oz) caster sugar
90ml (6 tblsp) marsala

Sieve the flour into a mixing bowl; make a well in the centre and pour in the egg yolks, white wine, salt and the oil. Mix well using a wire whisk, and leave the batter to stand for 20 minutes. Whisk the egg whites until stiff and fold in the sugar. Fold the egg whites into the batter. Carefully remove the stone from each prune and replace it with an almond. Spike the prunes with a fork and dip them into the batter. Fry the coated prunes in hot oil until they are golden brown; remove and drain them on absorbent paper. Scatter the grated chocolate over the prunes when they are nearly cold. Dust with icing sugar. To make the sauce: cream the egg yolks, whole egg and sugar together in a heatproof bowl over a saucepan of simmering water. Add the marsala to the mixture and beat it with a balloon whisk until it doubles in volume, and is foamy. Serve immediately with the Locksmiths Lads.

Strawberry Shortcake

PREPARATION TIME: 15 minutes

COOKING TIME: 7-10 minutes

OVEN TEMPERATURE: 230°C, 450°F, Gas Mark 8

SERVES: 6 people

A wonderful dessert for the summer, with a luxurious topping.

225g (8oz) plain flour
10ml (2 tsp) baking powder
50g (2oz) butter
25g (1oz) caster sugar
1 egg, lightly beaten
Milk
350g (12oz) strawberries, hulled
300ml (½ pint) double cream
1 recipe Chocolate Fudge Sauce (see recipe)

Chocolate Waffles and Fruit Kebabs (top right) and Strawberry Shortcake (right).

e the flour and baking powder
a mixing bowl. Rub the butter
the mixture until it resembles
dcrumbs. Stir in the sugar. Add
beaten egg, and enough milk to
the mixture into a stiff scone
gh. Roll out the dough to a
kness of approximately 1cm (½
) and cut out two circles. Put
circles of dough onto greased
ng sheets. Bake for 10 minutes
shortcakes should be pale
en). Cool on a wire rack. Slice
g (8oz) of the strawberries and
the cream. Place one circle of
hortcake on a plate. Spoon
of the cream onto it and top
the sliced strawberries. Add a
more cream and place the
nd shortcake on top. Top the
tcake with spoonfuls of the
aining cream and the remaining
vberries. Drizzle over a little
colate fudge sauce. Serve the
aining sauce separately.

Strawberry Fondue

PREPARATION TIME: 50 minutes
COOKING TIME: 20 minutes
SERVES: 6 people

Stand
Oasis cone (from a florist) 30-38cm (12-15 inches) high
Kitchen foil
Dress net
Ribbon bows

1kg (2lb) large strawberries, washed and hulled
Cocktail sticks

Vanilla Fondue
375g (12oz) white chocolate, grated
85ml (3 fl oz) evaporated milk
1.25ml (¼ tsp) vanilla essence

Grand Marnier Fondue
175g (6oz) plain chocolate, grated
175g (6oz) milk chocolate, grated
200ml (7 fl oz) double cream
30ml (2 tblsp) Grand Marnier

To make the stand: cover the oasis with kitchen foil and then cover it with the dress net (use a colour that will go with the strawberries and with your table decoration). Place ribbon bows at random, fixing them into the oasis. Stick the strawberries into the stand, using cocktail sticks, so that they almost cover the cone completely. To make the vanilla fondue: melt the white chocolate with ⅔ of the evaporated milk in a pan over a low heat. Add the vanilla essence and then add the remaining evaporated milk as required. (The fondue should coat the back of a spoon.) To make the Grand Marnier fondue: melt together the chocolates and then add the cream. Stir well and remove from the heat. Finally add the liqueur. Pour the two fondues into separate warmed bowls. Keep these on a warming tray, or fondue tray, or on stands with night light candles beneath. Your guests can then pick strawberries and dip them into the fondues.

Chocolate Apricot Horns

PREPARATION TIME: 15 minutes
COOKING TIME: 15-20 minutes
OVEN TEMPERATURE: 220°C, 425°F, Gas Mark 7
MAKES: 10

225g (8oz) puff pastry
Beaten egg to glaze
100g (4oz) plain chocolate
15g (½oz) butter
30ml (2 tblsp) brandy
175ml (6 fl oz) apricot puree
175ml (6 fl oz) double cream, whipped

To Decorate
Chocolate curls

Roll out the pastry into a rectangle about 25x33cm (10x13 inches) and trim the edges. Cut into strips 2.5cm (1 inch) wide. Dampen one long edge of each strip with water and wind round a metal cornet mould (start at the point and overlap the dampened edge as you go). Put the horns on a lightly dampened baking sheet and chill for 15 minutes. Brush the horns with beaten egg and bake for 15-20 minutes until golden brown. Leave for 5 minutes, before carefully removing the moulds; cool the pastry horns on a wire rack. Melt the chocolate with the butter on a plate, over a pan of hot water; dip each of the horns into the chocolate. Mix the brandy with the apricot puree and spoon a little into each of the horns. Fit a star nozzle to a piping bag and fill the piping bag with the whipped cream. Pipe the cream into the horns. Decorate with chocolate curls.

Profiteroles Vine

PREPARATION TIME: 30 minutes, plus cooling
COOKING TIME: 25-30 minutes
OVEN TEMPERATURE: 200°C, 400°F, Gas Mark 6
SERVES: 4-6 people

Choux Pastry
150ml (¼ pint) water
50g (2oz) butter
65g (2½ oz) flour, sieved
2 eggs, beaten

Filling
30ml (2 tblsp) instant custard powder
15ml (1 tblsp) cocoa powder
15ml (1 tblsp) caster sugar
300ml (½ pint) milk
150ml (¼ pint) double cream, whipped
175g (6oz) plain chocolate, melte
Chocolate Butter Sauce (see recip

For the pastry: heat the water a butter in a small saucepan until butter melts. Bring to the boil; remove the pan from the heat beat in the flour. Beat with a wooden spoon until it leaves th sides of the pan clean. Cool the mixture slightly, and gradually b in the eggs, beating between ea addition. (The mixture should smooth and glossy.) Fill a pipin bag fitted with a large plain noz with the choux pastry. Pipe 20 even-sized balls onto two dampened baking sheets. Bake pre-heated oven for 20-25 minutes, until well risen. Split of the choux balls and let the st escape; return to the oven for a further 2 minutes. To make the filling: mix the custard powder, cocoa and sugar with a little of milk. Boil the remaining milk an stir it into the custard powder. Rinse the saucepan. Return the custard to the pan and cook fo few minutes. Beat the custard with a wooden spoon, and pou into a bowl to cool (cover the b with cling film so that a skin do not form as the custard cools). the cream into the custard, ma sure that there are no lumps (w if necessary). Fill a large piping fitted with a plain nozzle, with custard cream and fill the chou buns. To decorate and serve: co large leaf with melted chocolate pipe a few curls and a stem ont sheet of silicone paper. Leave th to set; gently peel off the paper the leaf. Arrange the profiterole look like a bunch of grapes on a large serving tray or dish; add t chocolate leaf, stem and curls. Finally pour over the chocolate sauce.

This page: Strawberry Fondu (with Grand Marnier Fondu

Facing page: Profiteroles Vi (top) and Chocolate Apricot Horns (bottom).

Frozen Desserts

Mocha Ice Cream

PREPARATION TIME: 25 minutes, plus freezing

SERVES: 6 people

30ml (2 tblsp) instant coffee granules
50g (2oz) butter
100g (4oz) soft brown sugar
60ml (4 tblsp) cocoa powder
75ml (5 tblsp) water
450ml (¾ pint) canned evaporated milk, chilled

Put the coffee, butter, sugar, cocoa and water into a saucepan, and heat gently. Stir the mixture until melted, and bring it to the boil. Cool. Whisk the chilled evaporated milk in a bowl, until it is thick and frothy. Mix it into the cooled mixture, whisking until it is well blended. Turn the mixture into a freezer container and freeze uncovered until slushy. Beat the ice cream well and re-freeze until firm.

Rum Ice Cream Gateau

PREPARATION TIME: 30 minutes, plus freezing

COOKING TIME: 1 hour

OVEN TEMPERATURE: 150°C, 300°F, Gas Mark 2

SERVES: 6-8 people

Oil for greasing
225g (8oz) caster sugar
3 egg whites
15ml (1 tblsp) instant coffee
30ml (2 tblsp) boiling water
450ml (¾ pint) double cream
30ml (2 tblsp) dark rum
150ml (5 fl oz) chocolate ice cream

Lightly oil a baking sheet and line the base of an 18cm (7 inch) round loose-bottomed cake tin with greased greaseproof paper. Whisk 50g (2oz) of the caster sugar into the egg whites and continue to whisk until stiff. Add the remaining sugar and whisk until it peaks. Fill a piping bag, fitted with a star nozzle, with the meringue mixture. Pipe small rosettes onto the baking sheet, keeping them well apart. Bake them in a pre-heated oven for 1 hour; leave in the oven for a further 20 minutes, with the oven turned off. Remove the meringues from the oven and allow them to cool. Mix the coffee with the water in a small bowl. Whisk the cream until thick; fold in all but 4 of the meringues. Add the coffee and the rum, taking care not to crush the meringues. Use the mixture to fill the prepared cake tin. Cover and freeze until firm. Soften the ice cream. When the gateau is hard enough, remove it from the tin. Beat the ice cream and use it to fill a piping bag fitted with a 1cm (½ inch) star nozzle. Quickly pipe rosettes on top of the gateau. Return the gateau to the freezer and leave until firm. Put the reserved meringues in the centre of the gateau. Refrigerate for 10 minutes before serving.

This page: Mocha Ice Cream (top) and Rum Ice Cream Gateau (bottom).

Facing page: Chocolate Chip Cream (top) and Chocolate I Box Cake (bottom).

Chocolate Ice Cream

PREPARATION TIME: 1 hour 40 minutes, plus freezing time

COOKING TIME: 15-20 minutes

SERVES: 8 people

100g (4oz) plain chocolate, chopped or grated
600ml (1 pint) milk
7 egg yolks
100g (4oz) caster sugar

Put the chopped chocolate into a saucepan with a little milk. Stir over a low heat until the chocolate melts and forms a smooth paste. Add the remaining milk. Whisk the egg yolks and sugar together until thick and light. Whisk into the chocolate milk. Whisk continuously over a low heat until thick. Pour the mixture into a bowl and stand over ice. (If you do not have a lot of ice, chill in the refrigerator.) Either pour into an ice cream churn, and follow the manufacturer's instructions, or pour into ice trays and freeze for 30 minutes. Tip the par-frozen ice cream into a bowl and whisk until smooth. Return to the freezer. Repeat this process every 30 minutes, until the ice cream is really thick. Freeze until ready to serve.

Nougat Ice Cream Cake

PREPARATION TIME: 40 minutes, plus freezing

SERVES: 6-8 people

50g (2oz) ground hazelnuts
16 small wafer biscuits
425g (15½oz) can pineapple chunks, or
225g (8oz) crystallised pineapple
450ml (¾ pint) vanilla ice cream
450ml (¾ pint) chocolate ice cream
100g (4oz) plain chocolate, finely chopped
100g (4oz) nougat
450ml (¾ pint) whipping cream, whipped

Grease a 450g (1lb) loaf tin and sprinkle the inside with ground hazelnuts. Put 12 of the wafer biscuits around the sides and base of the tin. Drain the pineapple chunks (or chop the crystallised pineapple). Soften the ice creams by placing them in the refrigerator. Spoon the vanilla ice cream into the tin and smooth it down. Add the chopped chocolate to the chocolate ice cream, and ¾ of the chopped pineapple. Spoon this mixture on top of the vanilla ice cream. Chop the nougat into small pieces and sprinkle it on top of the chocolate ice cream. Cover the chocolate ice cream with the remaining 4 wafer biscuits. Freeze for 3-4 hours, until firm. Spoon or pipe the whipped cream over the unmoulded ice cream cake. Decorate with the reserved pineapple. Serve cut into slices

Chocolate Ice Box Cake

PREPARATION TIME: 1 hour, plus freezing

COOKING TIME: 25-30 minutes

OVEN TEMPERATURE: 190°C, 375°F, Gas Mark 5

SERVES: 8 people

Melted butter for greasing
7 eggs, separated
75g (3oz) vanilla sugar
75ml (5 tblsp) plain flour
Pinch of salt
Caster sugar

Filling
350g (12oz) plain chocolate, chopped or grated
30ml (2 tblsp) strong black coffee
50ml (2 fl oz) brandy
2 egg yolks
5 egg whites, stiffly beaten
120ml (4 fl oz) double or whipping cream, lightly whipped

Icing
150ml (¼ pint) double cream
150g (5oz) plain chocolate, chopped or grated

Grease and line two 23x30cm (9x12 inch) Swiss roll tins with greaseproof paper. Brush the paper with melted butter and dust with flour. Whisk the egg yolks and vanilla sugar together until thick and light; fold in the flour and salt. Whisk the egg whites until stiff but not dry. Gently fold the whisked egg whites into the mixture. Divide the mixture between the two tins. Bake in a pre-heated oven for 15-20 minutes, or until golden. When the sponges are baked, spread two tea towels on a work surface and cover each one with a sheet of greaseproof paper. Sprinkle with caster sugar and turn the sponges out onto the sugared paper. Peel off the lining paper and leave the sponges to cool. Line the bottom of a 20cm (8 inch) spring form cake tin with greased greaseproof paper. Cut a circle of sponge from each rectangular sponge to fit the tin. Put one on top of the paper lining. Reserve the other. Cut three strips of sponge, 5cm (2 inches) wide, to line the sides of the tin. Place in position. To make the filling: put the chocolate, coffee and brandy into a saucepan and stir over a low heat until the chocolate has melted. Leave to cool. Beat in the egg yolks, and then gently fold in the whisked egg whites, taking care not to over-mix. Finally, fold in the whipped double cream. Pour the mixture into the sponge-lined cake tin and put the remaining sponge circle on top as a lid. Cover the top of the tin with a plate 20cm (8 inches) in diameter, weighted down lightly. Put the cake tin into the freezer for 2-3 hours, or chill in the refrigerator for at least 5 hours. To make the icing: pour the cream into a pan and bring to the boil. Stir in the chocolate until it melts, and the mixture thickens. Carefully take the set cake out of its tin and pour icing over it. Open freeze, or refrigerate, until the icing has set.

Chocolate Chip Ice Cream

PREPARATION TIME: 30 minutes, plus freezing time

COOKING TIME: 6-8 minutes

SERVES: 8 people

90g (3½oz) plain chocolate, choppe or grated
300ml (½ pint) milk
3 egg yolks
75g (3oz) caster sugar
300ml (½ pint) double or whipping cream, lightly whipped
65g (2½oz) finely chopped chocola

Stir the chopped or grated chocolate into the milk in a small, heavy-based saucepan; stir over a gentle heat until the chocolate melts. Put the egg yolks into a bow with the sugar and whisk until thick and creamy. Add the chocolate milk and whisk. Return the chocolate mixture to the saucepan and stir continuously over a moderate heat until the mixture is thick, and will coat the back of a spoon. Strain the chocolate custard into a bowl and cool in the refrigerator. When qui cold, fold in the whipped cream. (you are using a churn, pour in the mixture and follow the manufacturer's instructions, adding the chopped chocolate at the appropriate stage.) Pour into ice trays and freeze until the mixture begins to set around the edges. Pour into a bowl and whisk. Stir in

Chocolate Ice Cream (above right) and Nougat Ice Cream Cake (right).

the chopped chocolate. Return the ice cream to the ice trays and freeze for 30 minutes. Repeat the whisking and freezing method every 30 minutes, until the ice cream is really thick. Freeze until firm.

Luxury Lace Ice Cream

PREPARATION TIME: 50 minutes, plus freezing

COOKING TIME: 6-8 minutes

SERVES: 6-8 people

300ml (½ pint) single cream
150g (5oz) plain chocolate, chopped or grated
5ml (1 tsp) instant coffee powder
4 egg yolks
100g (4oz) caster sugar
300ml (½ pint) double cream

To Decorate
100g (4oz) plain chocolate, chopped or grated

Put the single cream into a saucepan and heat gently. Add the chocolate and coffee powder and stir until the mixture is smooth, and the chocolate has melted. Whisk the egg yolks and sugar until thick, pale and creamy. Continue whisking, and slowly pour in the chocolate cream mixture. Return the mixture to the saucepan and stir it over a gentle heat until it reaches coating consistency. Remove from the heat and cool. Whip the cream lightly and fold it into the chocolate mixture. Pour the mixture into a shallow container and freeze it until firm. To make the chocolate lace decoration: put a large bun tray upside down. Smooth a piece of cling film over alternate domed shapes. Melt the plain chocolate and use it to fill a greaseproof piping bag fitted with a writing nozzle. Pipe around the edge of each dome and then pipe parallel lines in every direction over the dome, joining up all the lines with circles. Repeat the pattern so that it is "double" in thickness. Chill the chocolate domes until set. Carefully lift them off the bun tray. Keep them chilled until you are ready to serve the ice cream. To serve: put a generous scoop of ice cream into each chocolate lace cup and top it with another cup.

Frozen Chocolate Souffle

PREPARATION TIME: 30 minutes, plus freezing time

COOKING TIME: 15 minutes

SERVES: 6-8 people

This delicate and light chocolate dessert makes an unusual end to a meal.

50g (2oz) caster sugar
3 eggs, separated
90g (3½ oz) plain chocolate, melted and cooled
350ml (12 fl oz) double cream, lightly whipped

To Decorate
Chocolate scrolls
Icing sugar

Tie a collar of greased greaseproof paper around a 600ml (1 pint) souffle dish, making sure that it extends at least 5cm (2 inches) above the rim of the dish. Whisk the sugar and egg yolks in a bowl over a pan of simmering water, until thick and light. The mixture should fall off the whisk in ribbons). Remove from the heat and beat in the melted chocolate. Whisk until the mixture has cooled. Fold the lightly whipped cream into the chocolate mixture. Whisk the egg whites until stiff but not dry; fold lightly into the mixture. Pour the mixture into the prepared souffle dish. Freeze for at least 4 hours. Just before serving, remove the paper collar by gently easing it off. Decorate the top with chocolate scrolls and dust lightly with icing sugar.

Minted Chocolate Chip Gateau

PREPARATION TIME: 25 minutes, plus freezing

COOKING TIME: 20 minutes

OVEN TEMPERATURE: 200°C, 400°F, Gas Mark 6

SERVES: 6 people

3 large eggs
75g (3oz) caster sugar
75g (3oz) self-raising flour, sieved

Filling
6 scoops chocolate chip ice cream

To decorate
1 box chocolate mint sticks

To make the sponge: whisk the eggs and sugar together until they are thick and light in colour. Fold the sieved flour lightly but thoroughly into the mixture. Put into a greased and lined shallow loaf tin. Bake in the oven for 20 minutes. Turn out and cool. Slice the cake through into layers; sandwich together with 4 scoops of the ice cream. Spread the remaining ice cream over the sides of the cake, omitting the top; stick on the chocolate mint sticks (you may have to use a piece of string or ribbon to hold them in position). Freeze the cake until firm. Cut the cake into slices to serve.

Iced Lake

PREPARATION TIME: 35 min plus fre

COOKING TIME: 10-15 minut

OVEN TEMPERATURE: 180°C 350°F, Gas Mark 4

SERVES: 6 people

Lemon Ice Cream
Grated rind of 2 lemons
Juice of 3 lemons
175g (6oz) caster sugar
300ml (½ pint) double cream
300ml (½ pint) milk

Chocolate Biscuits
50g (2oz) butter
50g (2oz) caster sugar
1 egg yolk
50g (2oz) plain flour
25g (1oz) rice flour
5ml (1 tsp) cocoa powder

To Serve
Nouvelle Chocolate Sauce (see recipe)

To make the ice cream: put th lemon rind, juice and sugar int bowl and stir well. Add the cre and whisk until thick. Whisk i milk slowly. Pour the mixture i large freezer container and free until slushy. Tip the ice cream a bowl and whisk it until smoo Re-freeze in its container until To make the biscuits: lightly gr a baking sheet. Cream the but and sugar together. Add the eg yolk, beat the mixture well. Ad the plain flour, rice flour and c and work them well into the mixture. Lightly flour the work surface and roll out the dough out shapes with animal cutters Place on a baking sheet. Bake f 10-15 minutes. Cool on a wire To serve: place scoops of ice cr onto small serving plates and t each one with an animal biscui Spoon Nouvelle Chocolate Sa around each portion.

This page: Iced Lake (top) a Minted Chocolate Chip Gat (bottom).

Facing page: Frozen Chocol Souffle (top) and Luxury La Ice Cream (bottom).

Cookies and Confections

Chocolate Ravioli

PREPARATION TIME: 30 minutes, plus chilling

MAKES: 25 pieces

100g (4oz) roasted hazelnuts
15ml (1 tblsp) granulated sugar
30ml (2 tblsp) melted butter
50g (2oz) plain chocolate melted
15ml (1 tblsp) brandy
250g (9oz) white chocolate, melted

Line a square baking sheet with a rim of tinfoil, making sure that it is smooth and even, with neat corners. Crush the hazelnuts and mix them with the sugar and butter. Stir in the melted dark chocolate and brandy to form a paste. Form into 25 small balls and arrange them in rows over the bottom of the baking sheet, pressing the balls flat. Pour the melted white chocolate evenly over the small balls, so as to cover them completely. Place the tray in the refrigerator until firm. Cut the ravioli into rows with a knife or ravioli cutter, and then separate each one.

Chocolate Meringues

PREPARATION TIME: 35 minutes

COOKING TIME: 15-20 minutes

OVEN TEMPERATURE: 180°C, 350°F, Gas Mark 4

MAKES: about 8

2 egg whites
100g (4oz) icing sugar, sieved
50g (2oz) nuts

Filling
100g (4oz) plain chocolate, chopped or grated
60ml (4 tblsp) water
15ml (1 tblsp) strong black coffee
50g (2oz) butter
2 egg yolks
15ml (1 tblsp) dark rum

Whisk the egg whites until stiff and dry. Add the icing sugar a spoonful at a time and continue to whisk until very thick. Carefully fold in the chopped nuts; spoon or pipe small mounds onto a baking sheet lined with silicone paper. Bake for 15-20 minutes. Leave to cool slightly and then transfer onto a wire rack. Gently spoon out a little meringue from the underside of each of the meringues. For the filling: melt the chocolate and stir in the coffee and water; boil the mixture, stirring continuously for 2 minutes. Remove the pan from the heat and allow the mixture to cool; beat the butter into the cooled mixture, and blend in the egg yolks and the rum. Refrigerate until the mixture thickens. When cool, spoon it into a piping bag fitted with a plain nozzle, and pipe the filling into the meringues. Sandwich them together in pairs.

This page: Toffee Bars (top Chocolate Fudge (top right) Chocolate Ravioli (bottom).

Facing page: Florentines (to and Chocolate Meringue Biscuits (bottom).

Chocolate Eggs

PREPARATION TIME: 50 minutes
COOKING TIME: 12-15 minutes
MAKES: 6

6 small eggs
Food colouring
175ml (6 fl oz) double cream
257g (10 oz) plain or milk chocolate, melted
60ml (4 tblsp) white rum
Sticking plaster or tape

Using a needle, make a small hole in one end of each egg; carefully make a larger hole in the other end. Blow the egg contents out into a bowl. Pour running water into the egg shells and shake them well until clean. Put a little food colouring of your choice into a saucepan of water and boil the egg shells until they take on the colour. Dry the shells in a low oven for 5 minutes. Boil the cream and stir it into the melted chocolate. Stir in the rum. Put a small piece of plaster over the smallest hole in each egg shell; fill a piping bag fitted with a plain nozzle with the chocolate cream. Fit the nozzle gently into the egg shell and pipe in the chocolate cream until full. Clean off any chocolate on the shell and chill. Remove the plasters. These eggs are fun to give as gifts, or use uncoloured, as a joke for a chocolate breakfast. Note: stand the eggs in their box to make filling and chilling easier.

Artichoke

PREPARATION TIME: 1 hour 30 minutes, plus setting overnight
MAKES: 1 artichoke, serving 8-10 people

After dinner mints with a difference.

450g (1lb) plain chocolate, chopped or grated
30ml (2 tblsp) oil
Few drops of peppermint oil
1 globe artichoke

To Make the Artichoke
25g (1oz) caster sugar
25g (1oz) butter
30ml (2 tblsp) water
50g (2oz) icing sugar, sieved
25g (1oz) cocoa powder
A piece of cake the size of the artichoke

Artichoke (above), Chocolate Eggs (right) and Truffles (far right).

Ielt the plain chocolate with the
il and stir occasionally until
ielted. Cool this mixture slightly
nd stir in the peppermint oil. Take
ie leaves off the artichoke; dip the
ont of each leaf into the melted
iocolate and lay them on silicone
iper. Leave overnight to set,
efore peeling off the artichoke
aves. To make the icing: dissolve
ie caster sugar in the butter and
ater over a low heat; remove from
ie heat and stir in the icing sugar
id the cocoa powder. Cut the
ike into a pyramid shape and
over it with some of the cooled
ing. Stick the chocolate artichoke
aves around the cake, in the same
der as the real artichoke was
sembled. You will need to use
me of the icing to help them to
ick. Serve with the peppermint
eams at the end of the meal.

Chocolate Fudge

REPARATION TIME: 35 minutes

OOKING TIME: 10-15 minutes

AKES: about 750g (1½lbs)

This fudge is much easier to make if you have a sugar thermometer, but do not worry if one is not available; the temperature of the fudge can be tested without one.

25g (1oz) butter
225g (8oz) plain chocolate, melted
225g (8oz) granulated sugar
450ml (¾ pint) canned evaporated milk

To Decorate

25g (1oz) cocoa powder, or drinking chocolate

If you have a sugar thermometer put it in your saucepan before you start the fudge. Heat the butter, sugar and evaporated milk in the saucepan, stirring continuously, until the sugar has dissolved. Boil the mixture until the thermometer reads 116°C, 240°F (if you do not have a thermometer, take out a little of the fudge with a small spoon and drop it into a jug of cold water; if it stays in a ball it is ready). Remove the saucepan from the heat and plunge the bottom of the pan into cold water to stop it cooking. After a few minutes beat the fudge until it is thick and grainy. Beat in the melted chocolate. Butter a shallow 30x18cm (12x7 inch) cake tin and pour in the fudge. Cool until set. Cut the fudge into squares. Dust the fudge in either cocoa powder or drinking chocolate.

Truffles

PREPARATION TIME: 15 minutes

MAKES: about 10

100g (4oz) plain chocolate, chopped or grated
15ml (1 tblsp) dark rum
25g (1oz) unsalted butter
1 egg yolk
100g (4oz) ground almonds
100g (4oz) cake crumbs
50g (2oz) chocolate vermicelli

Melt the chocolate with the rum in a small bowl over a saucepan of hot water. Beat in the butter and egg yolk and remove the mixture from

the heat. Stir in the ground almonds and cake crumbs to make a smooth paste. Divide it into balls; roll them in the vermicelli until evenly coated.

Dipped Fruit

PREPARATION TIME: 10 minutes, plus drying

MAKES: 750g (1½lb) dipped fruit

750g (1½lb) prepared fruit (grapes, strawberries, etc.)
Melted plain chocolate

Wash the fruits, but leave the stems on them if possible. Holding each piece of fruit by the stem, dip into the melted chocolate, leaving the top section uncovered. Allow any excess to run off and leave to set on a tray lined with silicone paper.

Chocolate Meringue Biscuits

PREPARATION TIME: 20 minutes

COOKING TIME: 15-20 minutes

OVEN TEMPERATURE: 180°C, 350°F, Gas Mark 4

MAKES: about 10

100g (4oz) butter or margarine
50g (2oz) caster sugar
1 egg yolk
50g (2oz) ground almonds
175g (6oz) plain flour

Filling
100g (4oz) plain chocolate
15g (½oz) butter

Meringue Topping
For meringue ingredients see Chocolate Meringues recipe

Grease a baking sheet and line with silicone paper. Cream the butter or margarine and sugar together; add the egg yolk and beat well. Add the ground almonds and flour and mix well. Knead the mixture and roll it out thinly. Cut into rounds using a 6cm (2½ inch) cutter. Place the rounds on the prepared baking sheet and bake for 15-20 minutes. Make up the meringue mixture. Pipe into 2.5cm (1 inch) swirls on a baking sheet lined with silicone paper. Follow the baking instructions for chocolate meringues. When cool, gently ease them off the baking sheet. To make up the filling: melt the chocolate with the butter over a gentle heat. Mix them well and spread over the top of each of the almond biscuits. Top each one with a meringue and leave until set.

Florentines

PREPARATION TIME: 15 minutes

COOKING TIME: 8-10 minutes

OVEN TEMPERATURE: 180°C, 350°F, Gas Mark 4

MAKES: 12

75g (3oz) butter
75g (3oz) golden syrup
75g (3oz) flaked almonds, chopped
25g (1oz) plain flour
25g (1oz) chopped mixed peel
50g (2oz) glace cherries, chopped
5ml (1 tsp) lemon juice
100g (4oz) plain chocolate, chopped or grated

Line a baking sheet with silicone paper. Melt the butter and syrup together in a small saucepan. Stir in the almonds, flour, mixed peel, cherries and lemon juice. Put small spoonfuls of the mixture onto the prepared baking sheet. Keep them well apart and flatten with a fork. Bake in a pre-heated oven for 8-10 minutes. Remove the Florentines carefully to a wire rack to cool. Melt the chocolate in a bowl over a pan of hot water. Spread over the flat side of each Florentine. Place the biscuits chocolate sides uppermost, and mark the liquid chocolate with wavy lines, using a fork. Leave until set.

Toffee Bars

PREPARATION TIME: 40 minutes

COOKING TIME: 25-30 minutes

OVEN TEMPERATURE: 180°C, 350°F, Gas Mark 4

MAKES: 15 bars

Biscuit Base
100g (4oz) butter
50g (2oz) caster sugar
175g (6oz) plain flour, sieved

Toffee Caramel
100g (4oz) butter or margarine
50g (2oz) caster sugar
30ml (2 tblsp) golden syrup
150ml (5 fl oz) condensed milk

Chocolate Topping
100g (4oz) plain chocolate
15g (½oz) butter

For the biscuit base: cream the butter and sugar together until light and fluffy. Add the flour and knead until smooth. Press the dough into a greased 20cm (8 inch) square shallow cake tin, and pr with a fork. Bake in a pre-heate oven for 25-30 minutes. Cool. the ingredients for the toffee caramel into a small saucepan a stir until dissolved; bring slowl the boil, and cook stirring for 5 minutes. Cool slightly and ther spread over the biscuit base. Le to set. For thêtopping: melt the chocolate with the butter over low heat; spread it carefully ove the toffee. Leave it to set and c into fingers.

Chocolate Muesli

PREPARATION TIME: 25 minu

COOKING TIME: 10-12 minute

OVEN TEMPERATURE: 190°C 375°F, Gas Mark 5

MAKES: about 12

100g (4oz) margarine or butter
100g (4oz) caster sugar
1 egg, beaten
Few drops vanilla essence
100g (4oz) plain flour, sieved
2.5ml (½ tsp) bicarbonate of sod
50g (2oz) rolled oats
50g (2oz) cocoa powder

Chocolate Coating
100g (4oz) plain chocolate, chop or grated
15g (½oz) butter

Beat the margarine or butter w the sugar until light and fluffy. I in the egg, adding the essence, and bicarbonate of soda. Stir ir oats and the cocoa powder. Sp the mixture onto a lightly greas baking sheet, and mark out int bars with a knife. Bake for 10-12 minutes until lightly browned. mark with a sharp knife and co on a wire rack. To make the chocolate coating: melt the chocolate and butter together pour evenly over the bars. Sep the bars when set.

This page: Chocolate Meringues (top) and Dippe Fruit (bottom).

Facing page: Praline Orang Log (top), Chocolate Muesli (centre right) and Mint Crea (bottom left).

Chocolate Chip Cookies

PREPARATION TIME: 15 minutes, plus chilling

COOKING TIME: 10-12 minutes

OVEN TEMPERATURE: 180°C, 350°F, Gas Mark 4

MAKES: about 30

225g (8oz) self-raising flour
Pinch of salt
150g (5oz) butter
100g (4oz) caster sugar
1 egg, lightly beaten
50g (2oz) plain chocolate, grated

Sieve the flour and salt into a mixing bowl. Cut the butter into the flour and rub in until the mixture looks like breadcrumbs. Stir the sugar into the mixture. Add the egg and mix to a stiff dough. Knead the grated chocolate into the dough. Chill the dough for 30 minutes. Roll out the dough and cut into 5cm (2 inch) rounds with a plain cutter. Grease a baking sheet and put the rounds on it, placing them well apart. Prick the rounds with a fork. Bake in a pre-heated oven for 10-12 minutes until golden. Cool on a wire rack.

Chocolate Crunch

PREPARATION TIME: 20 minutes, plus chilling

MAKES: 1 450g (1lb) loaf

100g (4oz) chocolate shortbread finger biscuits
50g (2oz) whole hazelnuts
100g (4oz) firm margarine
75g (3oz) caster sugar
30ml (2 tblsp) cocoa powder
1 egg, beaten
50g (2oz) sultanas

To Decorate
Icing sugar

Line a 450g (1lb) loaf tin with cling film. Chop up the shortbread fingers. Brown the hazelnuts and rub off the skins. Put the margarine and sugar into a small saucepan and stir over a low heat until the sugar dissolves. Stir the cocoa into the mixture, and remove from the heat. Stir in the egg, hazelnuts, sultanas and chopped biscuits. Pour the mixture into the lined tin and smooth it level. Chill until set. Dust with icing sugar and serve cut in slices.

Chocolate Palmiers

PREPARATION TIME: 30 minutes

COOKING TIME: 12-15 minutes

OVEN TEMPERATURE: 220°C, 425°F, Gas Mark 7

MAKES: 6

225g (8oz) puff pastry
Caster sugar
75g (3oz) plain chocolate, coarsely grated

To decorate
175ml (6 fl oz) double cream, whipped
50g (2oz) strawberries, halved
Icing sugar for dusting

Roll out the pastry on a well-sugared surface to a rectangle measuring approximately 30x20cm (12x10 inches). Sprinkle with the chocolate and press down with a rolling pin. Take the shorter edge of the pastry and roll it up to the centre. Roll the opposite side to meet it at the centre. Moisten with water and press together the adjoining rolls. Cut into 1cm (½ inch) slices and place them cut side down on a dampened baking sheet. Keep them well apart and flatten them a little. Bake in a pre-heated oven for 12-15 minutes, until puffed and golden. (Turn the palmiers over once they begin to brown.) Cool them on a wire rack. Whip the cream and use it to fill a piping bag fitted with a 1cm (½ inch) fluted nozzle. Pipe swirls of cream on half of the palmiers and arrange the fruit on top of the cream. Use the other palmiers to sandwich the fruit. Sprinkle with icing sugar.

Praline Orange Log

PREPARATION TIME: 20-25 minutes, plus chilling

COOKING TIME: 30-35 minutes

OVEN TEMPERATURE: 180°C, 350°F, Gas Mark 4

MAKES: 30 slices

175g (6oz) plain chocolate, chopped or grated
15ml (1 tblsp) strong black coffee
25g (1oz) caster sugar
15ml (1 tblsp) orange liqueur
75g (3oz) butter
2 egg yolks

Praline
175g (6oz) shelled nuts (see below)
225g (8oz) granulated sugar
65ml (2½ fl oz) water
1 egg white, beaten

Use either almonds, hazelnuts, walnuts or pistachio nuts. Use the nuts chopped or whole, with or without the skins, toasted or plain. For praline powder, the nuts must be peeled.

Melt the chocolate in a bowl with the coffee, sugar, orange liqueur and butter, over a low heat. Remove from the heat and allow to cool thoroughly. Stir in the egg yolks. Chill for 3½-4 hours. To make the praline: put the nuts on a baking sheet and warm them in the oven for 10 minutes. Butter a marble slab or large baking sheet. Put the sugar and water into a small, heavy saucepan, stirring until the sugar has dissolved. Bring to the boil and boil until the sugar caramelizes; remove from the heat and plunge the base of the pan into cold water to halt the cooking process. Stir in the nuts. Pour onto the marble or onto a baking sheet. Spread out and leave until set and hard. Put the praline into a strong plastic bag and crush with a rolling pin. To make praline powder, grind it in a coffee grinder. Shape the chilled chocolate mixture into a log, 5cm (2 inches) in diameter. Brush the log with the beaten egg white and roll gently in the crushed praline, pressing firmly with the hands to help the praline stick. Chill the log until very firm. Cut into slices about 5mm (¼ inch) thick.

Chocolate Crunch (top right), Chocolate Palmiers (centre left) and Chocolate Chip Cookies (bottom).

Mint Creams

PREPARATION TIME: 20 minutes, plus setting overnight

MAKES: about 16

The white of 1 egg
1.25ml (¼ tsp) peppermint essence
350g (12oz) icing sugar
100g (4oz) plain or milk chocolate, chopped or grated

Beat the egg white and essence together in a bowl and gradually add the icing sugar. Lightly dust the work surface with extra icing sugar and knead the peppermint icing until smooth. Using plenty of extra icing sugar, roll out the icing to a thickness of about 5mm (¼ inch) and cut out shapes with a 4cm (1½ inch) cutter, either fluted or plain. Place the shaped mints on a baking sheet lined with greaseproof paper, and leave them in a warm place to dry out, preferably overnight. Melt the chocolate; dip the mints in so that half is coated in chocolate. Shake off any excess chocolate and place the mints on a sheet of buttered greaseproof paper or foil until set.

Dominoes

PREPARATION TIME: 25 minutes

COOKING TIME: 10-15 minutes

OVEN TEMPERATURE: 180°C, 350°F, Gas Mark 4

MAKES: about 14

100g (4oz) butter or margarine
100g (4oz) caster sugar
1 egg, beaten
250g (9oz) plain flour
25g (1oz) cocoa powder
Salt

Butter Icing
75g (3oz) butter
175g (6oz) icing sugar, sieved
Few drops of vanilla essence

Cream the butter and sugar together and add the egg. Sieve the flour, cocoa powder and salt together and work into the butter mixture. Knead the dough and roll it out between two sheets of greaseproof paper. Cut out rectangles, about 3x7cm (1¼x2¾ inches). Mark a line across the centre of the biscuits using a skewer. Bake the biscuits on a greased baking sheet for 10-15 minutes. Cool them on a wire rack. To make the icing: soften the butter and beat in the icing sugar. You may need to add a few drops of hot water if the icing is too firm. Add vanilla essence to taste. If you want to sandwich the biscuits together, do so with a little of the butter icing. Pipe the top of the dominoes with dots, using a piping bag fitted with a plain nozzle and filled with the remaining butter icing.

Zigzag Shortbread

PREPARATION TIME: 20 minutes

COOKING TIME: 30-35 minutes

OVEN TEMPERATURE: 160°C, 325°F, Gas Mark 3

MAKES: about 14 fingers

150g (5oz) plain flour
50g (2oz) caster sugar
100g (4oz) butter
15ml (1 tblsp) cocoa powder
15ml (1 tblsp) drinking chocolate

Grease an 18cm (7 inch) square cake tin. Sieve the flour into a bowl, reserving 15g (½oz). Add the sugar. Rub in the butter until it forms a crumble texture. Divide the mixture in half; add the cocoa and the drinking chocolate to one half. Add the remaining flour to the other half. Knead both mixtures to doughs. Turn the chocolate dough onto a lightly floured surface. Roll out and cut into strips 4cm (1½ inches) wide. Do the same with the plain dough. Lay the strips alternately in the tin, in a diagonal pattern, easing them in so that they fit. Bake until lightly crisp but not brown, for 30-35 minutes. Mark out into fingers and leave to cool in the tin. Note: the shortbread trimmings can be cut into small shapes and baked separately for 5 minutes.

Chocolate Whirls

PREPARATION TIME: 10 minutes

COOKING TIME: 15 minutes

OVEN TEMPERATURE: 180°C, 350°F, Gas Mark 4

MAKES: 10

50g (2oz) butter or margarine
25g (1oz) brown sugar
15ml (1 tblsp) black treacle
5ml (1 tsp) cocoa powder
Pinch of salt
100g (4oz) self-raising flour
10 hazelnuts

Grease a baking sheet. Put the butter and sugar into a mixing bowl and beat until soft and creamy. Add the treacle and stir well. Sieve the cocoa powder, flou and salt together and knead into the treacle mixture. Spoon the mixture into small balls on a floured work surface. Roll the ball into long sausage shapes; curve round one end and continue winding the rest of the sausage round so you have a Catherine wheel shape. Place the "wheels" o the baking sheet; push a hazelnut into the centre of each one. Bake for 15 minutes. Cool on a wire ra

This page: Chocolate Whirls (left), Zigzag Shortbread (cent and Dominoes (right).

Facing page: Iced Chocolate (left) and Chocolate Egg Crea Soda (right).

Drinks and Sauces

Iced Chocolate

PREPARATION TIME: 5 minutes, plus chilling

COOKING TIME: 15 minutes

MAKES: 8-10 drinks

175g (6oz) granulated sugar
200ml (⅓ pint) water
40g (1½oz) cocoa powder
Chilled milk

Put the sugar and water into a heavy-based saucepan and stir over a moderate heat until the sugar dissolves. Brush off any sugar crystals that may form on the inside of the pan with a pastry brush dipped in cold water. Raise the heat and boil the syrup until it spins fine threads from a spoon or fork. Remove from the heat. Add the cocoa powder and stir until well mixed over a low heat. Cool the chocolate syrup and chill in the refrigerator until required. To make the drink: put 15ml (1 tblsp) chilled syrup into a jug or blender with 300ml (½ pint) chilled milk and stir or whisk until blended. Pour the chocolate drink over ice cubes in chilled glasses.

Bittersweet Butter Cream

PREPARATION TIME: 15 minutes

MAKES: 400ml (14 fl oz)

300g (10oz) bitter chocolate
350g (12oz) butter softened
350g (12oz) caster sugar
10ml (2 tsp) vanilla essence
3 eggs
45ml (3 tblsp) cocoa powder
5ml (1 tsp) instant coffee powder
10ml (2 tsp) dark rum
Pinch of salt

Melt the chocolate. Beat the butter until creamy and add the sugar and vanilla. Add the eggs, one at a time, beating well after each addition. Stir cocoa and coffee powder into the melted chocolate and add it to the buttercream. Stir in the rum and salt, making sure that all the ingredients are well incorporated. Use to fill Chocolate Raspberry Torte, or other chocolate recipe.

Banana Shake

PREPARATION TIME: 10 minutes
MAKES: 1 drink

45ml (3 tblsp) chocolate ice cream
30ml (2 tblsp) drinking chocolate powder
150ml (¼ pint) milk
1 banana
Ice cubes

Blend together all the ingredients in a blender or food processor, or whisk with a hand whisk (if using a hand whisk, mash the banana first). Serve in a tall glass with ice cubes.

Chocolate Butter Sauce

PREPARATION TIME: 5 minutes
COOKING TIME: 10 minutes
MAKES: 450ml (¾ pint)

250ml (8 fl oz) water
225g (8oz) plain chocolate, chopped or grated
15ml (1 tblsp) brandy
90g (3½oz) butter, cut into small pieces

Put the water, chocolate and brandy into a saucepan. Stir over a low heat until the chocolate has melted. The mixture should be smooth. Remove from the heat and slowly stir in the butter until it melts. The sauce should then become thick and glossy. This sauce can be served hot or cold.

Praline Sauce

PREPARATION TIME: 40 minutes, including making of praline
MAKES: about 300ml (½ pint)

15ml (1 tblsp) cocoa powder
175ml (6oz) canned evaporated milk
75g (3oz) plain chocolate, chopped or grated
60ml (4 tblsp) crushed praline (see recipe)

Whisk together the cocoa and evaporated milk in a small saucepan. Heat the mixture and bring it to the boil. Remove the pan from the heat and stir in the chocolate. Return to the heat and continue stirring over a gentle heat until the chocolate has melted. Add the praline.

Chocolate Toffee Sauce

PREPARATION TIME: 10 minutes
COOKING TIME: 15 minutes
MAKES: about 300ml (½ pint)

100g (4oz) plain chocolate, chopped or grated
85ml (3 fl oz) water
50g (2oz) granulated sugar
45ml (3 tblsp) chilled unsalted butter
5ml (1 tsp) vanilla essence
225g (8oz) nut brittle, broken into small chunks

Using a small, heavy-based saucepan, gently heat the chocolate and water until the chocolate has melted. Stir continuously. Stir in the sugar and continue to heat gently for 2 minutes, until the sugar has dissolved and the mixture has thickened. Remove the sauce from the heat and beat in the butter. Stir in the vanilla and the broken nut brittle. Serve hot. This sauce can be kept in the refrigerator for a few days. To serve warm, heat it gently to a pouring consistency.

Peppermint Sauce

PREPARATION TIME: 15 minutes
MAKES: about 200ml (⅓ pint)

75g (3oz) chocolate covered peppermint creams
150ml (¼ pint) single cream

Break up the peppermint creams and melt over a pan of hot water. Remove from the heat and slowly stir in the cream. Serve the sauce hot or cold with ice cream.

This page: Praline Sauce – shown with Nougat Slice – (top), Bitter Chocolate Sauce – shown with Cherries – (centre right) and Chocolate Butter Sauce (bottom left).

Facing page: Hot Fudge Sauce (left) and Chocolate Toffee Sauce (right).

Chocolate Custard

PREPARATION TIME: 10 minutes
COOKING TIME: 3 minutes
MAKES: about 600ml (1 pint)

45ml (3 tblsp) custard powder
15ml (1 tblsp) caster sugar
600ml (1 pint) milk
100g (4oz) milk chococlate, chopped or grated

Put the custard powder and sugar into a bowl with 30ml (2 tblsp) of the milk; stir it into a paste. Boil the remaining milk and add it to the custard paste, stirring continuously. Return the custard to the saucepan and cook for 1 minute, stirring. Stir in the chocolate until it melts. Serve hot.

Bitter Chocolate Sauce

PREPARATION TIME: 5 minutes
COOKING TIME: 15 minutes
MAKES: 250ml (8 fl oz)

45ml (3 tblsp) strong black coffee
100g (4oz) plain dark chocolate, chopped or grated
120ml (4 fl oz) double cream
85ml (3 fl oz) apricot jam

Put all the ingredients into a small, heavy-based pan. Stir continuously over a low heat until smooth.

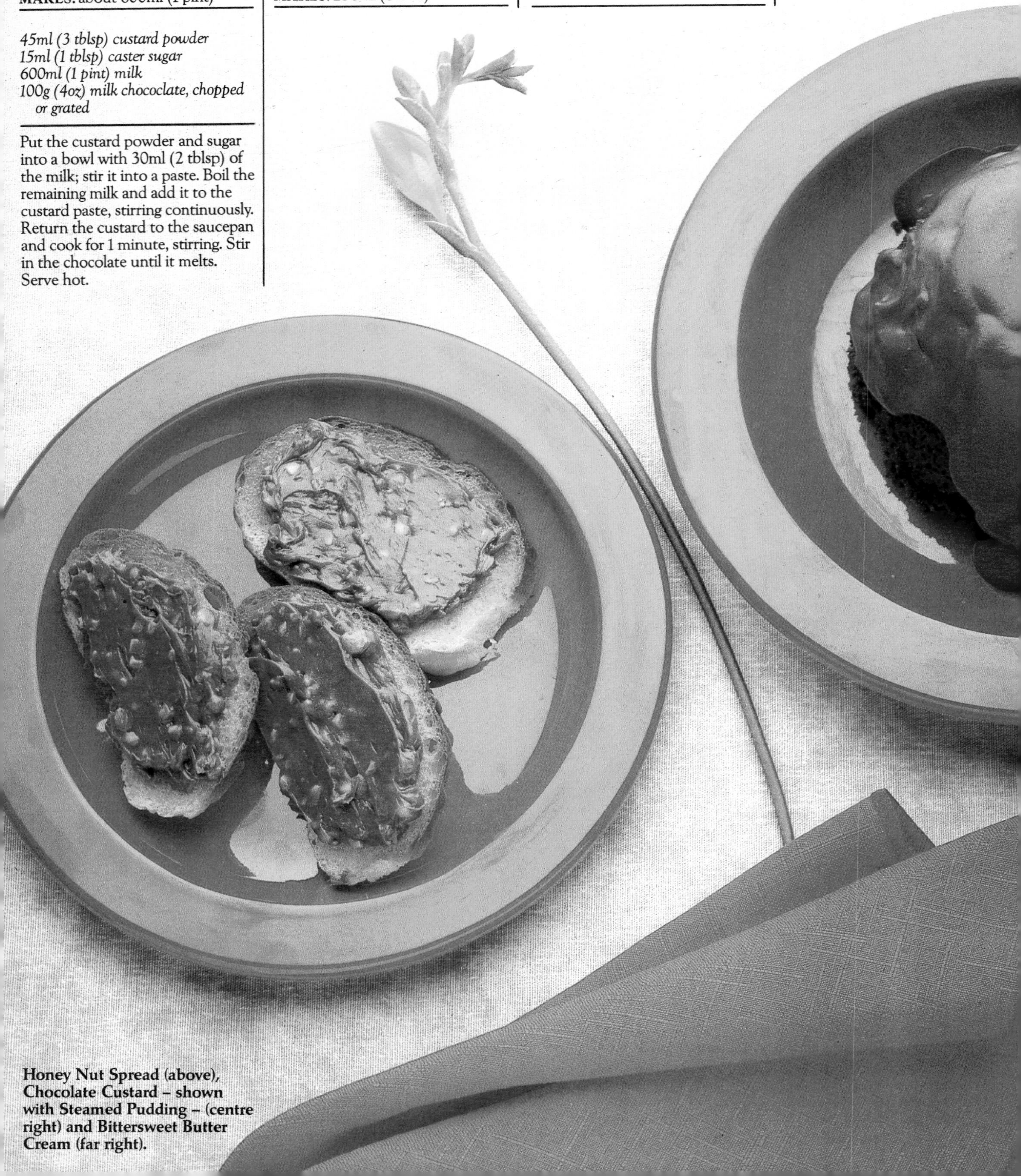

Honey Nut Spread (above), Chocolate Custard – shown with Steamed Pudding – (centre right) and Bittersweet Butter Cream (far right).

Nouvelle Sauce

PREPARATION TIME: 10 minutes
COOKING TIME: 5 minutes
MAKES: 450ml (¾ pint)

This is a thin chocolate sauce which is served slightly cooled.

225g (8oz) plain chocolate, chopped or grated
100g (4oz) granulated sugar
350ml (15 fl oz) water
10ml (2 tsp) brandy

Melt the chocolate with the sugar and water; simmer for 4-5 minutes, stirring continuously. Remove the pan from the heat and let the chocolate mixture cool. Stir in the brandy. Strain the sauce and serve.

Honey Nut Spread

PREPARATION TIME: 10 minutes
MAKES: about 175g (6oz)

50g (2oz) butter, softened
15ml (1 tblsp) cocoa powder
10ml (2 tsp) orange liqueur
30ml (2 tblsp) honey
25g (1oz) icing sugar
50g (2 oz) nuts, chopped

Cream the butter with the cocoa powder and the orange liqueur; beat in the honey and the icing sugar, and then fold in the nuts. This spread is now ready to serve on hot toasted crumpets, or muffins, and is delicious with pancakes.

Chocolate Cream Sauce

PREPARATION TIME: 5 minutes
COOKING TIME: 10-15 minutes
MAKES: 450ml (¾ pint)

300ml (½ pint) double cream
15ml (1 tblsp) brandy
15ml (1 tblsp) strong black coffee
225g (8oz) plain chocolate, chopped or grated

Pour the cream, brandy and coffee into a small, heavy-based saucepan and bring to the boil. Remove from the heat and add the chopped chocolate. Stir the chocolate until it melts and the sauce is smooth. Serve this sauce hot or cold.

Cocoa Rum

PREPARATION TIME: 5 minutes
MAKES: 1 drink

15g (½oz) plain chocolate, chopped or grated
150ml (¼ pint) milk
15ml (1 tblsp) rum
15ml (1 tblsp) whipped cream
Grated nutmeg

Put the chocolate and milk into a saucepan and bring it to the boil. Stir the chocolate milk a few times, and then remove it from the heat. Whisk in the rum and pour into a heatproof glass. Put a spoonful of cream on the top and sprinkle with grated nutmeg.

Malted Chocolate Shake

PREPARATION TIME: 10 minutes, plus chilling
COOKING TIME: 5 minutes
MAKES: 2 drinks

50g (2oz) soft brown sugar
40g (1½oz) cocoa powder
300ml (½ pint) milk
30ml (2 tblsp) vanilla ice cream
15ml (1 tblsp) whisky

Put all the ingredients except the whisky and ice cream into a saucepan and mix well. Bring gently to the boil. Cook gently for 5 minutes, stirring frequently. Remove from the heat and leave to cool. Whisk in the ice cream. Cover and chill in the refrigerator until required. Pour into two glasses and add the whisky.

Chocolate Egg Cream Soda

PREPARATION TIME: 8 minutes
MAKES: 2 drinks

50g (2oz) plain chocolate, melted
1 egg
300ml (½ pint) full cream milk
2 scoops chocolate ice cream
Chilled soda water
2 scoops vanilla ice cream

Put two tall glasses in the freezer until they are frosted. Put the melted chocolate, egg, milk and chocolate ice cream into the liquidiser; blend for 1 minute. Divide this mixture between two glasses; add a scoop of vanilla ice cream to each one and top up with chilled soda water. Serve while it is still frothing.

Hot Fudge Sauce

PREPARATION TIME: 10 minutes
COOKING TIME: 10 minutes
MAKES: about 450ml (¾ pint)

150g (5oz) unsalted butter
50g (2oz) cocoa powder
50g (2oz) plain chocolate, chopped or grated
75g (3oz) granulated sugar
120ml (4 fl oz) evaporated milk
Pinch of salt
A few drops of vanilla essence

Melt the butter in a small, heavy-based saucepan. Remove from h[eat] and add the cocoa powder. Whis[k] until smooth. Stir in the choppe[d] chocolate, sugar and evaporated milk; bring to the boil over a moderate heat, stirring continuously. Remove the sauce from the heat and stir in the salt and vanilla essence. This sauce w[ill] keep in the refrigerator for 2-3 days.

Coffolate

PREPARATION TIME: 10 minut[es,] plus chilling time
COOKING TIME: about 15 minu[tes]
MAKES: 4 drinks

15ml (1 tblsp) cornflour
450ml (¾ pint) boiling coffee
450ml (¾ pint) hot milk
50g (2oz) plain chocolate, choppe[d or] grated
2.5ml (½ tsp) ground cinnamon
100g (4oz) caster sugar

To Decorate
Whipped cream

Mix the cornflour to a paste wit[h a] little of the coffee. Place the hot milk in a bowl over a pan of simmering water (or into a doub[le] boiler). Mix in the cornflour pas[te] and stir well. Add the chocolate, cinnamon, sugar and remaining coffee. Simmer the mixture for 1[0] minutes, beating with a whisk; c[ool] and chill. Serve in tall glasses wit[h] the cream to decorate.

This page, top picture: Cocoa Rum (left) and Coffolate (righ[t]). Bottom picture: Nouvelle Sau[ce] (top left), Chocolate Cream Sauce (top right) and Peppermint Sauce – shown w[ith] Pear Flan – (bottom).

Facing page: Malted Chocola[te] Shake (left) and Banana Shak[e] (right).

SWEET SURPRISE

:hocolate Lime Flan

:EPARATION TIME: 20 minutes

5g (8oz) digestive biscuits
g (3oz) plain chocolate
g (1oz) butter
0g (12oz) white marshmallows
0ml (¼ pint) milk
imes
0ml (5 fl oz) double cream
g (2oz) plain chocolate, grated
e grated rind of 1 lemon
0ml (5 fl oz) double cream, whipped for decoration

ush the biscuits. Melt the ocolate and butter together and x in the biscuits. Lightly grease e sides and base of a 23cm (9 :h) flan dish. Press the biscuit xture onto the base and sides of e dish. Melt the marshmallows in asin over hot water and add the lk. Stir in the juice from one lime d grate the rind. Mix in the non rind, whip the double cream d fold into the marshmallow xture. Pour into the crumb base d leave to set. Decorate the flan th the remaining cream, grated ocolate and slices of the second e.

Cointreau and Mandarin Mousse

PREPARATION TIME: 10 minutes

290g (10½oz) tin of mandarin oranges
1 tablespoon gelatine
4 tablespoons Cointreau or orange liqueur
3 egg yolks
2 tablespoons caster sugar

Strain the mandarins, reserving the juice. Sprinkle the gelatine over the juice. Pour two tablespoons of Cointreau over the mandarins and leave them to soak. Add the remaining Cointreau, egg yolks and sugar to the gelatine. Whisk the egg mixture over a bowl of hot water until thick and frothy (with an electric whisk this should take 4 minutes). Pour into individual glass dishes and chill until set. Spoon the soaked mandarins on top. Serve.

Cheese Mousse with Strawberries

PREPARATION TIME: 45 minutes

200g (7oz) cottage cheese
150g (5oz) strawberries
25g (1oz) icing sugar
2 tablespoons Cointreau or orange liqueur
2 tablespoons lemon juice
2 tablespoons orange juice
1 tablespoon gelatine
150ml (5 fl oz) double cream
6 meringue rosettes

Chocolate Sauce
215g (8oz) plain chocolate
2 tablespoons milk
25g (1oz) butter

Put the cottage cheese into a bowl and add the strawberries, reserving a few strawberries for decoration. Sift the icing sugar over the cheese and sprinkle over the Cointreau. Cover and leave to stand in the fridge for about half an hour. Heat the orange and lemon juice and dissolve the gelatine in it. Whilst the gelatine is still warm, stir in the cheese mixture. Stiffly whip the cream and fold it in. Serve the mousse on the plate and decorate with the reserved strawberries. Serve with some chocolate sauce and meringue rosettes.

Chocolate Sauce
Melt the chololate, milk and butter in a bowl over hot water. Stir rapidly. Serve.

This page: Chocolate Lime Flan.

Facing page: Cointreau and Mandarin Mousse (top) and Cheese Mousse with Strawberries (bottom).

Special Desserts

Ginger Rum Trifle

PREPARATION TIME: 20 minutes

300g (12oz) ginger cake, sliced
300g (12oz) tinned pear quarters
9 tablespoons rum
450ml (¾ pint) cold thick custard
300ml (½ pint) double cream
2-3 teaspoons icing sugar
Toasted flaked almonds
Stem ginger cut into strips

Line the bottom of a glass dish with half the ginger cake. Drain the tinned pears and mix the rum with the juice. Sprinkle half over the cake. Place the pears on the top of the cake and cover with the remaining slices. Pour over a little more rum mixture. Spoon the custard over the cake. Whip the cream and gradually add icing sugar until it peaks. Spoon the cream over the custard and decorate with lightly toasted almond flakes and stem ginger strips.

Lemon Brandy Cream

PREPARATION TIME: 15 minutes

300ml (½ pint) single cream
300ml (½ pint) double cream
75g (3oz) soft brown sugar
2 large lemons
75g (3oz) sponge cake
30ml (2 tablespoons) brandy
25g (1oz) toasted flaked almonds

Mix the single and double cream in a small saucepan and add the sugar. Stir over a low heat until the cream begins to bubble. Grate the rind of the lemons and gently stir into the cream. Leave the mixture to cool and crumble the cake crumbs into glasses or serving dish. Stir the brandy into the cream mixture with the juice from both lemons. Pour the mixture into the glasses or dish over the cake crumbs and refrigerate for 30 minutes. Decorate with toasted almond flakes.

Exotic Fruit Salad Basket

PREPARATION TIME: 15 minutes

1 large melon
1 persimmon
3 kiwi fruit, washed
100g (4oz) blackberries, washed
175g (6oz) raspberries, washed
175g (6oz) redcurrants, washed
175g (6oz) strawberries, washed
175g (6oz) blackcurrants, washed
175g (6oz) grapes, red and green
1 mango, peeled and sliced
Strawberry leaves
Use as many fruits in season as are available
Sugar syrup (see Sauces)

Hollow out a melon and reserve the pulp. Slice the persimmon and kiwi fruit, and make melon balls using the reserved melon. Arrange the fruit in the melon basket and spoon over with sugar syrup (see Sauces).

Inset illustration: Lemon Brandy Cream (left), Berry Whip (right).

These pages: Exotic Fruit Salad (top left), Cranberry Fool (top right) and Ginger Rum Trifle (bottom).

Cranberry Fool, Chilled

PREPARATION TIME: 30 minutes

450g (1lb) cranberries
125g (5oz) sugar
2 tablespoons lemon juice
150ml (5 fl oz) carton soured cream

Bring the cranberries to the boil in 450ml (3/4 pint) water in a saucepan, then simmer for about 15 minutes. Cool and stir in the sugar until dissolved. Purée the mixture until most of it is smooth by rubbing it through a sieve to remove the cranberry skins. Make sure the mixture is cool, stir in the lemon juice, cover and chill. Spoon into serving dish and serve with sour cream.

Berry Whip

PREPARATION TIME: 15 minutes

3 egg whites
A few grains of salt
150g (6oz) icing sugar
200g (8oz) blackberries
Sponge fingers

In a deep bowl whisk the egg whites. Add the sugar and salt and beat until very stiff. Fold in the berries. Spoon into glasses and chill. Serve with sponge fingers.

Cremets

PREPARATION TIME: 10 minutes

300g (12oz) curd cheese
25g (1oz) vanilla sugar or caster sugar with a few drops of vanilla essence
300ml (½ pint) double cream

Beat the curd cheese until smooth. Add the sugar and gradually beat in the cream. Pile into a bowl and chill.

Almond Galette

PREPARATION TIME: 1 hour

COOKING TIME: 10 minutes for each batch of rounds

OVEN: 190°C (375°F) Gas Mark 5

350g (12oz) butter
450g (1lb) caster sugar
2 eggs
300g (11oz) plain flour
2 tablespoons ground almonds
900ml (1½ pints) double or whipping cream, whipped
Icing sugar
Double cream
Whole almonds

Cut out 12 22cm (9 inch) circles of non-stick baking paper. Cream the sugar and butter together and beat in the eggs. Fold in the sifted flour and ground almonds. Divide the mixture into 12 and using a large palette knife coat the individual paper rounds with the mixture. Work from the centre outwards with smooth strokes. Wet a baking sheet and bake the rounds. Leave until cool and carefully peel off the paper. When all the rounds are cooked use them to form layers spreading each one with whipped cream. Reserve 150ml (5 fl oz) of cream for decoration. Dust the top with icing sugar and decorate with almonds and cream.

Blackberry, Raisin and Walnut Jelly

PREPARATION TIME: 10 minutes
Note: In order that the fruit should be plump, soak overnight.

100g (4oz) seedless raisins
2 tablespoons rum
1 packet blackberry jelly
300ml (½ pint) port
400g (1lb) frozen blackberries (keep frozen)
6 walnuts halved
Cream
Flowers

Soak the raisins in the rum for a few hours, preferably overnight. Dissolve the jelly in 300ml (½ pint) of boiling water. Add the port and cool, making sure the jelly does not set. Put the fruit and nuts in individual glasses or a mould making sure they are quite full. Spoon over the jelly and leave to set. Decorate with flowers and/or cream.

French Plum Pudding

PREPARATION TIME: 20 minutes

COOKING TIME: 40 minutes

OVEN: 200°C (400°F) Gas Mark 6

175g (6oz) plain flour
175g (6oz) butter
75g (3oz) caster sugar
50g (2oz) ground almonds
1 egg yolk
1 tablespoon cold water
750g (1½lb) plums, halved and stoned

Sift the flour into a mixing bowl. Rub in two-thirds of the butter and 25g (1oz) of the sugar. Add the ground almonds and mix into a firm dough with the egg yolk and water. Chill. Melt the reserved butter in a 23cm (9 inch) round ovenproof dish. Add the remaining sugar until caramelised. Remove from heat. Arrange the plums, skin side down, in the ovenproof dish. On a lightly floured surface roll out the dough into a round slightly bigger than the dish. Place the dough on top of the plums and gently press down, tucking in the edges as you go. Bake in the oven until golden. To serve turn out onto a serving dish. Serve instantly.

Chocolate Meringues

PREPARATION TIME: 40 minut

COOKING TIME: 2 hours (leave the meringues to cool for long as necessary)

OVEN: 120°C (250°F) Gas Mark

4 egg whites
225g (8oz) caster sugar
50g (2oz) hazelnuts, finely ground
300ml (10 fl oz) double or whippi cream
1 tablespoon cocoa powder
Chocolate curls

Whisk the egg whites until stiff. Gently whisk in the sugar a little a time and fold in the hazelnuts with a metal spoon. Spoon out rounds of meringue onto a bakin sheet lined with non-stick silicon paper or lightly oiled greaseproo paper. Bake until well dried out. Cool on wire racks. Whip the cream until stiff and fold in the cocoa powder. Use the cream to sandwich the meringues and decorate with chocolate shaving or curls.

Coconut Cup

PREPARATION TIME: 35 minut

3 coconuts sawed in half
3 scoops soft-scoop vanilla ice crea per half coconut
3 tablespoons dark rum
450g (1lb) dried mixed fruit

Soak fruit in rum overnight. Saw coconuts in half and remove the flesh. Grate half the flesh, and incorporate in the ice cream alon with the fruit, reserving some of the fruit for decoration. Fill coconut halves with mixture and place in freezer until firm. To serv top with remaining fruit and grat coconut.

This page: Cremet (left), Almond Galette (right).

Facing page: Blackberry, Raisin and Walnut Jelly (to right), French Plum Puddin (centre left) and Chocolate Meringues (bottom).

Blackberry Ice Cream Dessert

PREPARATION TIME: 20 minutes plus freezing time

75g (3oz) sugar
1½ tablespoons Curaçao
300g (11oz) blackberry purée
175ml (6 fl oz) low-fat plain yogurt
Generous pinch of cinnamon
150ml (¼ pint) double or whipping cream, whipped
150ml (5 fl oz) water

Boil the sugar with the water for a minute and add the Curaçao. Stir in the blackberry purée (rub the fruit through a nylon sieve). Stir in the yogurt and cinnamon, and lastly fold in the whipped cream. Freeze until creamy and serve.

Kiwi Cheesecake

PREPARATION TIME: 45 minutes
COOKING TIME: 20 minutes
OVEN: 180°C (350°F) Gas Mark 4

Base
50g (2oz) soft margarine
50g (2oz) caster sugar
1 egg
65g (2½oz) self raising flour
½ level teaspoon baking powder
Finely grated rind of ½ medium orange

Filling
150g (6oz) cream cheese
50g (2oz) caster sugar
3 eggs, separated
Juice of 1 medium orange
Finely grated rind of ½ medium orange
15g (½oz) gelatine
4 tablespoons cold water
125g (5oz) natural yogurt
150ml (¼ pint) whipping cream

To decorate
150ml (¼ pint) whipped cream
3 kiwi fruit, peeled and sliced
Nuts

Base
Grease and line the base and sides of a 20cm (8 inch) loose bottom cake tin with greaseproof paper. Note: The paper should come over the top of the tin. In a mixing bowl add the margarine, egg and caster sugar and cream the mixture until fluffy. Sieve the flour and baking powder into the bowl and beat. Add the orange rind. Use either a wooden spoon or electric whisk for two or one minute respectively. Spoon the mixture into the cake tin and cook for 20 minutes, 180°C (350°F) Gas Mark 4. Leave in tin when cooked and allow to cool.

Filling
While the base is cooking, beat the sugar with cream cheese and add the egg yolks, orange juice and rind. Beat until very smooth. In a heatproof basin put the cold water and sprinkle in the gelatine, leaving it to stand for 10 minutes until soft. Stand the basin in a pan of simmering water until gelatine dissolves. Stir constantly. Leave to cool but not set. Pour the gelatine in a constant stream into the cheese mixture and stir. Whisk in the yogurt. Whip the cream and fold carefully into the mixture using a metal spoon. Whisk the egg whites in a clean bowl until stiff and fold into cheese mixture. Pour the cheese mixture over the base and smooth the top. Leave to set in the fridge for several hours.

To decorate
Remove from the tin and carefully peel off the paper, serve decorated with cream, kiwi fruit and nuts (an alternative could be orange segments). Serve chilled.

Poached Minty Pears

PREPARATION TIME: 40 minutes plus chilling

6 large pears, peeled
6 tablespoons sugar
Fresh mint leaves
6 tablespoons clear honey
3 tablespoons Creme de Menthe liqueur

Put the pears in a saucepan. Star upright and pour water over. Cover all the pears. Boil and the simmer for 30 minutes. Pour off half the water and sprinkle over with sugar. Add the fresh mint a simmer for 10 minutes. Transfer pears to a bowl. Reserve 150ml (pint) water from the pan and sti the honey and liqueur. Pour this mixture over the pears and allow to cool. Cover the pears and chi for 2 hours. Stand each pear on individual serving dish and spoo over the mint sauce.

This page: Blackberry Ice Cream Dessert (top), Cocon Cups (bottom).

Facing page: Kiwi Cheesecake (top), Poached Minty Pear (bottom).

Coffee Truffles

PREPARATION TIME: 10 minutes

200-225g (8oz) cake crumbs
25g (1oz) ground almonds
¼ teaspoon coffee powder
Heaped tablespoon apricot jam, melted
2-3 tablespoons coffee liqueur
50g (2oz) chocolate vermicelli

Put the crumbs and ground almonds into a bowl. Mix in the jam and coffee liqueur and mix together to form a stiff paste. Shape into small balls and roll in chocolate vermicelli.

Crystal Fruits

1 egg white
200g (8oz) bunch of grapes
2 large red apples
2 large pears
100g (4oz) plums
Any other soft fruit in season

Whisk up the egg white well and brush onto the fruit. Leave for a few minutes but not until dry. Dip the fruit into caster sugar and place on greaseproof paper until dry. Arrange in fruit bowl or stand.

Apricot Mountain

PREPARATION TIME: 20 minutes
COOKING TIME: 4 minutes or until meringue is brown
OVEN: 230°C (450°F) Gas Mark 8

About 350g (¾lb) tinned apricot halves
4-6 tablespoons Marsala or sweet sherry
3 egg whites
100g (4oz) caster sugar
1 x 20cm (8 inch) sponge flan case
450ml (¾ pint) vanilla ice cream

Strain the apricots and sprinkle them with the sherry. Whisk the egg whites until stiff and fold in the sugar. Whisk again until the meringue peaks. Stand the flan case on a heatproof dish and sprinkle with a little more sherry. Pile the apricots into the flan case. Cover the apricots with a mountain shape of ice cream. Using the meringue mixture, quickly cover the ice cream and the sponge base. Bake immediately until the meringue is light brown. Serve from the oven. For a very special effect bury half an egg shell at the top of the mountain before baking the meringue. As you serve fill it with warmed brandy, ignite and serve flaming.

Petits Fours

PREPARATION TIME: 40 minutes
OVEN: 200°C (400°F) Gas Mark 6

Sponge
3 eggs
125g (4oz) caster sugar
75g (3oz) plain flour
1 tablespoon hot water

Topping
Fruits in season
Apricot jam to glaze

Sponge
Whisk eggs and sugar until thick and creamy. Sift in flour and fold in with the hot water. Place mixture in a greased and floured swiss roll tin. Bake for 8 to 10 minutes until cake springs back when pressed. Turn out and cool. Cut shapes out of the sponge using pastry cutters.

Topping
Place sponge shapes on a wire rack and top with attractively arranged fruit. Melt apricot jam on low heat and spoon over shapes to glaze. When surplus has dripped off and jam has set remove and place on serving plate.

Chocolate Leaf, Filled with Orange Mousse

PREPARATION TIME: 1 hour plus chilling

For the Leaf
175g (6oz) plain chocolate
1 cabbage leaf (with veins)

Mousse
3 whole eggs plus 2 yolks
50g (2oz) caster sugar
Juice of ½ lemon
15g (½oz) powdered gelatine
150ml (¼ pint) double cream
150ml (¼ pint) freshly squeezed orange juice
Finely grated rind of 2 oranges

Leaf
Put the chocolate in a basin over simmering water and stir until smooth. With a pastry brush, paint the chocolate over a well-veined cabbage leaf and leave to cool and harden. Repeat the process until there is a thick build up of chocolate on the leaf. When hard the cabbage leaf can be easily removed.

Mousse
Put the eggs and yolks in a basin with the caster sugar. Whisk until pale and frothy. This can be done over a saucepan of simmering water, but make sure that the basin doesn't touch the water. Beat until thick. Remove from the heat and whisk until cold. Put the lemon juice and a little water into a small saucepan and sprinkle in the gelatine and leave it to soak for a few minutes. Whip the cream and stir it into the egg mixture, gradually adding the orange juice and grated rind. Gently heat the gelatine until clear and stir it quickly into the mixture. Fill the serving dish and refrigerate until set. This mousse can either be served with one leaf or several small leaves to go with each portion of mousse.

Crystal Fruits (left), Coffee Truffles (bottom left) and Petits Fours (bottom right).

Fruit Salad with Mango Purée

PREPARATION TIME: 20 minutes plus 1 hour chilling in the refrigerator

3 peaches
3 tamarillos (tree tomatoes)
3 kiwi fruit
1½ tablespoons lemon juice
3 tablespoons sugar syrup

Mango Purée
2 well-ripened mangoes weighing about 300g (12oz)
Juice of ½ a lime, or lemon
3 teaspoons honey
125g (5oz) redcurrants
Strawberry leaves for decoration

Blanch the peaches briefly and peel. Halve and remove stones and cut into delicate wedges. Peel and slice the tamarillos, nectarines and kiwi fruit, arrange in serving dish and scatter over with redcurrants. Pour over the lemon juice mixed with sugar syrup. Leave the fruits to stand in syrup for 1 hour in a cool place.

Mango Purée
Either liquidise or rub through a wire sieve the flesh of the mangoes and mix with the lime juice. Mix in the honey and pour the mixture over the fruit. Decorate with strawberry leaves.

Pineapple Malibu

PREPARATION TIME: 30 minutes

1 medium ripe pineapple
450ml (15 fl oz) double cream
75g (3oz) macaroons, roughly crushed
3 tablespoons coconut liqueur

Cut the pineapple a few inches below the top. Scoop out as much of the fruit as possible, discarding the core if hard. Chop the fruit into bite-size pieces. Whip two-thirds of the cream until it begins to stiffen and fold in the macaroons, having first soaked them in the coconut liqueur. In another bowl whip up the remaining cream and fold into the coconut cream. Spoon alternate spoonfuls of diced pineapple and cream mixture into the hollowed pineapple and chill. Serve straight from the fridge.

Chocolate Ginger Flan

PREPARATION TIME: 30 minutes

100g (4oz) plain chocolate
300ml (½ pint) milk
100g (4oz) caster sugar
3 tablespoons flour
100g (4oz) butter
2 egg yolks
150g (6oz) ginger nut biscuits
Whipped cream
100g (4oz) stem ginger cut into thin slices

Melt the chocolate in the milk in a saucepan, stirring constantly. Remove pan from heat. Mix the caster sugar, flour and 50g (2oz) butter into the chocolate milk and stir in the egg yolks. Put on a low heat and slowly bring to the boil. Simmer for 5 minutes until the mixture begins to thicken, stir until smooth. Remove from heat and cool. While the filling is cooling, melt the remaining 50g (2oz) of butter and crush the ginger nut biscuits. Mix the biscuits with the melted butter and press in a greased pie mould. When the filling is cool, pour onto the ginger nut base. Chill and decorate with whipped cream and sprinkle with stemmed ginger cut into thin slices (an alternative decoration is chocolate vermicelli).

Coffee Charlotte

PREPARATION TIME: 1½ hours
COOKING TIME: 12 minutes
OVEN: 220°C (475°F) Gas Mark

Sponge
4 egg yolks
50g (2oz) sugar
Generous pinch of salt
3 egg whites
60g (2½oz) flour mixed with 2 teaspoons coffee powder

75g (6oz) apricot jam
tablespoons brandy
tablespoons cornflour

Charlotte
apricot halves
tablespoon vanilla sugar
tablespoon brandy
egg yolks
0g (4oz) sugar
us 1 tablespoon sugar
0ml (8 fl oz) milk
vanilla pod
g (½oz) powdered gelatine
0ml (8 fl oz) double or whipping cream
ml (2½ fl oz) apricot glaze (warmed apricot jam)

Sponge
Beat the egg yolks with a spoonful of sugar and the salt. Whisk the egg whites and fold the egg yolk mixture into the meringue. Sift together the cornflour and flour and stir them in. Line a swiss roll tin with non-stick silicone paper or greaseproof paper. Spread the sponge mixture evenly in the swiss roll tin using a spatula. Bake until golden. Turn it out at once onto a damp tea towel and peel off the paper. Blend the jam with the brandy and spread the sponge cake with it. Roll it up. Let it cool and cut into thin slices 5mm (¼ inch) thick. Line the mould with the slices as close together as possible.

Charlotte
Place the apricot halves in a dish and sprinkle them with vanilla sugar. Pour over the brandy. Leave them to marinate in the refrigerator for half an hour. Cream the egg yolks and sugar together in a mixing bowl and put the milk in a small saucepan with the vanilla pod. Heat the milk and bring to the boil and pour into the egg yolks. Return the custard mixture to the saucepan and stir until it is thick enough to coat the spoon. Remove from heat. Dissolve the gelatine in warm water and stir in the tablespoon of brandy. Add to the custard mixture and stir well. Cool the custard. Meanwhile stiffly whip the cream, adding the remaining sugar. When the custard begins to set, carefully fold in the cream and fill the sponge-lined mould. Stir in the marinated apricot and cover the top of the mould with slices from the sponge roll. Let the charlotte set for three hours in the refrigerator and turn onto a serving dish. Brush with the apricot glaze.

Orange Campari Mousse

PREPARATION TIME: 45 minutes plus chilling

1 teaspoon powdered gelatine
2 medium oranges, washed and dried
75g (3oz) caster sugar
2 eggs, separated
3 tablespoons Campari
150ml (¼ pint) double cream
1 tablespoon cold milk
Red grapes

Add gelatine to two tablespoons of water in a saucepan. Leave to one side. Grate peel of 1 orange. Squeeze oranges and if necessary make up juice to 175ml (6 fl oz) with water. Melt gelatine and water over a low heat. Stir in orange juice. Pour mixture into a bowl, whisk in sugar, egg yolks, Campari and orange peel. Place in fridge until the mixture begins to thicken and set. In one bowl beat egg whites until stiff. In another whisk milk and cream together thick. Gradually mix egg whites and cream alternately into the orange mixture until totally incorporated. Pour into a bowl and place in refrigerator until firm and set. Serve in glasses decorated with sliced red grapes.

Facing page: Apricot Mountain (left), Orange Campari Mousse (right).

This page: Chocolate Leaf, Filled with Orange Mousse (top), Chocolate Ginger Flan (centre left) and Fruit Salad with Mango Purée (bottom right).

Chestnut Parfait

PREPARATION TIME: 40 minutes plus freezing

4 egg yolks
150g (5oz) sugar
150ml (¼ pint) milk, warmed and flavoured with a vanilla pod
200g (7oz) unsweetened chestnut purée
2 tablespoons dark rum
2 egg whites
50g (2oz) sugar
500ml (17 fl oz) double cream
Chocolate leaves
A few cranberries
Whipped cream

Beat the egg yolks with the sugar and add the warmed milk flavoured with the vanilla pod and cook until thickened, stirring gently. The mixture should coat the spoon. Transfer to a mixing bowl. Add the chestnut purée and rum while the mixture is still lukewarm. Chill well. Whip the egg whites with the sugar until very stiff. Whisk the cream until it peaks. Fold the egg white into the chestnut custard and carefully fold in the whipped cream. Pour into a 1.5 litre (2¾ pint) mould and freeze for 4 hours. Decorate with small rounds of sweetened chestnut purée dusted with chocolate powder or melted chocolate sauce.

Strawberry Shortcake

PREPARATION TIME: 1 hour
COOKING TIME: 25 minutes
OVEN: 220°C (425°F) Gas Mark 7

Shortcake
225g (8oz) plain flour
Pinch of salt
4 teaspoons baking powder
75g (3oz) butter
1 large egg
40g (1½oz) caster sugar
3 tablespoons milk
1 tablespoon melted butter

Filling
1 tablespoon custard powder
300ml (½ pint) milk
2 tablespoons sugar
150ml (¼ pint) double cream
450g (1lb) fresh or thawed, frozen strawberries
8 toasted almonds

Shortcake
Sift the flour, salt and baking powder into a bowl. With a knife mix in the butter. Beat in the egg, sugar and milk and pour into the centre of the dry ingredients. Mix into a dough. On a lightly floured surface knead gently and divide into two. Brush a 20cm (8 inch) sandwich tin with melted butter and shape half the dough into a circle to fit. Place the second circle on top and bake until risen and golden brown. Cool and separate the two halves.

Filling
Make up the custard using the milk and sugar. Cover and leave to cool. Whisk the cream until just stiff. Fold the cream into the cooled custard, reserving two tablespoons for decoration. Reserving 8 whole strawberries and one-third of the custard mixture, halve the remaining strawberries and mix into the custard cream. Spread the strawberry custard on the bottom layer of the shortbread and sandwich with the top layer. Spread the top with the reserved custard mixture and decorate with whole strawberries and almonds.

Green Devils

PREPARATION TIME: 20 minutes plus chilling

600g (1½lb) dessert gooseberries
150g (6oz) caster sugar
600ml (1 pint) water
3 tablespoons grenadine
Juice ½ lemon
1 level tablespoon cornflour
Cream

Rinse and top and tail the gooseberries. Put the caster sugar in a small saucepan and dissolve it in the water. Simmer and bring to the boil. Take off heat and stir in the grenadine, lemon juice and gooseberries and bring back to simmer. Cook very gently for five minutes until the fruit is tender. Remove from heat. Lift out the fruit and put into the serving dish. Mix the cornflour with a little water to make a thin paste. Stir into the fruit juice till it begins to thicken. Stir all the time. When the syrup is clear, pour over the fruit. Chill, preferably overnight, and serve with thick pouring cream.

Facing page: Pineapple Malibu (top), Coffee Charlotte (centre right) and Chestnut Parfait (bottom).

This page: Green Devils (top), Strawberry Shortcake (bottom).

CAKES AND CAKE DECORATION

Introduction

Cake decorating is both rewarding and interesting. It is hoped that this section of the book will show how simple it can be and encourage those who use it to improve on their basic skills.

Starting with the simplest icings, such as butter icing, which is easy to use and can create elaborate novelty cakes, the more complex techniques required to master the icing and decoration of wedding and other celebration cakes are gradually introduced.

Always try to avoid last-minute rushes; many of the decorations can be made in advance and stored. Try to plan ahead when you know that you will be making a special cake and remember that icing and decorating can take time and patience. If you have not had much practice, start with the simpler designs before trying to tackle a royal-icing celebration cake. You will be anxious that the result should be stunning, so practice first!

Never pipe the design straight onto the cake, as you may ruin the surface you have created. If you are using a complex design, pipe first in white icing then overpipe in colour. This way, if you make a mistake, you have not stained the surface of the cake. The cakes described here will certainly give you some new ideas and may encourage you to design versions of your own.

Cakes and their decoration is an absorbing hobby. By following and practising some of the designs suggested, it is hoped you will be able to produce a highly professional result – cakes for every occasion.

Note:
All eggs are size 2.
All spoon measures are level in both imperial and metric sizes. Some spoon measures even supply a spoon equivalent to a pinch.
Metric and imperial measurements have been calculated separately. Only use one set of measurements – they are not interchangeable.
Cooking times may vary as they depend upon the efficiency of your oven. Dishes should always be placed in the centre of the oven unless otherwise stated.
Fan-assisted ovens may cook slightly quicker, so follow the manufacturer's instructions. Always preheat the oven to the specified temperature.

Basic Cakes and Icing

Lining Cake Tins

All tins must be greased and lined unless you are using a non-stick cake tin, in which case follow the manufacturer's instructions.
If using a shallow tin, only the base needs to be lined for whisked sponges and the quick cake mixture.
If you are making a fruit cake, which will take longer to bake, then the sides as well as the base need lining using a double thickness of greaseproof paper.

To Grease the Tin

Brush with melted lard, margarine or oil. Grease the greaseproof paper with melted fat or oil; if you are using non-stick silicone paper do not grease it. In the preparation of tins, it is necessary to grease and dust them with flour if you are not lining them.

Round Tins

To line a deep, round tin, draw with a pencil round the edge of the cake tin on double thickness greaseproof paper and cut the resulting shape out.
Using a piece of string, measure round the tin. Use another piece of string to measure the height plus 2.5cm (1 inch). Cut out one long strip or two shorter lengths of greaseproof paper to the equivalent of these measurements. If making two lengths, add on a little extra for them to overlap. Make a fold 5mm (¼ inch) deep along one edge and cut into the fold at regular intervals at a slight angle. Place one of the circles of paper in the bottom of the tin, followed by the side pieces and, finally, the second paper circle which will cover the slashed edges.

Square Tins

To line a deep, square tin follow the instructions above for a round tin, but fold the long strips so they fit into the corners of the tin.

Rich Fruit Cake

CAKE SIZES	12cm (5in) round 10cm (4in) square	15cm (6in) round 12cm (5in) square	18cm (7in) round 15cm (6in) square	20cm (8in) round 18cm (7in) square	23cm (9in) round 20cm (8in) square	25cm (10in) r 23cm (9in) sc
APPROX COOKING TIME:	2½ hours	2¾ hours	3¼ hours	3¼ hours	4 hours	4¼-4½ hours
OVEN:	140°C/275°F Gas Mark 1	140°C/275°F Gas Mark 1	140°C/275°F Gas Mark 1	140°C/275°F Gas Mark 1	140°C/275°F Gas Mark 1	140°C/275°F Gas Mark 1
	Note for all recipes: First ⅔ of cooking time at 150°C/300°F Gas Mark 2					
Butter	65g/2½oz	75g/3oz	125g/4oz	150g/5oz	200g/7oz	250g/9oz
Eggs	2	2	3	4	5	6
Plain flour	75g/3oz	125g/4oz	175g/6oz	200g/7oz	250g/9oz	300g/11oz
Dark soft brown sugar	75g/3oz	90g/3½oz	150g/5oz	175g/6oz	225g/8oz	275g/10oz
Black treacle	½ tblsp	½ tblsp	1 tblsp	1 tblsp	1 tblsp	1 tblsp
Ground almonds	25g/1oz	25g/1oz	40g/1½oz	50g/2oz	65g/2½oz	75g/3oz
Ground mixed spice	½ tsp	½ tsp	¾ tsp	1 tsp	1¼ tsp	1½ tsp
Grated lemon rind	½ lemon	½ lemon	1 lemon	1 lemon	1 lemon	2 lemons
Grated orange rind	½ orange	½ orange	1 orange	1 orange	1 orange	2 oranges
Grated nutmeg	¼ tsp	¼ tsp	¼ tsp	½ tsp	½ tsp	¾ tsp
Chopped almonds	25g/1oz	40g/1½oz	50g/2oz	65g/2½ oz	90g/3½oz	125g/4oz
Currants	150g/5oz	175g/6oz	225g/8oz	275g/10oz	375g/13oz	450g/1lb
Raisins	25g/1oz	50g/2oz	75g/3oz	125g/4oz	150g/5oz	175g/6oz
Sultanas	75g/3oz	125g/4oz	150g/5oz	200g/7oz	250g/9oz	300g/11oz
Chopped mixed peel	25g/1oz	40g/1½oz	50g/2oz	65g/2½oz	90g/3½oz	125g/4oz
Glacé cherries	25g/1oz	40g/1½oz	50g/2oz	65g/2½oz	90g/3½oz	125g/4oz
Orange juice	1 tblsp	1 tblsp	1 tblsp	1 tblsp	2 tblsp	2 tblsp
Brandy	1 tblsp	1 tblsp	1 tblsp	2 tblsp	2 tblsp	3 tblsp

Swiss Roll Tins (Long, Shallow Tins)
Grease and line a shallow tin so that the cake may be easily removed. Line the sides of the tin with paper at least 4cm (1½ inches) longer than the tin, cutting into each corner.

Loaf Tins
When lining a loaf tin the method is again the same, but the paper should be 15cm (6 inches) larger than the top of the tin.

cm (11in) round	30cm (12in) round
cm (10in) square	28cm (11in) square
5¼ hours	6 hours
0°C/275°F s Mark 1	140°C/275°F Gas Mark 1
e note opposite	
0g/11oz	375g/13oz
	8
0g/14oz	450g/1lb
0g/12oz	400g/14oz
tblsp	2 tblsp
g/3½oz	125g/4oz
tsp	2 tsp
mons	2 lemons
anges	2 oranges
sp	1 tsp
g/5oz	175g/6oz
g/1¼lb	675g/1½lb
g/7oz	225g/8oz
g/13oz	450g/1lb
g/5oz	175g/6oz
g/5oz	175g/6oz
sp	3 tblsp
sp	4 tblsp

Oiling and lining cake tins.

Rich Fruit Cake

This is a traditional recipe which cuts well and is rich, dark and moist. Traditional fruit cake improves with keeping and is used for celebration cakes – weddings, birthdays and Christmas – marzipanned and royal iced.
Prepacked dried fruit is ready washed, but if you are buying your fruit loose, rinse it through with cold water and dry it well with kitchen paper or clean cloths. Then spread it out on a tea towel placed on a baking sheet in a warm (not hot) place for 24 hours. Do not use wet fruit in a cake as the fruit will sink.
Mix the sultanas, currants and raisins together. Cut the glacé cherries into quarters, rinse in warm water and dry with kitchen paper. Add the cherries to the fruit together with mixed peel, almonds, and grated orange and lemon rind.

Sift the flour with a pinch of salt, ground cinnamon and mixed spice. Cream the butter until soft, then add the sugar and cream until light and fluffy (do not overbeat). Add the eggs one at a time, beat well and after each egg add a spoonful of flour. Add the black treacle, orange juice and brandy, if desired. Spread the mixture evenly into a greased and double-lined tin. Use the back of a spoon to make a slight hollow in the centre of the cake so it will be flat when cooked. Tie two thicknesses of brown paper round the tin then bake in the centre of the oven at 150°C, 300°F, Gas Mark 2 (see chart for the suggested time). With large cakes turn the oven down to 140°C, 275°F, Gas Mark 1, after two-thirds of the cooking time. To test the cake, push a skewer into the centre. It should come out clean if the cake is cooked. When the cake is cooked, remove the tin from the oven and leave the cake in the tin to cool. Turn the cake onto a wire rack and remove the lining paper. Spike the top of the cake with a skewer and spoon a few tablespoons of brandy or other spirit over the top. To store the cake, wrap it in greaseproof paper and foil. If possible, repeat the spooning over of brandy or spirit every few weeks. The cake can be allowed to mature for 2-3 months.

Quick Mix Cake

This is a quick cake, which is ideal for novelty cakes, and the mixture is firm enough to cut into any shape; it is moist and crumbly and can be filled with cream, butter or jam.
Put the margarine, sugar, eggs, sifted flour and baking powder in a bowl. Mix together all the ingredients with either a wooden spoon or electric mixer. Beat for 1-2 minutes until the mixture is smooth and glossy. In a food processor this will take 30 seconds-1 minute. Put the mixture in a prepared tin. Level the top with the back of a spoon and bake in the centre of the oven at 160°C, 325°F, Gas Mark 3 (see chart for the suggested time). When baked, the cake will be firm to the touch and shrink away from the sides of the tin. Loosen the sides of the cake from the tin and leave it to cool on a wire rack. Turn the cake right way up onto another wire rack.

Whisked Sponge Cake

This cake mixture is ideal for afternoon tea and the cake may be filled with cream, butter icing or fruit. It does not keep well and is best eaten the same day it is made, although it can be kept in the freezer for up to 2 months.
Put the eggs and sugar in a

heatproof bowl over a saucepan of hot, not boiling, water. The bowl must not touch the water. Whisk the mixture until it becomes thick enough to leave a trail when lifted. Sift the flour and baking powder together and fold into the egg mixture with a metal spoon, taking care not to knock the air out. Pour the mixture into a prepared tin and gently shake the mixture level. Bake in the centre of the oven (see chart for oven temperature and suggested time). Remove from the tin and cool on a wire rack. When making a Swiss roll, turn out the cake onto a sheet of greaseproof paper sprinkled with caster sugar. Quickly peel off the lining paper and trim the cake edges. Fold and roll the cake up without cracking it. Let it cool a little, then unroll and remove the greaseproof paper. Fill and re-roll the cake.

Madeira Cake

Madeira cake is a moist cake that can be covered with marzipan and then iced with royal icing or any other icing.

PREPARATION TIME: 15 minutes

COOKING TIME: 1 hour 15 minutes to 1 hour 30 minutes

OVEN TEMPERATURE: 160°C, 325°F, Gas Mark 3

175g (6oz) butter
175g (6oz) caster sugar
Grated rind of 1 lemon
3 eggs
225g (8oz) plain flour
7.5ml (1½ tsp) baking powder
30ml (2 tblsp) warm water

Cream the butter and sugar until they are light and fluffy. Beat the eggs in one at a time, then after each egg add a spoonful of flour. Sift in the remaining flour and fold it into the flour with lemon rind and juice. Turn into a prepared cake tin and bake in the oven for 1¼-1½ hours. When cooked, the cake should be firm to the touch. Leave it in the tin to cool for 5-10 minutes, then turn onto a wire rack and remove the lining paper.

Whisked Sponge Cake

CAKE SIZES	2 x 18cm (7in) sandwich tins	20cm (8in) sandwich tin 18cm (7in) square tin	28 x 18cm (11 x 7in) Swiss roll tin	18 sponge drops	20cm (8in) round cake tin	2 x 20cm (8i sandwich tir
APPROX COOKING TIME:	20-25 minutes	25-30 minutes	10-12 minutes	5-10 minutes	35-40 minutes	20-25 minut
OVEN:	180°C/350°F Gas Mark 4	180°C/350°F Gas Mark 4	190°C/375°F Gas Mark 5	190°C/375°F Gas Mark 5	180°C/350°F Gas Mark 4	180°C/350°F Gas Mark 4
Eggs (sizes 1-2)	2	2	2	2	3	3
Caster sugar	50g/2oz	50g/2oz	50g/2oz	50g/2oz	75g/3oz	75g/3oz
Plain flour	50g/2oz	50g/2oz	50g/2oz	50g/2oz	75g/3oz	75g/3oz
Baking powder	½ tsp	½ tsp	½ tsp	½ tsp	½ tsp	½ tsp

Quick Mix Cake

CAKE SIZES	2 x 18cm (7in) sandwich tins	18 paper cake cases or patty tins	20cm (8in) sandwich tin 20cm (8in) ring mould 18cm (7in) deep square tin	*900ml (1½ pint) pudding basin **add 25g/1oz cornflour sifted with the flour*	About 26 paper cake cases or patty tins	2 x 20cm (8 sandwich ti
APPROX COOKING TIME:	25-30 minutes	15-20 minutes	35-40 minutes	about 50 minutes	15-20 minutes	30-35 min
OVEN:	160°C/325°F Gas Mark 3	160°C/325°F Gas Mark 3	160°C/325°F Gas Mark 3	160°C/325°F Gas Mark 3	160°C/325°F Gas Mark 3	160°C/325 Gas Mark
Soft tub margarine, chilled	100g/4oz	100g/4oz	100g/4oz	100g/4oz	175g/6oz	175g/6oz
Caster sugar	100g/4oz	100g/4oz	100g/4oz	100g/4oz	175g/6oz	175g/6oz
Eggs (sizes 1-2)	2	2	2	2	3	3
Self-raising flour	100g/4oz	100g/4oz	100g/4oz	100g/4oz	175g/6oz	175g/6oz
Baking powder	1 tsp	1 tsp	1 tsp	1 tsp	1½ tsp	1½ tsp
Vanilla essence	4 drops	4 drops	4 drops	4 drops	6 drops	6 drops

or Victoria Sponge see 'Tea ime Treats'.

ariations

hocolate Victoria Sponge
eplace 25g (1oz) flour with 25g oz) sifted cocoa powder. Add this the other flour.

offee Victoria Sponge
eplace the water with coffee sence, or dissolve 10ml (2 tsp) stant coffee powder in 15ml (1 sp) boiling water.

emon Victoria Sponge
dd the very finely grated rind of 1 non.

18 x 4cm 7 x 1½in) cake	30 x 23cm (12 x 9in) Swiss roll tin
5 minutes	12-15 minutes
C/350°F Mark 4	200°C/400°F Gas Mark 6
	3
3oz	75g/3oz
3oz	75g/3oz
)	½ tsp

ı (9in) wich tin	28 x 18 x 4cm (11 x 7 x 1½in) slab cake 20cm (8in) round tin 20cm (8in) square tin	1 litre (2 pint) pudding basin	29 x 21 x 4cm (11½ x 8½ x 1½in) slab cake	23cm (9in) round tin 23cm (9in) square tin	30 x 25 x 5cm (12 x 10 x 2in) slab cake
t 25 minutes	35-40 minutes	about 1 hour	about 40 minutes	about 1 hour	50-60 minutes
C/325°F Mark 3	160°C/325°F Gas Mark 3	160°C/325°F Gas Mark 3	160°C/325°F Gas Mark 3	160°C/325°F Gas Mark 3	160°C/325°F Gas Mark 3
/6oz	175g/6oz	175g/6oz	200g/8oz	200g/8oz	275g/10oz
/6oz	175g/6oz	175g/6oz	200g/8oz	200g/8oz	275g/10oz
	3	3	4	4	5
/6oz	175g/6oz	175g/6oz	200g/8oz	200g/8oz	275g/10oz
p	1½ tsp	1½ tsp	2 tsp	2 tsp	2½ tsp
ps	6 drops	6 drops	8 drops	8 drops	10 drops

Basic Icing Recipes and Their Uses

Quick Frosting

This is an easy white frosting which is a quick version of the traditional American frosting. A sugar thermometer is not required for this recipe, but the icing must be used very quickly before it sets.

PREPARATION TIME: 7-10 minutes

1 egg white
150g (6oz) caster sugar
Pinch of salt
30ml (2 tblsp) water
Pinch of cream of tartar

Put all the ingredients into a heatproof bowl and mix. Put the bowl over a pan of simmering hot water and beat the mixture. If possible, use an electric mixer until the icing peaks. Remove the icing from the heat and pour it over the cake, spreading it quickly. This will cover an 18cm (7 inch) cake.

Chocolate Fudge Icing

PREPARATION TIME: 10 minutes

This is a delicious chocolate icing which is quick and easy to make.

50g (2oz) butter
45ml (3 tblsp) milk
250g (8oz) icing sugar, well sifted
30ml (2 tblsp) cocoa powder, sifted

Melt the butter in a small saucepan with the milk. Add the icing sugar and cocoa and beat well until smooth and very glossy. Cool until lukewarm and pour over cake. This is enough to fill and ice the top of a 20cm (8 inch) cake.
NB: if the icing is too thick to pour, reheat gently to thin. This icing can also be made in a small bowl over a pan of gently simmering water.

Sponges: Whisked Sponge, Madeira Cake.

Marzipan or Almond Paste

This is a paste which is made firm and rollable, and is traditionally used as a base cover for fruit cakes before coating with royal icing or any other decorative icing.
Prepare the cake by levelling the top, if necessary. Dust a work surface with icing sugar and roll out half the almond paste 2.5cm (1 inch) larger than the top of the cake. Brush the top of the cake with the apricot glaze, or the egg white and brandy. Invert the cake onto the almond paste and, using a palette knife, draw up the top of the almond paste around the cake. Put the top of the cake down on a board and brush the sides of the cake with apricot glaze. Cut two pieces of string or thread, one the height of the cake and the other equal in length to the circumference. Roll out the remaining almond paste into a strip, equal in height and length of circumference of the cake, using the strings as a guide, or cut two short strips of paste instead. Carefully wrap the almond paste round the cake, pressing firmly round the sides and joins. For a square cake, cut the string into four lengths, equal to the sides of the cake and cut the paste to match. Press lightly on the paste when it is placed round the cake in order to produce sharp corners. When covered, leave the cake for 24 hours to dry. Wedding cakes should be left for up to 1 week before icing, otherwise almond oil will stain the icing if the cake is kept after the wedding.

Marzipan or Almond Paste

PREPARATION TIME: 15 minutes

100g (4oz) caster sugar
100g (4oz) icing sugar
200g (8oz) ground almonds
5ml (1 tsp) lemon juice
A few drops almond essence
1 or 2 egg yolks, beaten

Mix the sugars and the ground almonds in a bowl. Make a well in the centre and add the lemon juice, almond essence and egg yolk or yolks to the mixture and form into a pliable dough. Lightly dust the work surface with icing sugar and turn out the dough. Knead until smooth. The marzipan can be stored in a polythene bag or wrapped in foil for 2-3 days before use. Makes 450g (1lb).

Guide to Almond Paste Quantities Required for Cakes

Square	Round	Paste / marzipan
12.5cm (5 inch)	15cm (6 inch)	350g (12oz)
15cm (6 inch)	18cm (7 inch)	550g (1lb 4oz)
18cm (7 inch)	20cm (8 inch)	675g (1½lb)
20cm (8 inch)	23cm (9 inch)	675g (1½lb)
23cm (9 inch)	25cm (10 inch)	900g (2lb)
25cm (10 inch)	28cm (11 inch)	1kg (2¼lb)
28cm (11 inch)	30cm (12 inch)	1.25kg (2½lb)
30cm (12 inch)		1.5kg (3lb)

Apricot Glaze

PREPARATION TIME: 10 minutes

This glaze can be stored in an airtight container for up to 1 week, if kept in the refrigerator. Re-boil the glaze and cool before applying to the cake.

175-225g (6-8oz) apricot jam
30ml (2 tblsp) water

Put the jam and water in a saucepan and heat until the jam has melted, stirring occasionally. Pour the jam through a sieve and return it to a clean saucepan. Re-boil and simmer until you have a slightly thickened consistency. Cool before applying to the cake.

How to Royal Ice

It does not matter whether you ice the top or the sides first. The important point to remember is that the icing should be applied in several thin coats. Try icing a section first, rather than doing all of it in one go. Your aim is to achieve a smooth surface and you must let each coat dry before applying another. Most cakes require 2 coats on the top and sides, with maybe 3 on the top for a very smooth finish. Wedding cakes require three coats all over and the bottom tiers need 4 coats. For a 2 or 3-tier cake apply 4 coats to the bottom tier; for a 4-tier cake apply 4 coats to the bottom 2 tiers.

Method for Icing a Cake – Icing the Sides of a Round Cake

A flat-sided scraper is essential for producing smooth sides. Put plenty of icing on the side of the cake and, using a small palette knife, move it back and forth to get a relatively smooth surface and to remove little air pockets. For round cakes, put your arm round the back of the cake and move the scraper forwards on the cake as you can try to get a smooth, sweeping movement without stopping. The scraper should be upright against the side of the cake. Move the scraper off the cake at an angle so the join is not noticeable. If you use a turntable, it will make icing larger cakes easier. Hold the scraper to the side of the cake and use the other hand round the cake so the turntable moves round quickly and smoothly in one revolution. Scrape off any extra icing with a small palette knife. Wipe the cake board and allow each coat to dry for 2-3 hours or overnight before icing the top.

Icing the Top

When icing the base tier of a wedding cake, remember not to add glycerine. Spread the icing on the cake and, using a metal, or firm, plastic, ruler held at a 30° angle, draw it gently across the cake with a positive movement. Try not to press down too hard or the icing will be too thin. Remove any surplus icing from the sides of the cake with a clean palette knife. Leave the icing for at least a day to dry. Remove any rough edges round the joins with clean, fine-graded sandpaper. If the coating is not enough, repeat this 2-3 times. Wait 24 hours before piping decoration onto the cake.

Icing a Square Cake

Ice 2 opposite sides first, then the other 2 sides to produce sharp corners. Hold the palette knife parallel with the side of the cake when icing.

Royal Icing

The consistency of royal icing depends upon its use. For rosett and flat icing it should be quite firm, whereas for piping latticew and writing it should be a little thinner. When icing is required any flooding and runouts, it sho be thin and smooth. Royal icing can be made in any quantity in proportion of 1 egg per 225g (8 of sieved icing sugar. Keep the i bowl covered with a damp cloth keep it moist. As an egg substitu egg albumen (white) can be bou in specialist cake decoration sho and the instructions for use are given on the packet. The additi of glycerine will aid the softenin the icing when it is dry. This ma it easier to cut.

Wedding Cakes

When icing wedding cakes, do add glycerine to the two top lay of icing on the bottom tier, so t cake can support the other tiers Made icing can be stored in an airtight container in a cool atmosphere for 2 days. Before u the stored icing should be stirre well.
Beat the egg whites until frothy with a wire whisk, making sure the bowl is clean and dry first. Gradually beat in half the icing sugar using a wooden spoon. Be in the remaining half of the icin sugar with the glycerine and, if using lemon juice, add it now. B the mixture thoroughly until smooth and white. Beat in enou icing sugar to give the mixture a consistency which is stiff and stands in peaks. Add the colour, required. Cover the bowl with a damp cloth and leave the icing t stand for several hours. This all any air bubbles to rise to the surface of the icing and burst. Before using, stir well with a wooden spoon. Do not overbea Note: if you are using an electric mixer, use the slowest speed and leave the icing for 24 hours. It w incorporate more air and will ne longer to stand.

Facing page: covering with marzipan, and using apricot glaze.

Guide to Royal Icing Quantities Required to Flat Ice in Two Thin Coats

Square	Round	Icing Sugar
12.5cm (5 inch)	15cm (6 inch)	675g (1½lb)
15cm (6 inch)	18cm (7 inch)	900g (2lb)
18cm (7 inch)	20cm (8 inch)	1.25kg (2½lb)
20cm (8 inch)	23cm (9 inch)	1.5kg (3lb)
23cm (9 inch)	25cm (10 inch)	1.6kg (3½lb)
25cm (10 inch)	28cm (11 inch)	1.6kg (3½lb)
28cm (11 inch)	30cm (12 inch)	2kg (4½lb)
30cm (12 inch)	2kg (4½lb)	

Moulding Icing

PREPARATION TIME: 20 minutes

This is also known as kneaded fondant. It is very easy to use and can be rolled out like pastry. It is ideal for covering novelty cakes and even rich fruit cake. The icing sets and becomes firm. Moulding icing can be used to cover a cake directly or over almond paste or marzipan. If using marzipan first, allow the paste to dry before covering with the icing, which can also be used to make flowers and other decorations.

450g (1lb) icing sugar
1 egg white
50g (2oz) liquid glucose
Food colouring or flavouring, if desired

Sift the icing sugar into a mixing bowl and add the egg white and the liquid glucose to the centre of the sugar. Beat the ingredients with a wooden spoon, gradually incorporating the icing sugar to result in a stiff mixture. Knead the icing until you have a pliable paste. This icing can be stored by placing it into a bag, or wrapping it in cling film, or sealing it in a plastic container and storing it in a cool place for up to 3 days. If adding a colour, sprinkle with a little more sifted icing sugar to keep the icing the same consistency.

To Apply Moulding or Gelatine Icing
Attach the icing by first brushing either the cake with apricot glaze or the marzipan with egg white. Roll out the icing on a surface dusted with icing sugar or cornflour, or between two sheets of dusted polythene. Roll out the icing at least 7.5cm (3 inches) larger than the top of the cake. Support the icing on a rolling pin and drape it over the cake. Dust your hands with cornflour or icing sugar and rub the surface of the cake, working in circular movements with the palms of your hands to make the icing thinner and ease down the sides of the cake. Smooth out any folds in the icing and cut off the excess. If icing a square cake, mould the corners so that the square keeps it shape. Leave to dry.
NB: liquid glucose is available from chemists.

Gelatine Icing

PREPARATION TIME: 20 minutes

This icing can be used in the same way as moulding icing, but when it dries it becomes quite brittle. The icing can be used to make decorations such as flowers and leaves.

10ml (2 tsp) gelatine powder
30ml (2 tblsp) water to dissolve the gelatine
450g (1lb) icing sugar
1 egg white

Put the gelatine powder into the water, which is contained in a small heatproof basin held over a saucepan of hot water. Stir until the gelatine has dissolved. Sift the icing sugar into another bowl and add the dissolved gelatine and egg white. Stir well until firm, then knead with the fingers until smooth. Dust with extra icing sugar, if necessary. If adding food colouring, sprinkle with more icing sugar to keep the icing to the same consistency. This icing can be stored for 2 to 3 days before use. To do so, wrap it in cling film or a polythene bag and keep it in a sealed container. If it begins to dry, place or keep the icing in its sealed polythene bag and dip briefly in hot water. Leave for 1 hour and knead well before use.

Glacé Icing

PREPARATION TIME: 10 minutes

Probably the quickest icing to make, it is used on sponges, small cakes and biscuits. To keep the icing liquid, place the bowl over a pan of hot water.

250g (8oz) icing sugar
30ml (2 tblsp) warm water
Various flavourings and colourings

Sift the icing sugar into a mixing bowl and gradually add the water. The icing should be thick enough to coat the back of a spoon when it is withdrawn from the mixture. Add the flavouring and the colouring, if desired. This quantity will ice 18 small cakes and half the amount will ice the top of a 20cm (8 inch) cake.

Variations

Coffee
Replace 15ml (1 tblsp) warm water with 15ml (1 tblsp) coffee essence.

Orange or Lemon
Replace 15ml (1 tblsp) warm water with 15ml (1 tblsp) orange or lemon juice. Add the grated rind of one orange or lemon and a few drops of food colouring.

Chocolate
Sift 45ml (3 tblsp) cocoa powder with the icing sugar.
NB: you must be careful not to keep the icing in too hot a bowl of water, otherwise it will lose its gloss. Also, if a newly-iced cake is moved around without being given a chance to set, the glacé icing could crack and spoil the smooth surface.

Buttercream Icing

This icing is good for covering sponge and quick cake mixture cakes. Butter icing is ideal for covering novelty cakes, as it can be flavoured and coloured easily and is no problem to pipe.

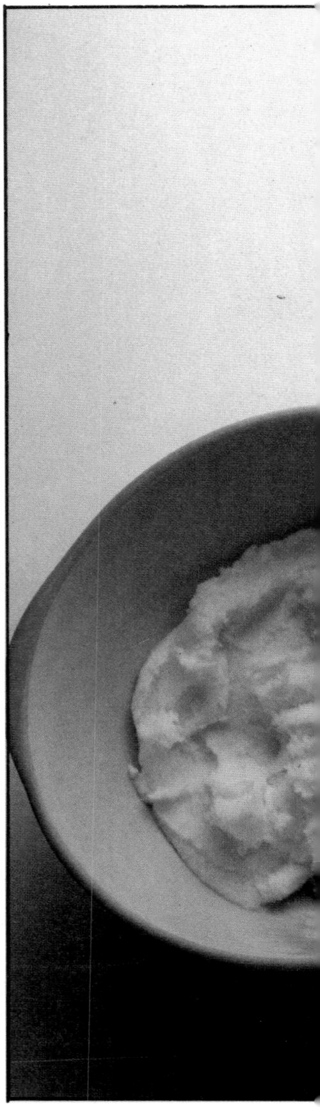

PREPARATION TIME: 10 minu

125g (4oz) butter
225g (8oz) sifted icing sugar
30ml (2 tblsp) milk
Flavourings (see 'Variations')

Beat the butter and some of the icing sugar until smooth. Add t remaining icing sugar with the r and flavouring. Beat until cream This icing will cover and fill a 2C (8 inch) sandwich cake. Store ir airtight container in the refrigerator, for several weeks if necessary.

Variations

Lemon or Orange
Add the grated rind of 1 lemon orange to the butter. Replace tl milk with lemon or orange juic Add a few drops of orange or lemon colouring.

Moulding icing, Royal icing, Butter icing, American frosting and Buttercream icing.

hocolate
end 30ml (2 tblsp) cocoa powder
th 30ml (2 tblsp) boiling water.
ool, then add to the mixture with
ml (1 tblsp) milk.

offee
place 15ml (1 tblsp) milk with
ml (1 tblsp) coffee essence.

rème au Beurre

PARATION TIME: 15 minutes

g whites
g (4oz) icing sugar, sifted
g (4oz) unsalted butter
ourings (see 'Variations')

e the egg whites and icing sugar bowl over a pan of simmering r. Whisk until the mixture ds its shape. Cool. Cream the butter until soft then beat into the egg white mixture, a little at a time. Flavour or colour as required.

Variations

Chocolate
Melt 50g (2oz) plain chocolate in a bowl over a pan of hot water. Cool and beat into the egg white mixture.

Coffee
Add 15ml (1 tblsp) coffee essence to the egg white mixture.

Praline
Gently heat 50g (2oz) of both caster sugar and blanched almonds in a small pan until the sugar turns brown round the nuts. Turn the mixture onto an oiled baking sheet, cool and crush with a rolling pin. Add the 45ml (3 tblsp) of this crushed praline to the egg white mixture.

NB: this icing can be stored in an airtight container in the refrigerator for several weeks.

Confectioner's Custard

PREPARATION TIME: 10-15 minutes

3 egg yolks
50g (2oz) caster sugar
25g (1oz) plain flour
300ml (½ pint) milk
25g (1oz) butter
10ml (1 dsp) sherry

Put the egg yolks and sugar in a bowl and beat until smooth and creamy. Stir in flour and mix well. Heat the milk until hot, but not boiling, and stir into the egg mixture. Return the mixture to the pan and stir, bringing it gently to the boil. Remove from the heat and beat in the butter and the sherry. Pour into a bowl, stirring occasionally to prevent a skin forming. Makes 450ml (¾ pint) of custard.
NB: the custard can be stored in the refrigerator for up to 48 hours.

Basic Equipment and Practising Skills
You will probably have most of the basic pieces of equipment needed for decorating simple cakes: various-sized bowls and basins, measuring jugs, measuring spoons, wooden spoons, spatula, pastry brush, rolling pin, kitchen scales, airtight containers, cocktail sticks, artist's brush and a skewer, to name but a few. However, special icing equipment is often required, so it is wise to invest in a good, basic selection. You can extend your

range as the need arises. Palette knives are ideal for smoothing and spreading icing. They come in various sizes and one would prove most useful. An icing ruler is essential for flat icing the tops of cakes. Choose a firm, not flexible, ruler – at least 30cm (12 inches long, but preferably 36cm (14 inches). An icing rule is even better. An icing turntable is invaluable for icing and decorating large cakes. There are several types of icing scrapers and these are used for pulling round the sides of the cake until it is smooth. Icing cones come into the same category and have serrated teeth of various sizes.

Piping Nozzles

Piping nozzles come in various forms, the metal types giving the best definition. Try to start with a few basic nozzles. The range available starts from size 00. A basic icing-nozzle kit should consist of a fine, a medium and a thick writing nozzle; a shell nozzle; a leaf and a scroll nozzle; a ribbon nozzle (which is also used for basketwork); a forget-me-not and an 8-point and 10-point star nozzle.

Nozzles are available in two styles: plain or screw-on types. Screw-on nozzles are used in conjunction with nylon piping bags and a screw connector. Plain nozzles can be used with paper or nylon icing bags. With this type of nozzle remember that the icing has to be removed in order to change a nozzle. You can either make your own, or use a nylon piping bag or icing pump.

To make a paper icing bag, cut a piece of good quality greaseproof paper or non-stick silicone paper into a 25cm (10 inch) square. Fold in half to form a triangle. Fold the triangle in half to make a yet smaller triangle. Open out the smaller triangle and re-shape into a cone. Turn over the points of the cone so that it stays conical. Secure the join with a little sticky tape. Cut about 1cm (½ inch) off the tip of the bag and push in a nozzle.

Nylon Piping Bags

Nylon bags are sold in various sizes and can be easily filled. These bags are used with a screw connector. The connector is pushed into the bag and protrudes through the hole at the tip of the bag. This allows the nozzle to be placed at the end and secured with a screw-on attachment, allowing the nozzle to be changed without emptying the piping bag.

Nylon piping bags are most useful for gâteaux as they can be filled with cream, and a meringue nozzle (a large decorative nozzle) can be attached to pipe rosettes.

Icing Pumps

These are bought as part of an icing set; some are made of metal and others of plastic. They consist of a tube with a screw attachment for the screw-on type of nozzle. The icing is controlled with a plunger and is unscrewed to refill the tube. Unfortunately, they are difficult to use for delicate work and you cannot feel the movement of the icing to help control it.

Piping Decorations

Stars

Stars, for example, can be piped with various-shaped nozzles ranging from 5 to 8, or more, points. With the 5-point star, use a nozzle number 13 or 8. These are the most useful sizes. Place the star nozzle in the bag and fill with icing. Hold the bag upright and pipe out enough icing to form a star. Remove the nozzle from the surface of the piped star swiftly. Stars should be fairly flat without a point in the centre.

Rosettes

These are piped with a star nozzle, but using a circular movement. Start at one side of the circle and finish slightly higher than the surface of the icing in the middle of the circle.

Shell

Use either a star nozzle or a special shell nozzle No. 12. Shell nozzles give fatter shells. Hold the icing bag at an angle to the surface on which the shell is required and start piping towards the centre of where the shell will rest. First move the nozzle away from you and then towards you. Push out more icing for the thicker parts of the shell. Link the shells together by starting the second shell over the tail of the first.

Leaves

Use a leaf nozzle, which is No. 10 and has a pointed tip, or sometimes an indentation in the centre of the point. Leaves can be piped straight onto the cake, or on non-stick silicone paper, left to dry and then placed onto the cake for decoration. When piping you can make two or three overlapping movements to give the leaf some form.

Basket Weaving

See 'Tracy Rose Wedding Cake'.

Templates

These are patterns made of paper or card which are used to transfer the pattern onto the top of a cake. It is easy to create your own or, for simple decorations, i.e. circles and squares, draw round a saucepan lid or plastic storage container. On the 21st birthday cake we use a round template. Draw a circle the size required onto a piece of greaseproof paper and cut it out with a pair of scissors.

Fold the circle in half, into quarters and into eighths, ending with a flattened cone shape. Draw a line in a concave shape from one point to another and cut it out. When the circle is opened, the edge of it will be scallop shaped.

Piped Flowers

Use a large, medium or fine petal nozzle, depending on the size of flower required, and an icing nail, or a piece of waxed paper cut into squares and attached to a cork. Once piped, leave the flowers to dry for at least 1 day before transferring them to a cake.

Rose

Hold the piping bag with the thin part of the nozzle upright. Pipe a cone of icing, twisting the nail quickly through the fingers and thumb. Pipe three, four or five petals round the centre of the rose by curving them outwards.

Forget-me-nots

Pipe these straight onto the cake, using a No. 2 writing nozzle for the petals, by joining five or six dots together round the edge of the piping nail and piping a curved petal in the centre. Alternatively use a forget-me-not nozzle.

Holly Leaves

Colour some marzipan green and roll out onto waxed paper and cut into rectangles. Using an icing nozzle, cut each holly leaf into shape by cutting first two corners of the rectangle and working your way down the sides until you have a holly leaf shape. Mark the 'veins' with a knife point. Roll out a little more marzipan and colour it red for the holly berries.

Christmas Roses

Cover the top of an essence bottle with a little foil and take a piece of moulding icing the size of a pea and dip it into cornflour and roll it into a ball. Shape another piece into a petal (see 'Moulded Roses'). Repeat until you have five petals. Place the small ball in the foil and surround it with the petals, overlapping them. Leave to dry. Remove from the foil and paint th centre yellow with a little food colouring.

Mistletoe

Roll out a little moulding icing, or marzipan, coloured green. Cut int tongue shapes and round the end Mark a definite vein down the middle of the leaf with a knife and leave it to dry. Make small, pea-sized balls out of either natural marzipan or white moulding icing.

Moulded Roses

Make a cone with a little coloured moulded icing and press it out at the base so that it stands. Place a piece of icing the size of a pea in a little cornflour and roll it into a ba Using a hard-boiled egg, flatten th icing in your hand with quick strokes. Use more cornflour if it gets too sticky. Gently try to get the icing very thin. Carefully wra the petals round the cone and tu the edges outwards. Repeat the process until a fully shaped rose i achieved. Leave the rose to dry a cut off the base. It may be necessary to use a cocktail stick t curl the petals.

Chocolate Leaves

Break the chocolate into small pieces and place in a bowl over a pan of hot water. Gently heat ur the chocolate melts. Do not overheat the chocolate or let an water dilute it. With an artist's small paintbrush, making sure tl the chocolate spreads evenly ov the surface of the leaf, paint the underside of the freshly-picked, undamaged and washed rose le Allow the chocolate to set and, when hard, carefully peel the le away from the chocolate, startir from the tip.

Facing page: a variety of cak decorations.

Novelty Cakes

These are fun cakes enjoyed by all ages, but particularly by children. There follows a variety of designs which can be used for every occasion. It is suggested that you use the quick cake mixture or maderia cake for these. Hopefully this will inspire you to design your own novelty cakes which might be more appropriate for a specific occasion. If you find it difficult to find a cake board for an unusual cake, make your own by covering a sheet of thick card with silver foil.

Birthday Box

30x25x5cm (12x10x2 inch) quick mix cake
Recipe apricot glaze
225g (8oz) marzipan (optional) – this makes the cake a little smoother
Recipe moulding icing
Thin 30x25cm (12x10 inch) cake board or piece of thick card
Food colouring – yellow
225g (8oz) sweets
225g (8oz) royal icing
Egg white, beaten, for attaching moulding icing

Put the cake on a larger cake board. Brush with apricot glaze and cover, if desired, with a thin layer of marzipan. Colour the moulding icing and save 100g (4oz) in a plastic bag. Brush the cake with egg white, roll out the moulding icing and use it to cover the marzipanned cake. With a knife or ruler press lines diagonally into the icing. Roll out the reserved 100g (4oz) of moulding icing and cove the white side of a thin, rectangu silver cake board (the same size a the top of the cake). Fit a piping bag with a small star nozzle and f with royal icing. Pipe shells rounc the bottom edge of the cake. Put the lid on a basin and pipe shells round the edge of the lid. Decora the lid with either fresh or piped flowers and a bow secured with royal icing. Place the sweets on to of the cake and put the lid on, leaving them partially revealed.

Clown

450g (1lb) moulding icing
75g (3oz) coloured pale orange
175g (6oz) coloured yellow
150g (5oz) coloured red
50g (2oz) coloured green
1 large Swiss roll
4 small Swiss rolls
2 sponge fingers (boudoir biscuits)
1 marshmallow
1 recipe apricot glaze
1 recipe royal icing, coloured red

Using the orange moulding icing, break off 2 small rounds and gen flatten them. Make 4 cuts halfwa into the balls, to make fingers. R out the remaining orange icing in a strip which is 20.5x7.5cm (8x3 inches). Brush the end of the Sw roll with the apricot glaze and us the orange strip to cover the end of the Swiss roll. Brush the rest o the Swiss roll with the glaze and with a third of the yellow icing rolled out into a strip 20.5x12.5c (8x5 inches), cover the glazed ar of the Swiss roll. Squeeze the joi of the yellow and orange icing so forms a head and body. Stand th Swiss roll upright on a cake boar with something for support. Put the small Swiss rolls lengthways f the legs and brush with glaze. Ta a small ball of yellow moulding icing and roll it out into a

This page: Birthday Box.

Facing page: Clown.

10x2.5cm (4x1 inch) width. Divide it into 2 and cut slashes in each halfway up. These will be used for the hair (reserve). Brush the sponge fingers with glaze and cover them with yellow fondant. Stick them with jam onto the sides of the body. Roll out the remaining yellow icing into a strip 20.5x12.5cm (8x5 inches) and cut it down the middle. Use each strip to cover the legs. Roll out a small piece of red icing and mould it over the marshmallow and leave to dry. Roll out 2 pea-sized balls of red icing and use them as buttons. Roll out another small piece of red icing and cut with a pastry cutter. Divide the green icing into two balls, rolling out one and cutting with the same round pastry cutter. Using a cocktail stick, create folds in the circles which radiate from the centre. Work your way round. Cut one of the circles in two and the other into four. Roll out the red icing into an oblong 18x7.5cm (7x3 inches) and attach it to the legs in thin strips. Using the reserved green icing, flatten it a little and cut it into two, shaping each half into an oval. Stick them upright on to the end of the legs as boots. Put half red and half green frills round the neck of the clown, securing them with a little apricot glaze. Put quarter frills round his wrists and ankles, with a little glaze to attach them to the hands. Secure the hair to his head with glaze. Do the same with the hat. Fill a piping bag fitted with a writing nozzle with the red icing and pipe his features onto his face. Surround him with sweets or put ballons in his hand.

Giant Sandwich Cake

30x25x5cm (12x10x2 inch) quick mix cake
Food colourings – brown, green, yellow, pink, red
Recipe moulding icing
Egg white to brush marzipan
½ x recipe butter cream icing
225g (8oz) marzipan, if required

Cut the cake diagonally so you have 2 triangles. Colour half of the icing pale brown. Divide a further quarter into four and colour the pieces green, yellow, salmon pink and red. Remember to keep icing in a plastic bag when you are not using it to prevent it drying out. For the lettuce, roll out an irregular shape with the green icing and crinkle it up using a cocktail stick so it looks like ruched material. Reserve on a sheet of non-stick silicone paper. To make the ham, roll out the pink icing with a pinch of white icing, making sure the colours stay separate. Roll out into an oval shape and reserve. For the cheese, roll the yellow icing into a 10cm (4 inch) square and reserve. For the tomato slices, roll the red icing into a 10cm (4 inch) square and with a small, plain round pastry cutter cut rounds. Roll out the pale brown icing into 6 strips all 5cm (2 inches) wide: two 30cm (12 inches) long, two 25cm (10 inches) long, two 40cm (16 inches) long. Use the egg white and brush the sides of the triangles. Stick the brown strips onto the appropriate length sides. The longest strips go along the cut diagonally. Roll out the remaining white icing into a triangle large enough to cover the top of one triangular cake piece. Brush the top of the cake triangle and fix on the moulding icing triangle. Spread the top of the other cake, the one without white moulding icing, with a little butter icing to make the bottom half of the sandwich and make sure it is on either a presentation plate or a cake board. Round the edges of the bottom triangle lay the lettuce, ham, tomato and cheese so they spill out of the cake. Sandwich together with the iced triangle. Fit a piping bag with a star nozzle and fill with the remaining butter icing. Pipe irregular swirls in between the lettuce, tomato, cheese and ham. Dust the top of the triangular cake with a little icing sugar.

Birthday Breakfast

Rich fruit cake (measure the size of your frying pan and bake a cake that will fit)
Recipe apricot glaze
100g (4oz) white moulding icing
Food colourings – brown, pink
425g (15oz) tin apricot halves

Transfer the fruit cake to the frying pan. Brush the top with apricot glaze. Roll out the white moulding icing and cut into several irregular shapes, rounding off any sharp corners. Roll the remaining icing into sausage shapes and brush them with a little brown and pink food colouring. Drain the tin of apricot halves. Place the irregular white moulding icing shapes on top of the cake, putting an inverted apricot half on each one. Put the sausages in the pan. Brush the sausages and the apricot halves with a little apricot glaze.

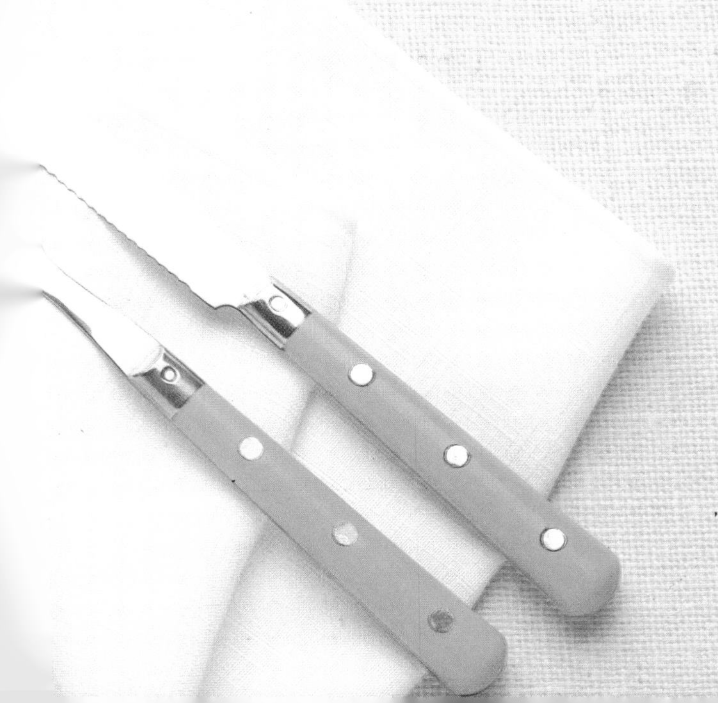

Giant Sandwich Cake (top left) and Birthday Breakfast (bottom left).

Camelot Castle

20cm (8 inch) square 6-egg Victoria sponge
Recipe butter cream icing
Recipe apricot glaze
4 ice-cream cones
4 miniature Swiss rolls
1 rectangular plain biscuit
1 water biscuit
100g (4oz) granulated sugar
100g (4oz) moulding icing
Recipe royal icing
Sugar flowers
Silver balls
3 or 4 small sandwich flags
Food colourings – pink, green, red

Toffee Water (To Fill Moat)
225g (8oz) granulated sugar
150ml (5 fl oz) water
Blue food colouring
Sugar thermometer, if available

Cut a 5cm (2 inch) wide slice from a cake. Put the other cake towards the back of the cake board. Sandwich the large section of cake to the cake on the board with some butter icing. Make sure it sits towards the back of the base cake. With apricot glaze, secure the 5cm (2 inch) slice on the front edge of the cake board. Using apricot glaze, brush the ends of the small Swiss rolls and place them in the four corners of the cake, placing the ice-cream cones on top. Cover the small Swiss rolls, ice-cream cones and the top and sides of the cake with butter icing. Also ice the 5cm (2 inch) slice. Put the water biscuit on the front side of the cake between the 2 Swiss roll towers. Put the granulated sugar, with a few drops of pink food colouring, in a bowl and stir well until the sugar takes up the colour. Sprinkle the coloured sugar over the ice-cream cones, the top of the castle and the grounds. Fit a star nozzle to a piping bag and fill with royal icing. Pipe round the top of the castle walls and over the front surface of the water biscuit. When the piped stars are just drying, go round the top of the walls and pipe another row of stars on top of each alternate star. Put a silver ball in the centre of each of the stars round the edge of the door and 2 for doorknobs. Colour a little of the royal icing green, and a little red, and pipe the green vine with red stars for flowers. You can also use sugar flowers.

To Make the Water to Fill the Moat
Colour the moulding icing green and roll it out to form a long sausage which will go round the

edge of the board. Use the icing to form a wall and stick it down by smoothing it onto the board, then leave it to dry for one hour. Heat the sugar and water so the sugar dissolves and boils. Continue to boil the mixture until it reaches 'soft crack' point, that is, just before it starts to colour. If a sugar thermometer is available, the reading should be 132-143°C, 270-290°F. Pour the sugar mixture into the moat. Put the sugar flowers on the green banks of the moat and lay the biscuit across from the castle to the land to form a drawbridge. Use the flags to decorate.

Ballet Shoes

2 Swiss rolls
30cm (12 inch) square cake board
900g (2lb) fondant icing
Food colouring – pink
Recipe apricot glaze
Cornflour to dust
60ml (4 tblsp) jam
1 metre (1 yard) pink satin ribbon (as an alternative to fondant ribbons)

To Make Shoes
Cut the edge of one end of the cake into a point. Then cut the tip of the point. This will be the toe end of the shoe. Repeat for the other shoe and place them both on the cake board. Cut the other end of the cake, rounding it slightly. Cut out a long oval towards the heel end of the cake. Press the cake in firmly, but gently, to create an instep. Colour all the fondant pale pink. Brush the cake with the glaze. Roll out the fondant on the cornflour-dusted work surface. Press the fondant down and smooth out any cracks. Mould it gently round the toe and take special care to squeeze and tuck it into the inside of the shoe. Cut off any excess and re-mould it into a ball. Roll out. Cut 4 long strips 2.5cm (1 inch) wide and cut the shortest ends with pinking shears or cut with a pastry wheel. With a little water attach the ribbons of fondant to the inside of the shoes approximately halfway between the toe and heel. With a cocktail stick, gently mark round the top of the shoe, then the sole. Cut two 15cm (6 inch) long, string-width strips of fondant and make a little bow out of each and put them in place. As an alternative, pink satin ribbon can be used in place of fondant. Fill the shoes with sweets.

Football Boot

25x20cm (10x8 inch) quick mix cake
Jam for filling
Recipe apricot glaze
Recipe moulding icing
Recipe butter icing
50g (2oz) desiccated coconut
50g (2oz) chocolate dots
Food colouring – red, yellow, black and green
Medium star nozzle and piping bag
2 liquorice laces
30cm (12 inch) square cake board
1 cocktail stick

Cut the cake horizontally and sandwich with jam for filling. Put the cakes on the board. With a cocktail stick mark out the outline of the boot. When you are happy with the outline, cut it out with a sharp knife and brush with apricot glaze. Divide the moulding icing into two, remembering to keep the icing in a plastic bag when not in use. Roll out half the icing into an oblong and cover the boot shape (top and sides). Do not ice the leg. Cut the icing at the ankle to indicate the top of the boot. Divide the remaining icing into two, colouring half red and the rest yellow. Draw out the shapes for the patches, tongue of the boot and the flash on some greaseproof paper. Draw a large 'E' with a double line and cut it out. This should be used as a template to guide you when you roll out the red icing to cover the ankle and th

This page: Camelot Castle.

Facing page: Ballet Shoes (to and Football Boot (bottom).

flash for the side of the boot. Roll out the yellow moulding icing and cut the same shapes, but smaller, to go on top of the red. Cut the liquorice laces and tie into a bow. With a little icing place it at the ankle. Mix half of the butter icing yellow and half red. Fill a piping bag with the red butter icing and pipe a band about 6 stripes wide, then repeat with the yellow icing. Work your way up the leg until you have 3 red bands and 2 yellow. Put rows of chocolate drops on the side of the boot to represent studs. Put the desiccated coconut in a bowl and add a few drops of green food colour. Stir in and use to sprinkle on the board to represent grass.

Shirt and Tie

13x9x2cm (15x3½x¾ inch) quick mix cake
2 x recipe butter cream icing
100g (4oz) coloured fondant, if using design with tie
1 small packet round sweets, e.g. jellies, fruit gums or milk drops
Food colouring – red

In a clean bowl reserve ¼ of the butter cream icing and with the food colouring make up a darker shade of the colour previously used. Wash the tin used for baking the cake and, if the tin is old or marked, line with foil so that the tin is totally covered both inside and out. You could otherwise find or make an old shirt box. Put the cake into the cake tin or box, and spread with the lighter icing. If the cake fits snugly into its box or tin, only ice the top; if not, ice all the visible cake. Make the neck and collar shaping by first marking it out. Draw a line in the icing with a cocktail stick 7.5cm (3 inches) from one end of the cake. (The 23cm (9 inch) sides are top and bottom). This marks the shoulder line, so use this line to guide you when building up the collar with more icing. Half the collar (front and back) should be on either side of the faint line. Fill the piping bag with the darker icing and with a writing nozzle outline the collar and shoulder seam. Roll out a thin strip of fondant 4cm (1½ inches) wide and 35cm (14 inches) long, pinch it in to form the knot and place on the cake. If you are using the design with centre placket (shirt front) pocket and sleeves use the darker icing in the piping bag and pipe the shirt front, pocket and sleeves. Put the sweets in position as buttons.

Artist's Palette

23cm (9 inch) square quick mix cake
Recipe apricot glaze
350g (¾lb) moulding icing
100g (4oz) granulated sugar
Food colourings – red, blue, green, yellow, orange, violet and brown

Cut a kidney shape out of the cake and carefully cut a circle slightly off centre. Place the cake on the cake board and brush with apricot glaze. Colour all except 50g (2oz) of the moulding icing pale brown. Roll out and use to cover the palette, pushing in gently at the hole so that the icing coats the inner wall of the circle. Push down to reveal the cake board. Using a dry brush, dip gently into the brown food colouring and drag hesitantly across the palette. Wipe the brush with kitchen paper to absorb some of the food colouring and continue to cover the palette with the wood grain. Leave to dry. Colour 15ml (1 tblsp) of granulated sugar with each of the food colourings. This is done by adding a few drops and stirring until the sugar absorbs the colour. Roll out the remaining moulding icing into a long sausage shape and cut into half. Make a point at the end of one sausage and leave to dry and gently flatten the end of the other.

To Make the Pencil and Paintbrush
When the moulding icing shapes are dry, copying a pencil, colour the one with the pointed end by painting in the lead and the outside. Copy the brush you are using and place them next to the palette. When the palette is dry, put little mounds of the coloured sugar on the top.

Artist's Palette (left) and Shirt and Tie (below).

Celebration Cakes

Mother's Day Cake

18cm (7 inch) or 20cm (8 inch) square or round cake
Recipe apricot glaze
675g (1½lb) marzipan
Royal icing, made with 900g (2lb) icing sugar
Food colourings – green, yellow
Green ribbon
Piped flowers

Brush the top and sides of the cake with apricot glaze and cover with marzipan; leave to dry. With a little icing, attach the cake to the cake board and flat ice the top and sides; leave to dry. Using a piping bag fitted with a leaf nozzle, pipe a row of leaves in white icing facing outwards around the bottom of the cake. Then pipe an overlapping circle of white leaves around the top edge of the cake. Fill another piping bag with green-coloured icing and pipe a row of leaves facing outwards on top. Finally, pipe an overlapping circle of green leaves on the top. Fill a piping bag with a little yellow-coloured icing and fit a medium writing nozzle and write 'Mother' on the top surface of the cake. Attach the piped flowers on the top surface with a dab of icing and, using the piping bag with green icing and the leaf nozzle again, pipe a few leaves around the flowers to finish. Decorate with the green ribbon.

Girl's Birthday Cake

20cm (8 inch) round, rich fruit cake
Recipe apricot glaze
800g (1¾lb) marzipan
Royal icing, made with 1.4kg (3lb) icing sugar
3 piped flowers
Food colouring – pink
Pink ribbon
Frond of asparagus fern

Brush the top and the sides of the cake with apricot glaze. Cover the cake with the marzipan. Attach the cake to the board with a little icing. Flat ice the top and the sides of the cake. Fit a piping bag with a large star nozzle and pipe a circle of stars round the top edge of the cake. Pipe a row of stars round the bottom of the cake. With a medium, plain nozzle pipe bulbs between each of the stars on the inner edge of the cake. Pipe another row of bulbs on the side o the cake above the stars. Colour a little of the icing pink and fit a piping bag with a writing nozzle. Pipe a row of dropped loops from each of the bulbs on the top of the cake. From the point of alternate stars on the top edge of the cake, pipe a row of dropped loops. Go round the cake again piping loops on the stars omitted on the first round. Pipe a bulb on the point of each of the stars. With the pink icing, pipe a scallop on the cake board round the stars. Pipe the message with swirls round it in the shape of 'S's and 'C's on the top of the cake and place the flowers, a little fern and the ribbon in position.

Boy's Birthday Cake

20cm (8 inch) square, rich fruit cake
Recipe apricot glaze
800g (1¾lb) marzipan
Royal icing, made with 1.4kg (3lb) icing sugar
Food colouring – blue
8 silver leaves for the top
16 silver leaves for the side panels

Brush the top of the cake with the apricot glaze. Cover the cake with the marzipan and leave it to dry. Attach the cake to the board with a little icing. Flat ice the sides and the top of the cake and let it dry. Fit a piping bag with a large nozzle and pipe a continuous 'S' pattern on the top edge and the base of th cake. Pipe 4 bars horizontally

This page: Girl's Birthday Cak and Boy's Birthday Cake.

Facing page: Mother's Day Cake.

Mother

across and down the corners of the cake. At each of the 4 corners, and on the top of the cake, pipe a single line from the flat surface of the cake crossing the continuous 'S' and ending in the corner. Fit a small star nozzle and pipe vertically down the corners of the cake, covering the ends of the bars. Pipe the decorative lines on the top of the cake, starting with a long line with a dot at each end and working out and down with shorter lines towards the outer edge. Write the name in the centre of the cake. Colour a little of the icing blue and fit a writing nozzle onto the piping bag. Pipe 2 rows of scallops on the top edge of the cake, a row on each side of the continuous 'S', ending at the corner where the corner bars start. Overpipe the name in blue. Pipe a dropped loop round the base of the cake, with the point of the loops at each of the corners. Attach 2 silver leaves at the base corners of each of the 4 side panels, and 2 silver leaves on the top of the cake at each of the 4 corners, attached to the flat surface of the cake.

It is most important that a celebration cake should feed the desired number of guests, so here is a guide:

Round	**Square**	**Portions**
15cm (6 inch)	13cm (5 inch)	20-30
20cm (7½-8 inch)	18cm (7 inch)	40-45
25cm (10 inch)	23cm (9 inch)	70-80
28cm (11 inch)	25cm (10 inch)	100-110
30cm (12 inch)	30cm (12 inch)	130-140

NB: for decorating simple cakes, sweets can be utilised and are easily applied to butter icing. These are much used in novelty cake designs.

Silver Wedding Anniversary Cake

20 or 23cm (8 or 9 inch) square, rich fruit cake
Recipe apricot glaze
800-900g (1¾-2lb) marzipan
Royal icing, made with 1.25kg (2½lb) icing sugar
8 silver leaves
Silver non-toxic colouring

Brush the top and the sides of the cake with apricot glaze and cover with marzipan. Leave the cake to dry. Attach the cake to the board with a little icing. Flat ice the top and sides of the cake, giving 2 or 3 coats. Fit your piping bag with a medium writing nozzle. Using a saucepan lid or a round template, draw a circle in the centre of the top of the cake. Using a medium-sized five-star nozzle, pipe a continuous swirl round the bottom edge of the cake and finish off each corner with a shell. With a smaller star nozzle, pipe a small dot on the top edge of the cake in the centre of the top edge of each of the side panels and divide the space between the original dot and the corner of the cake with a further dot. You should have 3 dots on each of the top sides of the cake. Using these as a guide, join them together by piping a scallop, with the dots marking the points of the scallop. Using a writing nozzle, pipe with a scribbling line between the scallop on the sides of the cake and the template circle drawn on the top of the cake. The scribbling should be done with a continuous line that never crosses itself. Using the same nozzle, overpipe the template-drawn circle with a continuously twisting line. On the side panels and on the corners of the cake, pipe three beads in descending size below each of the points of the scallop. Overpipe the continuous swirls round the bottom of the cake with a plain, continuous swirl beginning and ending with an 'S' shape. Pipe the '25' in the circle on top of the cake, then – when dry – overpipe this again with white. Fit your piping bag with a medium star nozzle and, having positioned the silver leaves, secure them with a piped rosette. Using a fine paintbrush, gently paint the continuous swirl overpiped on the circle on the top surface of the cake and also the top of the '25' with a single silver line.

Silver Wedding Anniversary Cake.

Golden Wedding Cake

25cm (10 inch) round, rich fruit cake
Recipe apricot glaze
1kg (2¼lb) marzipan
Royal icing, made from 1.4kg (3lb) icing sugar
Food colouring – yellow
6 gold leaves
Yellow ribbon

Brush the sides and top of the cake with the apricot glaze. Cover the cake with the marzipan and leave to dry. Attach the cake to the board with a little icing. Flat ice the top and sides of the cake. Fit a piping bag with a large star nozzle and pipe a row of shells round the top of the cake. Pipe a row of shells round the bottom of the cake. Fit the piping bag with a smaller star nozzle and pipe continuous 'C's on the shells on the top of the cake. Fit the piping bag with a medium-sized plain nozzle and pipe a scallop on the top of the cake round the shells. Round the bottom of the cake, on the board, pipe a scallop round the shells. Repeat the scallop on the side of the cake under the shells on the top edge of the cake. Colour a little of the icing yellow and, using a writing nozzle, repeat the pattern of continuous 'C's on the top edge of the cake. Pipe a dropped loop on top of the shell at the base of the cake. Fit the same piping bag with a leaf nozzle and pipe inverted leaves between the shells at the base of the cake, with the point of the leaves creeping up the sides of the cake. With a writing nozzle, pipe the words and surround them with 'S's and 'C's. Decorate with a real rose or any other flower, or piped flowers and/or gold leaves.

Diana Wedding Cake

Two-Tier Round Cake
25cm (10 inch) round, rich fruit cake
15 or 18cm (6 or 7 inch) round, rich fruit cake
2 x recipe apricot glaze
1.4kg (3lb) marzipan
Royal icing, made from 1.6kg (3½lb) icing sugar
Silver cake boards: 33cm (13 inch) and 20 or 23cm (8 or 9 inch)
32 silver leaves
8 piped flowers
4 round pillars

Brush the top and sides of the cake with apricot glaze and cover with marzipan. Leave the cake to dry. Attach the cake to the board with a little icing. Flat ice the top and sides of the cake, giving three coats and an extra coat on the base cake. Fit a piping bag with a large star nozzle and pipe shells round the bottom of each of the cakes. Using the same nozzle, mark the cake surface lightly at the edge as though it were square. That is, treat it as though it had four corners, putting a dab of icing in each of the four corners and a smaller dab at the centre of each of the four sides. From each of the dabs which mark the centre of the sides pipe an inverted 'S', finishing at the corner mark. Repeat this from where you started and mirror the original shape towards the other corner point. Repeat this round the cake. Pipe a 'C' facing the centre of the cake, with its back marking the centre point of the side. Overpipe all the decorative swirls, the 'S's and 'C's twice. Fit a piping bag with a medium-sized plain nozzle and pipe a continuously twisting scallop on the upper edge of the sides of the cakes. Repeat this pattern on the cake board around the shells. With the same nozzle overpipe the decorative swirls, 'S's and 'C's on the tops of the cakes. Pipe a scallop on the top surface of the cake, encompassing the 'C's in the curves; three curves to each

This page: Golden Wedding Cake. Facing page: Diana Wedding Cake.

Lindsey Jane Wedding Cake.

imaginary side. Pipe dropped loops under the continuously twisting scallop on the sides of cakes. On the sides of the cake below the loops, attach the flowers and leaves with a little icing, four flowers per cake below each 'C' and an icing rosette to attach the other leaves between each of the flowers. Assemble the cake using the pillars and decorate the top with flowers.

Lindsey Jane Wedding Cake

Two-Tier Square Cake
15cm (6 inch) square, rich fruit cake
25cm (10 inch) square, rich fruit cake
2 x recipe apricot glaze
1.5kg (3¼lb) marzipan
Royal icing made with 1.75kg (4lb) icing sugar
28 pink piped roses, to decorate
Asparagus fern, to decorate
Silver cake boards, 20cm (8 inch) and 30cm (12 inch)
4 square pillars
2 narrow ribbon bows

This design is suitable for a 1, 2 or 3-tier cake. The roses are chosen to match the bridal attire.
Brush the sides and tops of the cakes with apricot glaze and cover with marzipan. Leave to dry. Attach the cakes to the cake boards with a dab of icing. Flat ice the cakes, giving two or three coats all over. Fit a piping bag with a medium-sized shell nozzle and pipe shells on the top edge, the bottom edge and up each of the corners of the cakes. Pipe on the top of the cakes in each corner 2 shells facing each other. Fit the piping bag with a medium-sized plain nozzle and pipe a shallow scallop round the top side of the cake. Pipe with an 'S'-shaped swirl, filling each of the small scallops. On the bottom tier, put a cluster of roses in the middle of the cake, surrounded by fern, two roses in each of the corners and one rose at the base of each of the corners. On the top tier, repeat but with a single rose at the top of each corner and the ribbon bows on top of the cake. Assemble the cake using the pillars.

Christening Cake

20cm (8 inch) round, rich fruit cake
Recipe apricot glaze
800g (1¾lb) marzipan
Royal icing, made with 1.4kg (3lb) icing sugar
Food colouring – blue
15g (½oz) marzipan
1 narrow, white ribbon bow

Brush the top and sides of the cake with the apricot glaze. Cover the cake with the marzipan and leave it to dry. Attach the cake to the board with the royal icing. Fit a piping bag with a large star nozzle. With an icing comb, comb the sides of the cake with a swirling line and pipe a row of shells round the top of the cake. Fit a piping bag with a small star nozzle and pipe a scallop round the top of the shells. Pipe a graduated rope round the bottom of the cake, with a large, dropped loop round the rope. Fit the piping bag with a small, plain nozzle and pipe a scallop on the top of the cake next to the shells. Pipe the name of the baby on the top of the cake. Colour a little royal icing blue. Using a writing nozzle, pipe beads at the points of each of the nozzles. Pipe another scallop onto the silver board. Pipe over the name with the blue, piping small 'C's and scrolls. To make the bootees, colour a little moulding icing pale blue and shape into two. Press a small hole towards the end of each of the oval shapes. With a writing nozzle, pipe round the holes, making a little bow at the front. Decorate with a silver ball and put the small bow between the bootees.

Tracy Rose Wedding Cake

Three-Tier Square
13cm (5 inch) square, rich fruit cake
20cm (8 inch) square, rich fruit cake
28cm (11 inch) square, rich fruit cake
3 x recipe apricot glaze
2.25kg (5lb) marzipan
Royal icing, made with 3.3kg (8lb) icing sugar
2 x recipe moulding icing, peach colour (to make 60 moulded roses)
3 cake boards: 18cm (7 inch), 25cm (10 inch) and 35cm (14 inch)
Food colourings – green, peach (brown)
8 square cake pillars
2 rectangular silver boards

Brush the top and sides of the cakes with apricot glaze and cover with marzipan; leave to dry. Attach the cakes to the silver cake boards with a dab of icing. Flat ice the tops of the cakes with the royal icing, which is tinted peach in colour. Cut the thin, rectangular cake boards lengthways down the middle and then cut each widthways with a sharp knife. Cut the corners off each piece diagonally so that they will go together to form a square with a square hole in the centre. Place each on a sheet of greaseproof paper and flat ice onto the white side with a palette knife; leave to dry. Fill a piping bag with a medium writing nozzle and the other with a basket weave nozzle. Hold the basket weave nozzle sideways and on the side of the first cake pipe 3 lines, evenly spaced, one above the other and all of the same length. Pipe a vertical line using the writing nozzle along the edge of the basket weaving. Continue this process until the cake is covered. Repeat the basket weave method on each of the cardboard lids. To make the moulded flowers see chapter on decorations. Colour a little of the royal icing green and fit a piping bag with a leaf nozzle. Colour a little more royal icing a dark peach and use it to fill a bag fitted with a star nozzle. Continue to use the writing nozzle filled with the tinted peach royal icing as used in the basket weave. Position the moulded icing roses facing outward round the top edges of the 2 bottom tiers and in a radiating pattern on the small top tier. Pipe dark peach stars between each of the roses and dot the centre of each star using the tinted peach royal icing. Pipe leaves at random round the flowers. Place the pillars on a tray and pipe small stars dotted with tinted peach for the centre of the flower. Again, pipe leaves at random and leave to dry.

To Assemble the Cake

Place the basket lids round the outer edge of each of the cake's bottom two tiers and, with a little icing, secure them to the top of the cake. Make sure that there is enough room in the square at the centre of each cake for the four pillars.

Note: the cake board can be iced with a palette knife to surround each of the cakes, if required.

This page: Christening Cake.

Facing page: Tracy Rose Wedding Cake.

INDEX